**Insight Guides**

# SCOTLAND

**Discovery** CHANNEL.

**APA PUBLICATIONS**

Part of the Langenscheidt Publishing Group

# INSIGHT GUIDE
# SCOTLAND

# ABOUT THIS BOOK

## Editorial

**Project Editor**
**Josephine Buchanan**
**Editorial Director**
**Brian Bell**

## Distribution

**UK & Ireland**
**GeoCenter International Ltd**
Meridian House, Churchill Way West
Basingstoke, Hampshire RG21 6YR
Fax: (44) 1256 817988
***United States***
**Langenscheidt Publishers, Inc.**
36–36 33rd Street 4th Floor
Long Island City, NY 11106
Fax: 1 (718) 784 0640
***Australia***
**Universal Publishers**
1 Waterloo Road
Macquarie Park, NSW 2113
Fax: (61) 2 9888 9074
***New Zealand***
**Hema Maps New Zealand Ltd (HNZ)**
Unit 2, 10 Cryers Road
East Tamaki, Auckland
Tel: (64) 9 273 6459
Fax: (64) 9 273 6479
***Worldwide***
**Apa Publications GmbH & Co.**
**Verlag KG (Singapore branch)**
38 Joo Koon Road, Singapore 628990
Tel: (65) 6865 1600. Fax: (65) 6861 6438

## Printing

**Insight Print Services (Pte) Ltd**
38 Joo Koon Road, Singapore 628990
Tel: (65) 6865 1600. Fax: (65) 6861 6438

©2009 Apa Publications GmbH & Co.
Verlag KG (Singapore branch)
***All Rights Reserved***
First Edition 1984
*Fourth Edition (Updated) 2007*
*Reprinted 2008*

## CONTACTING THE EDITORS

We would appreciate it if readers
would alert us to errors or outdated information by writing to:
**Insight Guides, P.O. Box 7910,**
**London SE1 1WE, England.**
**Fax: (44) 20 7403 0290.**
**insight@apaguide.co.uk**

**www.insightguides.com**

The first Insight Guide pioneered
the use of creative full-colour
photography in travel guides in 1970.
Since then, we have expanded our
range to cater for our readers' need
not only for reliable information about
their chosen destination but also for
a real understanding of the culture
and workings of that destination.
Now, when the internet can supply
inexhaustible (but not always reliable)
facts, our books marry text and pictures to provide those elusive qualities: knowledge and discernment. To
achieve this, they rely heavily on the
authority of locally based writers
and photographers.

## How to use this book

The book is carefully struc-
tured both to convey an
understanding of Scotland
and its culture and to guide
readers through its sights and
attractions:

◆ The Features section, indicated
with a yellow colour bar, covers the
country's history and culture in
lively authoritative essays written by
specialists.
◆ The main Places section, indicated with a blue bar, provides full
details of all the sights and areas
worth seeing. The chief places of
interest are coordinated by number
with specially drawn maps.
◆ The Travel Tips section, indicated
with an orange bar, at the back of
the book, offers a convenient point
of reference for information on
travel, accommodation, restaurants and other practical aspects of the
country. Travel Tips
information may be
located quickly by using
the index printed on the
back cover flap – and the
flaps also serve as book-
marks.

An important contributor was Glasgow-born **Marcus Brooke**, a globe-trotting writer and photographer. A contributor to many Insight Guides and the author of *Insight Pocket Guide: Scotland,* he wrote the chapters on Skye, the Outer Hebrides and Orkney, and those on festivals, Highland games, golf, Edinburgh architecture, and the feature on castles and abbeys.

Also from Glasgow is the novelist and artist **Naomi May,** who wrote the chapters on art and religion.

Two contributors to *The Scotsman* – **Alastair Clark** and **Conrad Wilson** – add their insight to the music and food of Scotland, whilst **Stuart Ridsdale, Roland Collins,** and **Dymphna Byrne** share their enthusiasm for the Borders, Central Scotland and the Hebrides. **Andrew Eames,** who wrote the features on crofting and Highland flora and fauna, is a journalist and author of *Four Scottish Journeys.*

Insight Guides are as much about people as places and **Christopher Smout** offers a refreshing alternative to the myth of Highlanders and Lowlanders, drawing on his expertise as the author of the *History of the Scottish People.* Remaining chapters – on the Scottish character, early history, whisky, and Shetland – are written by Brian Bell. The book's main photograher is **Douglas Corrance.**

**Colin Hutchison,** a Glasgow-born, Edinburgh-based journalist, and travel writer thoroughly updated this version of Insight Guide Scotland.

**Paula Soper** edited the text and picture research was by **Tom Smyth.**

Thanks also go to **Neil Titman** who proofread the book, and to **Helen Peters** for indexing.

## The contributors

The book was edited by **Josephine Buchanan,** putting her Scottish ancestry to good use. The current edition builds on the original one produced by **Brian Bell,** a journalist with wide experience in newspapers and magazines.

A leading contributor – he wrote the chapters on Edinburgh, the age of rebellion, modern Scotland, Scots geniuses, tartan and hunting – is **George Rosie,** who began his career in Dundee with publisher D.C. Thomson. Rosie moved to London and joined the *Sunday Times* in 1974, but has since returned to Scotland and writes about it from the inside for newspapers and TV.

Other Scottish journalists who have contributed to this guide include **Julie Davidson,** who wrote five of the Places chapters (Glasgow, the Southwest, Forth and Clyde, the West Coast and the East Coast).

### Map Legend

|  |  |
|---|---|
| — — | State Boundary |
| – – – – | Region Boundary |
| ⚬ | National Park/ Nature Reserve |
| – – – – | Ferry Route |
| Ⓜ | Metro |
| ✈ | Airport: International/ Regional |
| 🚌 | Bus Station |
| 🅿 | Parking |
| ⓘ | Tourist Information |
| ✉ | Post Office |
| † | Church/Ruins |
| ☽ | Mosque |
| ✡ | Synagogue |
| ♜ | Castle/Ruins |
| ∴ | Archaeological Site |
| Ω | Cave |
| ★ | Place of Interest |

The main places of interest in the Places section are coordinated by number with a full-colour map (e.g. ❶), and a symbol at the top of every right-hand page tells you where to find the map.

# INSIGHT GUIDES
# SCOTLAND

# CONTENTS

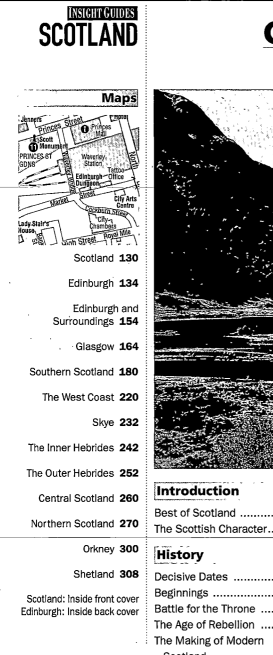

The monument at Glenfinnan, where Bonnie Prince Charlie raised the Stuart banner in 1745

## Insight on....

## Information panels

## Travel Tips

## Places

# THE BEST OF SCOTLAND

*From unique attractions and historic sights*

*to spectacular scenery and wonderful walks, here at a glance are our*

*recommendations, plus some handy money saving tips*

## BEST CASTLES

- **Edinburgh Castle**
High above the city stands Scotland's most popular tourist attraction. Listen out for the ritual firing of the One o'Clock Gun. *See page 141.*
- **Stirling Castle**
Perched atop a craggy outcrop, there's a wealth of Scottish history crammed into every corner of this ancient fortress. *See page 213.*
- **Dunvegan Castle**
Northwest of Portree, Dunvegan Castle has been the stronghold of the chiefs of MacLeod for more than seven centuries. *See page 234.*
- **Glamis Castle** This beautiful, turreted castle in Angus has a rich and royal history, not least as the former

home of Queen Elizabeth, the Queen Mother. *See page 272.*
- **Dunnottar Castle**
This ruined fortress, in a striking setting, has been witness to Scotland's stormy and bloodstained past. *See page 274.*
- **Eilean Donan**
Built against a backdrop of brooding mountains and a picturesque sea loch, every inch of Eilean Donan portrays the image of a Scottish romantic castle. *See page 226.*

## BEST MONUMENTS

- **Wallace Monument**
(Stirling) Built to commemorate the exploits of Scotland's 12th-century freedom fighter. *See page 213.*
- **Scott Monument**
(Edinburgh) The soaring Gothic spire on Princes Street was built as a tribute to the celebrated Scots

novelist, Sir Walter Scott. *See page 145*
- **Greyfriars Bobby**
(Edinburgh) In memory of the loyal Skye terrier who never left his master's graveside in Greyfriars Kirk. *See page 144.*
- **Glenfinnan Monument** On the "Road to the Isles", where the clans raised their Standard and gathered in support of Bonnie Prince Charlie's Jacobite cause. *See page 225.*
- **Robert the Bruce**
(Stirling) The victor of the Battle of Bannockburn in 1314 stands guard at Stirling Castle. *See page 214.*

**ABOVE:** Eilean Donan castle, Loch Duich.
**LEFT:** Scott Monument.

## STANDING STONES

- **Callanish** (Isle of Lewis) Nearly 50 stones occupy this monumental, megalithic site; many are aligned with the positions of the sun and stars. *See page 252.*
- **Ring of Brodgar** (Orkney) Constructed around 2500 BC and once a true circle; now only 27 of the 60 stones remain standing. *See page 301.*
- **Standing Stones of Stenness** (Orkney) On the shore of Stenness Loch stand four of the original thin stone slabs. The tallest is over 16ft (5m). *See page 301.*
- **Torhouse Stone Circle** (Wigtown) The three large upright stones in the centre of the circle are known as King Gauldus's Tomb. *See page 203.*

**ABOVE:** the standing stones of Callanish.
**BELOW RIGHT:** walking the West Highland Way at Auch.
**BELOW:** an exhibit from the Museum of Scotland.

## BEST MUSEUMS AND ART GALLERIES

- **Kelvingrove Art Gallery and Museum** (Glasgow) Housed in an imposing red sandstone building, this is Scotland's most popular gallery. Step inside this treasure trove of cultural antiquities and you'll understand why. *See page 169.*
- **Shetland Museum and Archives** (Lerwick) Housed in a striking timber-clad building, the museum charts Shetland's history and heritage with an amazing collection of over 3,000 artefacts and archives of written, photographic and musical records. *See page 308.*
- **Museum of Scotland** (Edinburgh) This remarkable museum charts the history of Scotland, bringing together under one roof a number of important artefacts, from neolothic standing stones to Viking treasures. *See page 144*
- **Aberdeen Art Gallery** The neoclassical building has a permanent collection of 18th–20th-century art including works by Toulouse Lautrec and Raeburn. *See page 283.*

## BEST WALKS

- **The West Highland Way** This is one of the greatest long-distance walks in Scotland, stretching 95 miles (153 km). Start north of Glasgow (Milngavie) passing Loch Lomond, through Glencoe to Fort William where you will reach the foot of Ben Nevis.
- **The Great Glen Way** The scenic route spans 73 miles (117 km), beginning at the Old Fort in Fort William and eventually leading you through the city to Inverness Castle. It is perfect for the less experienced walker because of the relatively flat terrain.
- **The Speyside Way** Starting at Buckie on the Moray Firth, the route takes you through the Tweed Valley towards the wilderness of the Cairngorm Mountains.

## PARKS AND GARDENS

● **Drummond Castle Gardens** (Crieff) This is one of the finest formal gardens with strong French and Italian influences. The boxwood parterre is laid out in the shape of a St Andrews Cross. *See page 264.*

● **Inverewe Gardens** (Perth) Created by Osgood Mackenzie in 1862, this sub-tropical oasis is one of Scotland's most popular, set on the shores of Loch Ewe. The diverse plant collection includes specimens from New Zealand and Chile. *See page 227.*

● **Royal Botanic Garden** (Edinburgh) The garden was founded as early as 1670 as a resource for medical research. The huge Victorian glasshouse, the Temperate Palmhouse, is impressive and packed with ferns and palms. *See page 150.*

● **Branklyn Garden** (Perth) An intensively cultivated garden with peat walls and a spectacular rock garden. One of the most striking plants to be seen is the Himalayan poppy. *See page 259.*

● **Arduaine Gardens** (Argyll) A 20-acre (8-ha) woodland garden, with superb coastal views, specialising in rhododendrons, ferns and azaleas. *See page 222.*

**ABOVE:** Highland cattle take a dip in Loch Lomond.
**BELOW:** autumnal shades in Drummond Castle Gardens.

## NATURE RESERVES AND PARKS

● **Balranald RSPB Nature Reserve** (North Uist) Large numbers of seabirds and waders can be seen here. In summer you can hear the corn bunting's song and see the redshanks and lapwing chicks in the marshes. *See page 254.*

● **Sands of Forvie** (Aberdeenshire) Part of the Forvie National Nature Reserve. The reserve has a large sand dune sytem, and the biggest breeding colony of eider duck in Britain. *See page 281.*

● **Beinn Eighe National Nature Reserve** (Wester Ross) Overlooking Loch Maree, parts of the reserve are home to the elusive pine marten, buzzards and golden eagles. Caledonian pinewood partly cover the forest. *See page 290.*

● **Kincraig Highland Wildlife Park** The park features wildlife that was once native to the Highlands, including wolves, wildcats and capercaillies, all in a spectacular setting. *See page 288.*

● **Hermaness National Nature Reserve** (Shetland) Overlooking Britain's most northerly tip, Hermaness is a haven to more than 100,000 nesting seabirds, including gannets, great skuas and puffins. *See page 309.*

## LOCAL DELICACIES

● **Lockfyne kippers**
These herrings are caught locally in Loch Fyne, north of Arran. They are soaked in brine and slowly cured over smouldering oak fires.

● **Forfar Bridies** This minced meat pie is said to have been made by Maggie Bridie of Glamis, when the county of Angus was called Forfarshire.

● **Arbroath Smokie**
A speciality from Arbroath, in Angus, of lightly smoked haddock.

● **Highland malts**
Among the famous Highland malts are Glenmorangie, Glenfiddich, Lochnagar and Tamnavullin.

● **Selkirk bannocks**
This rich fruit bun was originally made by a baker in Selkirk, and eaten at Christmas.

● **Moffat toffees** This is a toffee-based sweet with a sherbert centre, made in Moffat.

● **Scottish cheeses**
Lanark blue, Seater's Orkney and Isle of Mull, to name but a few of the best.

---

**ABOVE:** buttery Highland shortbread. **LEFT:** "have a wee dram 'afore ye go!" **RIGHT:** the sandy white dunes of Taransay.

## BEST BEACHES

● **Taransay (Outer Hebrides)** The idyllic island of Taransay, west of the Isle of Harris, has numerous sandy beaches. Access relies on the kindness of the Atlantic Ocean.

● **Sandwood Bay (north of Lochinver by Blairmore)** To enjoy the sweeping, pinky sands and tottering red-stone sea stack of Sandwood Bay, you must first negotiate a four-mile (6-km) stony track over rough moorland. Rest assured, it's well worth the trek.

● **Sands of Morar (Arisaig)** Along a twisting road that heads north to Mallaig from Arisaig, the visitor is met with a sublime seascape of azure waters and the silver-white beaches of Morar.

● **Scarista Beach (Harris, Outer Hebrides)** Scarista is just one of a dozen or more beaches that induce a deep sense of calm and wonder as you wander across deserted golden sands watching the waves roll off the eastern Atlantic.

## MONEY-SAVING TIPS

**Travel** Look out for the FirstScotrail explorer passes and Citylink bus passes. If sailing to several Scottish islands, it's worthwhile investing in a Caledonian MacBrayne Rover ticket. Remember that it costs considerably more to take your car on a ferry. It could save you a small fortune if you walk, cycle or use public transport on reaching your island destination.

**Eating** Many restaurants offer substantially reduced rates when you choose to eat between 5.30–7pm on a pre-theatre menu.

**Drinking** "Happy hour" continues to be a convenient way for pubs and clubs to entice office workers and visitors alike indoors for a drink. Most "happy hours" take place between 5–6pm or 6–7pm on weekdays when drinks are offered at substantially cheaper prices.

**Attractions** From Edinburgh Castle to wildlife cruises off Mull, it's definitely worthwhile asking about special family,
children and senior citizen prices. Cinemas also offer discounted prices for kids and over 60s.

**Paying for the view** The view from the ramparts of Edinburgh and Stirling Castle may be impressive, but if you are on a tight budget, don't forget the view is free from the respective Pentland and Ochil hills. Equally, with so many walking trails across the country, it can prove highly rewarding, financially, to take a picnic in a rucksack and head for the hills.

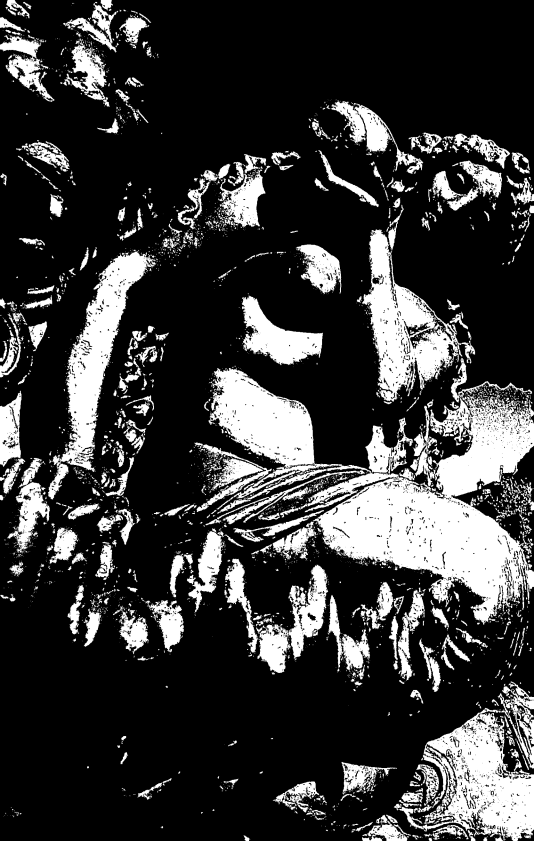

# THE SCOTTISH CHARACTER

*A confusing mix of dourness and humour, the Scots are unanimous only
when identifying the common cause of their problems: England*

Natives of Scotland, it has been said, consider themselves as Scots before they think of themselves as human beings, thus establishing a clear order of excellence. This attitude, naturally enough, wins them few popularity points from the rest of the human race and none at all from their nearest neighbour, England. Indeed, English literature is so peppered with anti-Scots aphorisms that the cumulative impression amounts to national defamation.

"I have been trying all my life to like Scotchmen," wrote the essayist Charles Lamb, "and am obliged to desist from the experiment in despair." P.G. Wodehouse was no kinder: "It is never difficult", he wrote, "to distinguish between a Scotsman with a grievance and a ray of sunshine." And Dr Samuel Johnson, whose tour of the Hebrides in 1773 was immortalised by his Scottish biographer James Boswell, produced the most enduring maxims: "The noblest prospect that a Scotchman ever sees is the high road that leads him to England" and "Much may be made of a Scotsman if he be caught young."

## Shotgun marriage

It is a road that many have taken: an estimated 20 million people of Scots descent, one of the most inventive peoples on earth, are scattered throughout every continent – four times as many as live in Scotland itself. Yet an unease towards the English, a suspicion that they are their social superiors, has for centuries blighted the Scots psyche. The union of the two countries in 1707, after centuries of sporadic hostility, was regarded by most Scots as a shotgun marriage, and over 300 years have scarcely diluted the differences in outlook and attitude between the ill-matched partners.

It is an old tune, often played. When the future Pope Pius II visited the country in the 15th century, he concluded: "Nothing pleases the Scots more than abuse of the English." In that respect, the Scots resemble England's other close neighbours, the French, with whom they have intimate historical connections.

Both share an outspokenness, which the English mistake for rudeness. Both are proud peoples, a characteristic which, in the case of the

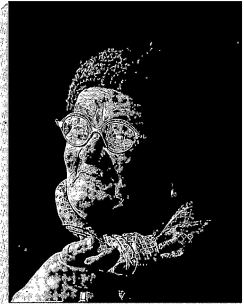

Scots, the English translate as ingratitude. "You Scots", the playwright J.M. Barrie once had one of his characters say, "are such a mixture of the practical and the emotional that you escape out of an Englishman's hand like a trout." Barrie, the creator of Peter Pan, was a Scot himself and often cast a cynical eye over his fellow countrymen. "There are few more impressive sights in the world", he declared, "than a Scotsman on the make."

It is noticeable that the butt of most of these waspish epigrams is the Scots *man*. Until recently, women, though no less strong in character, played a subsidiary role in the country's public affairs. It was very much a man's world:

---

**PRECEDING PAGES:** red deer grazing; Edinburgh Castle from Princes Street Gardens.
**LEFT:** on guard at Blackness Castle.
**RIGHT:** stallholder in Paddy's Market, Glasgow.

it has taken many centuries for a woman to be allowed to act as a Clan Chief. And although Scottish law introduced desertion as grounds for divorce in 1573 (364 years before England got around to doing so), it retained a robust, Calvinistic view about what wives ought to endure.

Certainly, the Calvinist tradition is central to the Scots character. While England absorbed the Reformation with a series of cunning compromises, Scotland underwent a revolution, replacing the panoply of Roman Catholicism with an austere Presbyterianism designed to put the ordinary people directly in touch with their God. No person was deemed inherently better than the next – and that included the clergy, who were made directly answerable to their congregations. This democratic tradition, allied with a taste for argument born of theological wrangling, runs deep and once led more than one English politician to label firebrand Glasgow shipyard workers, for example, as Communists. Some might have been; but most were simply exercising their right to be individualists. It was an attitude that would allow a riveter to regard himself as being every bit as good as the shipyard boss and, whenever necessary, to remind the boss of that fact. Deference? What's that?

## SCOTTISH HOME RULE

The long-standing resentment of Scotland towards England finally found a political focus in 1997, when the second referendum on autonomy within the UK in two decades resulted in a "yes" vote to the setting up of the first Scottish parliament since 1707. The lack of majority in 1999 forced Labour into a coalition with the Liberal Democrats, and the SNP formed the main opposition. Furthermore, the results of the 2007 Scottish elections, which have brought the SNP, led by Alex Salmond, to power (albeit narrowly) for the first time in its history, suggest the "hot potato" of Scottish independence is far from resolved.

In many other ways, too, the Scots character is a confusing one. It combines dourness and humour, meanness and generosity, arrogance and tolerance, cantankerousness and chivalry, sentimentality and hard-headedness. One aspect of these contradictions is caught by a *Punch* cartoon showing a hitch-hiker trying to entice passing motorists with a sign reading "Glasgow – or else!"

On the positive side, a bad climate and a poor soil forged an immensely practical people. But there was a price to be paid: these disadvantages encouraged frugality and a deep-seated pessimism. "It could be worse" comes easily to the lips of the most underprivileged.

The situation is redeemed by laughter. Scottish humour is subtle and sardonic and, in the hands of someone as verbally inventive as the Glasgow-born comedian Billy Connolly, can leave reality far behind with a series of outrageously surreal non-sequiturs.

It has also been used, over the years, to cement many a Scottish stereotype. "My father was an Aberdonian," the veteran comedian Chic Murray would say, "and a more generous man you couldn't wish to meet. I have a gold watch that belonged to my father, he sold it to me on his deathbed... so I wrote him a cheque, postdated of course."

even served to encourage more women into pubs for a drink and meal with friends.

## The cult of the kilt

Like the Irish, the Scots have realised that there's money to be made from conforming to a stereotyped image, however bogus it may be. If haggis isn't universally popular (once described as looking like a castrated bagpipe), it is offered to tourists as the national dish. Heads of ancient Scottish clans, living in houses large enough to generate cashflow problems, have opened their homes to tour groups of affluent overseas visitors. Others have opened "clan shops" retailing

Alcohol features prominently in Scottish jokes, as it does in many other aspects of the country's life. Until recently the single aim of Scottish pubs was to enable their clientele to get drunk as fast as possible, a purpose reflected in their decor. "Some of them", wrote the journalist Hugh McIlvanney, "are so bare that anyone who wants to drink in sophisticated surroundings takes his glass into the lavatory." Matters have greatly improved, with some commentators suggesting the introduction of Scotland's smoking ban in public places (since 2006) has

**LEFT:** passing the time of day with a pint.
**ABOVE:** ladies lunching in Princes Square, Glasgow.

an astonishing variety of tartan artefacts, including Hairy Haggisburger soft toys, and an abundance of tartan teddies. Still others have taken to appearing in Japanese TV commercials extolling their "family brand" of whisky. The cult of the kilt – based, someone mused, on the self-deception that male knees are an erogenous zone – is a huge commercial success.

But the image obscures the real Scotland. It's worth lingering long enough to draw back the tartan curtain and get to know one of Europe's most complex peoples. There's no guarantee that the more innocent tourists won't have the wool pulled over their eyes; but, if it's any consolation, it's sure to be best-quality Scottish wool.    ❑

los tuos quesum[us]
dñe deus ppetua men
tis et corporis salute gau
dere: et gloriosa beate ma
rie semp uirginis int[er]
cessione a presenti liba
ri tristicia et eterna pfru
i leticia. p dominum
Benedicamus dño.
Deo gras.

Dis omnia midi.

na dnitoriuz mcu i
tende

omine ad adiuuand
me festina.

la pzī    icut erat

en i ccreator sps:

# Decisive Dates

## Prehistoric times

*c.*6000 BC First sign of human settlement on west coast and islands.
*c.*3000 BC Village established at Skara Brae.
*c.*2000 BC Major burial sites such as Maeshowe and Clava Cairns set up.
*c.*1000 BC First invasion of Celtic tribes.

### THE ROMANS

AD 82 Agricola's forces enter Scotland and reach Aberdeenshire.

142 Second Roman invasion reaches Firth of Forth. Major fort established at Trimontium, near Melrose. Antonine Wall built from Forth to Clyde.
185 Withdrawal of Roman forces behind Hadrian's Wall.

### EARLY CHRISTIANS AND KINGDOMS

397 First Christian church founded at Whithorn by St Ninian.
400–600 Four "kingdoms" emerge – Dalriada, Pictland, Strathclyde and Bernicia.
563 St Columba lands on Iona and founds monastery.
775–800 Norse forces occupy Hebrides, Orkney and Shetland.

### THE BIRTH OF SCOTLAND

843 Kenneth MacAlpin becomes first king of Scots.
973 Kenneth II defeats Danish invaders at Luncarty, near Perth.
1018 Malcolm II defeats the Northumbrians at Battle of Carham.

### THE ENGLISH INFLUENCE

1040 Macbeth becomes king by murdering Duncan I.
1057 Macbeth killed at Lumphanan, succeeded by Malcolm Canmore. Anglicisation of Church and court started by his queen, Margaret.
1124–53 Reign of David I. Royal burghs founded, and Border abbeys established.
1138 David defeated by Norman forces at Battle of Northallerton.
1165 William I (the Lion) becomes king.
1174 William defeated at Battle of Alnwick and forced to do homage to English king.
1249 Alexander III becomes king. Start of "Golden Age".

### WARS OF SUCCESSION

1286 Death of Alexander III. Succeeded by infant granddaughter Margaret, but rival claimants to throne include John Balliol and Robert Bruce.
1290 Margaret dies en route to Scotland. Edward I of England declares himself feudal overlord of Scotland, selects Balliol as vassal king.
1291–6 Edward I (the Hammer of the Scots) invades Scotland, wins Battle of Dunbar, takes Stone of Destiny to London.
1297 Rebellion led by William Wallace. English forces defeated at Battle of Stirling Bridge.
1305 English put Wallace to death as a traitor.
1306 Robert the Bruce declares himself King Robert I and is crowned at Scone. Defeated at Methven and Dalry and goes into exile.
1314 Scots forces under Robert the Bruce defeat English at Battle of Bannockburn.
1320 Declaration of Arbroath sent to the Pope.
1333 English defeat Scots at Halidon Hill.
1346–57 David II held prisoner in London.

### THE EARLY STUARTS

1371 Robert II, first of Stuarts, becomes king.
1406–1542 Reigns of James I–V.
1513 James IV killed at Battle of Flodden.
1542 James V defeated at Battle of Solway Moss. Dies shortly after, succeeded by six-day-old daughter, Mary Queen of Scots.

**1547** Hertford wins Battle of Pinkie. Mary taken to France.

**1560** Protestants, led by John Knox, start to destroy religious houses.

**1561** Mary returns to Scotland to reclaim throne.

**1566** Birth of James VI.

**1568** Mary flees to England and is imprisoned.

### THE UNION OF CROWNS AND PARLIAMENTS

**1603** Elizabeth I dies. James VI becomes James I of England.

**1638** National Covenant signed in Edinburgh.

**1646** Solemn League and Covenant confirmed.

**1650** Cromwell seizes power in England. Scots proclaim Charles II as king in defiance. Cromwell's forces inflict heavy defeat at Dunbar.

**1660** Charles II restored as king. Covenanters continued to rebel.

**1689** James VII/II deposed by William and Mary. Scots supporters of James (Jacobites) win Battle of Killiecrankie.

**1692** Massacre of Glencoe.

**1707** Treaty of Union, abolition of separate Scottish parliament.

### JACOBITE REBELLIONS AND THE CLEARANCES

**1715** Rebellion led by Earl of Mar fails after abortive battle at Sheriffmuir.

**1722–40** Building of "Wade Roads".

**1745** Prince Charles Edward Stuart, "Bonnie Prince Charlie", sails to Scotland and raises clans at Glenfinnan. Success at Prestonpans, much of Scotland in Jacobite hands.

**1746** Campaign retreats and ends in débâcle at Culloden on 16 April.

**1765** James Watt invents steam engine.

**1780–** Highland Clearances, people evicted for sheep; "Age of Enlightenment" in literature and the arts.

### THE INDUSTRIAL AGE

**1812** *Comet*, the first passenger-carrying steamship, is launched.

**1823** Caledonian Canal opened.

**1836** Highland potato crop fails.

**1843** Disruption of Church of Scotland and formation of the Free Church.

**1847** Simpson introduces anaesthetics in childbirth and chloroform in surgery.

---

**PRECEDING PAGES:** *Annunciation to the Shepherds*, from early 14th-century Murthly Book of Hours.

**LEFT:** Robert the Bruce. **RIGHT:** Mary Queen of Scots.

**1850–** Massive expansion of heavy industry, particularly around Glasgow.

**1852** Victoria and Albert buy Balmoral.

**1865** Lister pioneers antiseptics in surgery.

**1882** The "Crofters War", including Battle of the Braes on Skye.

**1883** Highland Land League formed.

**1892** Free Presbyterians ("Wee Frees") split from Free Church.

### THE MODERN AGE

**1924** Ramsay Macdonald becomes first Labour Prime Minister.

**1934** Scottish National Party (SNP) formed.

**1964** Forth Road Bridge opened.

**1975** Start of North Sea gas and oil exploitation.

**1997** Referendum votes in favour of a 129-member Scottish Parliament with tax-varying powers. Stone of Destiny returned to Scotland.

**1999** A Scottish Parliament is elected.

**2002** The Falkirk Wheel, a rotating lift, links two canals between Edinburgh and Glasgow.

**2004** The Scottish Parliament's new building, budgeted at £40 million, opens in Edinburgh at a cost of more than £431 million. UNESCO names Edinburgh as the world's first City of Literature.

**2006** Scottish Parliament imposes a complete ban on smoking in public areas.

**2007** Alex Salmond (SNP) is elected First Minister of Scotland. ❑

# BEGINNINGS

*An endless battle for power, early Scottish history was dominated*

*by the continual conflicts of ruthlessly ambitious families*

On a bleak, windswept moor three witches crouch round a bubbling cauldron, muttering oaths and prophesying doom. A king is brutally stabbed to death and his killer, consumed by vaulting ambition, takes the throne, only to be killed himself soon afterwards. "Fair is foul, and foul is fair."

To many people, these images from William Shakespeare's *Macbeth* are their first introduction to early Scottish history. But of course, the Scots will tell you, Shakespeare was English, and, as usual, the English got it wrong. There is perhaps some truth to the tale, they admit – Macbeth, who reckoned he had a better hereditary claim to the throne than its occupant, did kill Duncan in 1040 – but thereafter he ruled well for 17 years and kept the country relatively prosperous.

## Power games

Where Shakespeare undeniably showed his genius, however, was in managing to heighten the narrative of a history that was already (and remained) melodramatic beyond belief. Scotland's story was for centuries little more than the biographies of ruthlessly ambitious families jostling for power, gaining it and losing it through accidents of royal marriages, unexpected deaths and lack of fertility.

A successful Scottish king needed cunning as well as determination, an ability to judge just how far he could push powerful barons without being toppled from his throne in the process. In a continuous effort to safeguard the future, marriage contracts were routinely made between royal infants, and, when premature death brought a succession of kings to the throne as children, the land's leading families fought for advancement by trying to gain control over the young rulers, occasionally by kidnapping them.

Summarise some of the stories and they seem more histrionic than historical. An attractive

young widow returns from 13 years at the French court to occupy the throne of Scotland, lays claim to the throne of England, conducts a series of passionate affairs, marries her lover a few weeks after he has allegedly murdered her second husband, loses the throne, is incarcerated for 19 years by her cousin, the Queen of

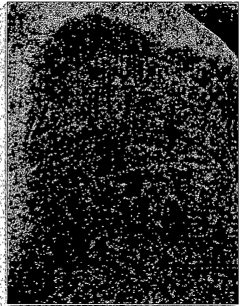

England, and is then, on a pretext, beheaded. No scriptwriter today would dare to invent as outrageous a plot as the true-life story of Mary Queen of Scots.

## Nameless people

Our earliest knowledge of Scotland dates back more than 6,000 years, when the cold, wet climate and the barren landscape would seem familiar enough to a time-traveller from the present day. Then the region was inhabited by nameless hunters and fishermen. Later, the mysterious Beaker People from Holland and the Rhineland settled here, as they did in Ireland, leaving as a memorial only a few tantalising

---

**LEFT:** Romans building Hadrian's Wall.
**ABOVE RIGHT:** evidence of the Picts near Inverary.

pots. Were the eerie Standing Stones of Callan-ish, on the island of Lewis, built by them as a primitive observatory? Nobody can be certain.

## A tribal society

Celtic tribes, driven by their enemies to the outer fringes of Europe, settled in Scotland, as they did in Ireland, Cornwall, Wales and Brittany, and mastered iron implements. The blueprint for a tribal society was in place.

It was the Romans who gave it coherence. The desire of Emperor Vespasian in AD 80 to forge northwards from an already subjugated southern Britain towards the Grampian Moun-

quell yet another rebellion and was never seen again. Was it really worth all this trouble, the Romans wondered, to subdue such barbarians?

Hadrian's answer, as emperor, was no. He built a fortified wall that stretched for 73 miles (117 km) across the north of England, isolating the savages. A successor, Antoninus Pius, tried to push back the boundaries in 142 by erecting a fortified wall between the Rivers Forth and Clyde. But it was never an effective exercise. The Roman Empire fell without ever conquering these troublesome natives, and Scottish life carried on without the more lasting benefits of Roman civilisation, such as good roads. A com-

tains and the dense forests of central Scotland united the tribes in opposition. To their surprise, the Romans, who called the natives Picti, "painted men", encountered fearsome opposition. An early Scots leader, called Calgacus by the Romans, rallied 30,000 men – a remarkable force but no match for the Roman war machine. Even so, the Romans respected their enemy's ability enough for the historian Tacitus to feel able to attribute to Calgacus the anti-Roman sentiment: "They make a wilderness and call it peace."

Soon, however, the "barbarians" began to perfect guerrilla tactics. In the year 118, for instance, the Ninth Legion marched north to

plex clan system evolved, consisting of large families bound by blood ties.

## The Dark Ages

Europe's Dark Ages enveloped the region. What records remain portray raiders riding south to plunder and pillage. True Scots were born in the 6th century when Gaels migrated from the north of Ireland, inaugurating an epoch in which beautifully drawn manuscripts and brilliant metalwork illuminated the cultural darkness.

Like much of Western Europe, Scotland's history at this time was a catalogue of invasions. The most relentless aggressors were the Vikings, who arrived in the 8th century in their

Scandinavian longships to loot the monasteries which had been founded by early Christian missionaries such as St Ninian and St Columba.

Eventually, in 843, the warring Picts – a fierce Celtic race who dominated the southwest – united with the Scots under Kenneth MacAlpin, the astute ruler of the west- coast kingdom of Dalriada. But Edinburgh was not brought under the king's influence until 962, and the Angles, a Teutonic people who controlled the south of the country, were not subjugated until 1018. Feuding for

> **ROYAL STANDARDS**
>
> Some believe Queen Margaret gave the Scots their inferiority complex by forcing them to measure themselves against the English.

Margaret, a Hungarian-born Christian reformer and strong supporter of English standards. Partly to please her, Malcolm invaded England twice. During the second incursion, he lost his life. This gave William Rufus, the Conqueror's son and successor, an opportunity to involve himself in Scottish affairs by securing the northern throne for Malcolm's eldest son, Edgar, the first of a series of weak kings. A successor, David I, having been brought up in England, gave many estates to his Norman friends. Also, he

power was continuous. It was in this period that Macbeth murdered his rival, Duncan, and was killed in turn by Duncan's son.

## The Norman conquest

The collapse of England to William the Conqueror in 1066 drove many of the English lords northwards, turning the Lowlands of Scotland into an aristocratic refugee camp. Scotland's king, Malcolm, married one of the refugees,

**LEFT:** Roman panel from Glasgow University's Hunterian Museum.
**ABOVE:** William Wallace rallies his Scottish forces against the English.

did nothing to stop English replacing Gaelic and introduced feudalism into the Lowlands.

But true feudalism never really took root. French knights, accustomed to deference, were surprised to find that, when they rode through a field of crops, the impertinent Scottish peasants would demand compensation. Although the Normans greatly influenced architecture and language, they in no sense conquered the country. Instead, they helped create a social division that was to dominate Scotland's history: the Lowlands were controlled by noblemen who spoke the same Norman French and subscribed to the same values as England's ruling class, while the Highlands remained untamed, under the influence of independent-minded Gaelic speakers, and the islands were loyal, more or less, to Norway.

The Highland clans, indeed, were virtually independent kingdoms, whose chiefs, under the old patriarchal system, had the power of life and death over their people. Feuds between clans were frequent and bloody, provoking one visiting scholar to pronounce: "The Scots are not industrious and the people are poor. They spend all their time in wars and, when there is no war, they fight one another."

Over the next three centuries the border with England was to be constantly redefined. The

seaport of Berwick-upon-Tweed, now the most northerly town in England, was to change hands 13 times. In the 1160s the Scots turned to French sympathisers for help, concluding what eventually came to be known as the Auld Alliance. In later years the pact would have a profound influence on Scottish life, but on this occasion it was no match for England's might.

After a comparatively peaceful interlude, England's insidious interference provoked a serious backlash in 1297. William Wallace, a violent youth from Elderslie, became an outlaw after a scuffle with English soldiers in which a girl (some think she was his wife) who helped him escape was killed herself by the

Sheriff of Lanark. Wallace returned to kill the Sheriff, but didn't stop there; soon he had raised enough of an army to drive back the English forces, making him for some months master of southern Scotland.

But Wallace, immortalised in the film *Braveheart*, wasn't supported by the nobles, who considered him low-born, and, after being defeated at Falkirk by England's Edward I (the "Hammer of the Scots"), he met his expected fate by being hanged, drawn and quartered. His quarters were sent to Newcastle, Berwick, Stirling and Perth.

## Bruce's victory

The next challenger, Robert the Bruce, who was descended from the Norman de Brus family, got further as a freedom fighter – as far as the throne itself, in fact, though he didn't sit on it long. During a year's exile on Rathlin Island, off the coast of Ireland, he is said to have been inspired by the persistence of a spider building its web in a cave, and he returned to Scotland full of determination and proceeded to win a series of victories. Soon the French recognised him as King of Scotland and the Roman Catholic Church gave him its backing.

England's new king, Edward II, although he had little stomach for Scottish affairs, could not ignore the challenge, and, in 1314, the two forces collided at Bannockburn, south of Stirling. Bruce's chances looked slim: he was pitching only 6,000 men against a force of 20,000 English. But he was shrewd enough to hold the high ground, forcing the English into the wet marshes, and he won.

Because the Pope did not recognise the new monarch, Bruce's subjects successfully petitioned Rome, and the Declaration of Arbroath in 1320 confirmed him as king.

Like the Romans, England's Edward III decided that Scotland was more trouble than it was worth and in 1328 granted it independence. He recognised Bruce as king and, cementing the treaty in the customary manner, married his young sister to Bruce's baby son. Peace had been achieved at last between two of the most rancorous of neighbours. It seemed too good to be true – and it was. ❑

**ABOVE LEFT:** Robert the Bruce's statue in Stirling.
**RIGHT:** Bruce kills Sir Henry de Bohun in single combat at Bannockburn.

Robert Bruce sends a defiance to Edward III.

# BATTLE FOR THE THRONE

*For centuries the throne of Scotland was a source of conflict,*

*inextricably part of the turbulent relationship with England*

The outbreak in 1339 of the intermittent Hundred Years War between England and France kept Edward III's mind off Scotland. He failed, therefore, to appreciate the significance of a pact concluded in 1326 between France and Scotland by Robert the Bruce. Yet the Auld Alliance, as the pact came to be known, was to keep English ambitions at bay for centuries and at one point almost resulted in Scotland becoming a province of France.

Principal beneficiaries of the deal were the kings of the Stuart (or Stewart) family. Taking their name from their function as High Stewarts to the king, they were descended from the Fitzalans, Normans who came to England with William the Conqueror in 1066.

When the Bruce family failed to produce a male heir, the crown passed in 1371 to the Stuarts because Marjorie, Robert the Bruce's daughter, had married Walter Fitzalan. The first of the Stuarts, Robert II, faced a problem that was to plague his successors: he had constantly to look over his shoulder at England, yet he could never ignore another threat to his power – his own dissident barons and warring chieftains.

## Youthful monarchs

His son, Robert III, trusted these ambitious men so little that he sent his eldest son, James, to France for safety. But the ship carrying him was waylaid and young James fell into the hands of England's Henry IV. He grew up in the English court and didn't return to Scotland (as James I) until 1422, at the age of 29. His friendliness with the English was soon strained to breaking point, however, and he renewed the Auld Alliance, siding with France's Charles VII and Joan of Arc against the English. But soon James was murdered, stabbed to death before his wife by his uncle, a cousin and another noble.

His son, James II, succeeded at the age of six, setting another Stuart pattern: monarchs who came to the throne as minors, creating what has

been called an infantile paralysis of the power structure. In 1460 James, fighting to recapture Roxburgh from the English, died when one of his own siege guns exploded. James III, another boy king, succeeded. He had time to marry a Danish princess (in the process bringing the Norse islands of Orkney and Shetland into the

realm) before he was locked in Edinburgh Castle by the scheming barons and replaced by his more malleable younger brother. The arrangement didn't last, and soon James's son, James IV, was crowned king, aged 15.

This latest James cemented relations with England in 1503 by marrying Margaret Tudor, the 12-year-old daughter of Henry VII, the Welsh warrior who had usurped the English throne 18 years before. The harmony was short-lived: the French talked James into attacking England, and he was killed at the battle of Flodden Hill. It was Scotland's worst defeat to the English, wiping out the cream of a generation, and some argue that the country never recovered

**LEFT:** Robert the Bruce meets with Edward III.
**RIGHT:** Edward III takes Berwick in 1333.

from the blow. James's heir, predictably, was also called James and was just over a year old. The power-brokers could continue plotting.

Torn between the French connection and the ambitions of England's Henry VIII, who tried to enrol him in his anti-Catholic campaign, the young James V declared his loyalties by marrying two Frenchwomen in succession. Life expectation was short, however, for kings as well as for peasants, and James V died in 1542 just as his second queen, Marie de Guise, gave birth to a daughter. At less than a week old, the infant was proclaimed Mary Queen of Scots.

Ever an opportunist, Henry VIII despatched an invasion force which reduced Edinburgh, apart from its castle, to rubble. It was known as the "Rough Wooing" and left hatred that would last for centuries. The immediate question was: should Scotland ally itself with Catholic France or Protestant England? In the ensuing tug-of-war between the English and the French, the infant Mary was taken to France for safety and, at the age of 15, married the French Dauphin. The Auld Alliance seemed to have taken on a new life, and Mary made a will bequeathing Scotland to France if she died childless.

When the King of France died in 1558, Mary, still aged only 16, ascended the throne with her

husband. Her ambitions, though, didn't end there: she later declared herself Queen of England as well, basing her claim on the Catholic assumption that England's new queen, Elizabeth I, was illegitimate because her father, the much-married Henry VIII, had been a heretic.

## Royal drama

When Mary's husband died in 1560, she returned to Scotland, a vivacious, wilful and attractive woman. She married a Catholic, Henry Darnley, who was by contemporary accounts an arrogant, pompous and effeminate idler, and soon she began spending more and more time with her secretary David Rizzio, an

Italian. When Rizzio was stabbed to death in front of her, Darnley was presumed to be responsible, but who could prove it? Mary appeared to turn back to Darnley and, a few months later, gave birth to a son. Immediately afterwards, however, Darnley himself was murdered, his strangled remains found in a building reduced to rubble by an explosion. Mary and her current favourite, James Hepburn, Earl of Bothwell, were presumed responsible – but again, who could prove it?

Bothwell, a Protestant, quickly divorced his wife and, with few fanfares, became Mary's third husband, three months after Darnley's

cousin, Elizabeth I. Her previous claim to the English throne, however, had not been forgotten. Elizabeth offered her the bleak hospitality of various mansions, in which she remained a prisoner for the next 19 years. In 1587 she was convicted, on somewhat flimsy evidence, of plotting Elizabeth's death and was beheaded at Fotheringay Castle.

## Southern prospects

Mary's son, by this time secure on the Scottish throne, made little more than a token protest. Because Elizabeth, the Virgin Queen, had no heir, James had his sights set on a far greater

death. Even Mary had gone too far this time. Protestant Scotland forced its Catholic queen, still only 24, to abdicate, locking her in an island castle on Loch Leven. Bothwell fled to Norway, where he died in exile. And so, in 1567, another infant king came to the throne: Mary's son, James VI.

Still fact rivalled fiction. Mary escaped from Loch Leven, tried unsuccessfully to reach France, then threw herself on the mercy of her

prize than Scotland could offer: the throne of England. On 27 March 1603 he learned that the prize was his. On hearing of Elizabeth's death, he set out for London, and was to set foot in Scotland only once more in his life.

Scots have speculated ever since about how differently history would have turned out had James VI of Scotland made Edinburgh rather than London his base when he became James I of England. But he was more in sympathy with the divine right of kings than with the notions of the ultra-democratic Presbyterians, who were demanding a strong say in civil affairs. And, as he wrote, ruling from a distance of 400 miles was so much easier.

**Left:** Robert Herdman's depiction of the execution of Mary Queen of Scots.
**Above:** Scottish border raiders.
**Above Right:** James I of England.

His son Charles succeeded to the throne in 1625, not knowing Scotland at all. Without, therefore, realising the consequences, the absentee king tried to harmonise the forms of church service between the two countries.

## Conflict and civil war

The Scots would have none of it: religious riots broke out, and one bishop is said to have conducted his service with two loaded pistols placed in front of him. A National Covenant was organised, pledging faith to "the true religion" and affirming the unassailable authority in spiritual matters of the powerful General Assembly

Cavalier supporters of the king. Charles tried to gain the Scots' support by promising a three-year trial for Presbyterianism in England. But his time had run out: he was beheaded on 30 January 1649.

Charles's execution came as a terrible shock north of the border. How dare England kill the King of Scotland without consulting the Scots! Many turned to Charles's 18-year-old son, who had undertaken not to oppose Presbyterianism, and he was proclaimed Charles II in Edinburgh. But Cromwell won a decisive victory at the Battle of Dunbar and turned Scotland into an occupied country, abolishing its separate parliament.

of the Church of Scotland. Armed conflict soon followed: in 1639 the Scots invaded northern England, forcing Charles to negotiate.

Soon the king's luck ran out in England too. Needing money, he unwisely called together his parliament for the first time in 10 years. A power struggle ensued, leading swiftly to civil war. At first the Scottish Covenanters (so named because of their support for the National Covenant of 1638) backed parliament and the Roundhead forces of Oliver Cromwell; their hope was that a victorious parliament would introduce compulsory Presbyterianism in English and Irish churches as well as in Scotland. Soon the Roundheads began to outpace the

By the time the monarchy was restored in 1660, Charles II had lost interest in Scotland's religious aspirations and removed much of the Presbyterian Church's power. Violent intolerance stalked the land during his reign and the 1680s became known as the Killing Time. The risk to Covenanters increased when, after Charles died of apoplexy in 1685, his brother James, a Catholic, became king. With the rotten judgement that dogged the Stewart line, James II imposed the death penalty for worshipping as a Covenanter. His power base in London soon crumbled, however, and in 1689 he was deposed in favour of his Protestant nephew and son-in-law, William of Orange.

Some Scots, mostly Highlanders, remained true to James. The Jacobites, as they were called, rose under Graham of Claverhouse and almost annihilated William's army in a fierce battle at Killiecrankie in 1689. However, Claverhouse was killed, leaving the Jacobites leaderless; most of them lost heart and returned to the Highlands.

Determined to exert his authority over the Scots, William demanded that every clan leader swear an oath of loyalty to him. Partly because of the bad weather, partly

**ACT OF DISUNION**

"We are bought and sold for English gold," the Scots sang following the Treaty of Union of 1707. Like so many Scottish songs, it was a lament.

MacDonald younger than 70 to the sword. The Campbells were only too pleased to carry out their commission, and the Massacre of Glencoe in 1692 remains one of the bloodiest dates in Scotland's bloodstained history. The barbarity of the massacre produced a public outcry, not so much because of the number killed but because of the abuse of hospitality.

Queen Anne, the second daughter of James II, succeeded William in 1702. Although she had given birth to 17 children, none had survived,

through a misunderstanding of where the swearing would take place, one chieftain, the head of the Clan MacDonald, took his oath several days after the king's deadline.

## Bloody massacre

Here was a chance to make an example of a prominent leader. Members of the Campbell clan, old enemies of the MacDonalds, were ordered to lodge with the MacDonalds at their home in Glencoe, get to know them and then, having won their confidence, put every

**LEFT:** Scottish Covenanters meet in Edinburgh.
**ABOVE:** grief after the Massacre of Glencoe.

and the English establishment was determined to keep both thrones out of Stuart hands. They turned to Sophie of Hanover, a granddaughter of James VI/James I. If the Scots would agree to accept a Hanoverian line of succession, much-needed trade concessions would be granted. There was one other condition: England and Scotland should unite under one parliament.

As so often before, riots broke out in Edinburgh and elsewhere. But the opposition was fragmented, and, in 1707, a Treaty of Union incorporated the Scottish parliament into the Westminster parliament to create the United Kingdom. Unknown to the signatories, the foundation of the British Empire was being laid. ❑

# THE AGE OF REBELLION

*The 18th and 19th centuries witnessed rebellions in Scotland not only against the Union, but also in ideas, industry, agriculture and the Church*

The ink was hardly dry on the Treaty of Union of 1707 when the Scots began to smart under the new constitutional arrangements. The idea of a union with England had never been popular with the working classes, most of whom saw it (rightly) as a sell-out by the aristocracy to the "Auld Enemy". Scotland's businessmen were outraged by the imposition of hefty, English-style excise duties on many goods and the high-handed government bureaucracy that went with them. The aristocracy who had supported the Union resented Westminster's peremptory abolition of Scotland's privy council. Even the hardline Cameronians – the fiercest of Protestants – roundly disliked the Union in the early years of the 18th century.

## Jacobite insurgency

All of which was compounded by the Jacobitism (support for the Stuarts) which haunted many parts of Scotland, particularly among the Episcopalians of Aberdeenshire, Angus and Perthshire, and among the Catholic clans (such as the MacDonalds) of the Western Highlands.

And, given that one of the main planks of Jacobitism was the repeal of the Union, it was hardly surprising that the Stuart kings cast a long shadow over Scotland in the first half of the 18th century. In fact, within a year of the Treaty of Union being signed, the first Jacobite insurgency was under way, helped by a French regime ever anxious to discomfit the power of the English.

In January 1708 a flotilla of French privateers commanded by Comte Claude de Forbin battered its way through the North Sea gales carrying the 19-year-old James Stuart, the self-styled James VIII and III. After a brief sojourn in the Firth of Forth near the coast of Fife the French privateers were chased round

PRECEDING PAGES: David Morier's portrayal of Culloden, painted in 1746. LEFT: Prince Charles Edward Stuart leaving Scotland, from a painting by J.B. MacDonald, and ABOVE: in his finery as the Young Chevalier.

the top of Scotland and out into the Atlantic by English warships, Many of the French vessels foundered on their way back to France, although James survived to go on plotting. On dry land, the uprising of 1708 was confined to a few East Stirlingshire lairds who marched up and down with a handful of men. They were

quickly rounded up, and in November 1708 five of the ringleaders were tried in Edinburgh for treason. The verdict on all five was "not proven" and they were set free. Shocked by this display of Scottish leniency, the British parliament passed the Treason Act of 1708, which brought Scotland into line with England, ensuring traitors a long and grisly death.

The next Jacobite uprising, in 1715, was a more serious affair. By then disaffection in Scotland with the Union was widespread, the Hanoverians had not totally secured their grip on Britain, there were loud pro-Stuart mutterings in England, and much of Britain had been stripped of its military.

## An odd outcome

But the insurrection was led by the Earl of Mar, a military incompetent known as "Bobbing John", whose support came mainly from the clans of the Central and Eastern Highlands. When the two sides clashed at Sheriffmuir near Stirling on 13 November, Mar's Jacobite army had a four-to-one advantage over the tiny Hanoverian force commanded by "Red John of the Battles" (as the Duke of Argyll was known). But, instead of pressing his huge advantage, Mar withdrew his

### SPANISH SURRENDER

Bealach-n-Spainnteach (the Pass of the Spaniards), a niche in the Kintail Mountains, recalls the rout suffered by the Spanish in 1719.

Stuarts trying again. In 1719 it was the Spaniards who decided to try to queer the Hanoverian pitch by backing the Jacobites. Again it was a fiasco. In March 1719 a little force of 307 Spanish soldiers sailed into Loch Alsh where they joined up with a few hundred Murrays, Mackenzies and Mackintoshes. This Spanish-Jacobite stage army was easily routed in the steep pass of Glenshiel by a British unit which swooped down from Inverness to pound the Jacobite positions with their mortars. The Highlanders simply vanished into the mist and snow

Highland army after an inconclusive clash.

The insurrection of 1715 quickly ran out of steam. The Pretender himself did not arrive in Scotland until the end of December, and the forces he brought with him were too little and too late. He did his cause no good by stealing away at night (along with "Bobbing John" and a few others), leaving his followers to the wrath of the Whigs. The Duke of Argyll was sacked as commander of the government forces for fear he would be too lenient. Dozens of rebels – especially the English – were hanged, drawn and quartered, and hundreds were deported.

Not that the débâcle of 1715 stopped the

of Kintail, leaving the wretched Spaniards in their gold-on-white uniforms to wander about the sub-arctic landscape before surrendering to the British troops.

## The Young Pretender

But it was the insurrection of 1745, "so glorious an enterprise", led by Charles Edward Stuart (Bonnie Prince Charlie), which shook Britain, despite the fact that the Government's grip on the turbulent parts of Scotland had never seemed firmer. There were military depots at Fort William, Fort Augustus and Fort George, and an effective Highland militia (later known as the Black Watch) had been raised. General Wade had thrown a network of military roads and bridges across the Highlands. Logically Charles, the Young Pretender, should never have been allowed to set foot out of the Highlands.

But having set up a military "infrastructure" in the Highlands, the British government had neglected it. The Independent Companies (the Black Watch) had been shunted out to the West Indies, there were fewer than 4,000 troops in the whole of Scotland, hardly any cavalry or artillery, and Clan Campbell was no longer an effective fighting force. The result was that Bonnie Prince Charlie and his ragtag army of MacDonalds, Camerons, Mackintoshes, Robertsons, McGre-

of Scotland. Few Jacobite troops had been raised in Edinburgh, and Glasgow and the southwest were openly hostile. Some men had been drummed up in Manchester, but there was no serious support from the Roman Catholic families of northern England. Charles got as far as Derby and then fled back to Scotland with two powerful Hanoverian armies hot on his heels.

## Dashed hopes

After winning a rearguard action at Clifton, near Penrith, and what has been described as a "lucky victory" at Falkirk in January 1746, the Jacobite army was cut to pieces by the Duke of

gors, Macphersons and Gordons, plus some Lowland cavalry and a stiffening of Franco-Irish mercenaries, was able to walk into Edinburgh and set up a "royal court" in Holyrood Palace.

In September the Young Pretender sallied out of Edinburgh and wrecked General John Cope's panicky Hanoverian army near Prestonpans, and then marched across the border into England. But Stuart's success was an illusion. There was precious little support for his cause in the Lowlands

LEFT: Culloden's victor, the Duke of Cumberland.
ABOVE: Prince Charlie's much romanticised farewell in 1746 to Flora MacDonald.
ABOVE RIGHT: Culloden remembered.

Cumberland's artillery on Drummossie Moor, Culloden, near Inverness on 16 April 1746. It was the last great pitched battle on the soil of mainland Britain. It was also the end of the Gaelic clan system, which had survived in the mountains of Scotland long after it had disappeared from Ireland. The days when an upland-chieftain could drum up a "tail" of trained swordsmen for cattle raids into the Lowlands were over.

Following his post-Culloden "flight across the heather", Charles, disguised as a woman servant, was given shelter on the Isle of Skye by Flora MacDonald, thus giving birth to one of Scotland's abiding romantic tales. He was then plucked off the Scottish coast by a French privateer and taken into exile, drunkenness and despair in France and Italy. A few dozen of the more prominent Jacobites were hauled off to Carlisle and Newcastle where they were tried, and some of them hanged. The estates of the gentry who had "come out" in '45 were confiscated by the Crown. And for some time the Highlands were harried mercilessly by the Duke of Cumberland's troopers.

In an effort to subdue the Highlands, the government in London passed the Disarming Act of 1746, which not only banned the carrying of claymores, targes, dirks and muskets, but also the wearing of tartans and the playing of bagpipes. It was a nasty piece of legislation, that impacted greatly on Gaelic culture. The British government also took the opportunity to abolish Scotland's inefficient and often corrupt system of "Courts of Regality" by which the aristocracy (and not just the Highland variety) dispensed justice, collected fines and wielded powers of life and wealth.

## The Age of Enlightenment

It is one of the minor paradoxes of 18th-century European history that, while Scotland was being racked by dynastic convulsions which were 17th-century in origin, the country was transforming itself into one of the most forward-looking societies in the world. Scotland began to wake up in the first half of the 18th century. By about 1740 the intellectual, scientific and mercantile phenomenon which became known as the Scottish Enlightenment was well under way, although it didn't reach its peak until the end of the century.

Whatever created it, the Scottish Enlightenment was an extraordinary explosion of creativity and energy. And while, in retrospect at least, the period was dominated by David Hume the philosopher and Adam Smith the economist, there were many others, such as William Robertson, Adam Ferguson, William Cullen and the Adam brothers. Through the multi-faceted talents of its literati, Scotland in general and Edinburgh in particular became one of the intellectual powerhouses of Western Europe.

But the Enlightenment and all that went with it had some woeful side-effects. The Highland "Clearances" of the late 18th and early 19th centuries owed much to the "improving" attitudes triggered by the Enlightenment, although the greed of the lairds played its part. The enterprising Sir John Sinclair, for example, pointed out that, while the Highlands were capable of producing from £200,000 to £300,000 worth of black cattle every year, "The same ground will produce twice as much mutton and there is wool into the bargain."

The argument proved irresistible. Sheep – particularly Cheviots – and their Lowland shepherds began to flood into the glens and straths of the Highlands, displacing the Highland "tacksmen" and their families. Tens of thousands were forced to move to the Lowlands, coastal areas, or in the colonies overseas, taking

with them their culture of songs and traditions.

The worst of the Clearances – or at least the most notorious – took place on the huge estates of the Countess of Sutherland and her rich, English-born husband, the Marquis of Stafford. Although Stafford spent huge sums of money building roads, harbours and fish-curing sheds (for very little profit), his estate managers evicted tenants with real ruthlessness. It was a pattern which was repeated all over Highland Scotland at the beginning of the 19th century, and then again later when people were displaced

**ABOVE:** a Skye crofter prepares some winter comfort.
**RIGHT:** Glasgow in the 18th century.

by the red deer of the "sporting" estates. The overgrown remains of villages all over the Highlands are a painful reminder of this sad chapter in Scottish history.

## Radicals and reactionaries

As the industrial economy of Lowland Scotland burgeoned at the end of the 18th century, it sucked in thousands of immigrant workers from all over Scotland and Ireland. The clamour for democracy grew. Some of it was fuelled by the ideas of the American and French revolutions, but much of the unrest was a reaction to Scotland's hopelessly inadequate electoral system.

At the end of the 18th century there were only 4,500 voters in the whole of Scotland and only 2,600 voters in the 33 rural counties.

And for almost 40 years Scotland was dominated by the powerful machine politician Henry Dundas, the First Viscount Melville, universally known as "King Harry the Ninth".

As Solicitor General for Scotland, Lord Advocate, Home Secretary, Secretary for War and then First Lord of the Admiralty, Dundas wielded awesome power.

But nothing could stop the spread of libertarian ideas in an increasingly industrialised workforce. The ideas contained in Tom Paine's

### INDUSTRIAL GLORY

The Enlightenment was not confined to the salons of Edinburgh. Commerce and industry also thrived. "The same age, which produces great philosophers and politicians, renowned generals and poets, usually abounds with skilled weavers and ship-carpenters," David Hume wrote in 1752.

By 1760 the famous Carron Ironworks in Falkirk was churning out high-grade ordnance for the British military. By 1780 hundreds of tons of goods were being shuttled between Edinburgh and Glasgow along the Forth-Clyde Canal. The Turnpike Act of 1751 improved the road system dramatically and created a brisk demand for carriages

and stagecoaches. In 1738 Scotland's share of the tobacco trade (based in Glasgow) was 10 percent; by 1769 it was more than 52 percent. There was a huge upsurge of activity in many trades: carpet-weaving, upholstery, glass making, china and pottery manufacture, linen, soap, distilling and brewing.

The 18th century changed Scotland from one of the poorest countries in Europe to a state of middling affluence. It has been calculated that between 1700 and 1800 the money generated within Scotland increased by a factor of more than 50, while the population stayed more or less static (at around 1½ million).

*Rights of Man* spread like wildfire in the Scotland of the 1790s. The cobblers, weavers and spinners proved the most vociferous democrats, but there was also unrest among farmworkers, and among seamen and soldiers in the Highland regiments.

Throughout the 1790s a number of radical "one man, one vote" organisations sprang up, such as the Scottish Friends of the People and the United Scotsmen (a quasi-nationalist group which modelled itself on the United Irishmen led by Wolfe Tone).

> **KING HARRY THE NINTH**
>
> Lord Cockburn summed up the relentless grip of Henry Dundas on Scotland: "Who steered upon him was safe; who disregarded his light was wrecked."

called Scottish Insurrection was brought to an end in the legally corrupt trial of the weavers James Wilson, John Baird, Andrew Hardie and 21 other workmen. A special (English) Court of Oyer and Terminer was set up in Glasgow to hear the case, and Wilson, Baird and Hardie were sentenced to be hanged, beheaded and quartered, after making resounding speeches. They were spared the last part of the gruesome sentence. The other Radicals were sentenced to penal transportation.

But the brooding figure of Dundas was more than a match for the radicals. Every organisation which raised its head was swiftly infiltrated by police spies and agents provocateurs. Ringleaders (such as the advocate Thomas Muir) were framed, arrested, tried and deported. Some, such as Robert Watt, who led the "Pike Plot" of 1794, were hanged. Meetings were broken up by dragoons, riots were put down by musket-fire and the Scottish universities were racked by witchhunts.

Although Dundas himself was discredited in 1806, after being impeached for embezzlement, and died in 1811, the anti-Radical paranoia of the Scottish ruling class lingered on. Establishment panic reached a peak in 1820 when the so-

## Reform and disruption

By the 1820s most of Scotland (and indeed Britain) was weary of the political and constitutional corruption under which the country laboured. In 1823 Lord Archibald Hamilton pointed out the electoral absurdity of rural Scotland. "I have the right to vote in five counties in Scotland, in not one of which do I possess an acre of land," he said, "and I have no doubt that if I took the trouble I might have a vote for every county in that kingdom." Hamilton's motion calling for parliamentary reform was defeated by only 35 votes.

But nine years later, in 1832, the Reform Bill finally passed into law, giving Scotland 30 rural constituencies, 23 burgh constituencies and a voting population of 65,000 (compared to a previous 4,500). Even this limited extension of the franchise – to male householders whose property had a rentable value of £10 or more – generated much wailing and gnashing of teeth among Scottish Tories.

No sooner had the controversy over electoral reform subsided than it was replaced by the row between the "moderates" and the "evangelicals" within the Church of Scotland. "Scotland", Lord Palmerston noted at the time, "is aflame about the Church question." But this was no genteel falling-out among theologians. It was a brutal and bruising affair which dominated political life in Scotland for 10 years and raised all kinds of constitutional questions.

At the heart of the argument was the Patronage Act of 1712, which gave Scots lairds the same right English squires had to appoint, or "intrude" clergy on local congregations. Ever since it was passed, the Church of Scotland had argued (rightly) that the Patronage Act was a flagrant and illegal violation of the Revolution Settlement of 1690 and the Treaty of Union of 1707, both of which guaranteed the independence of the Church of Scotland.

## A Free Church

But the pleas fell on deaf ears. The English-dominated parliament could see no fault in a system which enabled Anglicised landowners to appoint like-minded clergymen. Patronage was seen by the Anglo-Scottish establishment as a useful instrument of political control and social progress. The issue came to a head in May 1843 when the evangelicals, led by Dr Thomas Chalmers, marched out of the annual General Assembly of the Church of Scotland in Edinburgh to form the Free Church of Scotland.

Chalmers, theologian, astronomer and brilliant organiser, defended the Free Church against bitter enemies. His final triumph, in 1847, was to persuade the London parliament that it was folly to allow the aristocracy to refuse the Free Church land on which to build churches and schools. A few days after giving evidence, Chalmers died in Edinburgh.

LEFT: a 19th-century poster, now on display in Glasgow's People's Palace.
RIGHT: Scottish Presbyterians in the 17th century defying the law to worship.

The rebellion of the evangelicals was brilliantly planned, well funded and took the British establishment completely by surprise. Four hundred teachers left the kirk and, within 10 years of the Disruption, the Free Church had built more than 800 churches, 700 manses, three large theological colleges and 600 schools, and brought about a huge extension of education. After 1847, state aid had to be given to the Free as well as to the established Church schools, and in 1861 the established Church lost its legal powers over Scotland's parish school system. This prepared the ground for the Education Act of 1872, which set up a national system under

the Scottish Educational Department. And, although it ran into some vicious opposition from landowners, especially in the Highlands, the Free Church prevailed.

In fact, it can be argued that the Disruption was the only rebellion in 18th- or 19th-century British history that succeeded. Chalmers and his supporters had challenged both the pervasive influence of the Anglo-Scottish aristocracy and the power of the British parliament, and they had won. The Patronage Act of 1712 was finally repealed in 1874, and the Free Church re-merged with the Church of Scotland in 1929, uniting the majority of Scottish Presbyterians in one Church. ❑

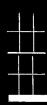

# THE MAKING OF MODERN SCOTLAND

*Despite the economic and social problems of the 20th century, Scotland remains fiercely confident, particularly in moves towards political independence*

During the Victorian and Edwardian eras, Scotland, like most of Europe, became urbanised and industrialised. Steelworks, ironworks, shipyards, coal mines, shale-oil refineries, textile factories, engineering shops, canals and, of course, railways proliferated all over 19th-century Scotland. The process was concentrated in Scotland's "central belt" (the stretch of low-lying land between Edinburgh and Glasgow), but there were important "outliers" like Aberdeen, Dundee, Ayrshire and the mill towns of the Scottish borders. A few smaller industrial ventures found their way deep into the Highlands or onto a few small islands.

It was a process which dragged in its wake profound social, cultural and demographic change. The booming industries brought thousands of work-seeking immigrants flocking into Lowland Scotland. Most came from the Highlands and Ireland, and many nursed an ancient distaste for the British establishment which translated itself into left-wing radicalism – one reason why Scottish politics are still dominated by the Labour Party today. The immigrants were also largely Roman Catholic, which did something to loosen the grip of the Presbyterian churches on Scottish life.

## A huge metropolis

Industry transformed the city of Glasgow and the River Clyde. Between 1740 and 1840 Glasgow's population leapt from 17,000 to 200,000 and then doubled to 400,000 by 1870. The small Georgian city became a huge industrial metropolis built on the kind of rectangular grid common in the United States, with industrial princes living in splendour while Highland, Irish, Italian and Jewish immigrants swarmed in the noisome slums.

In many ways 19th-century Glasgow had more in common with Chicago or New York than with any other city in Britain. Working-

**PRECEDING PAGES:** the elegant Edinburgh residence of Scotland's Secretary of State.
**LEFT:** *First Steamboat on the Clyde*, by John Knox.
**RIGHT:** slum-dwellers in Glasgow's Gorbals.

class conditions were appalling. Rickets, cholera, smallpox, tuberculosis, diphtheria and alcoholism were rampant. The streets were unclean and distinctly unsafe. Violence was endemic as Highlanders and Irishmen clashed in the stews and whisky dens, while Orangemen from Ulster were used as violent and murder-

ous strike-breakers. The city hangman was never short of work.

But there was no denying Glasgow's enormous industrial vitality. By the middle of the century the city was peppered with more than 100 textile mills (an industry which by that time employed more than 400,000 Scots). There were ironworks at Tollcross, Coatbridge and Monklands, productive coal mines all over Lanarkshire, and the River Clyde was lined with boiler makers, marine-engineering shops, and world-class shipyards. For generations the label "Clyde built" was synonymous with industrial quality.

Nor was industry confined to Glasgow and its environs. The Tayside city of Dundee forged close links with India and became the biggest jute-manufacturing centre in Britain. The Carron Ironworks at Falkirk was Europe's largest producer of artillery by the year 1800, while in West Lothian a thriving industry was built up to extract oil from shale. Scotland's east-coast fisheries also flourished, and by the end of the century the town of Wick in Caithness became Europe's biggest herring port.

As well as producing large quantities of books, biscuits and bureaucrats, Edinburgh was a centre of the British brewing industry; at one stage there were more than 40 breweries within the city boundaries. And, in the latter part of the 19th century, the Scotch whisky industry boomed, thanks to the devastation of the French vineyards in the 1880s by phylloxera which almost wrecked the thriving cognac industry.

## Rich and poor

By the end of the 19th century, Scotland, with its educated workforce and proximity to European markets, was attracting inward investment. The American-funded North British Rubber Company moved into Edinburgh in 1857. In 1884 the Singer Company built one of the biggest factories in the world at Clydebank to

### CASH INCENTIVES

The growth of industry in Scotland generated huge amounts of cash. Edinburgh and Dundee became centres for investment trusts which sunk cash into ventures all over the world, particularly the US. In 1873 the Dundee jute man Robert Fleming set up the Scottish American Investment Trust to channel money into American cattle ranches, fruit farms, mining companies and railways. The biggest cattle ranch in the US – Matador Land & Cattle Company – was run from Dundee until 1951. The outlaw Butch Cassidy once worked for a cattle company operating from the fastidious New Town of Edinburgh.

manufacture mass-produced sewing machines. It was the start of a 100-year trend which did much to undermine the Scottish economy's independence.

Despite the enthusiasm of Queen Victoria and the British gentry for the Highlands, dire poverty stalked upland Scotland. Land reform was desperately needed. Following riots in Skye in 1882 and the formation of the Highland Land League in 1884, Gladstone's Liberal government passed the Crofters (Scotland) Holdings Act of 1886, which gave crofters fair rents, security of tenure and the right to pass their croft on to their families. But it was Lord Salisbury's Conservative government which put the Scottish Secretary in the British cabinet, and established the Scottish Office in Edinburgh and London in 1886.

By the end of the 19th century the huge majority of the Scottish population was urban, industrialised and concentrated in the towns and cities of the Lowlands. And urban Scotland proved a fertile breeding ground for the British Left. The Scottish Labour Party (SLP) was founded in 1888, although it soon merged with the Independent Labour Party (ILP), which in turn played a big part in the formation of the (British) Labour Party. Britain's first Labour MP, Keir Hardie, was a Scot, as was Ramsay MacDonald, Britain's first Labour prime minister.

percent of the British Army. And when the butcher's bill was added up after the war it was found that more than 20 percent of all the Britons killed were Scots.

In addition to which, the shipyards of the Clyde and the engineering shops of west central Scotland were producing more tanks, shells, warships, explosives and fieldguns than any comparable part of Britain. That explains why the British government took such a dim view of the strikes and industrial disputes which hit the Clyde between 1915 and 1919 and led to the area being dubbed "Red Clydeside". When Glasgow workers struck for a 40-hour week in

## The Great War

When World War I broke out in 1914 the Scots flocked to the British colours with an extraordinary enthusiasm. Like Ireland, Scotland provided the British Army with a disproportionate number of soldiers. Like the Irish, the Scots suspended their radicalism and trooped into the forces to fight for King and Empire, to the despair of left-wing leaders like Keir Hardie and John Maclean. With less than 10 percent of the British population, the Scots made up almost 15

**LEFT:** herring drifters near the port of Peterhead.
**ABOVE:** Labour Party leader Ramsay MacDonald with his son and daughter in 1929.

January 1919, the Secretary of State for Scotland panicked and called in the military.

Glaswegians watched open-mouthed as thousands of armed troops backed by tanks poured onto the Glasgow streets to nip the Red Revolution in the bud. At a huge rally in George Square on 31 January 1919, the police baton-charged the crowd.

## The hungry years

The 1920s and 1930s were sour years for Scotland. The "traditional" industries of shipbuilding, steel-making, coal-mining and heavy engineering went into a decline from which they have never recovered. And the whisky industry reeled

# Laying down the Law

One curiosity of the Scottish legal system is Not Proven – "that bastard verdict", as Sir Walter Scott called it. At the end of a criminal trial the verdict can be "guilty" or "not guilty", as in England, or the jury may find the charge "not proven". It's an option that reflects Scots logic and refusal to compromise by assuming a person innocent until proved guilty, though it does confer a stigma on the accused.

The jargon of Scots lawyers is distinctive, too. If you embark on litigation you are a "pursuer". You sue a "defender". "Law Burrows" (nothing to do

with rabbits) is a way of asking the courts to prevent someone harassing you. If you disagree too outspokenly with a judge's decision, you may be accused of "murmuring the judge".

From the abolition of the Scottish Parliament with the 1707 Act of Union until its re-establishment in 1999, the UK parliament in London made laws for the country. Yet, though few outsiders realise it, the Scots managed to maintain a distinctive legal system despite those three centuries of political union with the rest of the UK.

Scottish law is quite different in origin from that of England and those countries (such as the US and many Commonwealth nations) to which the English system has been exported, and is closer to the legal systems of South Africa, Sri Lanka, Louisiana and

Quebec. It was developed from Roman law and owes much more to Continental legal systems than does that of England – thanks partly to the custom of Scottish lawyers, during the 17th and 18th centuries, studying in France, Holland or Germany. Solicitors, the general practitioners of the law, regard themselves as men of affairs, with a wider role than lawyers in some countries have adopted. Advocates, who are based in Parliament House in Edinburgh and to whom a solicitor will turn for expert advice, also refuse to become too narrowly specialised. This is important if they wish to become sheriffs, as the judges of the local courts are called.

Some practitioners have demonstrated outstanding talents beyond the confines of the law. Sir Walter Scott was, for most of his life, a practising lawyer. In Selkirk, near the palatial house he built at Abbotsford, can be seen the courtroom where he presided as sheriff. Robert Louis Stevenson qualified as an advocate, the equivalent of the English barrister, though he quickly deserted the law for literature.

Inevitably, English law has had its influence. Much modern legislation, especially commercial law, has tended to be copied from England. The traffic, however, hasn't been all one-way. In Scottish criminal trials, the jury of 15 has always been allowed to reach a majority verdict, a procedure only recently adopted by England. The English have also introduced a prosecution service, independent of the police, similar to that which operates in Scotland. Some in England would also like to import the "110-day rule": this requires a prisoner on remand to be released if his trial doesn't take place within 110 days of his imprisonment. More controversially, Scottish judges have power in criminal cases to create new crimes – a power they use sparingly.

Many in England envy the Scottish system of house purchase. Most of the legal and estate agency work is done by solicitors and seems to be completed far faster than in England. Scottish laws on Sunday trading are more liberal, and divorce was available in Scotland several centuries before it was south of the border.

Along with the kirk, the separateness of the Scottish legal system plays a vital part in establishing a sense of national identity. Many Scots lawyers resent the failure of Westminster to have proper regard to the fact that the law is different in Scotland. Whether it's better is a separate question; the best verdict in this case may be "not proven".  ❏

**LEFT:** time for legal exchange between sessions.

from the body-blow of American Prohibition.

The new light engineering industries – cars, electrics and machine tools – stayed stubbornly south of the border. Unemployment soared to almost three in 10 of the workforce, and Scots boarded the emigrant ships in droves. An estimated 400,000 Scots (10 percent of the population) emigrated between 1921 and 1931. And in 1937 Walter Elliot, Secretary of State for Scotland, described how in Scotland "23 percent of its population live in conditions of gross overcrowding, compared with 4 percent in England".

Most of urban Scotland saw its salvation in the newly formed Labour Party, which not only

the Scottish literary renaissance of the inter-war years the nationalist movement grew increasingly more political. In 1934 the small (but right-wing) Scottish Party merged with the National Party of Scotland to form the Scottish National Party (SNP).

## The world at war

It wasn't until World War II loomed that the Scottish economy began to climb out of the doldrums. And when war broke out in September 1939 the Clydeside shipyards moved into high gear to build warships like the *Duke of York*, *Howe*, *Indefatigible* and *Vanguard*, while the

promised a better life but also a measure of Home Rule. Support for the Labour Party began early. At the general election of 1922 an electoral pattern was set which has remained (with few exceptions) ever since: England went Conservative even if Scotland voted Labour.

The 1920s and 1930s also saw revival of a kind of left-wing cultural nationalism which owed a lot to the poetry of Hugh MacDiarmid, the writing of Lewis Grassic Gibbon and the enthusiasms of upper-crust nationalists like Ruaridh Erskine of Marr and R.B. Cunninghame-Graham. From

**Above:** the Hungry Thirties: Glasgow kids keep smiling through the hard times.

engineering firms began pumping out small arms, bayonets, explosives and ammunition. The Rolls-Royce factory at Hillington near Glasgow produced Merlin engines for the RAF's Spitfires. Clydeside became one of Britain's most important wartime regions.

The point wasn't missed by the Germans. On 13 and 14 March 1941, hundreds of German bombers, operating at the limit of their range, devastated Clydeside. More than 1,000 people were killed (528 in the town of Clydebank) and another 1,500 injured.

War killed more than 58,000 Scots (compared to the 148,000 who had lost their lives in World War I) but had the effect of galvanising the Scottish economy for a couple of decades. And there's no doubt that the Labour government which came to power in 1945 worked major improvements on Scottish life.

## The post-war period

The National Health Service proved an effective instrument against such plagues as infant mortality, tuberculosis, rickets and scarlet fever. Housing conditions improved in leaps and bounds as the worst of the city slums were pulled down and replaced by roomy (although often badly built) council houses. Semi-rural new towns like East Kilbride, Glenrothes, Cum-

land-based airline, was swallowed up by British Airways. To an alarming extent, Scotland's economy now has a "branch factory" status.

English enthusiasm for Labour's experiment flagged and in 1951 Sir Winston Churchill was returned to power. Scotland, of course, continued to vote Labour (although in the general election of 1955 the Conservatives won 36 of Scotland's 71 seats, the only time they have had a majority north of the border). And, while Home Rule for Scotland was off the political agenda, Scottish nationalism refused to go away.

In the late 1940s two-thirds of the Scottish electorate signed a "national covenant" demand-

bernauld, Irvine and Livingston were established throughout central Scotland.

What went largely unnoticed in the post-war euphoria was that the Labour government's policy of nationalising the coal mines and the railways was stripping Scotland of many of its decision-making powers, and therefore management jobs. The process continued through the 1960s and 1970s when the steel, shipbuilding and aerospace industries were also "taken into public ownership".

This haemorrhage of economic power and influence was compounded by Scottish companies being sold to English and foreign predators. In 1988 British Caledonian, originally a Scot-

ing Home Rule. In 1951 a squad of young nationalists outraged the British establishment by whisking the Stone of Destiny out of Westminster Abbey and hiding it in Scotland. And in 1953 the British establishment outraged Scottish sentiment by insisting on the title of Queen Elizabeth II for the new queen, despite the fact that the Scots had never had a Queen Elizabeth I.

## Industrial decline

But while Scotland did reasonably well out of the Conservative-led "New Elizabethan Age" of the 1950s and early 1960s, the old structural faults soon began to reappear. By the late 1950s the well-equipped Japanese and German shipyards were snatching orders from under the nose of the Clyde, the Scottish coalfields were proving woefully inefficient and Scotland's steelworks and heavy engineering firms were losing their grip on international markets.

And, although the Conservative government did fund a new steel mill at Ravenscraig, near Motherwell, and enticed Rootes to set up a car plant at Linwood and the British Motor Corporation to start making trucks at Bathgate, it was all done under duress, and all these projects were abandoned.

**ASSEMBLY ROOM**

In the 1970s the Royal High School in Edinburgh was purchased ready for the new assembly. After years of indecision it was sold again in 1994.

Labour Party. Although Ewing lost her seat at the 1970 general election, her success marked the start of an upsurge in Scottish nationalism that preoccupied Scottish – and, to some extent, British – politics for the next decade.

When Harold Wilson's Labour Government ran out of steam in 1970 it was replaced by the Conservative regime of Edward Heath – although, once again, the Scots voted overwhelmingly Labour. But in the early 1970s Scotland got lucky. The oil companies struck big quantities of oil. All

Scotland's distance from the marketplace continued to be a crippling disadvantage. The Midlands and south of England remained the engine-room of the British economy. The drift of Scots to the south continued.

Although the Scots voted heavily for the Labour Party in the general elections of 1964 and 1966, Labour's complacency was jolted in November 1967 when Mrs Winnie Ewing of the SNP snatched the Hamilton by-election from the

round Scotland engineering firms and land speculators began snapping up sites on which to build platform yards, rig repair bases, airports, oil refineries and petrochemical works. Nothing like it had been seen since the industrial revolution.

The SNP was quick to take advantage of the new mood of optimism. Running on a campaign slogan of "It's Scotland's Oil", the SNP won seven seats in the general election of February 1974 and took more than 20 percent of the Scottish vote. In October 1974 they did even better, cutting a swathe through both parties to take 11 seats and more than 30 percent of the Scottish vote. It looked as if one more push by the SNP would see

**LEFT:** shipbuilding on the Clyde, a dying industry; a Hebridean weaver makes Harris tweed on a traditional handloom. **ABOVE:** an Edinburgh piper blows hot air; victory for Alex Salmond.

the United Kingdom dissolved, and the hard-pressed British economy cut off from the oil revenues it so badly needed.

The Labour government responded to the nationalists' political threat with a constitutional defence. It offered Scotland a directly elected assembly with substantial (although strictly limited) powers if the Scottish people voted "yes" in a national referendum.

At which point Westminster changed the rules. At the instigation of Labour MP George Cunningham, parliament decided that a simple majority was not good enough, and that devolution would go ahead only if more than 40 percent of the Scottish electorate voted in favour. It was an impossible condition. Predictably the Scots failed to vote yes by a big majority in the referendum of March 1979 (although they *did* vote "yes") and the Scotland Bill lapsed. Shortly afterwards, the 11 SNP members joined a vote of censure against the Labour government – which fell by one vote. Margaret Thatcher was voted into power and promptly made it plain that any form of Home Rule for Scotland was out of the question.

### The Thatcher years

The devolution debacle produced a genuine crisis of confidence among Scotland's political classes. Support for the SNP slumped, the Alliance could do nothing. And the Labour Party, armed with the majority of the Scottish vote, could only watch helplessly as the aluminium smelter at Invergordon, the steel mill at Gartcosh, the car works at Linwood, the pulp mill at Fort William, the truck plant at Bathgate and much of the Scottish coalfield perished in the economic blizzard of the 1980s. Even the energetic Scottish Development Agency could do little to protect the Scottish economy. Unemployment climbed to more than 300,000, and the electronics industry's much-vaunted "Silicon Glen" proved far too small to take up the slack.

So the political triumph of Thatcherism in England found no echoes in Scotland. At the general election of June 1987 the pattern which first emerged in 1922 repeated itself; England voted Tory and Scotland voted Labour. Out of 72 Scottish MPs 50 were Labour and only 10 were Conservative. This raised the argument that the then Scottish Secretary, Malcolm Rifkind, was an English governor-general with "no mandate" to govern Scotland. Rifkind's

response was that the 85 percent of the Scottish electorate who voted for "British" parties were voting for the sovereignty of Westminster and therefore had to accept Westminster's rules.

At the end of 1987 the Labour Party tabled yet another Devolution Bill which was promptly thrown out by English MPs to the jeers of the SNP, who claimed that Labour's "Feeble Fifty" could do nothing without Westminster's say so.

### A new parliament

The commitment to devolution remained, however, and following Labour's landslide victory in the general election of May 1997, which left

Scotland with no Conservative MPs at all, the Scottish people were asked in a referendum whether they wanted their own parliament. The proposal received a ringing endorsement, a majority of two-to-one voting "yes". Proposals for the new parliament to have the power to vary taxes from UK standard rates were also approved.

In the first elections to the Edinburgh-based Scottish Parliament in 1999, only three out of five Scots bothered to vote. Labour won 53 of the 129 seats. This was not an overall majority, so Labour was forced to negotiate with the Liberal Democrats (17 seats) who became their coalition partners in a joint bid to keep at bay the pro-independence Scottish National Party (35 seats). The new parliament building finally opened at Holyrood in 2004, its construction costs having soared from an estimated £40 million to £431 million. Yet many voters regarded the assembly as a toothless beast, its energies sapped by the tendency of the more able politicians to direct their ambitions towards the London parliament rather than the Edinburgh one.

Land reform was one area where the Scottish Parliament did assert itself, notably by introducing the Land Reform (Scotland) Act to tackle the iniquity of most of the land of Scotland being owned by a few lairds, many

In 2002 Scotland reasserted itself in the world of engineering by unveiling an iconic landmark, the Falkirk Wheel. This, the world's only rotating boat lift, replaced derelict locks and transfers boats by means of gondolas between two canals – the Union and the Forth & Clyde – that stand at different levels and link Edinburgh and Glasgow.

Whilst Edinburgh is Scotland's powerful "financial hub", Glasgow's once-proud heavy industry has now been replaced by a thriving service sector. However, Glasgow and Edinburgh still both continue to have neighbourhoods plagued by poverty.

absentee and many foreign. The new law brought much of that land into public ownership by establishing two national parks – the Loch Lomond and Trossachs, and the Cairngorms. Other ground-breaking legislation abolished upfront tuition fees at universities, provided better care for the old and disabled, and gave mothers the legal right to breastfeed in public. Members voted to ban smoking in all public places (which came into effect in 2006), encouraging Westminster to bring forward similar proposals for England and Wales.

**ABOVE:** the Falkirk Wheel, a major engineering feat that links two canals between Edinburgh and Glasgow.

## The independence debate

Scots have now been members of the United Kingdom for over 300 years, and Scottish history is deeply enmeshed with that of Great Britain. With the Scottish National Party having seized power at the 2007 elections, and its leader, Alex Salmond now firmly installed as First Minister of the country, Scotland has once again taken a decisive step to challenge the status quo and the 1707 Treaty of the Union. Yet for those who dream of seeing Scotland achieve its independence, time will tell how much further public opinion and the fickle will of Scottish (and Westminster based) politicians will shift.                                    ❑

# HIGHLANDERS AND LOWLANDERS

*Although the distinctions between Highlanders and Lowlanders are disappearing, many of the original Gaelic traditions live on*

The division between the Highlander and the Lowlander was one of the most ancient and fundamental in Scotland's history. "The people of the coast", said John of Fordun, the Lowland Aberdeenshire chronicler, writing in 1380, "are of domestic and civilised habits, trusty, patient and urbane, decent in their attire, affable and peaceful.... The Highlanders and people of the islands, on the other hand, are a savage and untamed nation, rude and independent, given to rapine, easy-living, of a docile and warm disposition, comely in person but unsightly in dress, hostile to the English people and language and, owing to diversity of speech, even to their own nation, and exceedingly cruel."

The division was based on what Fordun called "the diversity of their speech": the Lowlanders spoke Scots, a version of Middle English, the Highlanders spoke Gaelic. The line between the two languages broadly coincided with the line of the hills. North of the Highland fault running from just above Dumbarton to just above Stonehaven, and west of the plains of Aberdeenshire and the Moray Firth, Gaelic was spoken. Outside that area, Scots was spoken, except in the northern isles of Orkney and Shetland, where a kind of Norse was spoken, and perhaps in a few pockets of the southwest where another form of Gaelic lingered until late in the Middle Ages.

## Lingering images

Four hundred years later, things hadn't changed that much. When Patrick Sellar, the Lowland sheep farmer, wrote to his employer, the Countess of Sutherland, about the nature of the people over whom he was appointed as estate manager, John of Fordun would have recognised the tone. Sellar spoke of "the absence of every principle of truth and candour from a population of several hundred thousand souls". He compared these "aborigines of Britain" with the

**PRECEDING PAGES:** the youth of Scotland demonstrate their loyalty; an Arinacrinachd weaver.
**LEFT:** Lonach Highlanders stop for refreshments.
**RIGHT:** starting young at Glenfinnan.

"aborigines of America", the Native American Indians: "Both live in turf cabins in common with the brutes: both are singular for patience, courage, cunning and address. Both are most virtuous where least in contact with men in civilised State, and both are fast sinking under the baneful effects of ardent spirits."

Then, in the 19th century, a startling turnabout occurred. Many Scots began to adopt as their national symbols the very trappings of the despised Highland minority – the kilt and the tartan, the bagpipe and the bonnet, the eagle's feather and the dried sprig of heather: it blended into a kitsch everyone across the world can recognise. In the late 1980s, when the American broadcasting networks wished to devote a minute of their national news bulletins to the question of why Scotland felt unsympathetic to the policies of Britain's then prime minister, Margaret Thatcher, they used 30 seconds setting the scene with men with hairy knees throwing pine trees about at a Highland gathering.

The fact that many Scots only wear a kilt on formal occasions and have never attended a Highland Games is not very relevant. The adoption of these public symbols has something to do with the campaigns of Sir Walter Scott to romanticise the Highlanders, something to do with the charismatic powers of the police pipe bands, which in Victorian days were largely recruited from Highlanders, and something to do with a music hall that loved a stereotype. The mask stuck.

At the same time, ironically, true Highland society was in a state of collapse. Ever since the 17th century its distinctive character and Gaelic culture had been eroded by the steady spread of

rides and a few other communities, mainly on islands, in the extreme west. In the current Scottish Parliament, however, members from those communities have tried to reverse the trend by introducing the Gaelic Language Bill. This aims to make more use of Gaelic in government matters and greatly strengthens its use within the education system. There are now Gaelic language centres on Islay and Skye, while the BBC airs news and cultural programmes in Gaelic.

## Blurred distinctions

So the Highland-Lowland division today has a different meaning from what it had in the past. It

hostile government power, the march of commercial forces tying Scotland together as one market, and the Lowlandisation of the clan chiefs as they sought wives with better dowries than the mountains could provide.

By 1800 Highland landowners wanted their estates to produce more cash more quickly, just as landowners did elsewhere in Scotland. Over the next 50 years they cleared most of the land of peasant farms, which paid little rent, in order to accommodate the Lowlander and his sheep, which paid a good deal more. Simultaneously, Gaelic began a catastrophic decline, from being the language of the Highland area to being the language, as it is today, only of the Outer Heb-

is certainly not any longer the most obvious or important division, ethnically and culturally, among the Scottish people as a whole. The Lowlanders themselves were never uniform: the folk of Aberdeenshire spoke "Doric", a dialect of their own, very different in vocabulary and intonation from, say, the folk of Lothian or Galloway. In the 19th century this sort of regionalism was greatly compounded and complicated by the immigration of the Irish, about two-thirds of them Catholic and one-third Protestant.

The Catholic Irish crowded into distinct areas – Glasgow and Dundee among the cities, and the small mining or iron-working towns of Lanarkshire, Lothian and Fife. Today, especially in the west, it is the Catholic-Protestant division that continues to have most meaning in people's lives. The Catholics are, overall, still a minority in Scotland, but their Church now has more attenders on Sundays than any Protestant denomination – even the Church of Scotland itself. Intermarriage between the two communities has dissolved animosities in the past half-century, but even today politicians deal cautiously with anything that touches, for example, on the right of Scottish Catholics to have their own state-aided schools.

**FOOTBALL FAITHFULS**

Sports allegiances in Scotland are a blend of the regional and the religious. Celtic is Glasgow Catholic, Rangers is Glasgow Protestant.

have a name with the prefix "Mac" or theoretically belong to some clan like Grant or Gunn, Murray or Munro; but, apart perhaps from a greater fondness for dressing in tartan and doing Highland reels at party time, there is little that is distinctive about being a Highlander in most communities that lie beyond the geological Highland line.

In the west, however, in the Inner and Outer Hebrides and along the extremities of the mainland coast from Argyll to Sutherland, the ancient significance and meaning of being a

Being a "Lowlander" has less meaning than having a religious affiliation, or coming from Edinburgh rather than Glasgow, or even than backing a particular football team.

Being a "Highlander" has an uncertain and ambiguous meaning over most of the area covered today by the Highland and Grampian region. The citizens of Pitlochry or Inverness don't, for the most part, speak Gaelic, are mostly ordinary lukewarm Protestants, and enjoy a lifestyle and a culture not obviously very different from that of the citizens of Perth or Aberdeen. They may

**LEFT:** sheep drovers in the 19th century.
**ABOVE:** assessing the form at the Braemar Gathering.

Highlander is very much alive. Not all these communities necessarily speak Gaelic rather than English, though in the Western Isles the power of the language is much less dimmed than elsewhere.

## Crofting communities
All of them are, however, historically "crofting communities": that is, they are the relics of a traditional peasantry who, thanks to a campaign of direct action in the 1880s, won from the British parliament the right to live under the same kind of privileged land law as their brethren in Ireland. The Crofters Holding Act in 1886 conferred on the crofting inhabitants of these areas

security of tenure, the right to hand on their holdings to heirs, and a rent which was fixed not by the whim of the estate manager but by the arbitration of a Land Court sitting in Edinburgh.

Crofting is still largely the economic foundation of these communities. It can best be described as small-scale farming that involves individual use of arable land and some communal use of the grazing on the hill and moor. It rarely provides a viable way of making a living. Very often, crofting is (or was) combined with some other activity, such as fishing or weaving, especially on the islands of Harris and Lewis. Today crofters often run bed-and-breakfast

establishments or some sort of outdoor tourist activity to supplement their income.

Today, inevitably, it involves regulation and subsidy on a massive scale, and the crofter becomes an expert in tapping the various grants available. Old animosities are sometimes rekindled when the Lowlander considers the Highlander's expertise in living off the handouts of the taxpayer, and the Highlander in return resents the indifference of Edinburgh and London towards the real problems of living in remote communities.

But the Highland way of life in these areas goes beyond the details of economic existence, and can best be understood in Scotland by a journey to the Outer Hebrides. In Lewis the visitor encounters the Protestant version of a Gaelic culture dominated, especially on Sundays, by grim Calvinist churches known to outsiders as the "Wee Frees". Jesus may have walked on water, but if he had dared walk on the glorious beaches of Harris or Lewis on a Sunday he would have been ostracised. In Barra and South Uist is the Catholic version, implanted by the 17th-century Counter-Reformation and not involving such denial of life's pleasures.

Some people argue that the Highland way of life exists in a still purer form in the Canadian Maritimes, especially in the Catholic Gaelic-speaking communities of Cape Breton Island, who trace their origins directly to the evictions and migrations that followed the 1745 Rebellion and the Clearances of the 19th century.

## Into the future

Wherever it survives, irrespective of religious background, the Gaelic tradition often defies the dominant world outside. In some ways, the Gaelic Highlander is indeed aboriginal, as the despised Patrick Sellar said, though he only meant it as an insult. The Highlander is often unmodern in priorities, is materialistic yet with little sense of individual ambition and attaches little importance to clock-watching. Gaelic society is supportive of its members, has an abiding sense of kinship and an unembarrassed love of a song and story, and a penchant for a dram.

With every passing year it appears superficially less likely that its distinctiveness can survive another generation, but its efforts to survive become more, not less, determined as Scotland enters the 21st century. The recent creation of a unified local government authority, the Western Isles Council, which conducts its business in Gaelic, has given a remarkable new confidence and ability to deal with modern political society. It is perhaps unlikely that any Ayatollah will arise in Stornoway, but the Highland way of life is far from finished on the islands.

On the other hand, elsewhere in Scotland, John of Fordun and Patrick Sellar have really had the last word. It is their Anglicised Lowland Scotland that now runs from the Mull of Galloway to John o' Groats. The tartan and the bagpipe ought not to fool the visitor: the Scots are not fooled, though they enjoy the pretence of it all.  ❑

**LEFT:** seeing red at Ibrox Park, Glasgow.

# Scots Idioms

There are moments in the lives of all Scots – however educated, however discouraged by school or station from expressing themselves in the vernacular – when they will reach into some race memory of language and produce the only word for the occasion.

The Scots idiom tends to operate at two ends of a spectrum: from abusive to affectionate. So the word for the occasion might well be "nyaff". There are few Scots alive who don't know the meaning of the insult nyaff – invariably "wee nyaff" – and there are few Scots alive who don't have difficulty telling you. Like all the best words in the Scots tongue, there is no single English word which serves as a translation. The most that can be done for nyaff is to say it describes a person who is irritating rather than infuriating, whose capacity to annoy and inspire contempt is just about in scale with his diminutive size, and the cockiness that goes with it.

The long historical partnership between Scotland and France has certainly left its mark on the Scots tongue. Scottish cooks use "ashets" as ovenware – a word which derives from *assiette*, meaning plate – while the adjective "douce", meaning gentle and sweet-natured, is a direct import of the French *douce*, meaning much the same thing. But the most satisfying Scots words – resounding epithets like "bauchle" (a small, usually old and often misshapen person) and evocative adjectives like "shilpit" (sickly-looking) and "wabbit" (weak and fatigued) – belong to that tongue which came under threat in the early 17th century when King James VI moved to London to become James I of England.

Until then, the Lowland Scots (as opposed to Gaelic-speaking Highlanders), whose racial inheritance was part-Celtic and part-Teutonic, spoke their own version of a northern dialect of English, and "Scots" was the language of the nobility, the bourgeoisie and the peasants. But when king and court departed south, educated and aristocratic Scots adopted the English of the "élite", and the Scots tongue received a blow from which it has never recovered.

Yet what could be more expressive than a mother saying of her child, "The bairn's a wee bit wabbit today"? What could be more colourful than the remark that the newspaper vendor on the corner is "a shilpit wee bauchle"? The words themselves almost speak their meaning, even to non-Scots, and they are beginning to creep back into the vocabulary of the middle classes.

The dialects of Glasgow and Scotland's urban west have been much influenced by the mass infusions of Gaelic and Irish from their immigrant populations from the Highlands and Ireland, but Glasgow's legendary "patter" has an idiom all its own, still evolving and still vitally conscious of every subtle shift in the city's preoccupations. Glasgow slang specialises in abuse which can be affectionate or aggressive. A "bampot" is a harmless idiot; a "heidbanger" is a dangerous idiot.

Predictably, there is a rich seam of Glasgow vernacular connected with drink. If you are drunk you might be steamin', stotious, wellied, miraculous or paralytic. If you are drinking you might be consuming a wee goldie (whisky) or a nippy sweetie (any form of spirits). And if you are penniless you might have to resort to electric soup, the hazardous mixture of meths and cheap wine drunk by down-and-outs.

If a Glaswegian calls you "gallus", it is a compliment. The best translation in contemporary idiom is probably streetwise, although it covers a range of values from cocky and flashy to bold and nonchalant. The word derives from gallows, indicating that you were the kind of person destined to end up on them. In Glasgow that wasn't always a reason for disapproval.  ❑

---

**RIGHT:** sales patter catching buyers' attention at Glasgow's Barras street market.

# HOW THE KIRK MOULDS MINDS

*The Church of Scotland has had a profound impact on the Scottish character, encouraging hard work, obedience and a rigorous independence of mind*

When Sunday was still solemnly observed as the Lord's Day, a young minister was asked to preach to George V at at his Highland palace, Balmoral. Nervous at such an honour, the minister enquired: "What would the King like the sermon to be about?" His Majesty replied: "About five minutes."

What he was dreading, of course, was an interminable exhortation to high moral endeavour. Until recent times the Sabbath was a day when profane activity ceased in some households. The intervals between services in the kirk (church) were spent in prayer or with improving books. The Presbyterian ethic is strict and challenging – well suited to promote survival in a poor country with a harsh climate. Whether the kirk has shaped the Scots or the Scots their kirk, it is impossible to understand Scottish character and attitude without taking into account the austere religious background.

## Vain outer show

Scots Protestants worship God, their Maker, in a plain dwelling dominated by a pulpit. There are no idolatrous statues or other Papist frumperies such as elaborate holy pictures, gorgeous surplices or altar hangings. The clergy are attired in sober black and a sparingly used Communion table replaces the altar. The appeal is to the conscience and to the intellect, with the minister's address based on a text from the Bible, the only source of truth. To avoid "vain repetitions", there's no liturgy, or even such set forms as the Apostles' Creed. Prayers, sometimes prolonged like the sermon, are extempore. The one concession to the senses is the singing of hymns and a psalm.

The reason for this lack of "outer show" is that ritual is thought irrelevant; what matters is the relation of the individual soul to his or her Maker. Hence the emphasis on self-reliance and personal integrity. With honesty a prime virtue,

the Roman Catholic practice of currying divine favour through bribing the saints is despised as devious. Presbyterians bow their heads in prayer, but feel no need to grovel on their knees; they talk to God directly. This directness characterises all other dealings, and strangers may be disconcerted by the forthright expression of opinion,

prejudice, liking or disapproval. The belief that all are equal in the eyes of the Lord has produced a people more obedient to the dictates of conscience than to rank or worldly status. The humble shepherd, who roves the mountains in communion with the Almighty, will stomach no affront from his so-called "betters". Even the Lord's anointed are not exempt: though a minister has no qualms about berating sinners from the pulpit, they in turn will take issue with him over errors in his sermon.

Unlike the English, who avoid confrontation, the average Scot has an aggressive zest for argument, preferably "philosophical". At its worst this fosters a contentious pedantry, at its best

---

**PRECEDING PAGES:** Presbyterian minister.
**LEFT:** Lorimer's *Ordination of the Elders*.
**RIGHT:** the reformer John Knox.

moral courage and the independence of mind which, from a tiny population, has engendered an astonishing number of innovative thinkers in many diverse fields.

The academic excellence of which the Scots are so proud owes its merit to John Knox, who insisted that every child, however poor, must attend a school supervised by the kirk. By the early 1700s Scotland was almost unique in having universal education.

Knox's concern, however, was more spiritual than scholastic: the newborn babe is not innocent but "ignorant of all godliness", his life thereafter being a thorny and arduous pilgrimage from moral ignorance at birth towards knowledge of the Lord. With the help of the *tawse* (a strap), children were brought up as slaves to the "work ethic": sober, frugal, compulsively industrious.

Values are positive: duty, discipline, the serious pursuit of worthwhile achievement and a role of benefit to the social good. Hard-headed and purposeful, Scots have no time to waste on frivolous poetics. Scotland has produced philosophers like David Hume, the economist Adam Smith, Watt, Telford and Macadam, whose roads revolutionised public transport; lawyers, doctors, scientists, engineers and radical politicians in search of Utopia – Knox's

## INDEPENDENT CHURCH

Rigorously democratic, the Church of Scotland is without bishops or hierarchy. In most other Churches, the attenders have no say in the appointment of clergy, who are imposed from above. The Scots minister, however, is chosen by the congregation, whose elders, having searched far and wide for a suitable incumbent, will invite the favourite candidate to test their worth by a trial sermon. Where other Churches' cardinals and archbishops hold office for life, the kirk's leader, the Moderator, is elected for one year only.

The kirk is also a symbol of national independence. At its General Assembly the Sassenach (English) queen or her representative, the Lord High Commissioner, is invited as a courtesy but is not allowed to take part in the debates. These are much publicised by the media, since, as there has been no Scottish parliament until now, politics and economics have been discussed along with matters clerical, and a report submitted to the government of the day. The General Assembly meets once a year in May for a week in Edinburgh (usually in the Assembly Hall on the Mound) and is chaired by the Moderator. It is attended by ministers and elders from almost every kirk in the land and its deliberations are keenly observed (sometimes critically) by the general public in the public gallery.

Godly Commonwealth in secular translation. And, although the General Assembly of 1796 declared that "to spread the Gospel seems highly preposterous, in so far as it anticipates, nay reverses, the order of Nature", yet Scotland would give the world, especially Africa, more Protestant missionaries – such as David Livingstone, John Phillip, Robert Moffat, Mary Slessor – than any other European country.

## Balance sheet

With the pressure to achieve so relentless, there's short shrift for the idle. Religious imagery is businesslike: at the Last Day people go to their *reckoning* to settle *accounts* with their Maker; it's not sins or trespasses for which pardon is implored but, "Forgive us our *debts* as we forgive our *debtors*." In a land where it's a struggle to survive, the weakest, who go to the wall, have *earned* their just deserts.

There's nothing meek and mild about the masculine virtues pleasing to God the Father, the Old Testament God of Wrath, who sets the tone for those in command, especially in the family. Some of the most powerful Scottish novels, such as Stevenson's *Weir of Hermiston*, show the terrifying impact of stern fathers on weak or hypersensitive sons.

But with one slip from the "strait and narrow" leading to instant perdition, it's said the Scots have a split personality: Jekyll and Hyde. God's Elect are teetotal, but alcoholism is "the curse of Scotland"; while it's almost unheard of for a kirk member to go to prison, Glaswegians proudly boast of having one of the busiest criminal courts in the UK. It would seem, therefore, that the unofficial influence of the kirk is defiance of all it stands for.

Its ministers have, at all times, lashed "the filthy sins of adultery and fornication", and the taboo on the flesh is so intense that some critics have accused mothers, fearing to "spare the rod and spoil the child", of showing too little physical affection towards their babies. Yet the poet Robert Burns, a flamboyant boozer and wencher, is a national hero, the toasting of whose "immortal memory" provides an annual excuse for unseemly revels. Visitors to puritan Scotland may be puzzled by the enthusiasm for

his blasphemous exaltation of sensual delights. But perhaps, if paradoxically, Burns's anarchic *joie de vivre* also stems from the teaching of the kirk, to whose first demand, "What is the chief end of man?" the correct response is: "To glorify God and *enjoy* Him for ever."

Though the kirk's faithful have declined – today fewer than one in five are regular communicants – its traditions die hard. Fire and brimstone sermons may be a thing of the past, and it's only in some of the outer isles that the Sabbath is kept holy. Sunday is a day, as elsewhere, for sport and idle leisure; even Christmas, once bypassed as Papist, is now approved

for uniting the family clan. The kirk, however, remains important both in politics, through the General Assembly, and socially as a principal dispenser of charitable aid to the poor and afflicted in this Vale of Tears.

More significant, though, than its public function is an enduring impact on the moulding of character. Scots are still brought up to be thrifty, upright and hard-working, while those who rebel put an energy into their pleasures that can often seem self-destructive. There's success or failure, no limbo in between. However secularised the goal, the spur remains: a punitive drive to scale impossible heights. The jaws of Hell still gape for those found "wanting".  ❑

LEFT: Sunday morning congregation in Stornoway in the Outer Hebrides.
ABOVE RIGHT: proselytizing on the streets of Edinburgh.

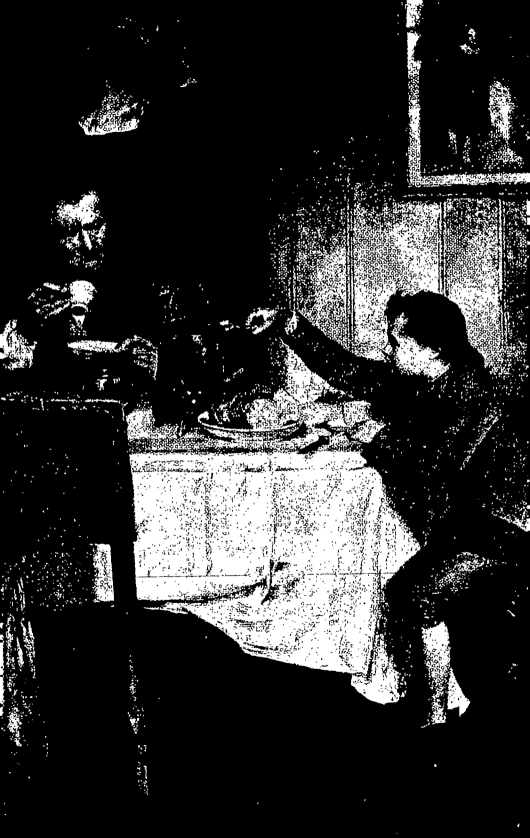

# SCOTS GENIUSES

*For its size, Scotland has produced a disproportionate number of intellectual*
*geniuses: great thinkers who have changed the face of the modern world*

When the English social scientist Have-lock Ellis produced his *Study of British Genius* (based on an analysis of the *Dictionary of National Biography*) he came up with the fact that there were far more Scots on his list than there should have been. With only 10 percent of the British population, the Scots had produced 15.4 percent of Britain's geniuses. And when he delved deeper into the "men of Science" category he discovered that the Scots made up almost 20 percent of Britain's eminent scientists and engineers.

Not only that, but the Scots-born geniuses tended to be peculiarly influential. Many of them were great original scientists like Black, Hutton, Kelvin, Ramsay and Clerk Maxwell, whose work ramified in every direction. Others were important philosophers like the sceptic David Hume or the economist Adam Smith, whose words, according to one biographer, have been "proclaimed by the agitator, conned by the statesmen and printed in a thousand statutes".

## Great Scots

Scotland, like Ireland, produced a long string of great military men such as Patrick Gordon (Tsar Peter the Great's right-hand man), James Keith, David Leslie and John Paul Jones. There are also great explorers such as David Livingstone, Mungo Park, David Bruce and John Muir, and accomplished financiers like John Law, who founded the National Bank of France, and William Paterson, who set up the Bank of England. Andrew Carnegie, also a Scot, ruthlessly put together one of the biggest industrial empires America has ever seen, sold it when it was at its peak, then gave much of his money away on the fine Presbyterian basis that "the man who dies rich dies disgraced".

Just why a small, obscure country on the edge of Europe should produce such a galaxy of tal-

**LEFT:** Eureka! A popular version of how James Watt discovered steam power.
**RIGHT:** the possibly apochryphal meeting between Robert Burns and the young Walter Scott.

ent is one of the conundrums of European history. As nothing in Scotland's brutal medieval history hints at the riches to come, most historians have concluded that Scotland was galvanised in the 16th and 17th centuries by the intellectual dynamics of the Protestant Reformation. This is a plausible theory. Not only did

the Reformation produce powerful and challenging figures such as John Knox and his successor Andrew Melville, but it created a Church which reformed Scotland's existing universities (Glasgow and St Andrews), set up two new ones (Edinburgh and Aberdeen) and tried to make sure that every parish in Scotland had its own school.

## Radical thinkers

When Thomas Carlyle tried to explain the proliferation of genius in 18th- and 19th-century Scotland, he found "Knox and the Reformation acting in the heart's core of every one of these persona and phenomena". This is a large claim, and overlooks the well-run network of primary schools inherited from the Roman Catholic authorities.

But, whatever the reason, 18th-century Scotland produced an astonishing number of talents. As well as David Hume and his friend Adam Smith, Scottish society was studded with able men like Adam Ferguson, who fathered sociology, William Robertson, one of the finest historians of his age, and the teacher Dugald Stewart. There were also gifted eccentrics like the High Court judge Lord James Monboddo, who ran into a barrage of ridicule by daring to suggest (100 years before Darwin) that men and apes might, somehow, be related. It was a sceptical, questioning, intellectually charged atmosphere in which talent thrived.

## Intellectual freedom

Interestingly, that talent didn't fall foul of established religion: few Scots had a problem squaring their faith with their intellectual curiosity. An extraordinary number of Scotland's ablest and most radical thinkers were "sons of the manse" – that is, born into clergy homes. This meant that, in 1816, when Anglo-Catholics were squabbling over the precise date of the Creation, the Presbyterian intellectual Thomas Chalmers

### LITERARY GENIUSES

As celebrated by the Scottish Writers' Museum in Edinburgh, Scotland has three international-class writers in Robert Burns (1759–96), Walter Scott (1771– 1832) and Robert Louis Stevenson (1850–94). Stevenson won acclaim with his travelogues, short stories, essays and novels such as *Treasure Island* and *Kidnapped*. To Scott, writing was as much a trade as an art, and he produced a long stream of work based on medieval and foreign themes. But it is Burns whose poetry and songs earned him pride of place in every Scottish heart, and whose birthday (25 January – Burns Night) is celebrated in rousing style around the world.

could ask: "Why suppose that this little spot (the planet earth) should be the exclusive abode of life and intelligence?"

And nothing thrived more than the science of medicine. In the late 18th and early 19th centuries Edinburgh and Glasgow became two of the most important medical centres in Europe and produced physicians such as William Cullen, John and William Hunter (who revolutionised surgery and gynaecology in London), the three-generation Munro dynasty, Andrew Duncan (who set up the first "humane" lunatic asylums), Robert Liston and James Young Simpson (who discovered the blessings of chloroform). It was a Scot, Alexander Fleming, who, in 1929, discovered the bacteria-killing properties of penicillin, the most effective antibiotic ever devised.

While Scotland has never produced a classical composer of any note, or a painter to compare with Rembrandt or Michelangelo, the reputation of 19th-century portraitists like Raeburn, Wilkie and Ramsay are now being upgraded. And in the Adam family (father William and sons Robert, John and James), Scotland threw up a dynasty of architectural genius which was highly influential. (One of the scandals of modern Scotland is the number of Adam-designed buildings which are collapsing into ruin.)

James "Paraffin" Young, who first extracted oil from shale; Alexander Graham Bell, who invented the telephone; and John Logie Baird, the father of television.

## Makers of the modern world

More important in world terms were Scotland's "pure" scientists, such as John Napier, who invented logarithms; Joseph Black, who described the formation of carbon dioxide; James Hutton, Roderick Murchison and Charles Lyell, who by their efforts created modern geology; and Lord Kelvin (an Ulster Scot), who devised, among much else, the second law of

However, the number of technologists born in Scotland is truly remarkable: they include James Watt, who improved the steam engine beyond measure; the civil engineer Thomas Telford; R.W. Thomson, who invented both the fountain pen and the pneumatic tyre (which was taken up commercially by John Dunlop); John Macadam, the engineer who gave his name to the metalled road; Charles MacIntosh, who did the same to waterproofed fabric; James Nasmyth, who dreamed up the steam hammer;

thermodynamics and whose name is remembered (like those of Fahrenheit and Celsius) as a unit of temperature.

Then there's the Scotsman who is said to have virtually invented the modern world: James Clerk Maxwell, the 19th-century physicist who uncovered the laws of electrodynamics. Albert Einstein described Clerk Maxwell's work as a "change in the conception of reality" which was the "most fruitful that physics has experienced since the time of Newton". And Max Planck, the German physicist, said Clerk Maxwell was among the small band who are "divinely blest, and radiate an influence far beyond the border of their land". ❏

**LEFT:** an 1827 view of the engineer John Macadam.
**ABOVE:** Alexander Graham Bell, the inventor of the telephone.

# THE GREAT TARTAN MONSTER

*Tartanry is a big, colourful business in Scotland, displaying*

*its gaudy wares to willing tourists at every opportunity*

When it comes to selling drink, the Mackinnons of Edinburgh (and formerly of Skye) are no slouches. In fact, their family company, the Drambuie Liqueur Co. Ltd, and their sweet-tasting liqueur continues to be successful as Scotch whisky enjoys a boom in worldwide sales.

And it has all been done on the coat-tails of that great loser, Bonnie Prince Charlie. Not only does Drambuie claim to be based on a "secret" recipe given to the Mackinnon family by the prince himself, but the Stuart's kilted portrait adorns every bottle. (On Skye, the drink became known locally as "dram buidhe", the yellow drink.) And the conference room in Drambuie's Edinburgh HQ is an exact replica of the 18th-century French frigate which sailed the Prince into exile (not to mention drunkenness and despair) in France and Italy.

But, thanks to Bonnie Prince Charlie, the Mackinnons are now turning over many millions of pounds. "The drink itself may be nothing famous," says one Edinburgh expert, "but the marketing has been superb." The Jacobite rising of 1745–6 was a major disaster for the Stuarts, but it was good news for the Mackinnon family.

## The power of tartan

The success of Drambuie – "the Prince's Dram" – is tartanry in action. The Mackinnon millions are yet another tribute to that *mélange* of chequered cloth, strident music, mawkish song and bad history which has stalked Scotland for generations and refuses to go away. Tartan tea-towels and tartan tea-cosies, tartan pencils and tartan postcards, tartan golf club covers and a wide assortment of comestibles packaged in tartan – all are eagerly purchased.

Tartanry is a vigorous subculture which, somehow, manages to lump together Bonnie Prince Charlie, John Knox, pipe bands, Queen Victoria, Rob Roy, Harry Lauder, Mary Queen of Scots, Edinburgh Castle and the White Heather Club dancers. It is a cultural phenomenon which has defied every attempt by the Caledonian intelligentsia to understand it or explain it away.

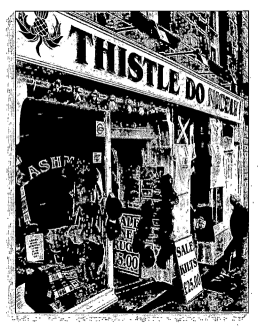

## Fun or frightful?

Many resent the fact that this debased and often silly version of Gaeldom has come to represent the culture of Adam Smith, David Hume, Robert Burns and James Clerk Maxwell. Others regard tartanry as a harmless effervescence which has kept alive a sense of difference in the Scottish people that may yet prove politically decisive. Even more think it is wonderful and buy Andy Stewart records.

But it certainly demands elaborate and expensive tribute. A full set of Highland "evening wear" consisting of worsted kilt, Prince Charlie Coatee, silver-mounted sporran, lace jabots and cuffs, ghillie shoes, chequered hose and

**LEFT:** tourists love tartan – the lure of the kilt is irresistible to some.
**RIGHT:** an assortment of tartanware on sale in Edinburgh's Old Town.

*sgian dubh* can cost up to £1,000. Even a "day wear" outfit of a kilt in "hunting" tartan, Argyle Jacket, leather sporran and civilian brogues will set the wearer back £600.

Of course, none of this applies to the Highlanders who actually live in the Highlands. As anyone who knows the area will confirm, the day dress of the Highland crofter or shepherd consists of boiler suit, wellington boots and cloth cap. For important evening occasions he takes off his cap.

Tartanry could be regarded as Gaeldom's unwitting revenge on the country which once despised and oppressed it. Right into the 19th century there was nothing fashionable (or even respectable) about Highlanders. They were about as popular in 18th-century Britain as the IRA is now. Their kilts, tartans and bagpipes were hopelessly associated in the public mind with the Jacobite assaults on the Hanoverian ascendancy in 1715, 1719 and 1745. In fact, in 1746 (following the 1745 Rising) the whole caboodle – bagpipes and all – was banned by the British government "under pain of death" and remained banned until 1782.

But, with the Jacobite menace safely out of the way, the élites of Hanoverian Britain began to wax romantic over the Highland clans. The

## REGIMENTAL COLOURS AND CHANGING OF THE GUARD

The popularity of tartan was helped along by the stirring performances of the Highland regiments in the Crimean War and the Indian Mutiny. In their "Government" tartans, red coats and feathered bonnets, the Highland battalions were an awesome sight. By 1881 the British military were so besotted with tartanry that the War Office ordered all Scotland's Lowland regiments to don tartan trousers and short Highland-style doublets. Venerable Lowland regiments were outraged and protested that their military tradition was both older and a lot more distinguished than that of the Highlanders. But their pleas fell on deaf ears. Only the Scots Guards, as members of the élite Brigade of Guards, were granted the right not to wear tartan on their uniforms. However, in 2006 an efficiency-inspired decision by the UK government to merge six Scottish infantry regiments, including the Royal Scots, the world's oldest active army regiment, into one "super-regiment", met with a storm of protest. Alas, the proud Black Watch, King's Scottish Borderers et al are now part of the new Royal Regiment of Scotland (www.royalregimentofscotland.org.uk). The new regimental cap badge incorporates the Saltire of St Andrew and the Lion Rampant, which are two recognisable symbols of Scotland. As a Royal regiment, the cap badge is surmounted by a crown.

bogus "Ossian" sagas of James Macpherson became the toast of Europe (Napoleon loved them), while Sir Walter Scott's romantic novels became runaway best-sellers. And it was Scott who orchestrated the first-ever outburst of tartan fervour: King George IV's state visit to Edinburgh in 1822.

## Tartan order

Determined to make the occasion high romance, Scott wheeled into Edinburgh dozens of petty Highland chieftains and their tartan-clad "tails" and gave them pride of place in the processions. The huge 20-stone (127-kg) frame

sheep. "It almost seems as if there was a cruel mockery in giving such prominence to their pretentions," Lockhart wrote.

But there was no stopping the tartan bandwagon. "We are like to be torn to pieces for tartan," wrote an Edinburgh merchant to the weaving firm of William Wilson and Son of Bannockburn in the wake of George IV's visit. "The demand is so great that we cannot supply our customers." Wilson took the hint and installed 40 extra looms.

The tartan business got another boost when a couple of amiable English eccentrics known as the "Sobieski Stuarts" (born Charles and John

of George IV himself was draped in swathes of Royal Stewart tartan over flesh-coloured tights. "Sir Walter Scott has ridiculously made us appear to be a nation of Highlanders," grumbled one Edinburgh citizen at this display of tartan power, "and the bagpipe and the tartan are the order of the day." Scott's own son-in-law, John Lockhart, pointed out that the same gentry strutting around Edinburgh in their Highland finery were the very people who were ousting their own clansfolk to make way for

**LEFT:** Sir Walter Scott and friends, who helped create the romantic Highland image.
**ABOVE:** more modern manifestations of tartanry.

Allen) popped up, claiming to be the direct descendants of Bonnie Prince Charlie and his wife Louisa of Stolberg. They also claimed to have an "ancient" (in other words fake) manuscript which described hundreds of hitherto unknown tartans.

## Royal favour

But the real clincher came in 1858 when Queen Victoria and Prince Albert bought Balmoral Castle as a summer residence and furnished it almost entirely with specially designed (by Albert) "Balmoral" tartan. After that, the English mania for Highland Scotland knew no bounds. Every Lancashire industrialist and City of London financier had to have his shooting lodge in the mountains, while every family name in Scotland was converted into a "clan" complete with its own tartan.

## Marauding bands

According to the Royal Scottish Pipe Band Association (RSPBA), there are now more than 400 pipe bands alive and wailing in the UK alone, with hundreds more all over the world. Every year the bands flock to the one or other of the RSPBA's five championships. The biggest prize is the World Pipe Band Championship, which invariably used to be won by a Scottish band, but which in 1987

had more than 20,000 members and 170 branches prancing and leaping around ballrooms all over the world. This may be understandable in Scot-infested corners of the globe like the United States, Canada and New Zealand, but it isn't so explicable in France, Holland, Sweden, Kenya or Japan. Just why the sensible citizens of Paris, The Hague, Gothenburg, Nairobi and Tokyo should want to trick themselves out in tartan to skip around in strict tempo to tunes like "The Wee Cooper O'Fife", "The Dukes of Perth", "Cadgers in the Canongate" or "Deuks Dang Ower My Daddie" is a deep and abiding mystery.

went to the 75th Fraser Highlanders from Canada and, in 1992 and 1993, to the Field Marshal Montgomery Band from Northern Ireland. Over 80 of the RSPBA's member bands are in Northern Ireland, where the hardline Protestants are happy to swathe themselves in the tartans of the Jacobite clans, most of whom were Catholic or Episcopalian. On the other side of the Irish fence, the saffron-kilted pipers of Ireland have abandoned their melodic "Brian Boru" pipes for the Great Highland Bagpipe.

Another (somewhat quieter) arm of tartan imperialism is the Royal Scottish Country Dance Society (RSCDS; www.rscds.org/dancing) which is run from Edinburgh and which, at the last count,

## Famous patrons

It may have something to do with Scottish country dancing's royal and aristocratic connections. The Queen herself is patron of the RSCDS, and the Royal prefix was granted by her father King George VI just before he died in 1952. Other exalted members include the Earl of Mansfield (who is president of the RSCDS) and the Right Honourable Peregrine Moncrieffe of Moncrieffe.

But it seems unlikely that the royal laying-on of hands will ever extend to the crowd of kilted warblers, accordion players, comics and fiddlers who make their living entertaining Scotland (and the Scottish diaspora). Usually showbiz tartanry finds its own niche, but occasionally, as in the case of the 70s band The Bay City Rollers or Rod Stewart's wearing of Royal Stewart tartan, it escapes into the mainstream of pop culture.

## Olympic efforts

Yet another manifestation of tartanry is the Highland Games circuit. Every year between May and September villages and towns the length of Scotland (plus a few in England) stage a kind of Caledonian Olympics in which brawny, kilted figures toss the caber, putt the shot and throw

> **LOUD MUSIC**
>
> In contrast to the loud dress sense of some of the Scottish pop world, the newer breed of Gaelic-speaking folk-rock bands has never been seen near a scrap of tartan.

Grandfather Mountain in North Carolina celebrated its 52nd anniversary in 2007 and is now one of the biggest of its kind in the world. American tartanry buffs are very keen on "clan gatherings" in which they get togged up in a kind of "Sword of Zorro" version of Highland dress, and march past their "chief" brandishing their broadswords.

But perhaps the daftest manifestation of competitive tartanry is "haggis-hurling". This is a sport that allegedly has its origins in the Highlands, when clansmen would catch a

the hammer while squads of little girls in velvets and tartans dance their hearts out to the sound of bagpipes.

The Scottish Games Association represents over 60 annually held Highland Games. Most attract crowds of up to 5,000, although the Braemar Gathering (with the royal family in attendance), can easily pull in more than 20,000. But even Braemar cannot compete with the 40,000 or 50,000-strong crowds who flock to watch the big Highland Games in the US. The event at

haggis thrown across the river by their wives at lunchtime. It was revived in 1977 by an Edinburgh public relations man, Robin Dunseath, as "a bit of an upmarket joke". To his astonishment the "ancient" sport of haggis-hurling (usually from standing on top of a whisky barrel) took off and went from strength to strength, with competitions taking place all over the globe.

So popular has the "sport" become that a world championship now takes place. The current world record was set in 1984 by Alan Pettigrew, who hurled a haggis a remarkable 180 feet 10 inches (55.11 metres) on the island of Inchmurrin, Loch Lomomnd. ❏

**LEFT:** tartan helps keep the Royal Family warm at the Braemar Gathering.
**ABOVE:** a sheaf of tartans.

# SCOTLAND'S PAINTERS

*From the Edinburgh Enlightenment to the Glasgow rebels, Scottish painting retains an exuberance that defies its Calvinistic background*

In spite of its puritanism and thunderings from the kirk against "vain outer show", Scotland is unique among the British provinces in having a distinctive painterly tradition. The art of Protestant Northern Europe tends to be tormented and morbid and, given a Calvinist shadow of guilt and sin, one would expect Scottish painting to be gloomily angst-ridden. Instead, as if in defiance of all that the kirk represents, it is extroverted, joyful, flamboyant, robust – much more sensuous (even if less complex) than English art with its inhibiting deference to the rules of good taste.

It is significant that young Scottish artists have mostly bypassed the Sassenach (English) capital to study abroad; those from Edinburgh in Rome, the Glaswegians a century later in pleasure-loving Paris. Growth of the arts in Scotland is linked to the relative importance of its two major cities, and the rivalry between them (culture versus commerce) has resulted in aesthetic dualism: where Edinburgh's painters are rational and decorous, raw but dynamic Glasgow has produced exuberant rebels.

## The Enlightenment

Before the 18th century, Scottish art scarcely existed. There was no patronage from the kirk, which forbade idolatrous images, or from the embattled aristocracy. In a country physically laid waste by the Covenanter Wars and mentally stifled by religious fanaticism, painters were despised as menial craftsmen.

The return of peace and prosperity, however, gave rise to a remarkable intellectual flowering, the Edinburgh Enlightenment, which lasted, roughly, from 1720 until 1830 and caused the city to be dubbed the "Athens of the North". The rejection of theology for secular thought was accompanied by a new enthusiasm for the world and its appearance, the brothers Adam

---

**PRECEDING PAGES:** Wilkie's *Pitlessie Fair.*
**LEFT:** Raeburn's perennially popular *Rev. Robert Walker Skating on Dunningston Loch.*
**RIGHT:** Ramsay's portrait of David Hume.

evolving a style in architecture and design that was adopted all over Europe and remains to this day the classic model of elegance and grace.

A need arose, meanwhile, for portraits to commemorate the city's celebrated sons. Though the earliest portrait painters, Smibert and Aikman, achieved modest recognition as

artists not craftsmen, Allan Ramsay, son of a poet and friend of the philosopher David Hume, expected to be treated as an equal by the intellectual establishment, many of whose members he immortalised with his brush.

Considering the visual austerity of his background – Edinburgh had no galleries, no art school and only a few enlightened collectors – Ramsay's rise to fame is astonishing. Leaving home to study in Italy, he returned to London in 1739 and was an instant success, finally ending up as court painter (in preference to Reynolds) to George III. Despite his classical training, Ramsay cast aside impersonal idealism for "natural portraiture", concentrating on light, space and atmosphere and the meticulous rendering of tactile detail: ribbons, cuffs, the curl of a wig, the bloom on a young girl's cheek. Above all, he was interested in the character of his sitters, combining formal dignity with intimacy and charm. The refined distinction of his best work, such as the portraits of his two wives, has earned him an honourable position in the history not just of Scottish but of British art.

## Scottish arts

Ramsay's achievement was rivalled in the next generation by Sir Henry Raeburn, knighted in 1822 by George IV and made King's Limner

genres, especially landscape. Though Alexander Nasmyth painted an Italianate Scotland, gilded and serene, the choice of local vistas – rather than a classical idyll in the manner of Claude – was startling in its novelty.

Equally novel was David Allan's transfer of the pastoral tradition of nymphs and shepherds into scenes from Scottish rural life. He was followed by David Wilkie, whose *Pitlessie Fair* (painted at 19) was the start of a career which earned him a knighthood and outstanding popularity; his "low-life" comedies like *The Penny Wedding* created a taste for such subjects that persisted throughout the Victorian era.

(painter) for Scotland. Raeburn also studied in Italy, and his *oeuvre*, like Ramsay's, was confined to portraiture with an emphasis on individual character: the fiddler Neil Gow or a homely matron receiving the same attention as a scholar or fashionable beauty. But his style is broader and more painterly, the poses more dramatic: Judge Eldin looking fierce in his study, the Clerks of Penicuik romantically strolling, the Rev. Robert Walker taking a turn on the ice.

Raeburn was the first Scottish painter of national renown to have remained in his native Edinburgh and, in doing so, he established the arts in Scotland and their acceptance by the public. Interested prestige led to ventures in other

Although no one equalled Raeburn or Wilkie, there was a new public interest in the arts, which continued to flourish in Edinburgh during the 19th century. Notable in landscape are David Roberts with his views of the Holy Land and, later, William McTaggart, "the Scottish Impressionist".

## The Glasgow Boys

The academic mainstream, however, was confined to historical melodrama, sentimental cottagers and grandiose visions of the Highlands as inspired by Sir Walter Scott. The 1880s saw a new departure when a group of students, nicknamed the Glasgow Boys, united in protest against Edinburgh's stranglehold on the arts. Due to rapid industrial expansion, Glasgow had grown from a provincial town into "the second city of the Empire" and, in contrast to 18th-century Edinburgh, there were galleries, an art school and lavish collectors among the new rich (one of whom was William Burrell), who were anxious to buy status through cultural patronage.

Initially, though, the Glasgow Boys scandalised their fellow citizens. Rejecting the turgid subjects and treacly varnish of the academic "glue-pots", they abandoned their studios to paint in the open air,

> ### ART ON SHOW
>
> Confidence in Scottish painting has been boosted by superb municipal collections, notably the Burrell in Glasgow which has always been a major tourist draw.

disgust to study in Paris – where they were subsequently acclaimed. This success abroad tickled civic pride (what Edinburgh artist could compete?) and the canny burghers, who had once been so hostile, began to pay high prices for their pictures, Sadly, the Glasgow Boys now lost their freshness and became respectable: Lavery a fashionable portrait painter, Guthrie a conservative president of the Royal Scottish Academy, while Hornel retreated into orientalism. Today, there is a revival of interest – and investment.

choosing earthy, peasant themes that lacked "message" or moral and gave offence to the genteel. The public, devoted to gain, godliness and grand pianos (whose legs were prudishly veiled) was both affronted and bemused by Crawhall's lyrical cows, the voluptuous cabbages tended by James Guthrie's farm hands, the indecent brilliance of the rhubarb on Macgregor's *Vegetable Stall*.

Influenced by Whistler and the European Realists, most of the Glasgow Boys left Scotland in

LEFT: close scrutiny of Sir James Guthrie's *Old Willie, a Village Worthy* on display in Glasgow.
ABOVE: MacGregor's *Vegetable Stall*.

## New experiments

The Glasgow Boys gave younger artists the courage to experiment through their flamboyant handling of paint and colour. Oppressed by the drab Calvinism of Scottish life, rebels of the next generation, led by Peploe, Cadell, Hunter and Fergusson, again fled to Paris, where they were intoxicated by the decorative art of Matisse and the Fauves. Discarding conventional realism, they flattened form and perspective into dancing, linear rhythm, with colour an expression of a pagan *joie de vivre*.

As with the Glasgow Boys, fame abroad brought the Scottish Colourists belated success at home. Peploe and Hunter returned to paint a

Scotland brightened by Gallic sunshine and the witty Cadell to transform Glasgow housewives into flappers of the Jazz Age.

A gloomier fate, though, awaited the architect and designer Charles Rennie Mackintosh. An originator of art nouveau, his distinctive style is typified by a simple geometrical manipulation of space based on combinations of straight line and gentle curves. Glasgow School of Art, his architectural masterpiece, is one of the city's most remarkable buildings, and the Glasgow Style he initiated in furniture and the decorative arts is now admired the world over. Yet in his day "Toshie" was dismissed as a drunken eccentric and was

such a failure professionally that he abandoned architecture to paint watercolours in France.

## Modern times

From the 1930s landscape has tended to predominate in Scottish painting. In a country where intellectual achievement allied to public service is so highly esteemed, it's curious that the arts in Scotland have mostly been devoted to expressing simple emotion and visual pleasure. In the 1950s, Colquhuon and MacBryde adopted Cubism, not for formal reasons but as a means of conveying romantic melancholia.

Since World War II, while modern trends have been pursued with characteristic vigour,

there's been a loss of optimism and sparkle. More poignant than the Modernists is Joan Eardley, who turned her back on artistic fashion to paint urchins in the Glasgow backstreets, then, after settling in a remote fishing village in the northeast, sombrely elemental landscapes.

John Bellany is unusual in that he has the tormented vision one might expect, but rarely finds, among artists brought up under Calvinism. Overwhelmed, after a visit to Buchenwald, by human wickedness, he gave up modish abstracts to return to figurative art of a tragic, often nightmarish monumentality. Later, after liver failure and confrontation with death, he unleashed intense energy with a prolific output of superb, lyrical autobiographical canvases.

## Glasgow graduates

Another post-war change is that German Expressionism, with its energy and gloom, has replaced the hedonistic influence of the French, especially in recent times when Glasgow School of Art has produced a new group of rebels. Known (unofficially) as the Glasgow Wild Boys, they have also rejected Modernism for gigantic narrative pictures with literary, political or symbolist undertones. The most successful, Adrian Wiszniewski and Stephen Campbell, have been rapturously received in New York.

Wiszniewski, a Pole born in Scotland, has adapted Slavic folk art to express nostalgia for the past, disenchantment with the present. Campbell, combining macho brutalism with whimsy, draws his inspiration from the contrasting writings of P.G. Wodehouse and Bram Stoker (author of *Dracula*). Although affecting social "concern" and apparently doom-laden, the most striking quality of these young painters is anarchic ebullience.

Other brilliant Glasgow graduates include Stephen Conroy, Peter Howson, Mario Rossi, Craig Mulholland and Steven Campbell, who, with the exception of Howson, are all from in and around Glasgow. And Allison Watt, Lesley Banks and Jenny Saville redress the balance for women, though their images of other women are far from conventional: Watt earned notoriety for her painting of the Queen Mother with a teacup on her head. ❑

**LEFT:** James Guthrie's *Hind's Daughter*.
**RIGHT:** Joan Eardley's *Street Kids*.

# SONG AND DANCE

*The folk music revival has had a profound effect in Scotland,*
*filling the clubs and pubs once more with traditional Celtic sounds*

The sound of Scottish music has changed dramatically in the past 25 years – and that's before you take into account the insidious influence exerted in recent years by phenomenally successful Scottish pop groups such as Simple Minds, Belle and Sebastian, Franz Ferdinand and Travis.

Nothing has been more dramatic than the forging of an alliance between two previously alien schools. On the one hand, the inheritor of the bagpipe tradition, regarded until then as a musical law unto themselves. On the other hand, the young adventurers of the folk music revival, ready to play and sing anything that had its roots embedded somewhere in Celtic culture.

## Piped music

Whether the piping Establishment has benefited is debatable. They are a gritty, stubborn lot, much given to internecine warfare over the etiquette and mystique of piping disciplines which have been handed down like family heirlooms through the generations. Discipline still rules at the sponsored competitions, where pipers from all over the world challenge each other at what in Gaelic is called *pìobaireachd* (pibroch).

Just to confuse the uninitiated, *pìobaireachd* has another title, *ceòl mór* (Great Music). This is a truly classical music, built to complex, grandiloquent proportions and actually playable only after years of study and practice. Those who *can* play it do so by memory, in the manner of the great Indian raga players. The pipe music that most of us are familiar with – stretching from "Mull of Kintyre" to reels, marches, jigs and strathspeys – is referred to by the classicists as *ceòl beag* (Small Music).

Great or Small, much of it has survived thanks to patronage rather than household popularity. The earliest royal families in Scotland are credited with having a piper, or several, on

their books, and no upwardly mobile landlord of ancient times could afford to be without his piper. But it was in the warring Highland clan system that the pipes flourished. The blood-tingling quality of the Great Highland Bagpipe, with its three resonant drones, was quickly recognised by the early Scottish regiments, and

the military connection remains to this day. Even now, the Scots use the pipes to soften up the English at football and rugby internationals.

Despite being bearers of the country's national music, the pipes can offer nothing to compare with the phenomenal resurgence of Scots fiddle music, which had thrived only in certain areas until the folk music revival got its full head of steam in the 1960s. Today, there are probably more fiddlers in Scotland than ever before. The best-known folk musicians are the Shetland fiddler Aly Bain and accordionist/songwriter Phil Cunningham, who perform widely at home and abroad. A few groups such as Blazing Fiddles are also making their mark.

**PRECEDING PAGES:** Fiona Middleton and her daughter Hannah play to the seals on the island of Islay.
**LEFT:** taking the tunes to the people.
**RIGHT:** making a traditional Scottish fiddle.

Another traditional instrument that has become increasingly popular is the *clarsach*, or Scots harp, which first appeared in 8th-century Pictish stone carvings. Some of the great *clarsach* music came from Ruaridh Dall Morrison (the Blind Harper) in the 17th century. Much smaller than the modern concert harp, the *clarsach* had become virtually extinct until it was revived in the early 1970s.

If the fiddle and the *clarsach* have fought their way back into the mainstream of Scottish culture, they were both a long way behind folksong in doing so. The classic narrative ballads and *pawky bothy* (a Gaelic term meaning "hut") bal-

lads had survived largely in the hands of farm workers and the travelling folk (the tinkers) of Perthshire and the northeast. The advent of the tape recorder enabled collectors like the late Hamish Henderson to bring their songs to the ears of the young urban folk revivalists. Today's best-known singers are Fife-based Sheena Wellington (traditional song) and Ishbel MacAskill from Lewis (Gaelic song).

The folk clubs served, too, as spawning grounds for new songwriting, especially of the polemical brand, producing some of the best songs since Robert Burns. Burns is credited with more than 300 songs, many of them set to

**FIDDLERS ON THE HOOF**

The fiddle has been part of Scottish music for more than 500 years – King James IV had "fithelaris" on his payroll in the 15th century. The fiddle reached its Golden Age in the 18th century, when Scots musicians sailed to Italy to study and brought back not only the tricks of the classical trade, but also a steady supply of exquisite violins, which were soon copied by enterprising local craftsmen. At the same time, the dancing craze had begun.

Country fiddlers found their robust jigs and reels much in demand at balls, parties and other social gatherings, and the first major collections of Scots fiddle tunes were published, making the music widely accessible.

By the early 19th century, though, high society had turned its fancy to the new polkas and waltzes that were flooding in from Europe. The rural fiddlers played on regardless, and it was the Aberdeenshire village of Banchory that produced the most famous Scots fiddler of all – James Scott Skinner, born in 1843. Classically trained, and technically virtuosic, the "King of the Strathspey" won international acclaim, and the arrival of recording in the later part of his career helped to spread the message – even as far as fiddle-packed Shetland, which had until then resolutely stuck to its own Norse-tinged style.

traditional fiddle tunes, and you can still hear them in all sorts of venues. You'll also hear Scotland's unofficial national anthem, the sentimental "Flower of Scotland", written by the late Roy Williamson of folk duo The Corries. Recalling the Scots victory over the English at Bannockburn in 1314, it is sung at major sporting events in the hope of firing the national teams on to equal success.

## Clubs and festivals

Many of the early folk clubs are still in existence – notably those in Edinburgh, Aberdeen, Kirkcaldy, Stirling and St Andrews. Sadly, the type of *ceilidh* laid on for tourists tends to be caught in a time warp of kilt, haggis and musical mediocrity. In the Gaelic, *ceilidh* means a gathering. The Gaelic-speaking community, now mostly confined to the West Highlands and islands, holds its great gathering, the Royal National Mod, in different parts of Scotland every October. At the Mod – dubbed "the Whisky Olympics" by those who regard Gaelic as a largely archaic language – you can sample some beautiful competitive singing.

From Easter until autumn, there's hardly a weekend when there isn't a folk festival somewhere in Scotland. In cities like Edinburgh and Glasgow, the festivals are among the biggest of their kind in the world; Edinburgh's (before Easter) lasts for 10 days and Glasgow's Celtic Connections for two weeks in January. But there's nothing to beat the smaller traditional folk festivals in rural areas, where the talent tends to be local rather than imported. Among the best events, the Isle of Skye Music Festival (May) was voted the UK's most fan-friendly festival at the 2006 Festival Awards. Kirriemuir (September) and Orkney (May) are also famous for their annual celebrations of traditional music.

Most folk festivals have their unofficial "fringe", and many pub sessions can match the finest organised *ceilidh*.

## Highland flings

The cunning Irish centuries ago devised a way of dancing in tight cottage corners: they keep their arms rigid at the sides of the body. For the Scots, dancing is reserved for the village hall or the ballroom. Many of the traditional dances, including the famous Highland Fling, call for the raising of the arms to depict the antlers of the red deer – splendidly symbolic but treacherous at close quarters. Popular formations like the Eightsome Reel and the Dashing White Sergeant also involve much whirling around in large groups.

Like the accordion-pumped music which fires these breath-sucking scenes, Scottish dancing has its more rarified moments. There are country dance societies in various districts, and when the members get together they dance with the kind of practised precision that must have been essential at the earliest Caledonian Balls.

In the 1980s and '90s, Scottish rock began to sit up and notice its Celtic heritage, with folk-rock bands such as Runrig and Wolfstone, which were all-electric but hitched musically to ancient Gaelic themes. In songwriting, too, folk music has made its mark in the rock venues. The leading singer-songwriters – men such as Dougie MacLean, Rab Noakes and the brilliant Dick Gaughan – have found eager new audiences there, and their influence can be heard in the music of contemporary rock groups. One such group is Capercaillie, whose charismatic lead singer, Karen Matheson, comes from Oban and whose musical roots lie much closer to their Hebridean origins than most. ❑

**LEFT:** "T in the Park" music festival, Balado, Kinross. **RIGHT:** scores of young dancers compete in the Highland Gatherings around Scotland every year.

# GAMES HIGHLANDERS PLAY

*A traditional Highland Gathering, with the skirl of pipes, tartan-clad dancers and muscular athletes, is a wonderfully colourful – and noisy – experience*

Highland Gatherings, which are sometimes described as "Oatmeal Olympics", are much more than three-ring circuses. As the Gathering gets going, a trio of dancers are on one raised platform; a solitary piper is on another; a 40-piece pipe band has the attention, if not of all eyes, at least of all ears; the "heavies" are tossing some unlikely object about; two men are engaged in some strange form of wrestling; a tug-of-war is being audibly contested and an 880-yard (800-metre) race is in progress.

Track events are the least important part of these summer games – but don't tell the runners. The venue has been chosen for its scenic beauty rather than its "Tartan" track. At the Skye Games, milers literally become dizzy as they run round and round the track's meagre 130 yards (117 metres).

## Pipers and dancers

Everywhere the sound of pipes can be heard. It is not only the piper playing for the dancers, another solitary piper playing a mournful dirge in the individual piper's competition, or the 40-strong pipe band being judged in the arena. Around the arena, behind marquees, under trees, in any place which offers some slight protection to muffle the sound, those still to compete are busy rehearsing under the sharp ear of their leaders and coaches.

The solo pipers are undoubtedly the aristocrats of the Games, and the highest honour – and the biggest prize – is awarded to the pibroch winner. There are three competitions for solo pipers: pibrochs (classical melodies composed in honour of birthdays, weddings and the like), marches (military music); and strathspeys and reels (dance music). While playing a pibroch the piper marches slowly to and fro, not so much in time to the music, but in sympathy with the melody. On the other hand, when playing dance music, the pipers remain in one position tapping

their foot; and, understandably, when playing a march – for who can resist the skirl of the pipes? – they stride up and down the platform.

Most dancers at Games are female, although occasionally a thorn appears among the roses. Seldom are any girls older than 18, and competitions are even held for three- and four-year-olds.

King Malcolm Canmore is credited with being responsible for one of the more famous dances seen at the Games. In 1054 he slew one of King Macbeth's chieftains and, crossing his own sword and that of the vanquished chieftain, performed a *Gille Calum* (sword dance) before going into battle. The touching of either sword with the feet was an unfavourable omen.

The origin of the Highland Fling is also curious. A grandfather was playing the pipes on the moors and his young grandson was dancing to them. Two courting stags were silhouetted against the horizon. The grandfather asked the lad: "Can ye nae raise yer hands like the horns of yon stags?" And so originated the Highland

---

**Left:** hammer-throwing at a Highland meeting.
**Right:** tossing the caber.

Fling. The dance is performed without travelling (that is to say, on one spot) and the reason is that the Scot, like the stag, does not run after his women: he expects them to come to him. A more mundane explanation for the dance being performed on one spot is that it was originally danced on a shield.

In the dance called *Sean Truibhas* – the Gaelic for old trews (trousers) – the performer's distaste for his garb is expressed. This dance originated after Culloden when the wearing of the kilt was proscribed.

One of the original aims of the Games was to select the ablest bodyguards for the king or chieftain, and this is perpetuated in today's heavy events. The objects used in these have evolved from what would be found in any rural community, such as a blacksmith's hammer or even a stone in the river bed.

## Olympic strength

Hurling the hammer and putting the shot are similar, yet different, to these events as practised at the Olympics. At the "Oatmeal Olympics" the hammer has a wooden shaft rather than a chain, and the weight of the shot varies. The 56-lb (25-kg) weight is thrown by holding, with one hand, a short chain attached to the weight; the

**ROYAL CONNECTIONS**

The Highlands of Scotland are famous for their Games. Some claim that Games were first held in 1314 at Ceres in Fife, when the Scottish bowmen returned victorious from Bannockburn. Others believe that it all began even earlier when King Malcolm organised a race up a hill called Craig Choinnich. The winner received a *baldric* (warrior's belt) and became Malcolm's foot-messenger. A race up and down Craig Choinnich became a feature of the Braemar Gathering, which is the highlight of the circuit. However, this isn't so much because of the calibre of the competition but because, since the time of Queen Victoria, it is often attended by the Royal Family.

length of weight and chain must not exceed 18 inches (45 cm). Then there is the tossing of the 56-lb (25-kg) weight. In this event it is not distance but height that counts. The competitor stands below and immediately in front of a bar and with his back to it. Then, holding the weight in one hand, he swings it between his legs and throws it up and, with luck, over the bar. A correct throw will just miss the thrower on its way down, while a bad throw is liable to cause untold mischief.

The most spectacular event is tossing the caber, a straight, tapered pine-tree trunk shorn of its branches. It weighs about 125 lbs (57 kg) and is about 19 ft (6 metres) long. The diameter at one end is about 9 inches (23 cm) and at the other about 5 inches (13 cm). Two men struggle to carry the caber to a squatting competitor. They place it vertically with the narrow end in his cupped hands. The competitor gingerly rises and, with the foot of the caber resting against his shoulder, and the remainder towering above, starts to run. Finally, at a suitably auspicious moment, the competitor stops dead, lets out an almighty roar, and thrusts his hands upwards. The wide end of the caber hits the ground; now is the moment of truth: will the quivering pole tumble backwards towards the hopeful competitor or will it attain the perpendicular and then

Caber-tossing is believed to have evolved from throwing tree trunks into the river after they had been felled. They would then float to the sawmill. It was important to throw the trunks into the middle of the river or they would snag on the banks.

## Colour codes

Colour is the keynote of the Games. All dancers and musicians are dressed in full Highland regalia, as are many of the judges and some spectators. Competitors in the heavy events all wear the kilt. The reds of the Stuarts, the greens of the Gordons and the blues of the Andersons

turn over completely and fall away from him?

But why does an empty-handed, puffing judge trot alongside the competitor? Tossing the caber is judged not on distance but on style. An imaginary clockface is involved, and the athlete is presumed to be standing at the figure 6 when he makes his throw. A perfect throw lands at 12; a somewhat less perfect one at 11 or at 1 and so on. Naturally, the athlete will attempt, after throwing, to swivel his feet so that his throw appears perfect. Hence the puffing judge.

---

**ABOVE LEFT:** judges deliberate at the Braemar Games.
**ABOVE:** the tug-of-war team flexes its porridge-fed muscles.

all mingle with the green of the grass and the purple of the heather to produce a muted palette.

Highland Games are very much in vogue, and new venues are constantly announced. Currently, more than 60 Gatherings are held during the season, which extends from the end of May until mid-September. In spite of the spectacular appeal of the great Gatherings (Braemar, Cowal, Oban), the visitor might find that the smaller meetings (Ceres, Uist in the Hebrides) are more enjoyable. These have an authentic ambience, and competitors in the heavy events are certain to be good and true Scots and not professional intruders from foreign parts. What's more, you may not even have to pay admission! ❑

# A FONDNESS FOR FESTIVALS

*The Scottish calendar is bursting with local festivals: very different in origin but all offering an excuse to celebrate in spectacular style*

Until the middle of the 20th century puritanical Scotland completely ignored Papist Christmas: offices, shops and factories all functioned as usual on 25 December. The great event in the Scottish calendar was the night of 31 December (Hogmanay) and New Year's Day (which was called *Nollaig Bheag* – Little Christmas – in many parts of the Highlands).

Traditionally, as the bells struck midnight, the crowds gathered around the focal points of towns would join hands and sing "Auld Lang Syne" and then whisky bottles would be passed around before all dispersed to go first-footing. It is important that the first-foot (the first person to cross a threshold in the new year) should be a tall, dark-haired male who brings gifts of coal and salt which ensure that the house won't want for fire or food in the coming year. Also, the first-foot will normally carry a bottle of whisky.

## Hot stuff

Fiery New Year processions which will drive out and ward off evil spirits have been held for centuries at Comrie, Burghead and Stonehaven. At the Comrie Flambeaux procession, locals walk through the town carrying burning torches; at Stonehaven, participants swing fireballs attached to a long wire and handle. Some suggest that the swinging of fireballs is a mimetic attempt to lure back the sun from the heavens during the dark winter months.

The Burning of the Clavie at Burghead is held on 11 January. (This is when Hogmanay falls according to the Old Style calendar, which was abandoned in 1752 but which still holds sway when deciding the date of many celebrations.) The ceremony begins with the Clavie King lighting a tar-filled barrel, which is then carried in procession through the town and from which firebrands are distributed. Finally, the Clavie is placed on the summit of Doorie Hill and left to burn for a time before being rolled down the hill.

**LEFT:** the Beltane Fire Festival, held in Edinburgh, celebrates the arrival of summer.
**RIGHT:** dressed up for the Galashiels Common Riding.

More recent in origin is the torchlight procession on Edinburgh's Princes Street on 31 December, the highlight of a five-day Hogmanay extravaganza. However, by far the greatest and most spectacular fire ceremony is Up-Helly-Aa, held at Lerwick in the remote Shetland Islands on the last Tuesday in January.

Up-Helly-Aa (compare the old Scots name for Twelfth Night, *Uphaliday*) begins with the posting of "The Bill", a 10-ft (3-metre) high Proclamation, at the Market Cross, and the displaying of a 30-ft (9-metre) model longship at the seafront, which is ceremonially burned.

Come evening, and with the Guizer Jarl magnificently dressed in Viking costume at the steering oar, the longship is dragged to the burning site. Team after team of *guizers*, each clad in glorious or grotesque garb and all carrying blazing torches, follow the ship. When the burning site is reached the "Galley Song" is sung; the Guizer Jarl leaves the longship; a bugle sounds; and hundreds of blazing torches are hurled upon and consume the hull. Celebrations continue all through the night.

At Kirkwall, capital of Orkney, those who survived the Hogmanay celebrations gather on New Year's Day at the Mercat Cross for the "Ba' Game". Two teams attempt to carry a leather ball, about the size of a tennis ball, against all opposition, to their own end of the town. A giant scrum forms, becoming so torrid that steam rises from its centre. A good game lasts for several hours.

Later in the month, Burns Night (25 January) honours the birth of the national poet. In villages and cities throughout the land, Burns clubs and others toast the haggis *(see page 122).*

A different kind of game can be seen at Lanark on 1 March. The church bells peal out and the children of Lanark, armed with home-made weapons of paper balls on strings, race three times around the church, beating each other over the head as they go. Town officials then throw handfuls of coins for which the children scramble. Some say Whuppity Scoorie is a ridding of the town of evil spirits by scourging the precincts of the church. A more mundane explanation is that the festival represents the chasing away of winter and the welcoming of spring.

In April, students at St Andrews University stage the Kate Kennedy pageant, in which they

### THE RIDING OF THE MARCHES

Throughout the early summer months the clippity-clop of horses' hoofs is heard on the cobblestones of Border towns. The Riding of the Marches, introduced in the Middle Ages, is the custom of checking the boundaries of common lands owned by the town. In some cases, the Riding also commemorates local historical events which invariably involved warfare between the English and the Scots in the Middle Ages. The festivities often last for several days and are always stiff with protocol.

The Selkirk Gathering, held in June, is the oldest, the largest and the most emotional of the Ridings. It concludes with the Casting of the Colours, which commemorates Scotland's humiliating defeat at the Battle of Flodden. At the "casting", flags are waved in proscribed patterns while the band plays a soulful melody.

Each town – including Dumfries, Duns, Galashiels, Jedburgh, Lanark, Langholm and Lauder – has its own variations of the Riding ceremonies; all have other activities which include balls, concerts, pageants and sporting events. In Annan, the Riding of the Marches have been ridden since the town was created a Royal Burgh over 600 years ago. At Peebles the Riding incorporates the Beltane Fair, which is the great Celtic festival of the sun and which marks the beginning of summer.

play the parts of distinguished figures associated with the university or the town. Lady Kate, a niece of the university's founder, was a great beauty to whom the students are said to have sworn everlasting allegiance. Women are banned from taking part in the procession, and the role of Kate is played by a first-year male student.

## Summer festivals

Traditional summer fairs are held throughout the country. Until quite recently, farm employees who wished to change their jobs would seek out new employers at Feeing Markets, and one such market, enlivened with Highland dancing, country music and other entertainments, is still held in June at Stonehaven. Later in the month, a similar event, the Maggie Fair, is held at Garmouth: it commemorates the landing of Charles II at nearby Kingston after he had been proclaimed king of Scotland following the execution of his father, King Charles I.

The Beltane Festival, held on Edinburgh's Calton Hill on Midsummer's Eve, revives one of the major events of the Celtic calendar. Weirdly costumed, and often largely naked, revellers wielding flaming torches make this a dramatic welcome for the season of plenty.

The first day of August is Lammas Day, or Lunasdal – the feast of the sun god, Lugh – and was formerly a popular day for local fairs. Such fairs are still held in August, although not on the first day, at St Andrews and Inverkeithing. Also at this time a bizarre ritual occurs on the day before the South Queensferry Ferry Fair. A man, clad head to toe in white flannel, is covered with an infinite number of burrs until he becomes a moving bush. Bedecked with flowers and carrying two staves, this strange creature makes his way from house to house receiving gifts. One theory for this strange practice equates the Burryman with the scapegoat of antiquity.

The Highland Festival, a more recent event, is centred on the city of Inverness, but many of its musical, artistic and theatrical performances are staged throughout the region.

## Fleet of foot

In late August, the ancient west-coast burgh of Irvine holds its Marymass Fair, which dates from the 12th century. Horse races, very much a part of this fair, are said to be even older. These races are not only for ponies but also for Clydesdale carthorses which, in spite of their great size, are remarkably fleet of foot.

"Horses" of a different kind are involved in a mid-August festival on the island of South Ronaldsay in Orkney. The "horses" are young boys or girls dressed in spectacular costumes. Pulling beautifully wrought miniature ploughs, often family heirlooms, and guided by boy ploughmen, these "horses" compete to turn the straightest furrows on a sandy beach.

Hallowe'en, on 31 October, is popular with

children, who dress up as witches and ghouls in order to frighten off the "real" evil spirits abroad at All-Hallows Eve. The imported American custom of "trick or treat" is threatening to reduce the charm of this ancient ritual. On 5 November, towns and villages commemorate with bonfires and firework displays the anniversary of the Gunpowder Plot in 1605, when Guy Fawkes tried to blow up parliament in London.

St Andrew's Day (30 November), the national day, is mostly ignored. It does offer excuses for society types to dress in their finery, attend balls, toast the haggis, and imbibe unwise quantities of whisky. So, inexorably, the festive year rushes headlong towards another Hogmanay. ❏

**LEFT:** the Galashiels Braw Lads gallop out.
**RIGHT:** the climax of Lerwick's Up-Helly-Aa Viking Festival.

# THE LURE OF THE GREEN TURF

*To play on the hallowed ground of Scotland's ancient golf courses*

*is the ambition of amateur and professional golfers alike*

Visit the 19th hole at any of Scotland's 400 golf courses and you're almost certain to hear a heated argument, over a dram or two of whisky, as to where the game of golf originated. The discussion doesn't involve geography but rather topography: the "where" refers to *which* part of Scotland. All know that, in spite of the Dutch boasting of a few old paintings which depict the game, it all began in Scotland centuries ago, when a shepherd swinging with his stick at round stones hit one into a rabbit hole. Little did the rustic know the madness he was about to unleash when he murmured to his flock: "I wonder if I can do that again?"

## Scottish links

Few courses have the characteristics of the quintessential Scottish course. Such a course, bordering the seashore, is called a links. It is on the links of Muirfield, St Andrews, Troon and Turnberry that the British Open – or "the Open" – is often played.

The word links refers to that stretch of land which connects the beach with more stable inshore land, and a links course is a sandy, undulating terrain which borders the shore. One feature of such a course is its ridges and furrows, which result in the ball nestling in an infinite variety of lies. Another feature is the wind, which blows off the sea and which can suddenly whip up with enormous ferocity. A hole which, in the morning, was played with a driver and a 9-iron can, after lunch, demand a driver, a long 3-wood and a 6-iron.

Summer days in Scotland are long, and the eager beaver can tee off at 7am and play until 10pm – easily enough time for 54 holes, unless you're prone to slice, hook or pull. But the rough of gorse, broom, heather and whin is insatiable, and a great deal of time can be lost searching for balls.

Most golfers will immediately head for St Andrews. They will be surprised to find that the

Old Course has two, rather than the customary four, short holes and has only 11 greens. Yet it is categorically an 18-hole course: seven greens are shared. This explains the enormous size of the greens, on which you can find yourself facing a putt of almost 100 yards (90 metres). Remember it is the homeward-bound player who has the

right of way on these giant double greens.

Don't be too distressed if you fail to obtain a starting time on the Old (half of starting times are allocated by ballot: contact the starter before 2pm on the day before you wish to play). The New Course is even more difficult, but St Andrews still has five other courses from which to choose *(see Travel Tips, page 352)*.

Ancient as the Royal and Ancient Golf Club of St Andrews is, it must bow the knee to the Honourable Company of Edinburgh Golfers, which was formed in 1774 and is generally accepted as the oldest golf club in the world. Its present Muirfield course – which is at Gullane (pronounced *Gillun*), 13 miles (21 km) east of

**LEFT:** St Andrews, a magnet for all golfers.
**RIGHT:** teeing off beside the sea.

Edinburgh and was the venue for the 2002 Open Championship – is considered to be the ultimate test of golf. The rough here is ferocious, and if, on looking around, you lose your partner, don't panic: they will merely be out of sight in one of the nearly 200 deep pot-bunkers which litter the course.

And not to worry if you can't play on Muirfield: the tiny village of Gullane is also the home of the three challenging Gullane courses (simply called 1, 2 and 3) and to Luffness New. The latter is "New" because, by Scotland's standards, it is just that, having been founded as recently as 1894.

## Capital courses

Back in the city of Edinburgh are more than a score of courses, two of which are home to very ancient clubs. The Royal Burgess Golfing Society claims to be even older than the Hon. Coy, while the neighbouring Bruntsfield Links Golfing Society is only a few years younger.

On the road from Gullane to Edinburgh you pass through Musselburgh, where golf is known to have been played in 1672 and, most probably, even before that. Was this where Mary Queen of Scots was seen playing a few days after the murder of Lord Darnley, her second husband? Was Mary the world's first golf widow?

## CLUB FORMALITIES

At the majority of courses no formal introduction is necessary: as a visitor, you just stroll up, pay your money and play. Some clubs do ask that you be a member of another club. Others require an introduction by a member, although if you are an overseas visitor this formality is usually waived. And the better courses demand a valid handicap certificate, which usually must be below 20 for men and 30 for ladies.

Access to the course doesn't mean you will gain entry to the clubhouse – that remains the private domain of a particular club whose members happen to make use of the adjacent course.

Glasgow, never outdone by Edinburgh, has nearly 30 courses. Outstanding among these are Killermont and Haggs Castle. The latter is less than 3 miles (5 km) from the city centre. While golfers thrill over birdies and eagles at Haggs, their non-playing partners can enthuse over the renowned Burrell Collection, which is less than half a mile (1 km) away. Even closer to the Burrell is the excellent Pollok course. Further afield at Luss (23 miles/37 km northwest of the city) by the bonnie banks of Loch Lomond is a course designed by Tom Weiskopf and Jay Morrish. Ranking 21st (in 2005) out of the 100 best courses in the world, the Loch Lomond Golf Club is one of the best in Britain.

Troon, 30 miles (48 km) south of Glasgow and frequently the scene of the Open, is the kingpin in a series of nearly 30 courses bordering the Atlantic rollers. Here, hardly ever stooping to pick up your ball, you can play for almost 30 miles (48 km). Troon itself has five courses.

To the north is Barassie with one, and then Gailes with two courses. South of Troon are three courses at Prestwick – scene of the first Open in 1860 – and Ayr, also with three courses. Fifteen minutes further down the "course" are the exclusive Arran and Ailsa links of Turnberry. There's an excellent courseat Brunston Castle, a few miles to the southeast,

Over on the east coast is another remarkable conglomerate of courses, with St Andrews as its kingpin. About 30 miles (48 km) to the north, across the Tay Bridge, are the three Carnoustie courses. The Medal course here, formerly scene of many Opens, has been called brutal, evil and monstrous.

Then, 20 miles (32 km) south of St Andrews and strung, like a priceless necklace, along the north shore of the Firth of Forth, are the Elie, Leven, Lundin Links and Crail golf courses. The Crail course is claimed by golf-storians to

**LEFT:** caught in a bunker at Muirfield.
**ABOVE:** golf can sometimes be a risky business.

be the seventh-oldest in the world.

Other glittering gems are found in the northeast. Here are Balgownie and Murcar, two of Aberdeen's half a dozen courses; nearby is Cruden Bay; Nairn, which is close to Inverness; and Dornoch, which stands in splendid isolation in the extreme northeast. The Balgownie and Cruden Bay clubs are both 200 years old; the founders of the latter are probably turning in their graves at the new name of their club – the Cruden Bay Golf and Country Club.

Dornoch is, even for a Scottish course, underplayed and may be Britain's most underrated course. Authorities believe that this course, all of whose holes have a view of the sea, would be on the Open rota if it was closer to the main centres of population.

Down at the extreme southwest of the country is Machrihanish, another underrated, underplayed links. Its turf is so naturally perfect that "every ball is teed, wherever it is". And if the views from here, which include Ireland and the Inner Hebrides, seduce you then you might wish to make your way over the seas to Islay, which is renowned for both its whisky and its Machrie course.

## New additions

Scotland, home of golf, also boasts some superb inland courses. Many aficionados consider the King's at Gleneagles to be the best inland course in Britain. Certainly nowhere in the world can there be a championship course set in such dramatically beautiful scenery. In 1993, it was joined by the PGA Centenary Course, which is from the drawing board of Jack Nicklaus and has the flavour of an American rather than a Scottish course. These are just two of the four courses which make up the luxurious Gleneagles complex.

If these four aren't enough, a mere 30 miles (48 km) to the north is Blairgowrie with its fabled Rosemount course. Here, among parasol pines, larches, silver birch and evergreens, you'll come upon lost golf balls, partridges, pheasant and otter. And new courses are still being created: the 18-hole par 72 Spey Valley Championship Golf Course opened in 2006 in Aviemore and was designed by Ryder Cup player, Dave Thomas.

The billionaire American Donald Trump also hopes to create a £1 billion golf course development north of Aberdeen. ❑

# HUNTING, SHOOTING AND FISHING

*The natural assets of Scotland are eagerly exploited by wealthy proprietors,*

*satisfying the continuing demand for upmarket sports*

**W**hile Scotland may have been blessed with more deer, grouse, salmon and trout than most small European countries, a significant proportion of these assets are controlled by a small number of wealthy estates, whose owners may live a long way from Scotland. This means that "field sports" such as deer stalking, salmon fishing and grouse shooting are touchy political issues, bound up with memories of the Highland Clearances and the ownership and use of the land.

Ownership of large Highland estates varies from local aristocrats who have been there for centuries to southern financiers, European entrepreneurs and oil-rich Arabs. While "traditional" estate owners retain a paternalistic approach, some of the newer proprietors arrive with little or no knowledge of the Scottish way of life, and try to recoup their investment any way they can, often at the expense of local interests.

## Clash of interests

Rights enjoyed and shared by local people can suddenly vanish. This happened when the then North of Scotland Hydroelectric Board (now Scottish Hydro-Electric) sold its fishing rights on the River Conon north of Inverness to a City of London financier for a reputed £1.5 million. He promptly divided the river into weekly time-share "beats" which were sold at up to £15,000 per person per week. Not unnaturally, locals who had long fished the river, but who could not afford such prices, were incensed.

There have also been problems in the past with estates covering large areas of prime hill-walking country trying to deny access to walkers and climbers during the shooting seasons. Many walkers regard access as a right, not a privilege, and have been prone to ignore aggressive or intimidating "keep out" notices.

The situation has eased considerably, thanks to greater cooperation between the various factions.

---

**PRECEDING PAGES:** fishing holiday.
**LEFT:** trophies from hunts in Brodick Castle, Arran.
**RIGHT:** a Highland gamekeeper.

In 1996, a national Access Forum was set up by Scottish Natural Heritage, to draw up a "Concordate on Access" recognising both the needs of the estates and the ambitions of walkers. Subsequently, the Land Reform (Scotland) Act 2004 now gives the public statutory rights to Scotland's mountains, moorlands, lochs and rivers. Based on

the premise of "responsible access", the Act aims to balance the interests of land managers with conservationists and recreations such as hill-walking. In sensitive areas, a "Hillphone" system operates under which walkers can phone a recorded message which tells them where stalking or grouse shooting is taking place.

## Health and safety

The health of Scotland's field sports depends heavily on the state of the ecology, so environmental groups and estate owners can have similar concerns. Uneasy bedfellows in the past, they are now working together on such matters as scientific studies into the reasons for the dramatic decline in grouse numbers in many areas. Other common concerns include acid rain and the damage caused by tributyl tin to salmon and sea trout. Overenthusiastic conifer-planting of large areas has, happily, been reined in, with many areas now being replanted with native tree species.

## Chasing the deer

Stalking the magnificent red deer is one of Scotland's prime attractions for wealthy foreign sportsmen. According to the Deer Commission for Scotland, in 2000 there were 300,000–350,000 red deer in Scotland, most of them north of the "highland line" between Helensburgh and Stonehaven. Since 1950, numbers have more than doubled, the increase in recent years being partly due to more animals living in woodland – the cover is opening up as forests reach maturity. The annual cull, necessary to maintain a sustainable population level, is based on estimates of the numbers and density of deer herds.

The vast majority of the shooting is by professional stalkers, foresters or sporting parties under professional guidance. After the stag season ends, hind culling, though not for sport, continues until February. Although the stag stalking season officially runs from 1 July to 20 October, very little shooting is done before mid-

August. For the next two months, shooters from all over Britain, Europe and North America descend on the Highlands in pursuit of a stag. All-terrain vehicles are increasingly used to get them onto the hill, but the final part of the stalk can still be an exhausting belly-crawl through heather or peat until the stalker decides the prey is close enough to get off a clean shot.

Nor does this pleasure come cheap. A week's stalking (six days) can cost over £2,000, and only the trophy (the head) belongs to the hunter; the venison will be sold by the estate. Accommodation is extra. Rifles can be hired, but most sportsmen bring their own. A decent stalking rifle will cost anything from £500 to £5,000.

There are between 200,000 and 400,000 roe deer in Scotland, and shooting roe deer bucks (males), often from high seats fixed in the trees, is becoming more popular. It is less expensive, costs being roughly between half and two-thirds those for a red deer stag shoot.

## Seeking the salmon

The upmarket sport par excellence has to be salmon fishing in one of Scotland's great salmon rivers such as the Dee, the Spey, the Tay, the Tweed or the Conon. One survey estimated that it cost the affluent angler over £2,000 to land an Atlantic salmon from a prime stretch of a Scottish river. Certainly, a week's fishing on a good stretch (called a "beat") at the height of the season (July to September) on one of the classier rivers is likely to set the fisherman back between £1,500 and £2,000.

Yet demand is so high that a number of specialist firms, and even some estates, have taken to operating salmon beats on a "timeshare" basis. It works like this. The company buys a decent stretch of a good salmon river for a very large sum of money. The river is then divided into beats, and on each beat a week's fishing is sold "in perpetuity" for up to £30,000 (depending on when the slot occurs in the season and the quality of the fishing). All this is much against the wishes of those, like the Scottish Campaign for Public Angling (SCAPA), who believe that everyone should have the right to fish where they want and that no waters should be closed to the public.

With so much money at stake, it is little wonder that river proprietors have grown anxious as they have seen salmon stocks decline. Some commentators believe stocks of wild salmon could even be wiped out in a matter of decades. The drop has been attributed to net fishing at river mouths, river and sea pollution, global warming, intensive salmon farming and declining fertility in the fish.

The net fishing has almost died out, thanks partly to the efforts of the Atlantic Salmon Conservation Trust, set up in 1986. The Trust rapidly raised several million pounds and acquired the rights to many net fishing operations, then simply closed them down. However, problems still exist. Drift netting still takes place

in the far North Atlantic, off Greenland, Iceland and the Faroe Islands, and poachers are still busy along Scotland's rivers.

While salmon fishing may be the glamour end of the sport, many anglers feel that too much is made of it. They argue that there is much better sport in the brown trout fishing which is available – for far less outlay – on countless Scottish lochs, particularly on the west coast and in the northern Highlands, where the salmon are not abundant. Some remote lochs are still only visited by a few enthusiasts, and 100 fish in a day on two rods from a boat is not just a dream.

## Trout are tops

Tourist authorities promote this valuable resource through schemes whereby a single ticket will get the angler access to a variety of waters during a holiday. Angling is worth millions of pounds per year to the Scottish economy, and this figure is bound to grow as the hitherto secret delights of the upland rivers and lochs become better-known.

Who knows, you might get lucky and snag one of the ferocious ferox trout found in the West Highlands. They weigh up to 20 lbs (9 kg) and are cannibals, but as one angler said, "a hell of an exciting fish to get on the end of your line". And a great tale to tell afterwards in the pub. ❑

**LEFT:** a catch from the River Don.
**RIGHT:** fishing in the River Spey.

# A WEE DRAM

*While many dispute the secret of the unique taste of Scotch whisky,*
*few deny the pleasures to be had from the "water of life"*

At the end of sophisticated dinner parties in London, guests are invariably offered a choice of brandy or port but seldom a glass of Scotch. Familiarity, perhaps, has produced contempt for the native product – or, the Scots would argue, the English are showing their customary ignorance of all things Scottish.

The prejudice is an ill-founded one because good malt whiskies have a wider range of flavour and aroma than brandy and – an extra bonus – they are less likely to make the over-indulger's head throb the morning after. Snobbery probably accounts for the attitude, too, for Scotland's unique drink has never quite managed to cultivate the exclusive image of cognac.

For one thing, there's a lot more of it on the international market. Scotch is one of Britain's top five export items, contributing £2 billion annually to the balance of trade: even the Vatican, on one recent annual reckoning, bought 18,000 bottles. More than 2,500 brands of Scotch whisky are sold around the world with the major export market being the United States. However, both India and China are seen as potentially huge untapped markets.

## Toddler's tipple

The lowly origins of Scotch may also be partly to blame for its fluctuating fortunes. In the 18th century, it was drunk as freely as the water from which it was made, by peasants and aristocrats alike. A spoonful was given to newborn babies in the Highlands, and even respectable gentlewomen might start the day with "a wee dram". The poorest crofter could offer the visitor a drink, thanks to the ubiquity of home-made stills which made millions of bottles of "mountain dew" in the remote glens of the Highlands. Excise officers estimated in 1777 that Edinburgh had eight licensed stills and 400 illegal ones.

Yet something as easy to make cannot be made authentically outside Scotland. Many have tried, and the Japanese have thrown the most modern technology at the problem; but the combination of damp climate and soft water flowing through the peat cannot be replicated elsewhere.

Some historians believe that the art of distilling was brought to Scotland by Christian mis-

sionary monks. But it is just as likely that Highland farmers discovered for themselves how to distil spirits from their surplus barley. The earliest known reference to whisky occurred in 1494, when Scottish Exchequer Rolls record that Friar John Cor purchased a quantity of malt "to make aquavitae".

These days there are two kinds of Scotch whisky: *malt*, made from malted barley only; and *grain*, made from malted barley together with unmalted barley, maize or other cereals. Most popular brands are blends of both types of whisky – typically 60 percent grain to 40 percent malt.

A single malt, the product of one distillery, has become an increasingly popular drink,

**PRECEDING PAGES:** whisky maturing under the eye of the customs officer.
**LEFT:** whisky still.
**RIGHT:** tools of the distiller's trade.

thanks largely to the aggressive marketing by William Grant & Sons of their Glenfiddich brand. But sales of single malts still account for only one bottle in 20 sold around the world, and most of the production of single-malt distilleries is used to add flavour to a blended whisky.

## Making whisky

So automated are Scotland's 100-plus distilleries that visitors, sipping an end-of-tour glass of the product they have watched being manufactured, are left with an image of the beautifully proportioned onion-shaped copper stills and a lingering aroma of malted barley – but not

with any clear idea of the process by which water from a Highland stream is transformed into *uisgebeatha*, the water of life.

What happens is this. To make malt whisky, plump and dry barley (which, unlike the water, doesn't have to be local) sits in tanks of water for two or three days. It is then spread out on a concrete floor or placed in large cylindrical drums and allowed to germinate for between eight and 12 days. It is dried in a kiln, which ideally should be heated by a peat fire. The dried malt is ground and mixed with hot water in a huge circular vat called a mash tun. A sugary liquid, "wort", is drawn off from the porridge-like result, leaving the remaining solids to be sold as cattle food. The wort is fed into massive vessels containing up to 9,900 gallons (45,000 litres) of liquid, where living yeast is stirred into the mix in order to convert the sugar in the wort into crude alcohol.

After about 48 hours, the "wash" (a clear liquid containing weak alcohol) is transferred to the copper pot stills and heated to the point at which alcohol turns to vapour. This vapour rises up the still to be condensed by a cooling plant into distilled alcohol which is then passed through a second still.

## Tricks of the trade

The trick is to know exactly when the whisky has distilled sufficiently. Modern measuring devices offer scientific precision, but the individual judgement of an experienced distiller is hard to beat. Once distilled, the liquid is poured into oak casks which, being porous, allow air to enter. Evaporation takes place, removing the harsher constituents of the new spirit and enabling it to mellow. Legally it can't be sold as whisky until

---

### TASTE THE DIFFERENCE

Despite the claims of distillers that each whisky blend has a unique taste, the truth is that most people, in a blind tasting, would be hard-pressed to say whether they were drinking Bell's, Teacher's, Dewar's, Johnnie Walker or J&B. Pure malt whis-kies, on the other hand, are more readily identifiable. The experienced Scotch drinker can differentiate between Highland malts, Lowland malts, Campbeltown malts and Islay malts, and there is certainly no mistaking the bouquet of a malt such as Laphroaig, which is usually described as tasting of iodine or seaweed. So which is best? Whole evenings can be whiled away in Scotland debating and

researching the question with no firm conclusions being reached. It all comes down to individual taste – after all, in the words of Robert Burns: "Freedom and Whisky gang thegither [together]."

However, the one point of agreement is that a good malt whisky should not be drunk with a mixer which would destroy the subtle flavour. Yet, although it is said there are two things which a Highlander likes naked, connoisseurs may be permitted to add a little water to their single malt. After dinner, malts are best drunk neat, as a liqueur. Blended whisky, in contrast, is refreshing in hot weather when mixed with soda.

it has spent three years in the cask, and a good malt will stay casked for at least eight years.

It wasn't until the 1820s that distilling began to develop from small family-run concerns into large manufacturing businesses. What accelerated the change was the invention in 1830 by Aeneas Coffey of a patent still. This was faster and cheaper than traditional methods; more importantly, it did not need the perfect mix of peat and water, but could produce whisky from a mixture of malted and unmalted barley mashed with other cereals.

But was the resulting grain whisky a real Scotch? Some dismissed it as flavourless surgical spirits; others approved of it as "lighter-

duce a palatable compromise between taste and strength. What's more, an almost infinite variety of combinations was possible, enabling each brand to claim its own unique taste.

## Old favourites

In sales terms, it's estimated 31 bottles of whisky are sold around each second, while more Scotch is sold in one month in France than cognac in a year. The Scots themselves tend to favour Glenmorangie, which is matured in old Bourbon casks, charred on the inside, for at least 10 years to produce a smooth spirit with hints of peat smoke and vanilla. The most popular

bodied". The argument rumbled on until 1905, when one of London's local authorities decided to test in the courts whether pubs could legally sell the patent-still (as opposed to the pot-still) product as "whisky". Even the courts couldn't agree. It was left to a Royal Commission to deliver the verdict that both drinks were equally wholesome and could call themselves whisky.

The industry's future, however, lay in the marriage between malt and grain whiskies. Blending tiny amounts of 30 or 40 malt whiskies with grain whisky, distillers found, could pro-

malt in the United States is The Macallan, which is produced on Speyside and matured in 100 percent sherry casks seasoned for two years in Spain with dry oloroso sherry; connoisseurs argue that the 10-year old is a better drink than the more impressive-sounding 18-year old.

The brave should sample Glenfarclas (with over 60 percent alcohol). Those desiring a more diluted sample need only take one of the many distillery tours on the Scotch Whisky Trail or enjoy the annual Speyside Whisky Festival (May). Because whisky "breathes" while maturing in its casks, as much as 4 million gallons (20 million litres) evaporate into the air each year. All you have to do is inhale.  ❑

**Left:** an Oban bar's whisky selection.
**Above:** rolling out the barrels on Islay.

# PORRIDGE, HAGGIS AND COCK-A-LEEKIE

*Cooked breakfasts, high teas and smoked salmon for supper:*
*traditional Scottish food satisfies the heartiest of appetites*

Scotland, as the writer H.V. Morton once remarked, is the best place in the world to take an appetite. No doubt his appetite was coaxed by the abundance of fresh food and the freshness of the air, which in the Highlands (and even the Lowlands) remains remarkably pure.

Scots cuisine, uninspired and uninspiring for many years, has been largely transformed in recent years. Some of Britain's top chefs now produce award-winning food in Scotland, relying on top-quality, locally produced fresh meat and fish prepared with an international twist – particularly Mediterranean flavours and the exotic tastes of Asian and Eastern food, which the Scots have long had a penchant for.

The Scottish diet also has its hazards, however. Local tastes, especially the love of fried food, are held to be a major contributory factor to the Scots' internationally appalling level of heart disease. This is the home of the deep-fried Mars bar and the Scotch egg, a more traditional fast-food snack consisting of a hard-boiled egg wrapped in sausage meat, coated in breadcrumbs and then fried.

## Scottish roots

Despite the recent rise in international influences, Scottish cookery still has its roots in the soil, especially in some of those isolated hotels and restaurants far from the main cities. There, real Scottish cuisine is something the proprietors are genuinely proud of serving, notably the "traditional full Scottish breakfast". This generally starts with kippers (smoked herring) or porridge, similar to polenta and made from oatmeal. Traditionalists take it with salt, but many prefer it with sugar. This is followed by bacon, egg, sausage, and perhaps black pudding (a variety of sausage made with blood). Expect also an array of breads, rolls, oatcakes and scones, topped off with an assortment of (often home-made) jams and conserves.

**LEFT:** only the finest ingredients will do.
**RIGHT:** time for afternoon tea and cakes.

Scottish bakery can often be really delectable, but can sometimes be stodgy, heavy and mass-produced. Not too long ago in Scotland, there were fewer restaurants than tearooms. Here, people ate not only lunch and afternoon tea but also "high tea", which usually consisted

of fish and chips and a generous selection of scones and cakes. High teas are still on offer in some hotels.

It is also significant that biscuit-making remains an extensive and popular industry in both Edinburgh and Glasgow and as far north as Kirkwall in Orkney (where the oatcakes are arguably the best in the land). Dundee is renowned for its eponymous cake and for orange marmalade, its gift to the world's breakfast and tea tables – though the theory that the name "marmalade" derives from the words *Marie est malade* (referring to the food given to Mary Queen of Scots when she was ill) must be considered rather far-fetched.

### Flavoursome fish and meat

Kippers, too, are a treat. The best of them are from Loch Fyne, where their colour emerges properly golden, not dyed repellent red as they are in so many places. Arbroath smokies or finnan-haddies (types of smoked haddock) are a tasty alternative, simmered gently in milk and butter. Salmon and trout, sadly, are just as likely to come from some west-coast or northern fish farm as fresh from the river, but the standard remains high.

If you're buying from a fishmonger, ask for "wild" salmon, more flavoursome than the farmed variety. On the other hand, farmed fish is

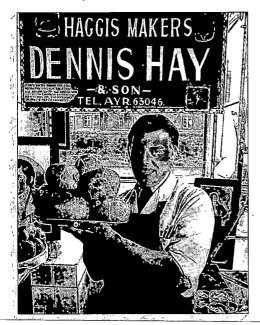

generally preferred, to help ensure uniformity, in the production of justifiably renowned smoked salmon and trout.

The beef of the Aberdeen Angus cattle remains the most famous in the world (escaping the worst of the BSE scares). Good Scottish meat, the experts claim, should be hung for at least four weeks or even for eight – unlike supermarket steak, which is not aged at all – and should never be sliced less than 1¼ inches (3 cm) thick.

Venison, pheasant, hare and grouse are also established features of the Scottish kitchen. Admittedly, the romance of eating grouse after it has been ritually shot on or around the glorious 12 August should be tempered (if you are

honest with yourself) by this bird's depressing fibrous toughness, which makes grouse shooting seem, at least to a gourmet, an unutterable waste of time.

### The national dish

As for haggis – though it, too, is hardly a gourmet delight – it does offer a fascinating experience for brave visitors. Scotland's great mystery dish is really only a sheep's stomach stuffed with minced lamb and beef, along with onions, oatmeal and a blend of seasonings and spices. After being boiled, the stomach is sliced open, as spectacularly as possible, and the contents served piping hot.

Butchers today often use a plastic bag instead of a stomach; this has the advantage that it is less likely to burst during the boiling process, resulting in the meat being ruined. But no haggis devotee would contemplate such a substitute.

The tastiest haggis, by popular acclaim, comes from Macsween's of Edinburgh, who also make a vegetarian haggis. (That's progress, as the Orkney poet George Mackay Brown would cynically say.) Small portions of haggis are sometimes served as starter courses in fashionable Scottish restaurants, though the authentic way to eat it is as a main course with chappit tatties (potatoes), bashed neeps (mashed turnips) and a number of nips (Scotch whisky, preferably malt). This is especially so on Burns Night (25 January), when the haggis is ceremonially piped to table, and supper is accompanied by poetry reading, music and Burns's own "Address to the Haggis"; or on St Andrew's Night (30 November), when haggis is again attacked with gusto by loyal Scots the world over.

### Colourful cuisine

Many of Scotland's national dishes have names as rugged as Scottish speech. Soups such as the ubiquitous Scotch broth (made with mutton stock, vegetables, barley, lentils and split peas), cock-a-leekie (made from chicken and leeks, but authentic only if it also contains prunes) and cullen skink (soup made from smoked haddock, cream and potatoes) are widely available, but other dishes may be harder to track down: hugga-muggie (Shetland fish haggis, using the fish's stomach), crappit heids (haddock heads stuffed with lobster), partan bree (a soup made from giant crab claws, cooked with rice), stovies (potatoes cooked with onion), carageen mould (a Hebridean dessert), cranachan (a mixture of cream, oatmeal, sugar and rum), or hattit kit (an ancient Highland sweet made from buttermilk, milk, cream, sugar and nutmeg).

Though the Scots are said to like far more salt in their soup – and with their fish and vegetables – than the English, they also possess an exceptionally sweet tooth, as some of the above dishes confirm. This is also seen in their penchant for fizzy lemonade and the Glaswegian's favourite thirst-quencher, Irn-Bru, a sparkling concoction said to be

**GOOD TASTE**

The best places to eat in Scotland are members of "A Taste of Scotland": over 500 establishments where you will be served good quality, fresh Scottish produce.

in Ayreshire from goat's cheese. Cheese on Arran also finds favou palate. Crowdie, Scotland's origi cottage cheese, has evolved into Caboc from the Highlands; with its original oatmeal coating, it is almost as creamy as France's crème fraîche. Pentland and Lothian cheeses are Scotland's answer to camembert and brie.

Cheese before pudding, as a running order, reflects Scotland's Auld Alliance with France, as does the large amount of fine claret to be

"made from girders". And don't miss the chance to sample the enormous variety of puddings and desserts, often served with a generous helping of butterscotch sauce.

Real cheese, at last fighting back against the marketing boards' anonymous mass production, has been making progress in Scotland. Lanark Blue, handmade from unpasteurised sheep's milk, has been one recent success, worth looking out for in go-ahead restaurants. Popular, too, is Cairnsmore, a hard ewe's-milk cheese from Wigtownshire, and Bonnett, made

**LEFT:** on offer: Scotland's most famous dish.
**ABOVE:** salmon ready for smoking in North Uist.

found on the wine lists of good restaurants and hotels and in many homes. But pudding before savoury is also an admirable tradition, for a long time almost defunct but now showing happy signs of revival.

Hot savouries have always tended to have mysterious, sometimes misleading names. Scotch woodcock, for instance, is no more a bird than Welsh rarebit is a rabbit; a woodcock, in this context, is a portion of anchovies coated with scrambled eggs and served on small fresh slices of toast. At best, it rounds off a meal most piquantly as an after-dinner savoury, as do Loch Fyne toasts, where kipper fillets replace the anchovies. ❑

# PLACES

*A detailed guide to Scotland and its islands, with principal sites clearly cross-referenced by number to the maps*

Scotland has something to suit all tastes. Whether you want the peace of wide, open spaces or the excitement of dynamic cities, you can find it here. Even the unpredictable weather cannot dull Scotland's charm, as the wildest Highland thunderstorm only enhances the magnificence of the hills.

Edinburgh, a majestic capital city, enchants effortlessly, its castle towering over it on a rugged crag as a daily reminder of its turbulent history. When the new Scottish Parliament set up shop in 1999, Edinburgh became a "court city" for the first time since 1707 and had reason to revive its old appellation of "the Athens of the North". Just 40 miles (64 km) away, Glasgow, by contrast, is Britain's great unknown city, still suffering from an outdated image of industrial grime and urban decay. Yet, having had its heart ripped out by motorways in the 1960s, it remodelled itself to take centre stage as European City of Culture in 1990, while the city is justly proud of the 9,000 works of art housed in the Burrell Collection and the £2.8 million renovation of its favourite building, Kelvingrove Art Gallery.

Outside the two great cities lies an astonishingly varied landscape. To the southwest are the moorlands, lochs and hills of Dumfries and Galloway, haunt of Scotland's national poet Robert Burns; to the southeast, the castles, forests and glens of the Borders, one of Europe's unspoilt areas; to the west, the rugged splendour of the West Highlands, a fragmented wilderness of mountain and moor, heather and stag, and the jumping-off point for Skye and the Western Isles; to the northeast, the farms and fishing villages of Fife and the swing along the North Sea coast through Dundee towards the granite city of Aberdeen, Scotland's oil capital; and, to the north, the elusive monster of Loch Ness, splendour of the Highlands, and the islands of Orkney and Shetland, more Norse than Scottish.

Scotland's greatest appeal is to people who appreciate the open air, whether scenery or outdoor pursuits. The attractions range from pleasant rambling across moors and treks along long-distance footpaths to arduous hill-walking and hair-raising rock climbs and mountain-bike trails. You can ski down snow-capped mountains, canoe in fast-flowing white water, thrill to some of Europe's best surfing, fish for salmon in crystal-clear streams or play golf in the country that invented the game.

And the people? They have a reputation for being dour – but, as long as you avoid saying anything which might be construed as being even faintly complimentary about the English, you are likely to find that the Scots character often contains a carefully concealed warmth.     ❑

**PRECEDING PAGES:** Blackrock Cottage, Glencoe; the much-photographed Eilean Donan Castle, Wester Ross; Edinburgh Castle from the air.

# EDINBURGH

*Set among a series of volcanic hills, Edinburgh is a stunning confection of late medieval tenements and neoclassical terraces, whose new status is supported by grand building projects*

N ot for nothing was that great parable of the divided self, *Dr Jekyll and Mr Hyde*, written by an Edinburgh man, Robert Louis Stevenson. He may have set the story in London, but he conjured it out of the bizarre life of a respectable Edinburgh tradesman. More than one critic has taken the Jekyll and Hyde story as a handy metaphor for the city of Edinburgh itself: something at once universal yet characteristically Scottish. Where else does a semi-ramshackle late medieval town glower down on such Georgian elegance? What other urban centre contains such huge chunks of sheer wilderness within its boundaries? Does any other city in Europe have so many solid Victorian suburbs surrounded by such bleak housing estates? Stevenson himself was inclined to agree. "Few places, if any," he wrote, "offer a more barbaric display of contrasts to the eye."

Just as Edward Hyde "gave an impression of deformity without any nameable malformation", so the meaner side of Edinburgh tends to lurk unnoticed in the beauty of its topography and the splendour of its architecture. Even the weather seems to play its part. "The weather is raw and boisterous in winter, nifty and ungenial in summer, and downright meteorological purgatory in spring," Stevenson wrote of his home town. But the Jekyll and Hyde metaphor can be stretched too far. For all its sly duality and shifty ways, Edinburgh remains one of Europe's most beautiful and amenable cities.

## Living theatre

To the south the city is hemmed in by the Pentland Hills some of which are almost 2,000 ft (600 metres) high – and to the north by the island-studded waters of the Firth of Forth. In 1878 Stevenson declared himself baffled that "this profusion of eccentricities, this dream in masonry and living rock is not a drop-scene in a theatre, but a city in the world of everyday reality".

Which, of course, it is. At the last count, Edinburgh contained just under half a million people rattling around a 100 sq. miles (39 sq. km) on the south bank of the Firth of Forth. While the city's traditional economy of "books, beer and biscuits" has been whittled away by the ravages of recession and change, there is a powerful underpinning of banking, insurance, shipping, the professions (especially the law), the universities, hospitals, and, of course, government bureaucracies (local and central). By and large, the North Sea oil boom passed Edinburgh by, although some of the city's financiers did well enough by shuffling investment funds around, and for a while Leith Docks was used as an onshore supply base, to coat pipes and to build steel deck modules.

And like every other decent-sized city in the western hemisphere, Edinburgh thrives on a rich cultural mix.

**LEFT:**
fireworks close the
Edinburgh Festival.
**BELOW:**
on parade at the
Thistle Ceremony.

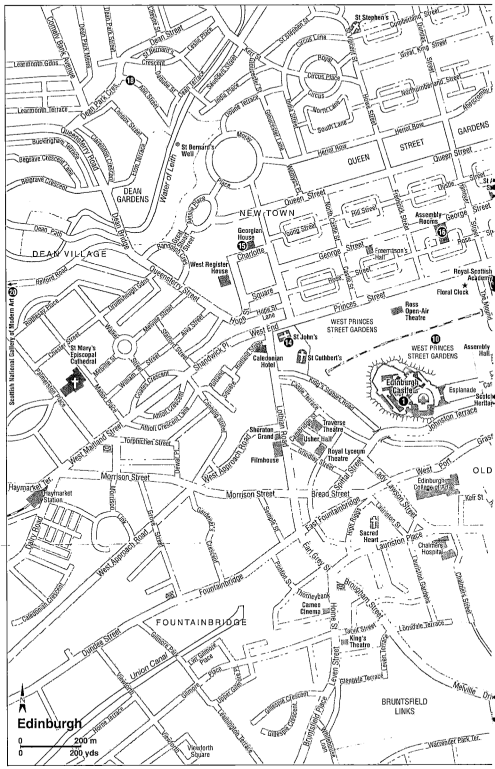

Edinburgh

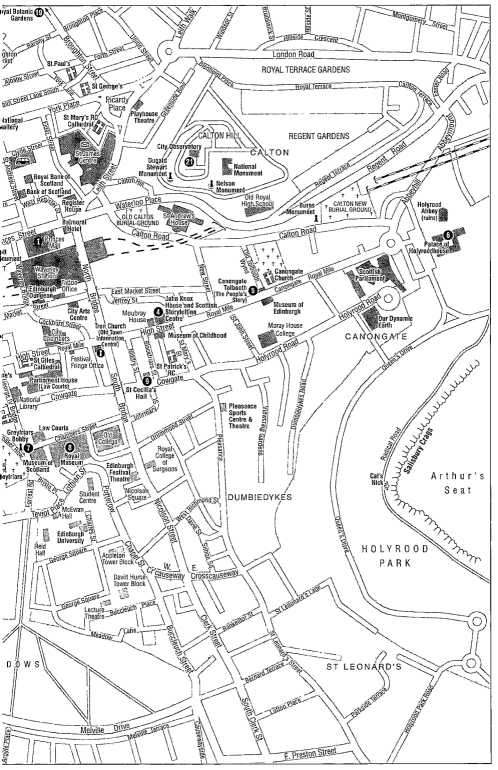

The Scotsman *news-paper, published in Edinburgh, is still arguably the most influential piece of media north of the border, acting as a kind of noticeboard of the Scottish establishment.*

The "base" population is overwhelmingly Scots with a large Irish content (muc of it from Northern Ireland), but there are also communities of Poles, Italians Ukrainians, Jews, Pakistanis, Sikhs, Bengalis, Chinese and, of course, English

In 2004, one aspect of Edinburgh's heritage was celebrated when it was name as UNESCO's first City of Literature. Its current residents include Ian Rankir creator of Inspector Rebus, and J.K. Rowling, begetter of Harry Potter.

## Capital city

In 1999 Edinburgh once again became a capital city with a parliament (initiall meeting at the Church of Scotland Assembly Hall, at Holyrood). Following strong endorsement from the Scottish people in the referendum of Septembe 1997, the devolved parliament signalled a significant start to the new millennium

The new Scottish Parliament was elected by a form of proportional represen tation (unlike elections to Westminster, which uses a traditional "first past th post" system) and it administers a wide range of local matters, although majo areas such as defence and foreign policy are still dealt with by the United King dom Parliament in London. A Secretary of State for Scotland still represent Scotland's interests in the UK parliament, but many regard this as an increas ingly redundant post.

Even before the Parliament was set up, Edinburgh wielded more power an influence than any British city outside of London. It has long been the centre o the Scots legal system, home to the Court of Session (the civil court) and th High Court of Justiciary (criminal court), from which there is no appeal to th House of Lords: Edinburgh's decision is final. Edinburgh is also the base of th Church of Scotland (the established church), whose General Assembly ever

**BELOW:** bric-a-brac stalls in the Grassmarket.

~y floods Edinburgh with sober-suited Presbyterian ministers. And anyone
:king to consult the records of Scotland (land titles, company registration,
vernment archives, lists of bankrupts, births, marriages, deaths) must make
ilgrimage to Edinburgh.

## ~e early days

~ one is quite sure just how old Edinburgh is, only that people have been liv-
; in the area for more than 5,000 years. But it seems certain that the city grew
·m a tiny community perched on the "plug" of volcanic rock which now sup-
·ts **Edinburgh Castle**. With steep, easily defended sides, natural springs of
ter and excellent vantage points, the Castle rock was squabbled over for hun-
:ds of years by generations of Picts, Scots, British (Welsh) and Angles, with
: Scots (from Ireland) finally coming out on top. It was not until the 11th cen-
y that Edinburgh settled down to be the capital city of an independent Scot-
~d, and a royal residence was built within the walls of Edinburgh Castle.
But Edinburgh proved to be a strategic liability in the medieval wars with the
glish. It was too close to England. Time after time, English armies crashed
·oss the border laying waste the farmlands of the southeast, and burning Edin-
·gh itself. It happened in 1174 (when the English held Edinburgh Castle for 12
ars), in 1296, in 1313 (during the Wars of Independence), in 1357, in 1573,
1650, and as late as 1689, when the Duke of Gordon tried, and failed, to hold
·inburgh Castle against the Protestant army of William of Orange.
The hammering of Edinburgh by the English came to an end in 1707 when
: Scottish Parliament, many of whose members had been bribed by English
~erests, voted to abandon the sovereignty of Scotland in favour of a union with

Map pages 134–5

*Ready for visitors at
Edinburgh Castle:
after London,
Edinburgh is the
UK's most popular
tourist destination.*

**BELOW:** a City
Halberdier, called
after the halberd
(pike) he carries.

*The concentration of talent in 18th-century Edinburgh led John Amyat, the king's chemist, to remark that he could stand at the Mercat Cross and "in a few minutes, take 50 men of genius by the hand".*

**BELOW:** a city by design: Edinburgh's West End.

England. "Now there's an end of an auld sang," the old Earl of Seafield w heard to mutter as he signed the Act. But in fact, power and influence had be haemorrhaging out of Edinburgh ever since the Union of the Crowns in 16 when the Scottish King James VI (son of Mary Queen of Scots) became the fi monarch of Great Britain and Ireland.

Stripped of its royal family, courtiers, parliament and civil service, 18th-ce tury Edinburgh should have lapsed into a sleepy provincialism. But the Treaty Union guaranteed the position of Scots law and the role of the Presbyteri Church of Scotland. With both these powerful institutions still firmly entrench in Edinburgh, the city was still a place where the powerful and influential met make important decisions.

## The Scottish Enlightenment

In fact, for reasons which are still not clear, 18th-century Scotland became o of Europe's intellectual powerhouses, producing scholars and philosophers li David Hume, Adam Smith and William Robertson, architect-builders li William Adam and his sons Robert and John, engineers like James Watt, Thom Telford and John Rennie, surgeons like John and William Hunter, and painte like Henry Raeburn and Allan Ramsay.

That explosion of talent became known as the Scottish Enlightenment, a one of its greatest creations was the **New Town** of Edinburgh. Between 17 and 1840 a whole impeccable new city – bright, spacious, elegant, rational a symmetrical – was created on the land to the north of the **Old Town**.

It was very quickly occupied by the aristocracy, gentry and "middling" class of Edinburgh, who left the Old Town to the poor and to the waves of Irish a

Map pages 134-5

ghland immigrants who flooded into Edinburgh from the 1840s onwards. Like most British (and European) cities, Edinburgh's population burgeoned in ʒ 19th century, from 90,786 in 1801 to just over 413,000 in 1901. There was no ʌy that the Old Town and the New Town could house that kind of population, ·d Victorian Edinburgh became ringed by a huge development of handsome ›ne-built tenements and villas in suburbs such as **Bruntsfield, Marchmont,** ·e **Grange** and **Morningside**, which in turn became ringed about by 20th-ʌtury bungalows and speculative housing.

Beginning in the 1930s, the Edinburgh Corporation (and later the Edinburgh strict Council) outflanked the lot by throwing up an outer ring of huge coun--housing estates.

Although the Old Town had been allowed to deteriorate in a way that is noth-ʒ short of disgraceful, it is steadily being revived. Serious efforts have been ade to breathe new life into its labyrinth of medieval streets, wynds and ›ses. As a way of rescuing Edinburgh's many architectural treasures, the city :hers have almost been giving away buildings (along with handsome grants) private developers. Restored 17th-century tenements and converted 19th-ʌtury breweries now cater for those who have discovered the delights of city-ʌtre living.

## ʌe Old Town

ʾen after two centuries of neglect, Edinburgh's Old Town packs more historic ildings into a square mile than just about anywhere in Britain. Stevenson, ain, provides the reason. "It [the Old Town] grew, under the law that regu-:es the growth of walled cities in precarious situation, not in extent, but in

**BELOW:** looking for something new in the Old Town: shopping in Victoria Street.

*Pub signs recall Edinburgh's royal history: Mary Queen of Scots.*

height and density. Public buildings were forced, whenever there was room x them, into the midst of thoroughfares; thoroughfares were diminished into lan houses sprang up storey after storey, neighbour mounting upon neighbou shoulder, as in some Black Hole in Calcutta, until the population slept 14 to deep in a vertical direction."

In this late medieval version of Manhattan, the aristocracy, gentry, merchan and commoners of Edinburgh lived cheek by jowl. Often they shared the sa "lands" (tenements), the "quality" at the bottom and hoi polloi at the top. Th rubbed shoulders in dark stairways and closes, and knew one another in a w that was socially impossible in England. Any Lord of Session (High Court judg whose verdict was unpopular could expect to be harangued or even pelted wi mud and stones as he made his way home.

Not that life in the Old Town was entirely dominated by mob rule. Until the e of the 18th century the Old Town was the epicentre of fashionable society, a ti little metropolis of elegant drawing rooms, fashionable concert halls, danci academies, and a bewildering variety of taverns, *howffs* (meeting places), coff houses and social clubs. "Nothing was so common in the morning as to meet m of high rank and official dignity reeling home from a close in the High Street wh they had spent the night in drinking," wrote Robert Chambers, a lively chronicl

The heady social life of the Old Town came to an end at the turn of the 19 century, when it was progressively abandoned by the rich and the influenti whose houses were inherited by the poor and the feckless. "The Great Flittin it was called, and crowds used to gather to watch all the fine furniture, croc ery and painting being loaded into carts for the journey down the newly creat "earthen mound" (now called **The Mound**) to the New Town.

**BELOW:**
the Royal Mile.

## THE RULE OF THE MOB

Politicians, aristocracy and Church leaders came under clc scrutiny of the citizens of Edinburgh during the 18th centu. When the Scottish parliament voted itself out of existence approving the Treaty of Union with England in 1707, the Edi burgh mob went on the rampage trying to track down the "tr tors" who, they felt, had sold Scotland out to the "Auld Enem (the English). The Edinburgh mob was a formidable political for The Porteous Riot of 1737, involving a crowd of 4,000, show how strong feelings in Scotland could be, and the government London was sufficiently alarmed that it decided to demolish Nether Bow Port in order to make it easier for its troops to en Edinburgh in the event of further rebellions. (It is an episode th is described in vivid detail in the opening chapters of Sir Wal Scott's novel *The Heart of Midlothian*.)

For much of the 18th century the Edinburgh mob was led b certain "General" Joe Smith, a bow-legged cobbler who believe passionately in the inferiority of women (his wife had to walk se eral paces behind him) and who could drum up a crowd of tho sands within a few minutes. With the mob at his back, Joe Sm could lay down the law to the magistrates of Edinburgh, and r a kind of rough justice against thieving landlords and dishone traders. His career came to an abrupt end in 1780 when, de drunk, he fell to his death from the top of a stagecoach.

## e Royal Mile

spine of the Old Town is the **Royal Mile** a wide road which runs down from
Castle to the **Palace of Holyroodhouse**, and comprises (from top to bottom)
stlehill, Lawnmarket, the High Street and the Canon'gate. This street was
cribed by the author of *Robinson Crusoe*, Daniel Defoe (who lived in Edin-
gh in the early 18th century), as "perhaps the largest, longest and finest Street
Buildings, and Number of Inhabitants, not in Britain only, but in the world".

Map,
pages
134–5

The **Castle** ❶ (open daily; admission charge) is well worth a visit, if only for the
ws over the city. Many of the buildings are 18th- and 19th-century, although
tiny Norman chapel dedicated to the saintly Queen Margaret dates to the 12th
tury. Worth seeking out are the **Scottish National War Memorial**, **Great Hall**
nich has a superb hammerbeam roof), and the **Crown Room**, which houses the
galia (crown jewels) of Scotland, which were lost between 1707 and 1818 when
ommission set up by Sir Walter Scott traced them to a locked chest in a locked
m in the castle. Also here is Scotland's symbolic coronation seat, the Stone of
stiny, returned from London in 1996 after a 700-year absence.

**TIP**

For an introduction to
Edinburgh's colourful
past, you can join one
of the excellent guided
tours around the
Castle or the Old Town.

ust below the Castle esplanade, on **Castlehill**, are an iron fountain marking the
t where between 1479 and 1722 Edinburgh burned its witches; **Ramsay Gar-**
n, the tenements designed by the 19th-century planning genius Patrick Ged-
; and a **Camera Obscura** ❷ (open daily; admission charge) built in the 1850s.
Across the road is the **Scotch Whisky Heritage Centre** (open daily), where
itors can learn about the drink's origin from an audio-visual show and by
velling in a whisky barrel through 300 years of history. The shop sells a good
ection of whiskies.

Next door, Tolbooth Kirk, where the city's Gaelic speakers used to worship,

**BELOW:** on display in
Princes Street.

has reopened as **The Hub** (Edinburgh's Festival Centre; open daily), wit[
booking office, exhibition area, shop and café-bar.

*Even though it's doubtful that the religious reformer John Knox actually lived in the house that bears his name, it's likely that he preached from its window.*

On the north side of the Lawnmarket is **Gladstone's Land** ❸ (open da[
Apr–Oct; admission charge), a completely restored six-storey 17th-century te
ement now owned by the National Trust for Scotland (NTS), which gives so[
insight into 17th-century Edinburgh life (dirty, difficult and malodorous). N[
door is Lady Stair's House, now the **Writers' Museum** (open Mon–[
10am–5pm, Sun during Aug noon–5pm; free), dedicated to Robert Burns,
Walter Scott and Robert Louis Stevenson, and **Deacon Brodie's Tavern**, nam[
after William Brodie, the model for the Jekyll and Hyde story.

Further along, on what is now **High Street**, are **Parliament House** (now [
Law Courts); the **High Kirk of St Giles** (open daily; free); the **Mercat Cro[**
from which kings and queens are proclaimed; and the **City Chambers**, wh[
was one of the first buildings in the great drive to "improve" Edinburgh in [
late 18th century. Below, visitors can explore haunted **Mary King's Close** (o[
daily; admission charge). The lower part of the High Street contains the 15[
century **Moubray House**, which is probably the oldest inhabited building
Edinburgh; **John Knox House** ❹ (open daily; admission charge) and the ad[
cent **Scottish Storytelling Centre**; and the **Museum of Childhood** (o[
Mon–Sat; free) with displays of historical toys, dolls and books. Across the r[
in **Trinity Church** in **Chalmer's Court** enthusiasts can make rubbings of r[
Scottish brasses and stone crosses in the **Brass Rubbing Centre** (o[
Mon–Sat, Easter–Sept; free).

**BELOW:** the new Scottish Parliament building.

Further east, **Canongate** is particularly rich in 16th- and 17th-century bu[
ings. These include the **Tolbooth** ❺, which houses *The People's Story* (o[

n–Sat; free), an exhibition about ordinary Edinburgh folk from the late 18th
tury to the present; **Bakehouse Close**; the **Museum of Edinburgh**, the city's
.in museum of local history (open Mon–Sat; free); **Moray House**, the most
ish of the aristocracy's town houses; the Dutch-style **Canongate Church**;
hite Horse Close (once a coaching inn); and the 17th-century **Acheson
~use**. Beyond the Canongate Church is the **"mushroom garden"**, a walled
·den laid out in the 17th-century manner, and almost completely unknown.
The **Palace of Holyroodhouse** ❻ (open daily with exceptions; tel: (0131) 556
)0; admission charge) began as an abbey in the 12th century, grew into a royal
.ace in the early 16th century, and was much extended in the late 17th century
· Charles II, who never set foot in the building. It was here that Mary Queen
Scots witnessed the butchery of her Italian favourite, David Rizzio, in 1558.
The new **Scottish Parliament** building (open daily with exceptions; tel: 0131
3 5000; www.scottishparliament.uk; free) opened its doors at Holyrood in 2004
a final cost of £431 million. Barcelona architect Enric Miralles's innovative
·hitecture was described by one critic as being "like a cluster of boats, a sweep-
; of leaves, a collection of seaside shells, a Pandora's box of architectural motifs
ed together ingeniously, this side of pandemonium." I ·
)pposite is a stunning, tented tourist attraction, **Our Dynamic Earth** (open
~r–Oct daily, Nov–Mar Wed–Sun; admission charge). This is a family-oriented
dio-visual "experience" of the formation and evolution of the planet.

## )uth of the Royal Mile

ose to the Royal Mile, on George IV Bridge, are the **Scottish Parliament
sitor Centre**, with various exhibitions on the parliament's workings; the

*When Bobby's master died in 1858 the loyal terrier refused to leave him: he kept watch over the grave in Greyfriars Church-yard every day for 14 years.*

**BELOW:** Holyrood Palace.

National **Library of Scotland** (a UK copyright library); and the little bron: statue of **Greyfriars Bobby** , the devoted Skye terrier immortalised by W Disney. In Chambers Street are two linked national museums: the **Royal Museu**  and the **Museum of Scotland** (both open daily; free). The former has a d: zling collection of 19th-century machinery, scientific instruments and natural h tory, plus the preserved remains of Dolly the sheep (1996–2003), the world's f cloned mammal. In the striking building of the Museum of Scotland are displa that tell the history of Scotland and national treasures.

On the corner of Chambers Street and the South Bridge lies Robert Adan **The Old College**, the finest of the university's buildings.

Running roughly parallel with the Royal Mile to the south are the **Grassma ket** – lined by cosy pubs and once the site of riots and public excutions – an long and rather dingy street called the **Cowgate**, which in the 19th century w crammed with Irish immigrants fleeing the Great Famine. The Irish Catho nature of the Cowgate is testified to by the huge but inelegant bulk of **St Patrick Roman Catholic Church**. A more interesting building is **St Cecilia's Hall** which now belongs to Edinburgh University, but was built by the Edinbur Musical Society as a concert hall in 1762, modelled on the opera house at Parr

## A landmark of Europe

"A sort of schizophrenia in stone" is how the novelist Eric Linklater once describ **Princes Street,** going on to contrast the "natural grandeur solemnised by mem ries of human pain and heroism" of the Castle rock with the tawdry commerci ism of the north side of the street. Thanks to the developers and retailers of 20th century it is no longer one of Europe's more elegant boulevards. Just abc

ery decent building has been gouged out of the north side of the street and )laced by some undistiguished piece of modern architecture. Fortunately, on the ıth side **Princes Street Gardens**  remain as the "broad and deep ravine planted ;h trees and shrubbery" that so impressed the American writer Nathaniel Willis 1834. Furthermore, with Princes Street packed with visitors throughout the year, ınblings continue of pedestrianising the famous thoroughfare.

With the exception of the superb **Register House** by Robert Adam at the far rtheast end of the street, and a few remaining 19th-century shops (such as •ners), everything worthwhile is on the south side of the street. The most star- ıg edifice, which may be ascended for splendid views, is the huge and intricate ıthic **monument to Sir Walter Scott**  (open daily) erected in 1844 and signed by a self-taught architect called George Meikle Kemp. The unfortu- ke Kemp drowned in an Edinburgh canal shortly before the monument was ımpleted, and was due to be buried in the vault under the memorial until some kty-minded member of Scott's entourage persuaded the Court of Session to /ert the funeral. Another blow for Edward Hyde.

Much more typical of Edinburgh are the two neoclassical art galleries at the ıction of Princes Street and The Mound. Since the completion of a multi- llion pound project in 2004 , both the **Royal Scottish Academy**  (open ıly 10am–5pm, Thur until 7pm; free) and the **National Gallery of Scotland** (same hours; free) have been connected by an underground passageway 'eston Link), accessed off Princes Street Gardens East. Both buildings were signed by William Playfair between 1822 and 1845. The space surrounding : galleries has long been Edinburgh's version of London's Hyde Park Corner, ł is heavily used by preachers, polemicists and bagpipers.

*At the foot of The Mound is the world's oldest floral clock. Laid out annually with more than 20,000 plants, it has electrically driven hands.*

**BELOW:** lunchtime refreshment.

## WEE DRAM – OR REAL ALE?

" dinburgh's scores of "watering holes" suggest its 457,000 -residents are spoilt for choice. Yet it is an extraordinary fact :dinburgh life that there is not one pub the whole length of ıces Street. A few plushy clubs, certainly, but no pubs. But ıent George Street and workaday Rose Street, a narrow and :e infamous thoroughfare that runs just behind it, have more ı their share. The more diverting Rose Street hostelries are **Kenilworth** (which has a lovely ceramic-clad interior), **Dirty k's** and the **Abbotsford.** A favourite Edinburgh sport has been ry to get from one end of Rose Street to the other, downing ł a pint of real ale or a dram in every pub and still remain ıding. In Rose Street you will also find a *howff* (meeting place) ed **Milnes Bar**, which was once the haunt of 20th-century ıburgh literati – writers like Hugh MacDiarmid and Norman ɔCaig and jazz musicians like Sandy Brown. Live music is ırd in many Edinburgh pubs today, particularly during the .ual Edinburgh Jazz Festival. And the main August Festival ısforms the pubs of Edinburgh, which are granted extended ınces to cope with the increased custom in these summer ⋅ks. Not that drinkers here usually have a problem: ever since relaxation of licensing regulations in 1976 genteel Edinburgh long been one of the easiest places in Britain in which to buy ink, with bars open well into the "wee sma' hours".

**TIP**

To escape the summer throng, wander and picnic in Princes Street Gardens.

Exhibitions at the Royal Scottish Academy come and go, but the Nation Gallery of Scotland houses the biggest permanent collection of Old Masters ou side London. There are paintings by Raphael, Rubens, El Greco, Titian, Goy Vermeer and a clutch of superb Rembrandts. Gauguin, Cézanne, Renoir, Deg; Monet, Van Gogh and Turner are well represented, and the gallery's Scotti collection is unrivalled. There are important paintings by Raeburn, Rams; Wilkie and the astonishing (and underrated) James Drummond.

At the southwest end of Princes Street is a brace of fine churches, **St John's** (Episcopalian) and **St Cuthbert's** (Church of Scotland). St John's support· lively congregation which is forever decking the building out with paintings support of various Third World causes and animal rights. The church, a Gotl Revival building designed by William Burn in 1816, has a fine ceiling whi John Ruskin thought "simply beautiful".

## The New Town

What makes Edinburgh a truly world-class city, able to stand shoulder to sho der with Prague, Amsterdam or Vienna, is the great neoclassical New Tow built in an explosion of creativity between 1767 and 1840. The New Town the product of the Scottish Enlightenment. And no one has really been able explain how, in the words of the historian Arthur Youngson, "a small, crowdt almost medieval town, the capital of a comparatively poor country, expand in a short space of time, without foreign advice or foreign assistance, so as become one of the enduringly beautiful cities of Western Europe".

It all began in 1752 with a pamphlet entitled *Proposals for carrying on ci tain Public Works in the City of Edinburgh*. It was published anonymously, t

**BELOW:** fanlight in Queen Street.

as engineered by Edinburgh's all-powerful Lord Provost (Lord Mayor), George ummond. Drummond was determined that Edinburgh should be a credit to the noverian-ruled United Kingdom which he had helped create, and should seek rid itself of its reputation for overcrowding, squalor, turbulence and Jacobitism. To some extent the New Town is a political statement in stone. It is Scotland's oute to the Hanoverian ascendancy. Many of the street names reflect the fact, witnessed in their names: **Hanover Street**, **Cumberland Street**, **George reet, Queen Street, Frederick Street**.

The speed with which the New Town was built is still astonishing, particu- ly given the sheer quality of the building. Built mainly in calciferous sand- ne from Craigleith Quarry to a prize-winning layout by a 23-year-old hitect/planner called James Craig, most of the more important New Town dings were in place before the end of the century: **Register House** (1778), north side of **Charlotte Square** (1791), the **Assembly Rooms and Music ill** (1787), **St Andrew's Church** (1785), most of **George Street, Castle reet, Frederick Street** and **Princes Street**.

The stinking Nor' Loch (north loch) under the castle rock was speedily drained make way for the "pleasure gardens" of Princes Street. By the 1790s the New wn was the height of fashion, and the gentry of Edinburgh were abandoning ir roots in the Old Town for the Georgian elegance on the other side of the wly built North Bridge. Some idea of how they lived can be glimpsed in the orgian House ⑮ (open daily; admission charge) at 7 Charlotte Square (on block designed by Robert Adam). The house has been lovingly restored by National Trust for Scotland. It is crammed with the furniture, crockery, glass- re, silver and paintings of the period, and even the floorboards have been

*Register House was built especially to store public records: its thick stone walls guard against the risk of fire.*

**BELOW:**
the Georgian House in Charlotte Square.

# Edinburgh's Money Men

With Scottish investment houses managing over £500 billion in funds and one in 10 people in Scotland employed in financial services, the sector is big business for the nation. It is also the second-biggest financial centre in the UK outside the City of London. According to a spokesperson for Scottish Financial Enterprises (the Edinburgh financiers' mouthpiece), it's also one of the largest financial hubs in Europe.

Naturally, this huge community of bankers, investment-fund managers, stockbrokers, corporate lawyers, accountants and insurance executives has to be "serviced". This means nice business for Edinburgh's glossier advertising agencies, public relations firms, design studios and photographers – not to mention restaurants, wine bars and auction houses. Just as "the City" is shorthand for London's vast financial community, so Edinburgh's was

known as "Charlotte Square" until the 1990s, when the square and connecting George Street were the centre of the financial district. Many of the finance houses relocated to the Exchange Office district west of Lothian Road when they encountered difficulties in upgrading the listed buildings. George Street is now lined with plush restaurants and shops, and Bute House in Charlotte Square is the official residence of Scotland's First Minister.

Edinburgh's star role in the financial world can be traced back to the enthusiasm of the Scots for making and then keeping money. The Scots have always been among the modern world's best and canniest bankers. This is why the Scottish clearing banks, including Clydesdale Bank and the Royal Bank of Scotland, have a statutory right (dating from 1845) to print their own distinctive banknotes. This is a right the Scottish banks relish, particularly as the English banks were stripped of it following a string of bank failures in the 19th century, and the Scots are remarkably attached to their Edinburgh-based banks.

Probably the biggest fish in Edinburgh's financial pond are the giant Scottish insurance companies, which handle funds in excess of £100 billion. The most important is the Standard Life Assurance Company, with its prominent position off Lothian Road and offices all over Britain, Ireland and Canada. Like most of the Edinburgh insurance companies, the Standard Life is a vintage operation (1825). Some are even older, with names that have a satisfyingly old-fashioned ring, like the Scottish Widows Fund and Life Assurance Society or the Scottish Provident Institution for Mutual Life Assurance.

Although Charlotte Square took much stick for being slow to get in on the booming unit trust business (a complaint it fast put right), there is no shortage of old-fashioned "investment trusts". It was with money from these trusts that much of the American West was built. In the 19th century, Charlotte Square was heavily into cattle-ranching, fruit-farming and railways in the United States. Nowadays it prefers to sink its "bawbees" into the high-tech industries. While Edinburgh as a whole benefited little from North Sea oil, parts of Charlotte Square did very nicely, thank you. ❏

**LEFT:** the Standard Life building.

yscrubbed in the original manner. The basement kitchen is a masterpiece of ↲e 18th-century domestic technology.

Also in Charlotte Square is **West Register House** (part of the Scottish Record ↲ffice) which was built by Robert Reid in 1811 and began life as St George's ↲hurch. Just along George Street are the **Assembly Rooms and Music Hall** ↲787) , once the focus of social life in the New Town, and still a top venue dur- ↲g the festival. Across the road is the **Church of St Andrew and St George** ↲785), whose oval-shaped interior witnessed the "Great Disruption" of 1843. ↲e Church of Scotland was split down the middle when the "evangelicals", led by ↲homas Chalmers, walked out in disgust at the complacency of the Church "mod- ↲ates" who were content to have their ministers foisted on them by the gentry (as ↲as the custom in England). Chalmers went on to form the Free Church of Scot- ↲nd, which proclaimed a sterner but more democratic form of Presbyterianism.

Parallel to George Street lies **Queen Street**, whose only public building of ↲ly interest is an eccentric Doge's Palace housing the **Scottish National Por- ↲ait Gallery** (open daily 10am–5pm, Thur until 7pm; free). The gallery is ↲ell stocked with pictures of generations of Scots worthies.

Although St Andrew Square at the east end of George Street has been knocked ↲out a bit, it is still recognisable, with the most noteworthy building in the ↲quare being the head office of the Royal Bank of Scotland. Originally built in ↲74 as the town house of Sir Laurence Dundas, it was remodelled in the 1850s ↲hen it acquired a quite astonishing domed ceiling with glazed star-shaped cof- ↲↲s. The 150-ft (45-metre) high monument in the centre of St Andrew Square is ↲ Henry Dundas, 1st Viscount Melville, who was branded "King Harry the ↲inth" for his autocratic (and probably corrupt) way of running Scotland.

Map pages 134–5

**TIP**

During the weeks of the Festival in August many of Edinburgh's attractions have longer opening hours.

**BELOW:** resting amid grand surroundings in St Andrew Square.

*Ann Street was the creation of the painter Henry Raeburn, who named it after his wife. It was described by the English poet Sir John Betjeman as "the most attractive street in Britain".*

**BELOW:** tickets for the Festival Fringe, anyone?

To the north of the Charlotte Square/St Andrew Square axis lies a huge acreage of Georgian elegance which is probably unrivalled in Europe. Most of it is private housing and offices. Particularly worth seeing are **Heriot Row, Northumberland Street, Royal Circus, Ainslie Place, Moray Place** and **Drummond Place. Ann Street**  near the Water of Leith is beautiful but atypical, with its gardens and two- and three-storey buildings. Nearby **Danube Street** used to house Edinburgh's most notorious whorehouse, run by the flamboyant Dora Noyes (the house has reverted to middle-class decency).

The **Stockbridge** area on the northern edge of the New Town is an engaging bazaar of antique shops, curiosity dealers, picture framers and second-hand bookstores, with a sprinkling of decent restaurants and pubs. The **Royal Botanic Garden** (open daily; free), half a mile (0.8 km) north of Stockbridge, comprises 70 acres (28 hectares) of woodland, green sward, exotic trees, heath garden, rockeries, rhododendron walks and elegant zoned plant houses.

Also in this area, on Belford Road, is the **Scottish National Gallery of Modern Art**, with a fine permanent collection of 20th- and 21st-century art, including works by Matisse and Picasso, Magritte and Hockney. The **Dean Gallery**, in another fine 19th-century building across the road (open Mon–Sat and Sun pm; free) features the Paolozzi Collection of modern art donated by the Edinburgh sculptor, major Dada and Surrealist works and temporary exhibitions.

## Pleasure-seekers

Edward Hyde lurks in the New Town, too. The designers of the New Town provided it with a plethora of handsome "pleasure gardens" which range in size from small patches of grass and shrubbery to the three **Queen Street Gardens**, which cover more than acres (4.5 hectares). All three are closed to the public and accessible only to the "key-holders" who live nearby. One of the drearier summer sights is to see puzzled tourists shaking the gates, at a loss to understand why they are barred from ambling round the greenery.

Between 1815 and 1840 another version of the New Town grew beyond the east end of Princes Street and Waterloo Place. **Regent Terrace, Royal Terrace, Blenheim Terrace** and **Leopold Place** were its main thoroughfares.

This eastward expansion also littered the slopes of **Calton Hill** with impressive public buildings, which probably earned Edinburgh the title "Athens of the North" (although a comparison between the two cities had been made in 1762 by the antiquarian James Stuart). On the hill are monuments to Dugald Stewart, the 18th/19th-century philosopher, and Horatio Nelson, whose memorial in the shape of a telescope may be ascended for great views, and the old **City Observatory**, where Edinburgh's Astronomical Society conducts public meetings most Friday evenings.

The oddest of the early 19th-century edifices on the Calton Hill is known as "Scotland's Disgrace". It is a war memorial to the Scots killed in the Napoleonic War, which was modelled on the Parthenon in Athens. The foundation stone was laid with a great flourish during

eorge IV's visit to Edinburgh in 1822, but the money ran out after 12 columns
ere erected and the monument remains incomplete to this day.

Beyond Calton Hill, on Regent Road, are the former **Royal High School**
alled "the noblest monument of the Scottish Greek Revival"), the **Robert
urns Monument**, modelled on the Choragic Monument of Lysicrates in
thens, and the **Old Calton Burial Ground**, with 18th- and 19th-century
emorials (including one honouring David Hume), in the lee of the empty, semi-
relict **Governor's House** of the Old Calton Jail.

## Maritime Edinburgh

though more ships now sail in and out of the Firth of Forth than use the Firth
Clyde, maritime Edinburgh has taken a terrible beating since the 1980s. Edin-
rgh's port of **Leith** ② was, until recently, one of the hardest-working har-
urs on the east coast of Britain (the city's coastline on the Firth of Forth is
dded with former fishing villages: **Granton, Newhaven, Portobello, Fish-
row**, and, further east, **Cockenzie, Port Seton** and **Prestonpans**). Ships from
ith exported coal, salt fish, paper, leather and good strong ale, and returned
th (among much else) grain, timber, wine, foreign foods and Italian marble.
e destinations were Hamburg, Bremen, Amsterdam, Antwerp, Copenhagen
d occasionally North America and Australia.

Right up to the mid-1960s at least four fleets of deep-sea trawlers plied out
Leith and the nearby harbour of **Granton**, and the half-Scottish, half-Nor-
egian firm of Christian Salvesen was still catching thousands of whales every
ar into the 1950s (which is why there is a Leith Harbour in South Georgia).
e 2-mile (3-km) stretch of shore between Leith and Granton was once littered

**BELOW:** street art
defies Scotland's
rainy climate.

*The rules drawn up by the Honourable Company of Edinburgh Golfers at Leith Links in 1774 still form the basis of golf today.*

with shipyards, ship repair yards and dry docks. The streets of Leith itself we full of shipping agents, marine insurance firms, grain merchants, ships' cha-dlers, plus a burgeoning "service sector" of dockside pubs, clubs, dosshouse bookies and whores.

But most of this is gone. The trade has shifted to the container ports on th east coast of England, and Leith now has uneasy neighbours in the olde deprived residential areas and the increasingly upmarket Shore, with "yupp flats, offices and restaurants. The whole area continues to be under siege by p vate developers with old warehouses, office buildings, lodging houses and least one veteran cooperage converted into high-priced flats and houses. Leith also now home to the gigantic Scottish Executive building (with, opposite, row of smart new restaurants). In all, the port hosts a cluster of fashionab restaurants, an art gallery and, in a conversion of one of the dock-gate buil ings, the successful Waterfront Wine Bar.

Meanwhile, Scottish Enterprise and the local authorities have been spendi millions restoring the exteriors of some of Leith's handsome commercial buil ings, such as the old **Customs House**, the **Corn Exchange**, the **Assemb Building**, and **Trinity House** in the Kirkgate. In Bangor Road is **Scotland Clan Tartan Centre** (open daily; free) where with the assistance of compute you can learn that you too are a clan member. Also resident in Leith docks is t decommissioned **Royal Yacht *Britannia*** (visitor centre and yacht open dai pre-booking required, tel: (0131) 555 5566). It was used by the royal family 44 years for state visits and royal holidays. The adjacent **Ocean Terminal** now one of Edinburgh's flagship shopping and leisure complexes, designed Sir Terence Conran.

**BELOW:** Leith's stylish waterfront.

The old port is still worth a visit, too, if only for its powerful sense of what it ;ed to be. And many of the buildings on **Bernard Street, Commercial Street, ·onstitution Street** and **The Shore** are handsome and interesting. Leith has an triguing constitutional history, first part of Edinburgh, then a separate burgh, ıd then swallowed up by Edinburgh again (in 1920). Halfway up the street ﹏own as **Leith Walk** is a pub called the Boundary Bar, through which the ·unicipal border between Edinburgh and Leith used to run.

## ·ewhaven

ever a village had been killed by conservation it must be the little port of ·ewhaven ㉓, a mile west of Leith. Into the 1960s this was a brisk community, ﹏th a High Street and a Main Street lined with shops and little businesses ﹏ough which tram-cars and later buses used to trundle. But now that the pic-·resque houses have been "restored" there is hardly a shop left in the place, the ﹏ce-crowded Main Street is a ghostly dead end, and Newhaven harbour is occu-·ed by a few pleasure yachts. The Ancient Society of Free Fishermen, the trade ﹏ild founded in 1572, still exists but lists few fishermen among its members.

All of this is a great pity. Newhaven is one of Edinburgh's more interesting ·rners. The village was founded in the late 15th century by James IV to build· ㏈ *Great Michael*, then the biggest warship on earth and destined to be the flag-· ip of a new Scottish navy. But like many such grandiose schemes – particularly ·e grandiose schemes hatched in Scotland – the *Great Michael* was never a ·ccess. After the ruin of the Scots army (and the death of James IV) at Flod-·n in 1513, the great ship which was the pride of Newhaven was sold to the ·ench, who left her to rot in Brest harbour.

**TIP**

You can enjoy fish and chips at their best at the famous Harry Ramsden's restaurant on Newhaven's harbourside.

**BELOW:** enjoying a drink at The Ship in Leith.

*The walk from Dean to Stockbridge takes you past St Bernard's Well, whose natural spring inspired the creation in the 18th century of a Roman temple with a statue of Hygeia, the Greek goddess of health.*

## The villages

Like most other cities sprawling outwards, Edinburgh has enveloped a numb
of villages. The most striking of them is probably **Dean Village** , a few mi
utes' walk from the West End of Princes Street. Now one of Edinburgh's mo
fashionable corners, Dean Village is at least 800 years old, and straddles th
Water of Leith at a point which was once the main crossing on the way
Queensferry. The Incorporation of Baxters (bakers) of Edinburgh once ope
ated 11 watermills and two flour granaries here. Its most striking building
**Well Court**, an unusual courtyard of flats built in the 1880s as housing for th
poor by John Findlay, proprietor of *The Scotsman* newspaper.

Other villages which have been swallowed by the city include **Corstorphi**
in the west of the city, where Edinburgh keeps its famous **Zoological Garden**
(open daily; tel: (0131) 334 9171; admission charge), with a fine collection
penguins in the world's largest enclosure, plus endangered species includi
snow leopards and white rhinos. There is also **Colinton** in the south, whi
features an 18th-century parish church and a "dell" beside the Water of Leit
and **Cramond** on the Firth of Forth, which used to sport an ironworks an
which was the site of a Roman military camp.

Also interesting is **Duddingston**, tucked under the eastern flank of Arthu
Seat, beside a small loch which is also a bird sanctuary. Duddingston claims th
its main pub, The Sheep's Heid, is the oldest licensed premises in Scotland.
also has a fine Norman-style church and a 17th-century house which was us
by Bonnie Prince Charlie in 1745. On the northern slopes of the Pentland Hi
lies **Swanston**, a small huddle of white-painted cottages, near where th
Stevenson family used to rent Swanston Cottage as a summer residence for th

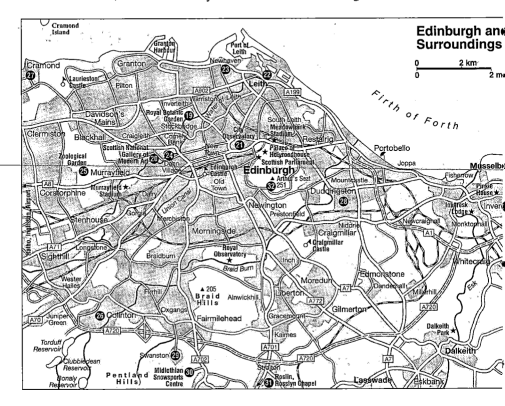

Edinburgh and
Surroundings

Map page 154

:kly Robert Louis Stevenson. For some odd reason, the gardens of Swanston ·e decorated with statuary and ornamental stonework taken from the High Kirk ' St Giles when it was being "improved" in the 19th century.

## ιe hills of Edinburgh

there is such a creature as the urban mountaineer, then Edinburgh must be s or her paradise. Like Rome, the city is built on and around seven hills, none ' them very high, but all offering good stiff walks and spectacular views of ε city. They are, in order of altitude, Arthur's Seat (823 ft/251 metres), Braid ‹ll (675 ft/205 metres), West Craiglockhart Hill (575 ft/173 metres), lackford Hill (539 ft/162 metres), Corstorphine Hill (531 ft/159 metres), ιstle Hill (435 ft/131 metres) and Calton Hill (328 ft/98 metres).

In addition, Edinburgh is bounded to the south by the Pentland Hills, a range amiable mini-mountains which almost (but not quite) climb to 2,000 ft (600 εtres), and which are well used by Edinburgh hill-walkers, fell-runners, moun-‹n bicyclists, rock-scramblers and the British Army. Here, too, is the **Mid-·thian Snowsports Centre** ⑨ (open daily; tel: (0131) 445 4433), the longest ·tificial ski and snowboarding slope in Britain. Non-skiers can take the lift and εn a short walk to Caerketton Hill for magnificent panoramic views of Edin-‹rgh, the Firth of Forth and the hills of Fife and Stirlingshire.

In the village of Roslin is **Rosslyn Chapel** ⑨ (Mon–Sat 9am–6pm, Sun ·on–4.45pm; admission charge). It is claimed that the Holy Grail and other ligious relics are contained in the Chapel. This theory appears in Dan Brown's ·st-selling book, *The Da Vinci Code* and film starring Tom Hanks, and has led an increasing number of visitors to the Chapel. The interior is decorated with

**TIP**

The penguin parade at Edinburgh Zoo (www.edinburghzoo. org.uk), which takes place at 2.15pm daily, is now rivalled by the zoo's big new lion enclosure.

**BELOW:** on parade at Edinburgh zoo.

Map page 154

*Dorothy Wordsworth (sister of the poet William) wrote in 1803 how she found Arthur's Seat "as wild and solitary as any in the heart of the Highland mountains".*

**BELOW:** the ornate Apprentice Pillar at Rosslyn Chapel.

remarkable carvings, notably the elaborately carved columns decorated wi flowers. The **Apprentice Pillar** is so called because it was carved by an appre tice stonemason while the master mason was absent. So jealous was the old mason that he killed the apprentice with a mallett.

Of the "city-centre" hills, Calton Hill at the east end of Princes Street prob bly offers the best view of Edinburgh. But it is **Arthur's Seat** ㉜, that crag; old volcano in the Queen's Park, which must count as the most startling piece urban mountainscape. It is one of the many places in Britain named after th shadowy (and possibly apocryphal) King Arthur. The area surrounding Edi burgh was one of the British (Welsh) kingdoms before it was overrun by th Angles and the Scots. On the flanks of Arthur's Seat, the feeling of *rus in ur* can be downright eerie. And its 823-ft (251-metre) high bulk provides son steep climbing, rough scrambling and fascinating geology on **Salisbury Cra**

## The outer darkness

Although Edinburgh may not have an "inner city" problem, it certainly has h. its "outer city" difficulties. It is ringed to the east, south and west with sprawli; council-housing estates, places like **Craigmillar** and **Niddrie, Alton, Mu**i **house** and **Wester Hailes**. Some the people who live here were "decanted" the from the High Street, the Cowgate and Leith, and perhaps many would eage go back if only they could find an affordable house in Edinburgh's boomi property market. But respectable Edinburgh has long since learned to conte plate the other Edinburgh with the equanimity of Henry Jekyll seeing the face Edward Hyde in the mirror for the first time. "I was conscious of no repu nance," Dr Jekyll says, "rather of a leap of welcome. This, too, was myself."

# The World's Biggest Arts Festival

When the Edinburgh International Festival explodes into life every August, the city, as the *Washington Post* once pointed out, becomes "simply the best place on Earth". Certainly the display of cultural pyrotechnics is awesome. Every concert-hall, basement-theatre and church hall in the centre of Edinburgh overflows with dance groups, theatre companies, string quartets, puppeteers, opera companies and orchestras. And for three weeks the streets of Edinburgh are awash with fire-eaters, jugglers, bagpipers, clowns, warblers, satirists and theatrical hopefuls of every shape, size and colour.

All of which is a distant cry from the dead and dreary days after World War II when the idea of the festival was hatched by Sir John Falconer, then Lord Provost of Edinburgh, Harry Harvey Wood of the British Council, and Rudolf Bing, the festival's first artistic director. The notion was, said the novelist Eric Linklater, "the triumph of elegance over drab submission to the penalties of emerging victorious from a modern war".

In 2006 alone, almost 2½ million tickets were issued for the "highbrow" International Festival, "fringe" and nightly stunning spectacle of the Edinburgh Military Tattoo. Indeed, according to Event Scotland, Edinburgh's summer diet of cultural festivals annually generate over £140 million for the Scottish economy.

Of course, it's not all plain sailing. During the 1980s artistic director Frank Dunlop sounded off regularly about upstart arts festivals trying to "poach" Edinburgh's hard-won commercial sponsors. Today, festival director Jonathan Mills, must continue to juggle financial and artistic priorities, and, with the box office generating over £30 million, one could argue it's a welcome sensual and visceral assault.

Edinburgh's "other" festival, the Festival Fringe (which also began in 1947), has become a behemoth – so big, in fact, that it threatens to outgrow the city. It's now the largest arts festival in the world. In 2006, the Fringe offered over 28,000 performances in over 250 venues. Of over 1,800 different shows, almost 180 were free. The Fringe has grown to eclipse its more staid official brother, selling over one million tickets a year. Over the years it's been a nursery for new talent: Maggie Smith, Tom Stoppard (*Rosencrantz and Guildernstern Are Dead* was premiered here), Rowan Atkinson, Billy Connolly and Emma Thompson all made their entrance into the business on the Festival Fringe. Every year the cream of artistic talent makes its way to Edinburgh, and the Fringe has grown into arguably the largest showcase for performers in the world.

Nor is that all. On the fringe of the Fringe (as it were) there is also a Television Festival (full of heavyweight discussions about the role of the media), a Film Festival (which gets many a good movie long before London), an acclaimed International Book Festival (held in Charlotte Square), and a Jazz Festival (staged in just about every pub in the city centre). ❑

**RIGHT:** the Festival Fringe Society headquarters.

# OLD AND NEW TOWN ARCHITECTURE

*Declared a UNESCO World Heritage Site in 1995, the centre of Edinburgh is a fascinating juxtaposition of medieval confusion and classical harmony*

Architecturally, Edinburgh's Old and New Towns are utterly disparate. In the Old, everything is higgledy-piggledy; in the New – now more than 200 years old – order and harmony prevail.

The Old Town lies to the south of Princes Street Gardens. Its backbone is the Royal Mile, described by the writer Daniel Defoe in the 1720s as "perhaps the largest, longest and finest Street for Buildings, and Number of Inhabitants...in the world". Then it was lined with tall, narrow tenements, some with as many as 14 storeys, where aristocracy, merchants and lowly clerks all rubbed shoulders in friendly familiarity in dark stairways and through which ran a confusing maze of wynds (alleys), courts and closes.

## A NEW ORDER

In 1766 James Craig, an unknown 23-year-old, won a competition for the design of the New Town. His submission was a "gridiron" consisting of two elegant squares – Charlotte and St Andrew – linked by three wide, straight, parallel streets: Princes, George and Queen. Robert and John Adam, Sir William Chambers and John Henderson, premier architects of the day, all contributed plans for glorious Georgian buildings. During the first part of the 19th century the New Town was extended by the addition of an extraordinary grouping of squares, circuses, terraces, crescents and parks, all maintaining the neoclassical idiom and permitting the New Town to boast the largest area of Georgian architecture in all Europe.

JOHN KNOX HOUSE

▷ **STATELY ELEGANCE**
New Town architecture reached its apotheosis with Robert Adam's superb design for Charlotte Square. The north frontage – the most magnificent – houses Bute House, official residence of the First Minister, and the Georgian House. On the west side is West Register House with its green dome. The statue in the centre of the Square is of Prince Albert, consort to Queen Victoria.

**◁ HOME DECORATION**
A picturesque late 15th-century building, John Knox's house is a splendid example of overhanging wooden upper floors with crow-stepped gables. Its outside stairway and fanciful decorations provide an idea of how the Royal Mile once looked.

**△ REST IN PEACE**
Greyfriars churchyard is a haven for the living as well as the dead, with magnificent 17th-century monuments and tombstones.

Two of the finest examples of Edinburgh's Old and New Towns have been restored to their former glory and are open to visitors, thanks to the National Trust for Scotland (NTS), a charity founded in 1931 to promote the conservation of landscape and of historic buildings.

The Georgian House in Charlotte Square *(above and below)* evokes elegant living in the New Town: it has been beautifully furnished to show how a wealthy family lived in the 18th century. Gladstone's Land on the Old Town's Royal Mile is a skilful restoration of a merchant's house. The six floors behind its narrow frontage were once occupied by five families: an example of a 17th-century Edinburgh skyscraper. The arcaded ground floor has been restored to its original function as a shopping booth.

**NLT TO DESIGN**
last detail in 12-sided
/ Place was included in
sign; this is New Town at
ndest, including Tuscan
os and a central garden.

**FENDERS OF THE FAITH**
ple stone monument in
d Town's Grassmarket
s the occasion in 1638
"For the Protestant Faith
s spot many Martyrs
ovenanters died".

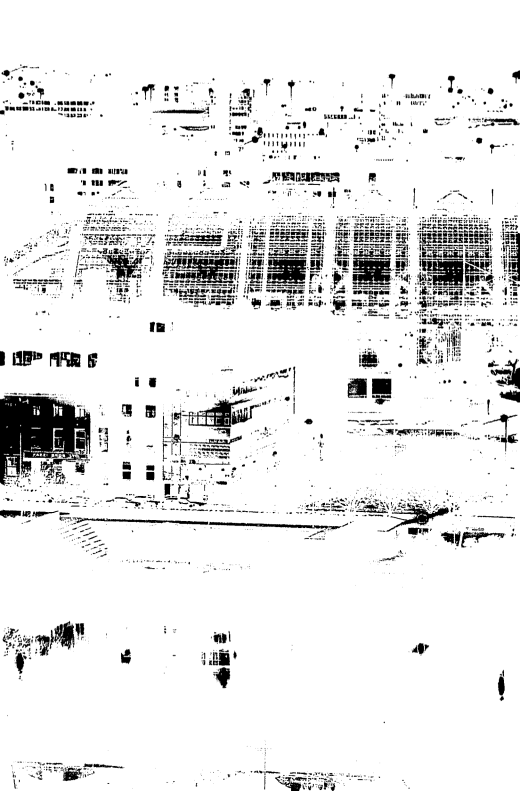

# GLASGOW

*A city of noble character, handsome buildings and invincible spirit, Glasgow accommodates no neutrality: it is either loved or loathed by native Scots and admired or avoided by visitors*

Map pages 164–5

lasgow is a city for connoisseurs. It always has been, from the days when one of its earliest tourists, the 18th-century writer Daniel Defoe, described it as "the cleanest and beautifullest and best built city in Britain", to its ore recent endorsement by Bill Bryson, author of *Notes from a Small Island*. et there are few places in Europe that have been more publicly misunderstood d misrepresented than this monstrous, magnificent citadel to the worst and e best of commerce and capitalism, to the price and the prizes of Empire and e Industrial Revolution. And few cities can have inspired more furious con-cts of opinion of its worth, or ignited so much controversy.

## vincible spirit

et even in the darkest days of its reputation, when Glasgow slums and Glas-w violence were the touchstone for every sociologist's worst urban night-ares, it was still a city for connoisseurs. It appealed to those who were not sensitive to the desperate consequences of its 19th-century population explo-on, when the combination of cotton, coal, steel and the River Clyde trans-rmed Glasgow from elegant little merchant city to industrial behemoth; and ho were not blind to the dire effect of 20th-century economics which, from 'orld War I onwards, presided over the decline of its ipbuilding and heavy industries; but who were nev-theless able to uncover, behind its grime and grisli-ss, a city of nobility and invincible spirit.

Its enthusiasts have always recognised Glasgow's ualities, and even at the height of its notoriety they ve been able to give Glasgow its place in the pantheon great Western cities. Today, it is fashionable to :scribe Glasgow as European in character, for the markable diversity of its architecture and a certain lev-/ of heart, or to compare it with North America for its idiron street system and wisecracking street "patter". But these resonances have long been appreciated by perienced travellers. In 1929, at a time when social nditions were at their worst, the romantic but per-ptive travel writer H.V. Morton found "a transatlantic ertness about Glasgow which no city in England pos-sses" and – the converse of orthodox opinion – was le to see that "Edinburgh is Scottish and Glasgow is smopolitan". And in 1960 the "British place-taster" n Nairn discovered with a sense of shock that "Glas-w was without doubt the friendliest of Britain's big ies", noting that "Any Glasgow walk is inflected by a altitude of human contacts – in shops, under umbrel- ; (there *is* a good deal of rain in Glasgow), even from licemen – and each of them seems to be a person-to-rson recognition, not the mutual hate of cogs in a achine who know their plight but cannot escape it".

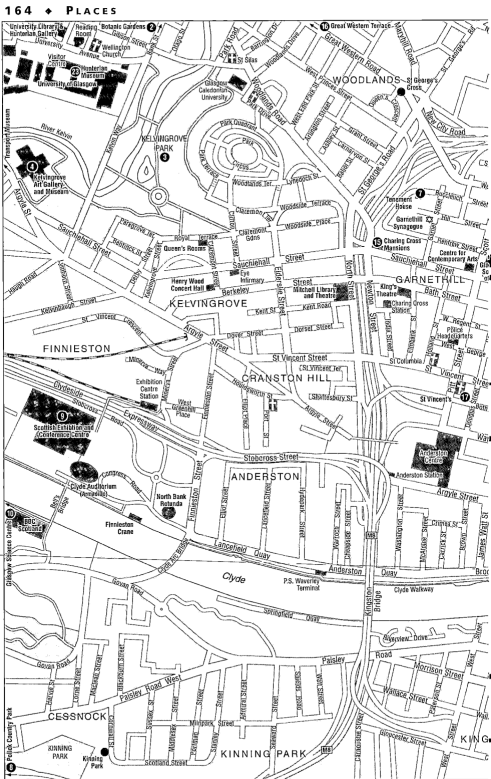

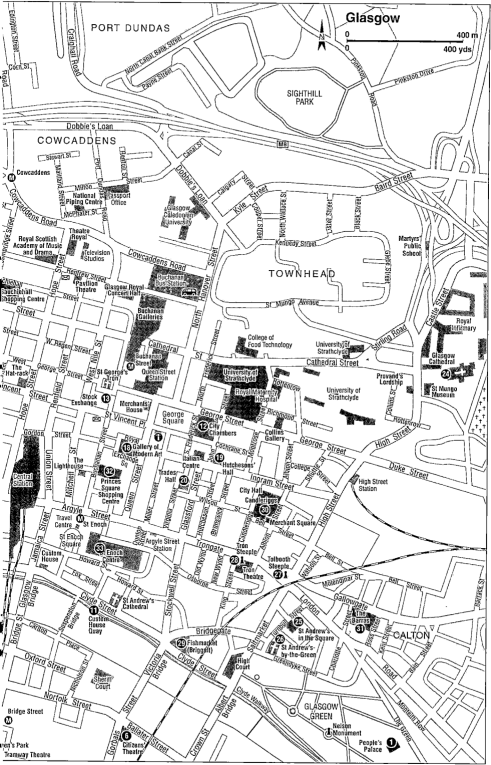

Glasgow

## Culture city

Glasgow today is visibly, spectacularly, a city in transformation. It hasn
allowed its "hard, subversive, proletarian tradition" to lead it into brick wall
of confrontation with central government. The result? A city which has ma:
sively rearranged its own environment; which sees its future in the service indu:
tries, in business conferences, exhibitions and indeed in tourism; which ha
already achieved some startling coups on its self-engineered road to becomin
"Europe's first post-industrial city"; and which has probably never been mo
exciting to visit since, at the apogee of its Victorian vigour, it held the Intern:
tional Exhibition of Science and Art more than 100 years ago.

Glaswegians allow themselves a sly smile over their elevation to the first ran
of Europe's cultural centres. (It was European City of Culture in 1990 and U
City of Architecture and Design in 1999, and it is hotly tipped to host the 201
Commonwealth Games.) But the smile becomes a little bitter for those who li
in those dismal areas of the city as yet untouched by the magic of stone-cleanin;
floodlighting or even modest rehabilitation. Defenders of the new Glasgo
argue that their turn will come; that you can't attract investment and emplo
ment to a city, with better conditions for everyone, unless first you shine up i
confidence on the inside and polish up its image on the outside.

Like the other four Scottish cities, Glasgow is defined by hill and water. I
suburbs advance up the slopes of the vast bowl which contains it, and the pi
nacles, towers and spires of its universities, colleges and cathedral occupy the
own summits within the bowl. It is, therefore, a place of sudden, sweeping vi:
tas, with always a hint of ocean or mountain just around the corner. Look nor
from the heights of **Queen's Park** and you will see the cloudy humps of tI

## FISTS OF IRON

The Glaswegian comedian Billy Connolly said of Glasgow: "There's a
lightness about the town, without heavy
industry. It's as if they've discovered how
to work the sunroof, or something." Yet
Glaswegians themselves will admit that
their positive qualities have a negative
side. Even today, mateyness can turn to
menace in certain dismal pubs where too much whisky
chased by too much beer. The working man's tipple-here-h
traditionally been "a wee hauf and hauf" – a measure of whis
pursued by a half pint of beer, often replaced today by a letI
mixture of vodka and cheap wine. Religious bigotry, the obve
of honest faith, simmers below the surface, spilling out onto t
streets and football terraces. And Glasgow's legendary humo
made intelligible even to the English through the success
comedians like Billy Connolly but available free on every str
corner, is the humour of the ghetto. It has been nurtured on h:
times. It is dry, sceptical, irreverent and often black. It's I
humour of self-defence, the wit of people who know if they dc
laugh they will cry. The Glasgow writer Cliff Hanley compares it
American-Jewish humour in its fast pace, but places it in "I
hard, subversive proletarian tradition of the city".

Map pages 164–5

ampsie Fells and the precipitous banks of Loch Lomond. Look west from ilmorehill to the great spangled mouth of the Clyde and you will sense the a fretting at its fragmented littoral and the islands and resorts that used to bring ousands of Glaswegians "doon the watter" for their annual Fair Fortnight.

The antiquity of this July holiday – Glasgow Fair became a fixture in the local alendar in 1190 – gives some idea of the long-term stability of the town on the lyde. But for centuries Glasgow had little prominence or significance in the istory of Scotland. Although by the 12th century it was both a market town and cathedral city (with a patron saint, St Mungo) and flourished quietly through-ut the Middle Ages, it was largely bypassed by the bitter internecine conflicts f pre-Reformation Scotland and the running battles with England. Most of cotland's trade, too, was conducted with the Low Countries from the east coast orts. But it had a university, now five centuries old, and a distinguished centre f medical and engineering studies, and it had the Clyde. When trade opened p with the Americas, Glasgow's fortune was made.

*Today, the names of the streets of 18th-century Glasgow – like Virginia Street and Jamaica Street – tell something of the story which turned a small town into the handsome fief of tobacco barons, and hint at a shameful "profit" from the slave trade.*

## ıstant city

he tobacco trade with Virginia and Maryland brought the city new prosper-y and prompted it to expand westwards from the medieval centre of the High reet. (Little of medieval Glasgow remains.) In the late 18th century the urban-ation of the city accelerated with an influx of immigrants, mainly from the /est Highlands, to work in the cotton mills with their new machines intro-uced by merchants who were forced to desert the tobacco trade. The Indus-ial Revolution had begun, and from then on Glasgow's destiny – grim and lorious – was fixed.

**BELOW:** motorways cut a swathe through the city.

*A tribute to the working people of Glasgow, the decoration on the facade of the People's Palace includes allegorical figures representing the textile industry, shipbuilding and engineering.*

**BELOW:** the Kelvingrove Art Gallery and Museum.

The deepening of the Clyde up to the Broomielaw, near the heart of the city, the 1780s and the coming of the steam engine in the 19th century consolidated process of such rapid expansion that Glasgow has been called an "instant city" In the 50 years between 1781 and 1831 the population of the city quintupled, an was soon to be further swelled by thousands of Irish immigrants crossing the Iris Sea to escape famine and seek work. The Victorians completed Glasgow's indu trial history and built most of its most self-important buildings as well as the co gested domestic fortifications which were to become infamous as slum tenement Since World War II, its population has fallen below the million mark to fewer tha 600,000, the result of policies designed to decant citizens into "new towns" and tl growing appeal of commuting from "green-belt" villages and towns.

## The dear green place

One translation of the original Celtic is that the city's name, Glasgow, mea "dear green place". Other translations include "dear stream and "greyhound (which some say was the nickname of St Mungo), but the green reference most apt, for Glasgow has, after all, over 70 parks – "more green space per hea of population than any other city in Europe", as the tour bus drivers tell you.

The most unexpected, idiosyncratic and oldest of its parks – in fact, the olde public park in Britain – is **Glasgow Green**, once the common grazing ground the medieval town and acquired by the burgh in 1662. To this day Glaswegia have the right to dry their washing on Glasgow Green, and its Arcadian sward still spiked with clothes poles for their use, although there are few takers. Munic pal Clydesdale horses, used for carting duties in the park, still avail themselves the grazing, and the eccentricity of the place is compounded by the proximity

Map pages 164-5

mpleton's Carpet Factory, designed in 1889 by William Leiper, who aspired to plicate the Doge's Palace in Venice. (The factory is now a business centre.)

Here, too, you will find the **People's Palace ❶** (open daily; free), built in '98 as a cultural centre for the East End community, for whom its red sand-ne munificence was indeed palatial. It's now a museum dedicated to the social d industrial life of the 20th-century city.

The most distinguished of the remaining 69-odd parks include the **Botanic ardens ❷** (open daily; free) in the heart of Glasgow's stately West End, with other palace – the **Kibble Palace** – the most enchanting of its two large hot-uses. It was built as a conservatory for the Clyde coast home of a Glasgow sinessman, John Kibble, and shipped to its present site in 1873. The architect s never been identified, although legend promotes Sir Joseph Paxton, who signed the Crystal Palace in London.

**Kelvingrove Park ❸**, in the city's West End, was laid out in the 1850s and as the venue of Glasgow's principal Victorian and Edwardian international hibitions, although that function is now performed by the modern Scottish hibition and Conference Centre. It is a spectacular park, traversed by the River elvin and dominated on one side by the Gothic pile of **Glasgow University** is seat of learning was unseated from its original college in the High Street d rehoused on Gilmorehill in 1870) and by the elegant Victorian precipice of rk Circus on the other side.

Reopened in 2006 following a three-year, multi-million-pound renovation, the elvingrove Art Gallery and Museum ❹** (open daily; free) includes a major llection of European paintings and extensive displays on the natural history, chaeology and ethnology of the area. Its magnificent organ is regularly used

**TIP**

The much-loved Kelvingrove Art Gallery and Museum is the largest civic museum and art gallery in the UK, attracting over 1 million visitors a year.

**BELOW:** traditions live on at Glasgow University.

# Culture Comes in from the Cold

Glasgow's elevation to the position of European City of Culture 1990 (a title bestowed by the Ministers of Culture of the 12 member states of the European Community) was received with a mixture of astonishment and amusement in Edinburgh, which had long perceived itself as guardian of Scotland's most civilised values.

But, ever so quietly, Glasgow had been stealing the initiative. Edinburgh had been trying to make up its mind for nearly 30 years about building an opera house, but Glasgow went ahead and converted one of its general-purpose theatres, the Theatre Royal, into a home for the Scottish Opera and regular venue for Scottish Ballet. The city is also the home of three major orchestras and the Royal Scottish Academy of Music and Drama.

Besides its traditional theatres – the King's and the Pavilion – the city boasts the cav-

ernous **Tramway Theatre ❺**, the former home of the city's tram-cars, in which Peter Brook staged his ambitious *Mahabharata*. Studio theatres include the Tron, founded in 1979, the Mitchell Theatre, housed in an extension of the distinguished Mitchell Library, and two small theatres in the multimedia complex of the dynamic Centre for Contemporary Arts on Sauchiehall Street. However, Glasgow's most distinctive stage is the innovative **Citizens' Theatre ❻**.

Each year, it seems, Glasgow adds a new festival to its calendar. Mayfest, a general celebration of the arts, has been followed by international jazz, folk music and early music festivals, each held during successive months of the summer to keep the visitors coming.

The turning point in Glasgow's progress towards cultural respectability came with the opening, in 1983, of the striking new building in Pollok Country Park to house the Burrell Collection bequeathed to the city in 1944. Until recently. the enormous popularity of the Burrell Collection has tended to overshadow Glasgow's other distinguished art galleries and museums: Kelvingrove, at the western end of Argyle Street, which has a strong representation of 17th-century Dutch paintings and 19th-century French paintings as well as many fine examples of the work of the late 19th-century Glasgow Boys; the Gallery of Modern Art (GOMA), opened in 1996; the university's Hunterian Museum and Art Gallery, and the St Mungo Museum of Religious Life and Art. The McLellan Galleries, built in 1856, are currently closed. In 1999, The Lighthouse, designed by Charles Rennie Mackintosh and formerly the offices of the *Glasgow Herald*, reopened as an architecture and design centre, with displays on the work of Mackintosh and exhibition galleries.

Other museums of note are the Museum of Transport, which contains the UK's largest range of vehicles and an unsurpassed collection of model ships; Haggs Castle, a period museum, on the South Side; and the charming miniature repository of social history, the red sandstone **Tenement House ❼** (open Mar–Oct daily 1–5pm) a two-room-and-kitchen flat in an 1892 tenement in Garnethill, wonderfully preserved.  ❏

**LEFT:** a night at the opera.

Map, pages 164–5

recitals, and a WWII Spitfire hangs in the main hall. Nearby is the intriguing **Museum of Transport** (open daily; free) with cars, trams and model ships on display. **Victoria Park**, near the north mouth of the Clyde Tunnel, has a glasshouse containing several large fossil trees of some 350 million years' antiquity.

**Pollok Country Park** ❽ on the city's south side (those who live south of the Clyde consider themselves a separate race of Glaswegian) has a well-worn path beaten to the door of the **Burrell Collection** (open daily; free), where there are over 8,000 exhibits, from artefacts of ancient civilisations to Impressionist paintings. The park is also the home of the 18th-century **Pollok House**, designed by William Adam (open daily summer; admission charge). It, too, is an art gallery, with works by El Greco, Murillo, Goya and William Blake. The windows look out on a prizewinning herd of Highland cattle and Pollok Golf Course.

Also on the south side, south of Queen's Park in Cathcart, lies **Holmwood House**, the best domestic example of Alexander "Greek" Thomson, Glasgow's most famous Victorian architect. It was built in 1857–8 for a paper manufacturer, James Couper (open daily Easter–Oct; admission charge).

*The Glasgow Harbour project is an ambitious, multi-million-pound residential and leisure development transforming the banks of the Clyde.*

## Old and new by the Clyde

Abcross Quay is the site of the **Scottish Exhibition and Conference Centre** ❾ and the Clyde Centre, known as **The Armadillo**, a 3,000-seater conference and concert venue designed by Lord Foster. You can also marvel at the industrial colossus of the **Finnieston Crane** and the **Tall Ship** (open daily; admission charge), a three-masted Clyde-built barque (1896), with adjoining Pumphouse visitor centre and exhibition gallery. Across Bell's Bridge is the **Glasgow Science Centre** ❿, a collection of futuristic buildings that includes Scotland's only IMAX **Cinema**, with

**BELOW:** the titanium-clad Scottish Exhibition and Conference Centre.

*Glasgow District Subway, opened in 1896, was one of the earliest underground train systems in Britain and the only one in the country that is called, American-style, "the Subway".*

an 80-ft (24-metre) wide screen; the **Science Mall**, a hands-on extravaganza whe visitors can explore, create and invent; and the **Glasgow Tower**, the tallest fre standing structure in Scotland and the only one in the world that will rotate throu 360 degrees; the views are spectacular.

Stobcross Quay is also a terminus of the **Clyde Walkway**, an area that's pa of a £1 billion nine-year-long "Clyde Waterfront Regeneration" scheme intr ducing new residential and leisure developments to the once heavily indust alised banks of the Clyde. You can walk from the quay through the centre of t city past Glasgow Green to the suburb of **Cambuslang**, but somehow the jou ney eastwards isn't as cheerful as it should be, still lacking the kind of vigorc commercial, social and domestic life which has turned other derelict waterfro into major attractions.

The central section is the most interesting, taking in the city's more disti guished bridges and many of the buildings associated with its maritime li (The architectural historians Gomme and Walker identify only two bridges, the pedestrian Suspension Bridge and the Victoria Bridge, as worthy of notice, d missing the others as "a sorry lot".) The Victoria Bridge was built in 1854 replace the 14th-century Old Glasgow Bridge, and the graceful Suspensi Bridge was completed in 1871 and designed by Alexander Kirkland, who la became Commissioner of Public Buildings in Chicago.

**Custom House Quay** ⓫, which looks across to the delicately restor Georgian façades of Carlton Place on the south bank, has opulent sandsto landscaping, a bandstand and a pub.

**BELOW:** taking a stroll by the River Clyde.

Regeneration is continuing of the **Broomielaw**, an area rich in sailing histo To the west of George V Bridge and Central Station's railway bridge, it w

## DEATH ON THE CLYDE

The old adage that "the Clyde made Glasgow and Gla gow made the Clyde" can no longer be taken as a tr description of the relationship today. In his book *In Sea of Scotland*, H.V. Morton describes the launching of a sl on the Clyde in a passage which brings tears to the ey "Men may love her as men love ships… She will beco wise with the experience of the sea. But no shareholder w ever share her intimacy as we who saw her so marvellou naked and so young slip smoothly from the hands th made her into the dark welcome of the Clyde". That w written in 1929 – at a time when the Clyde's shipbuildi industry was on the precipice of the Great Depression fr which it never recovered.

Soon another writer, the novelist George Blake, was ca ing the empty yards and silent cranes "the high, tra pageant of the Clyde", and today that pageant is noth more than a side-show. Not even the boost of demand d ing World War II, nor replacement orders in the 1950s, even the work on supply vessels and oil platforms for the industry in the 1970s, could rebuild the vigour of the Cly Today Glasgow no longer depends on the river for its ec nomic survival. Developments like the Clyde Walkway sh a new future for the river in the leisure industry.

the departure point for regular services to Ireland, North America and the -coast towns and islands of Scotland. You can sail "doon the watter" from on the world's last sea-going paddle-steamer, the *Waverley*, which cruises mmer to the Firth of Clyde and the Ayrshire coast.

ere is new life stirring, however, on the inner-city banks of the Clyde, as s and wharves are replaced by modern residential apartments. On the south , near Govan, upmarket apartments have been built at the old **Princes Dock**, 20 million Clyde Arc links the Finnieston Quay with the new BBC Scotland plex on the south bank, and the massive Rotunda at the north of the old e Tunnel, designed for pedestrians and horses and carts, has been restored restaurant complex.

her opportunities to get on the river are offered by Seaforce, which runs rboat trips from beside the Tall Ship, and the Clyde Waterbus, a river taxi een Broomielaw and Braehead.

## gh sentimentalism

gh, careless, vulnerable and sentimental." That's how the writer Edwin Mor- lescribed Glaswegians, and they are certainly qualities which Glaswegians brought to their environment. The city has been both brutal and nostalgic t its own fabric, destroying and lamenting with equal vigour. When the city rs built an urban motorway in the 1960s they liberated Glasgow for the rist but cut great swathes through its domestic and commercial heart, and only just prevented from extending the Inner Ring Road, which would have lished in the process much of the Merchant City. But the disappearance of st tramcars in the 1960s has been regretted ever since, even though Glaswe- have grown to love the "Clockwork Orange" – the ntly coloured underground transport system.

t to Morgan's list of adjectives might have been d "pretentious" and "aspirational", two sides of the tectural coin which represents Glasgow's legacy agnificent Victorian buildings. They aren't hard to the dense gridiron of streets around George Square westwards invites the neck to crane at any number aring façades, many bearing the art of the sculptor ll signifying some chapter of the city's 19th-cen- history.

## orian splendour

ge Square is the heart of modern Glasgow. Like Scottish squares, it contains a motley collection of es, commemorating 11 people who seem to have chosen by lottery. The 80-ft (24-metre) column in ntre is mounted by the novelist Sir Walter Scott, g southwards, so they say, to the land where he all his money. But the square is more effectively nated by the grandiose **City Chambers** 🖘 (guided Mon–Fri at 10.30am and 2.30pm; free) designed illiam Young and opened in 1888. The marble-clad or is even more opulent and self-important than the ior. The pièce de résistance is the huge banqueting 110 ft (33 metres) long, 48 ft (14 metres) wide and (16 metres) high; it has a glorious arched ceiling,

Map pages 164–5

**TIP**

Hampden Park, in the south of the city, has been redeveloped as Scotland's National Football (soccer) Stadium, with a museum of Scottish football (open daily; admission charge).

**BELOW:** the Clyde Arc.

leaded glass windows and paintings depicting scenes from the city's history. south wall is covered by three large murals, works of the Glasgow Boys *pages 86–7*).

George Square's other monuments to Victorian prosperity are the for Head Post Office on the south side (now the main **Tourist Information Cen** and the noble **Merchants' House** on the northwest corner (now the home o Glasgow Chamber of Commerce). Its crowning glory is the gold ship o dome, drawing the eye ever upwards – a replica of the ship on the original I chants' House.

Just off Buchanan Street is **Nelson Mandela Place** (its name having changed from St George's Place in tribute to the South African political lea Here you will find the **Glasgow Stock Exchange** , designed in the 1870 John Burnet, whose reputation was to be eclipsed by his celebrated son J.J. net, and the **Royal Faculty of Procurators** (1854).

Nearby are examples of the work of another distinguished Glasgow archi the younger James Salmon, who designed the **Mercantile Building** (1897–8) in Bothwell Street and the curious **Hat-rack** in St Vincent St named for the extreme narrowness and the projecting cornices of its tall faç Further west, J.J. Burnet's extraordinary **Charing Cross Mansions** of 1 with grandiloquent intimations of French Renaissance style, were spare surgery of motorway development which destroyed many 19th-century b ings around Charing Cross.

On the other side of one of these motorways are the first buildings of the **Conservation Area**. These buildings have given rise to the statement that C gow is the "finest piece of architectural planning of the mid-19th century". S

**BELOW:** all lit up in George Square.

wards through this area to a belvedere above Kelvingrove Park and marvel the glorious vistas. The belvedere is backed by **Park Quadrant** and **Park** **rrace**, which are probably the most magnificent of all the terraces in the Park nservation Area. Still in the west end, in Great Western Road, you will find **eat Western Terrace ⑯**, one of the best surviving examples of the work of exander "Greek" Thomson, the architect who acquired his nickname as a ult of his passion for classicism.

3ack towards the city centre in St Vincent Street is Thomson's prominent **Vincent Street Church ⑰**. It is fronted by an Ionic portico, with sides more yptian than Greek and a tower that wouldn't have been out of place in India ring the Raj. Here the streets rise towards **Blythswood Square**, once a haunt prostitutes but now, with its surroundings, providing a graceful mixture of e Georgian and early Victorian domestic architecture.

## t and architecture

Buchanan Street is the **Glasgow Royal Concert Hall**, a purpose-built venue ich regularly attracts top artists and orchestras. Behind **St Vincent Place** is **yal Exchange Square**, which is pretty well consumed by the city's **Gallery Modern Art ⑱** (open daily; free). The glorious building in which it is used began life as the 18th-century mansion of a tobacco lord, and has since n a bank, the Royal Exchange, and more recently a public library and exten- e archive.

\mong the city centre's most distinguished Georgian buildings are, in Ingram eet, **Hutcheson's Hall ⑲** (open Mon–Sat; admission charge), designed by vid Hamilton and now housing National Trust for Scotland offices, visitor

*No. 7 Blythswood Square was where Madeleine Smith poisoned her French lover in 1858. She later moved to London, entertained George Bernard Shaw and married a pupil of the designer William Morris.*

**BELOW:**
Great Western
Terrace in winter.

*Mackintosh's startling design for the School of Art was inexpensive to build, thanks to its lack of ornamentation.*

**BELOW:** behind the Necropolis are the Cathedral and Royal Infirmary.

centre and shop; and, in nearby Glassford Street, **Trades Hall ㉒**, which, des[ alterations, has retained the façade designed by the great Robert Adam.

But any excursion around Glasgow's architectural treasures must include work of the city's most innovative genius, Charles Rennie Mackintosh, w overturned the Victorians in a series of brilliant designs between 1893 and 19 Mackintosh's influence on 20th-century architecture, along with his lead contribution to art nouveau in interiors, furniture and textile design, has lo been acknowledged and celebrated throughout Europe, although all his fir work was done in and around Glasgow.

His sometimes austere, sometimes sensuous style, much influenced by n ural forms and an inspired use of space and light, can be seen in several imp tant buildings: his greatest achievement, designed in 1896, the **Glasgow Sch of Art ㉑** (guided tours Mon–Sat, plus Sun Apr–Sept; admission charge; pr booking advisable) in Renfrew Street; **Scotland Street School**, on the So Side, opened in 1904 and now a Museum of Education (open daily; free); and **Martyrs' Public School** (open daily; free), perched above a sliproad to the motorway near Glasgow Cathedral, and now housing Glasgow Museum's C servation Department.

In Sauchiehall Street the façade of his **Willow Tea Rooms ㉒** (19( remains, and a room on the first floor has been turned over to teatime aga with reproduction Mackintosh furniture. But more stunning examples of interior designs can be seen at the **Mackintosh House** at the University Glasgow's **Hunterian Art Gallery ㉓** (open Mon–Sat; free) on Gilmoreh There, rooms from the architect's own house have been reconstructed a exquisitely furnished with original pieces of his furniture, watercolours a

designs. Also worth a visit are the **House for an** **Lover** (open summer Sat–Thur; winter Sat and S weekdays vary; admission charge) in Bellahous Park, erected long after his death, but to his exact sp ifications; the **Queen's Cross Church** (open Mon– and Sun pm; admission charge) in Garscube Road, a **The Lighthouse** in Mitchell Lane near Central S tion, now a Mackintosh study centre as well a broad-based architecture and design centre (op Mon–Sat and Sun pm; admission charge to Mack tosh Interpretation Centre).

### Old and new

There's not much left in Glasgow which is old British standards. The oldest building is **Glasg Cathedral ㉔** (open Mon–Sat and Sun pm; free), m of which was completed in the 13th century, thou parts were built a century earlier by Bishop Jocelyn was completed by the first bishop of Glasgow, Rob Blacader (1483–1508). The only pre-Reformati dwelling house is **Provand's Lordship** (open Mon– and Sun pm; free), built in 1471 as part of a refuge poor people and extended in 1670. It now contain museum of medieval material.

Both old buildings stand on **Cathedral Street**, at top of the High Street – the cathedral on a site wh has been a place of Christian worship since it w blessed for burial in AD 397 by St Ninian, the earli

ssionary recorded in Scottish history. A severe but satisfying example of early
)thic, it contains the tomb of St Mungo.
)Behind the cathedral, overseeing the city from the advantage of height, are more
nbs – the intimidating Victorian sepulchres of the **Western Necropolis**. This
metery is supervised by a statute of John Knox, the 16th-century reformer, and
ong the ranks of Glaswegian notables buried there is one William Miller, "the
reate of the nursery". He wrote the popular bedtime jingle, "Wee Willie Winkie".
A cream-coloured Scottish baronial building in front of the cathedral is home
the **St Mungo Museum of Religious Life and Art** (open daily; free), with
Japanese Zen garden. Don't miss the comments on the visitors' board.
The two oldest churches in Glasgow, other than the cathedral, are **St Andrew's
rish Church ㉕**, which contains some spectacular plasterwork, and the Epis-
pal **St Andrew's-by-the-Green ㉖**, once known as the Whistlin' Kirk because
its early organ. Both were built in the mid-18th century and both can be found
the northwest of Glasgow Green, in the Merchant City.
There you will also find two remnants of the 17th century, the **Tolbooth
eeple ㉗** and the **Tron Steeple ㉘**. The Tolbooth Steeple, at Glasgow Cross
here the Mercat Cross is a 20th-century replica of a vanished one) is a pretty
bstantial remnant of the old jail and courthouses, being seven storeys high
h a crown tower. The Tron Steeple was once attached to the Tron Church, at
Trongate, and dates back to the late 16th and early 17th centuries. The orig-
l church was burned down in the 18th century and the replacement now
commodates the lively Tron Theatre.
Those truly dedicated to the pursuit of antiquity, however, could always pro-
d to the refined northwest suburb of **Bearsden**, where once rough Romans

Map pages 164–5

**TIP**

It's advisable to book
ahead if planning to
tour the Glasgow
School of Art (tel:
(0141) 353 4526;
www.gsa.ac.uk)

**BELOW LEFT:**
a Mackintosh room
in the Hunterian Art
Gallery.
**BELOW:**
inside Glasgow's
School of Art.

**Map pages 164–5**

*Tobias Smollett, writing in 1771, had no doubts about Glasgow's standing as a commercial centre: "One of the most flourishing in Great Britain... it is a perfect bee-hive in point of industry."*

**BELOW:** the Barras: Scotland's largest flea market.
**RIGHT:** modern shopping in the St Enoch Centre.

roamed. Bearsden lies on the line of the Antonine Wall, built during the 2nd century, and chunks of the Roman occupation remain to be seen.

## Market forces

Heavy industry has come and gone, but Glasgow still flourishes as a city of independent enterprise – of hawkers, stallholders, street traders and marketeers. Even the dignified buildings of its old, more respectable markets – fish, fruit and cheese – have survived in a city which has often been careless with its past, and have now become part of the rediscovery of the Merchant City area, which stretches from the **High Street** and the **Saltmarket** in the east to **Union Street** and **Jamaica Street** in the west. It contains most of the city's remaining pre-Victorian buildings. The old **Fishmarket** ❷ in Clyde Street is in fact Victorian, but accommodates a perpendicular remnant of the 17th-century Merchants' House, which was demolished in 1817.

In **Candleriggs** ❸, slightly to the north, the old Fruitmarket now houses a variety of cafes, restaurants and shops, while Glasgow's market celebrity still belongs to the **Barras** ❸, in the Gallowgate to the east, where both repartee and bargains were once reputed to rival those of Paris's Flea Market and London's Petticoat Lane. Founding queen of the Barras was Mrs McIver, who started her career with one barrow, bought several more to hire out on the piece of ground she rented in the Gallowgate, and was claimed to have retired a millionaire.

More local colour and open-air tat, useful or useless, can be found in **Paddy's Market**, in the lanes between Clyde Street and the Bridgegate, many of the stalls occupying the arches of an old railway bridge. This market has its genesis in Ireland's "Hungry Forties", when the great potato famines of the 1840s sent hundreds of thousands of destitute Irish people to Glasgow.

## Commercial interests

**Argyle Street**, traversed by the railway bridge to Central Station, **Sauchiehall Street** and the more upmarket **Buchanan Street**, with the Buchanan Galleries complex, are Glasgow's great shopping thoroughfares, while the cosmopolitan cafe culture area round **Byres Road**, in the West End, is a centre for interesting bric-a-brac and boutiques. **West Regent Street** has a Victorian Village (small antique shops in old business premises) and the area around the **Italian Centre** in the Merchant City buzzes with stylish cafe-bars.

Glaswegians have always spent freely, belying the slur on the open-handedness of Scots, and the city's commercial interests seem to believe that the appetite for shopping is insatiable. Just off Buchanan Street, upmarket **Princes Square shopping centre** ❷ is worth visiting even for those who don't wish to shop or eat. The site of the demolished St Enoch Railway Station and hotel (one of Glasgow's major acts of vandalism) is now occupied by the **St Enoch Centre** ❸, a spectacular glass-covered complex of shops, a fast-food "court", ice rink and car park. The latest "leisure and retail" development is the huge waterside **Braehead Centre**, at Renfrew on the western edge of the city.

"Edinburgh is the capital," as the old joke goes, "but Glasgow *has* the capital." And it flaunts it.

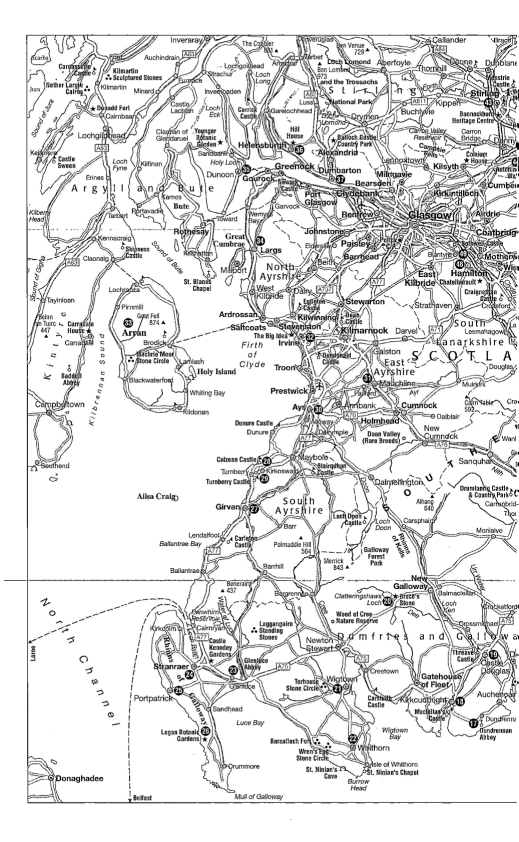

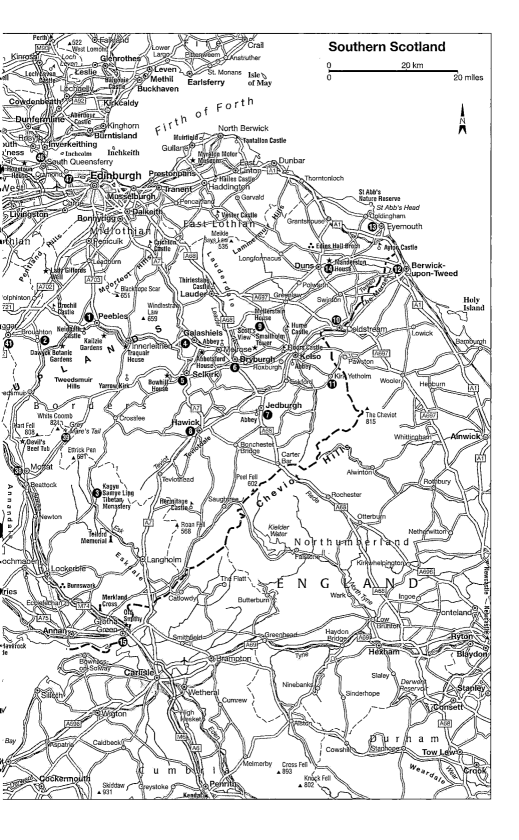

# THE BORDERS

*Castles, ruined abbeys, baronial mansions and*
*evidence of past turbulent struggles against the English give the*
*green hills of the Borders a romance all of their own*

There's a mistaken assumption that, compared with all those northerly lochs
and glens, rushing rivers and barren moors, the Borders have only border-
line appeal. In reality this area of proud rugby-loving communities enjoys
inning scenery and a reputation for world-class mountain biking and fishing.
Administratively, the Borders include the four "shires" of Peebles and Berwick
the north (though Berwick-upon-Tweed is in England) and Selkirk and Rox-
urgh in the south.

## Quiet beginnings

irectly south of Edinburgh, **Peebles** ❶ owes much of its charm to its Tweedside
cation. Here the river already runs wide and fast. Peebles' central thoroughfare
equally wide but much more sedate. The town was never renowned for its hus-
and bustle; an 18th-century aristocrat coined an ungenerous simile: "As quiet
the grave – or Peebles." This is no longer apt, for each June things liven up
nsiderably with the week-long "Riding of the Marches" Beltane festival.

The **Cross Kirk** was erected in 1261 after the discovery of a large cross on
is site. The remains include a large 15th-century tower and foundations of clois-
and monastic buildings. St Andrew's Collegiate Church, the forerunner to the
ross Kirk, sits in a cemetery on the Glasgow Road.

**PRECEDING PAGES:**
beauty in the
Borders.
**LEFT:** a shepherd
near Moffat.
**BELOW:** crossing the
Tweed into Peebles.

ere, too, only a tower remains; the remainder was
rned by the English at the time of the sacking of the
ur great Border abbeys. At the bottom of Peebles High
reet, the Gothic outline of Peebles Parish Church adds
the town's air of sobriety.

The **Chambers Institute**, Peebles' civic centre and
me of the Tweeddale Museum, was a gift to the place
om William Chambers, a native of the place and the
unding publisher of Chambers Encyclopedia.

## Following the Tweed

st a few minutes out of Peebles (west on the A72),
rched high on a rocky bluff overlooking the Tweed,
**eidpath Castle** (open May–Sept Wed–Sat and Sun
n; tel: (01721) 720333; admission charge), a well-pre-
rved example of the many medieval tower houses in
e region, offers more excitement. Wordsworth visited
1803 and wrote a famous poem lamenting the deso-
tion caused in 1795 when the absentee landowner, the
h Duke of Queensberry, cut down all the trees for
oney to support his extravagant London lifestyle.
'ordsworth would have been happier had he journeyed
miles (13 km) southwest of Peebles on the B712 to
awyck Botanic Garden (open Feb–Nov daily; tel:
1721) 760254; admission charge), an outstation of
linburgh's Royal Botanic Garden, containing some of
e oldest and tallest trees in Europe.

*Robert Smail's
Printing Works in
Inverleithen is a
working museum
with early 20th-
century machinery
and equipment,
including a restored
waterwheel. Visitors
can watch the
printer at work and
can try their hand at
typesetting.*

Continue via the B712 to **Broughton** ❷, the site of **Broughton Place**, a imposing 20th-century castellated house that looks much older. Insid Broughton Gallery (open Apr–Sept and during special exhibitions; tel: (0189 830234) has a fine collection of work by British artists and craftsmen for sal John Buchan, author of the classic *The Thirty-Nine Steps*, grew up in this vi lage, and just to the south is the **John Buchan Centre** (open Easter a May–Sept daily pm; tel: (01899) 221050; admission charge), a small museu dedicated to the man who eventually became Governor General of Canada.

Buchan frequented the **Crook Inn**, just outside **Tweedsmuir**, 15 miles (2 km) south of Broughton. One of the oldest Border coaching inns, it has strong l erary associations. Robert Burns was inspired to write his poem "Willie Wastle Wife" in the kitchen (now the bar, with the original flagstone floor). Sir Walt Scott also visited, as did his lesser-known contemporary James Hogg, the po known locally as "The Ettrick Shepherd".

Step southwards outside the Borders towards Eskdalemuir, and you'll k greeted by a real surprise: the **Kagyu Samye Ling Tibetan Monastery** ❸ (op daily; tel: (01387) 373232). Founded in 1967 for study, retreat and meditatio it's the first and largest Tibetan centre and Buddhist monastery in the West. Vi itors, regardless of faith, can join free tours around the centre's facilities.

East of Peebles on the A72 is **Traquair House** (open Apr–Oct daily p June–Aug daily, Nov weekends; tel: (01896) 830323; admission charge), Scc land's oldest continually inhabited house (since 1107), where Mary Queen Scots stayed with her husband Darnley in 1566. Its full history dates from th 12th century. After Bonnie Prince Charlie visited in 1745, the 5th Earl of Traqua closed the Bear Gates after him and swore they would not open until a Stuart kin

**BELOW:**
Sir Walter Scott
towers over Selkirk.

## BORDER COUNTRY

The River Tweed has inspired roman-tic Borders ballads for hundreds of years and was held by the novelist Sir Walter Scott to be the most precious river in the world. Its source is just a few miles south of the village of Tweeds-muir, and the river cuts right through three of the most important Border towns: Peebles, Melrose and Kelso. Here, too, you will find rugg moorland and craggy terrain, reminiscent of the Scottish Hig lands. The two highest points in the Borders, Broad Law and D lar Law, rise to more than 2,750 ft (840 metres) and 2,680 ft (8 metres) respectively.

Draw a line between Hawick and Broughton and then st south of it and you'll see the best the Border has to offer. A pc ular route is the side road out of Tweedsmuir up to the Talla a Megget Reservoirs. Steep slopes and rock-strewn hillsides pr vide a stunning panorama as you twist and turn down to t A708, where, to the south, is another favourite spot: St Mar Loch, the only loch in the Borders region. If you are fit, you shou forsake the car and follow the Southern Uplands Way, which ru alongside the loch and north across the moors to Traquair Hous or south to the valley of Ettrick Water.

d been restored to the throne. The wide avenue from the house to the gates has
en disused ever since. The surrounding gardens include a hedge maze, crafts
ops and a tearoom.
·On the road west back to Peebles, **Kailzie Gardens** (open daily; tel: (01721)
0007; admission charge) adds to the beauty of the Tweed Valley with its for-
ıl walled garden, greenhouses and woodland walks.

## eart of the Borders

ıough it has little to tempt today's visitor, **Galashiels ❹** has played a pivotal role
the Borders economy as a weaving town for more than 700 years. The School of
xtiles and Design, founded in 1909, has helped to cement the reputation of the tar-
ıs, tweeds, woollens and other knitted materials sold in the mills here. Although
ε industry across the region has gone into decline, there are numerous working
ɹlls open to the public: **Lochcarron of Scotland** in Huddersfield Street (open
ʻ1–Dec Mon–Sat 9am–5pm and June–Sept including Sun pm; tel: (01896)
·1100); admission charge) which holds conducted tours (Mon–Thur and Fri am)
d features a textiles museum.
It's not only Galashiels that lets you sample the Borders textiles. Tourism
s fashioned the Borders Woollen Trail, which includes eight other towns
volved in this industry. One of them, **Selkirk ❺**, became a textile centre in
ε 19th century when the growing demand for tweed could no longer be met
the mills of Galashiels. Other than shopping, there are several interesting
aces to visit, including the 18th-century **Halliwell's House Museum** (open
ʌster–Oct Mon–Sat and Sun am; tel: (01750) 20096; free) a former old iron-
ɔngers which now tells the story of Selkirk in entertaining detail. Nearby is

**TIP**

Just 1 mile (1.6 km)
east of Peebles, the
forests of Glentress are
riddled with purpose-
built mountain-biking
tracks (www.thehub-
intheforest.co.uk).

**BELOW LEFT:**
on parade at
Traquair House.
**BELOW:**
peace at Samye
Ling Monastery.

*Sir Walter Scott wrote all the Waverley novels at Abbotsford House, but only admitted to being the author late in life, feeling that it wasn't "decorous" for a Clerk of Session to be seen writing novels.*

**BELOW:**
Dryburgh Abbey: a brooding reminder of bloody history.

**Sir Walter Scott's Courtroom** (open Easter–Oct Mon–Sat, pm only in Oc May–Aug also Sun pm; tel: (01750) 20096; free) where the great writer di pensed justice during his 35 years as sheriff here. Down by the Ettrick Wat is Selkirk Glass (open daily; tel: (01750) 20954).

Don't leave the locality without visiting **Bowhill House and Country Pa** (house open July daily pm; country park open late Apr–Aug: daily 10am–5p except Fri; tel: (01750) 22204; admission charge). Bowhill is the home of th Scotts of Buccleuch and Queensberry, once one of the largest landowners of a the Border clans. More than 300 years of discerning art collecting has amasse works by Canaletto, Guardi, Raeburn, Reynolds and Gainsborough.

If the Borders have a sort of visitors' mecca, then **Abbotsford House** (op mid-Mar–May and Oct Mon–Sat and Sun pm, June–Sept daily; tel: (0189 752043; admission charge), home of Sir Walter Scott from 1811 to 183 undoubtedly lays claim to that title. Scott spent £50,000 and the rest of his li turning a small farm into an estate befitting his position as a Border laird.

Scott was buried at **Dryburgh** , one of the four great 12th-century abbeys the Borders (open Apr–Sept daily, winter Mon–Sat and Sun pm; tel: (0183 822381; admission charge). While the ruins at Jedburgh, Kelso and Melrose near the edge of their respective towns, Dryburgh, founded by Hugh de Morvi for monks from Alnwick in Northumberland, is tucked away in an idyllic locatio among trees by the edge of the Tweed.

Dryburgh's setting is no match for **Scott's View** on the B6356, which offer: sweeping view of the unmistakable triple peaks of the **Eildon Hills** (reputed be the legendary sleeping place of King Arthur and his knights) and a wi stretch of the Tweed Valley. Scott came here many times to enjoy the panoram

The town of **Melrose,** between Dryburgh and Galashiels, escaped much of the industrialisation that affected Selkirk, Hawick and Galashiels. **Melrose Abbey** (open daily Oct–Mar, closed Sun am; tel: (01896) 822562; admission charge) seals the town's pedigree. The abbey was founded in 1136 by King David I, who helped to found all four of the great Border abbeys, and was the first Cistercian monastery in Scotland. Tragically, it lay in the path of repeated English invasions long before Henry VIII made his presence felt in the 16th century. An attack in 1322 by Edward II prompted Robert Bruce to fund its restoration. The heart of King Robert I is buried in the abbey.

Also in Melrose is Scotland's only **Teddy Bear Museum** (open daily in summer, winter Fri–Sun; tel: (01896) 823854), where bears are made to order; **Priorwood Garden**, a walled garden specialising in plants suitable for drying; and the **Trimontium Exhibition** outlining the Roman occupation of the area. Melrose is also the starting point on the 60-mile (100-km) **St Cuthbert's Way** walk to Lindisfarne (Holy Island) and in April, annually hosts the Melrose (rugby) Sevens Tournament.

North of Melrose, on the outskirts of **Lauder**, is **Thirlestane Castle** (open Apr–Oct Sun–Fri; tel: (01578) 722430; admission charge), once the seat of the Earls of Lauderdale and still owned by their descendants. It is one of Scotland's oldest castles and has renowned 17th-century plaster ceilings.

## Roman reminders

Historically, **Jedburgh** ❼ is the most important of the Border towns. It was also strategically important; as the first community across the border it often bore the full brunt of invading English armies. Earlier invaders came from even further

*The heart of Robert the Bruce was said to be buried near the high altar of Melrose Abbey, but subsequent excavations have failed to locate any trace of it.*

**BELOW:** arms and armour at Abbotsford House.

*Contrary to popular belief, the word "tweed" does not come from the river; in fact, it was originally a misprint – by an English publisher – for tweels, the Border name for woollen fabrics.*

**BELOW:** the stately interior of Floors Castle.

afield: 2 miles (3km) north of Jedburgh one can follow the course of Dere Str the road the Romans built in southern Scotland over 1,900 years ago.

The oldest surviving building, **Jedburgh Abbey** (open Apr–Sept daily Oct–M closed Sun am; tel: (01835) 863925; admission charge), was founded in 1138 Augustinian canons from northern France. Stonework in the abbey's museu dates from the first millennium AD and proves that the site had much older re gious significance. Malcolm IV was crowned here, and Alexander III married second wife in the abbey in 1285. Their wedding feast was held at nearby Je burgh Castle, which occupied a site in Castlegate. It was demolished in 1409 keep it out of English hands. In 1823 the **Castle Gaol** (open Easter–Oct Mon–S and Sun pm; tel: (01835) 864750; admission charge) was built on the old castl foundations; its museum of social history is well worth a visit.

Near the High Street, displays in **Mary Queen of Scots' House** (op Mar–Nov daily; tel: (01835) 863331; admission charge) tell a short but cruc chapter in Scotland's history. It was in this house in late 1566 that Queen Ma spent several weeks recovering from serious illness after her renowned dash horseback to Hermitage Castle to see her injured lover James Hepburn, Earl Bothwell. Her ride resulted in scandal that was made all the worse by the mu der of her husband Darnley in the following February. From there on, her dow fall was steady. Years later, during her 19 years of imprisonment, Mary regrett that her life hadn't ended in the Borders: "Would that I had died in Jedburgh

If you decide to retrace Mary's footsteps to Hermitage Castle, you're likely pass through **Hawick** ❽ (pronounced *Hoik*). The Borders' textile industry is around you here, not least at the Cashmere Visitor Centre (open daily; (0145 371221). At the **Hawick Museum** in **Wilton Lodge Park** (open Mon–F

ıster–Sept and Sat and Sun pm, Jan–Mar Mon–Fri and Sun pm; tel: (01450) '3457; free) a fascinating collection of exhibits picks up older sartorial threads. Still retaining its cobbled streets leading into a spacious square, **Kelso** is one 'the most picturesque Border towns. Close to the town centre is **Kelso Abbey** pen Mon–Sat and Sun pm; free), once the largest and richest of the Borders 'beys. It suffered the same fate as the abbeys at Melrose, Jedburgh and Dry- ırgh and is today the least complete of all of them.

It's ironic that, while the English destroyed Kelso's abbey, the Scottish were sponsible for the much greater devastation of the town of **Roxburgh** and its ıstle. Roxburgh had grown up on the south bank of the Tweed around the ıighty fortress of Marchmount. An important link in the chain of border forti- ıations, Marchmount controlled the gateway to the north. In the 14th century ıe English took Roxburgh and its castle and used it as a base for further incur- ıns into Scottish territory. In 1460 James II of Scotland attacked Marchmount ıt was killed by a bursting cannon. His widow urged the Scottish troops forward. On achieving victory they destroyed Roxburgh's castle (to make sure it stayed ıt of enemy hands for good) with a thoroughness that the English would have ıund hard to match. Today, on a mound between the Teviot and the Tweed just ıst of Kelso (the plain village of Roxburgh a few miles on is no direct relation the ancient town), only fragments of Marchmount's walls survive.

*Floors Castle is the largest inhabited castle in Scotland.*

## ırt and architecture

ı the north bank of the Tweed, Kelso thrived, however. **Floors Castle** (open ıster–Oct daily; tel: (01573) 223333; admission charge) was designed by Robert ıdam and built between 1721 and 1726. It owes its present flamboyant appearance William Playfair, who remodelled and extended the ıstle between 1837 and 1845. An outstanding collection German, Italian and French furniture, Chinese and ıresden porcelain, paintings by Picasso, Matisse and ıgustus John, and a 15th-century Brussels tapestry are ıne of the many glittering prizes that give Floors an air palatial elegance. There's also a licensed restaurant ıd coffee shop.

**Smailholm Tower** (open Apr–Sept daily, Oct–Nov ı day Sat and Sun pm; tel: (01573) 460365; admission ıarge) stands gaunt and foreboding 6 miles (10 km) ırthwest of Kelso (B6404). Walter Scott made a deal ıth the owner of this superb 16th-century peel tower: exchange for saving it, Scott would write a ballad – ıe Eve of St John – about it. Today, the stern-faced rtress is a museum of costume figures and tapestries ılating to Scott's *Minstrelsy of the Borders*.

Northwest from Kelso on the A6089 is **Mellerstain ıouse ⑨** (open Easter, May, June and Sept, Sun–Wed, ıly–Aug Sun–Mon, Wed and Thur; tel: (01573) ı0225; admission charge), one of Scotland's finest ıeorgian mansions and the product of the combined ınius of William Adam and his son Robert. Externally ıhas the dignity, symmetry and well-matched propor- ıns characteristic of the period. Inside there's furni- ıre by Chippendale, Sheraton and Hepplewhite; ıintings by Gainsborough, Constable, Veronese and ın Dyck; and some exquisite moulded plaster ceilings,

**BELOW:** the ruins of Kelso Abbey.

Map pages 180–1

Berwick-upon-Tweed retains its medieval street plan and has several steep, cobbled streets that are worth exploring if you are feeling energetic.

doorheads and light fittings. As if all this weren't enough to impress, form-Italian gardens were laid out in 1909 to create a series of gently sloping terrac and the house became a popular venue for fashionable dances.

## Border crossings

East of Kelso the Tweed marks the natural boundary between England and Scc land. **Coldstream ⑩**, one of the last towns on this river before Berwick, has li tle to offer the visitor other than history. The town's name was taken by th famous regiment of Coldstream Guards that was formed by General Monck 1659 before he marched south to support the restoration of the Stuart mona chy. The regiment today loans material to the **Coldstream Museum** (op Easter–Oct Mon–Sat and Sun pm; tel: (01890) 882630; free), set up in a house th was Monck's headquarters.

Nearly 150 years earlier, in 1513, James IV of Scotland crossed the Tweed Coldstream to attack the English with a much larger force. Though Henry VⅪ was at that time fighting in France (James IV's invasion was a diversion intend to aid the French) an English army was sent north to meet the threat. Th encounter, which took place near the English village of Branxton but was knov as the Battle of Flodden, was a military disaster for Scotland: the king, his so and as many as 46 nobles and 9,000 men were slain.

Happier endings are to be had at **Kirk Yetholm ⑪**, just 1 mile (1.6 km) fro the English border. Overlooking the village green, the Border Hotel bills itself the "End of the Pennine Way". A few miles away **Linton Kirk**, said to be tl oldest building in continuous use for Christian worship in the area, sits proud on a hummock of sand in a picturesque valley.

**BELOW:** Mellerstain: one of Scotland's most glorious Georgian houses.

When it comes to identifying precise borderlines, **Berwick-upon-Tweed** ⓬ ı be forgiven for feeling a little confused. Boundaries around here lack a sense fair play: Berwick is not part of Berwickshire. And although the town takes its ⸱me from a river that has its source in the Scottish Borders, Berwick-upon-⸱eed is not part of Scotland. It's in Northumberland, England. It wasn't always ⸱e that. The town changed hands 13 times between 1147 and 1482 (when it was ally taken for England by Richard, Duke of Gloucester – later Richard III).

Historically Berwick is very much a part of the Borders. The town's castle, ⸱ılt in the late 12th century by Henry II, once towered high above the Tweed. ⸱ıch of it was demolished in 1847 to make space for the station, which bears an propriate inscription by Robert Stephenson: "The Final Act Of Union". ⸱rwick's town wall, built on the orders of Edward I, has fared better and is one the most complete of its kind in Britain.

Situated in Scotland, along the coast just north of Berwick, **Eyemouth** ⓭ is ⸱mall working fishing town whose **museum** (open Apr–Oct Mon–Sat and Sun ⸱₄; tel: (01890) 750678; admission charge) vividly outlines Eyemouth's long ⸱dition as a fishing port. The museum's centrepiece is the Eyemouth Tapes-⸱⸱, made by local people in 1981 to commemorate the great disaster of 1881 ⸱₄en 189 fishermen were drowned, all within sight of land, during a storm.

A few miles north, **Coldingham's Medieval Priory** and **St Abbs' Head ⸱ture Reserve** (open daily; free; tel: (018907) 71443) are two further justifi-⸱ions for making this detour off the A1 to Edinburgh. An alternative route to ⸱linburgh is the A6105/A697. If you do, stop at **Manderston House** ⓮ (open ⸱d May–Sept Thur and Sun pm; tel: (01361) 882010; admission charge), just ⸱tside Duns, to enjoy "the finest Edwardian country house in Scotland".    ❑

*Each of the 36 bells in the servants' quarters of Manderston House has a different tone: the cacophony must have been deafening when the servants were summoned to clean the silver staircase, the only one in the world.*

**BELOW:** the old bridge over the River Tweed in Berwick.

# HISTORIC CASTLES AND ABBEYS

*An Englishman's home may be his castle, but for centuries and, in some instances, even today, a Scotsman's castle has been his home*

Dotted throughout the Scottish landscape are more than 2,000 castles, many in ruins but others in splendid condition. The latter, still occupied, do not fulfil the primary definition of "castle" – a fortified building – but rather meet the secondary definition: a magnificent house, such as Fyvie *(above)*.

Either way, all are not merely part of Scottish history: they are its essence. Many carry grim and grisly tales. Thus, Hugh Macdonald was imprisoned in the bowels of Duntulm Castle and fed generous portions of salted beef, but he was denied anything – even whisky – to drink.

In 1746 Blair Castle was, on the occasion of the Jacobite uprising, the last castle in the British isles to be fired upon in anger. Today, the Duke of Atholl, the owner of Blair Castle, is the only British subject permitted to maintain a private army, the Atholl Highlanders. Prior to the siege, Bonnie Prince Charlie slept here (visitors might be excused for believing there are few castles in Scotland where the Bonnie Prince and Mary Queen of Scots did not sleep).

You, too, can sleep in Scottish castles. Culzean, Skibo (where Madonna and Guy Ritchie were married) and Inverlochy all have rooms to let. And, for those eager to become a laird, don the kilt and own a castle, several are invariably on the market.

◁ **STRONGHOLD**
In 1314 Robert the Bruce reaffirmed Scottish supremacy won at Bannockburn by reclaiming Stirling Castle from the English.

△ **RELIGIOUS RELICS**
The ruins of St Andrews Cathedral give some idea the grandeur of ecclesias building: this was once the greatest church in Scotla

◁ **GUARDING THE GLEN**
Urquhart Castle was built to guard the Great Glen. It played an important role in the Wars of Independence, being taken by Edward I and later held by Robert the Bruce. During the Jacobite troubles part of the castle was blown up to prevent it falling into "rebel" hands. Today, its walls are a strategic spot from which to sight the Loch Ness Monster.

▽ **ROYAL RESIDENCE**
Stirling Castle, once called "the key to Scotland" because of its strategic position between the Lowlands and Highlands, witnessed many bloody battles between the Scots and English. Later, it became a favourite residence of Stuart monarchs. Nowadays it is also the home of the regimental museum of the Argyll and Sutherland Highlanders.

◁ **BARONIAL SPLENDOUR**
Dunrobin, the largest pile in the Highlands, is the seat of the Dukes of Sutherland, who once owned more land than anyone in Europe. Originally a fortified square keep, it was transformed into a castle and then in the 19th century into a French château with Scottish baronial overtones. The gardens are magnificent.

# SCOTTISH BORDER ABBEYS

Scotland, especially the Borders, is full of abbeys that now lie ruined but were once powerful institutions with impressive buildings. During the reign of David I (1124–53), who revitalised and transformed the Scottish Church, more than 20 religious houses were founded. Outstanding among these is a quartet of Border abbeys – Dryburgh (Premonstratensian), Jedburgh (Augustinian), Kelso (Tironensian) and Melrose (Cistercian). All have evocative ruins, though perhaps it is Jedburgh *(above)*, with its tower and remarkable rose window still intact, which is Scotland's classic abbey.

It was not the Reformation (1560) that caused damage to these abbeys but rather the selfishness of pre-Reformation clergy, raids in the 14th–16th centuries by both English and Scots, the ravages of weather and activities of 19th-century restorers. The concern of the Reformation, spearheaded by firebrand John Knox, was to preserve, not to destroy, the churches they needed.

Monasteries continued to exist as landed corporations after the Reformation. Why upset a system that suited so many interests? After all, the Pope, at the king's request, had provided priories and abbeys for five of James V's bastards while they were still infants.

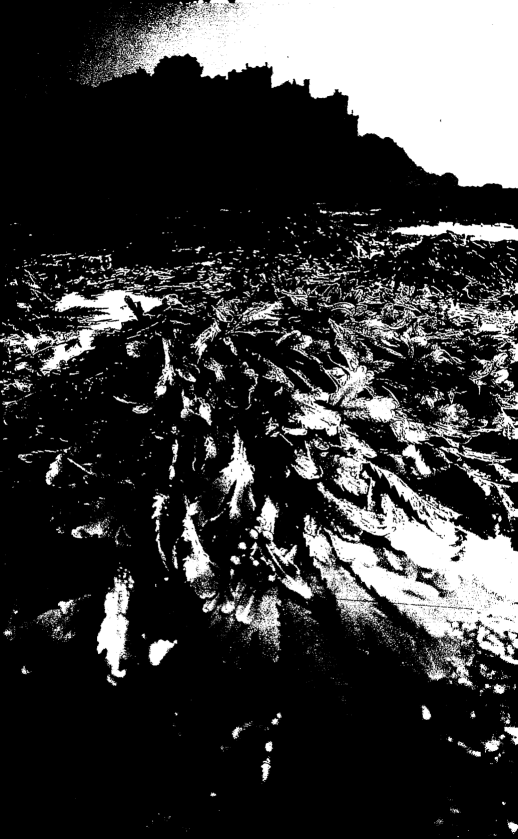

# THE SOUTHWEST

*The Southwest is gentle country, with a dense concentration of literary associations and a colourful history whose sometimes brutal nature belies the comeliness of the land*

n the landscape and seascapes of Southwest Scotland, in the pretty villages of Dumfries and Galloway and the hill farms of South Lanarkshire, in the industrial townships of Ayrshire and the ports and holiday resorts of the Clyde coast, ou will find something of the rest of Scotland. All that is missing, perhaps, is the spiring grandeur of the West Highlands. The **Galloway Hills** are lonely, lovely aces in their own right, but none rises to more than 2,800 ft (850 metres).

Yet travellers from England often bypass the Solway with its pastoral hinternd in their scamper up the M74 to points north and the Highlands, hesitating ·ly at a name which is legendary for just one reason. **Gretna Green** , just ·er the border (until the boundary between England and Scotland was agreed 1552, this area was known simply as the Debatable Land), became celebrated ·r celebrating marriages. It was the first available community where eloping ·uples from England could take advantage of Scotland's different marriage ·ws. Many a makeshift ceremony was performed at the **Old Blacksmith's**, ·hich is now a visitor centre with exhibits telling the story of the town's claim fame (open daily; tel: (01461) 338441), and many a romantic bride and Gretna football fan, still chooses to be married at Gretna Green today.

## ·e Burns legend

few miles farther north is **Ecclefechan**, where the ·etty white **Arched House** in which the man of letters ·iomas Carlyle was born in 1795, is now a modest lit·ary shrine (open May–Sept Thur–Mon; tel: (01576) ·0666; admission charge). But the Southwest is more ·escapably identified with the poet Robert Burns, ·hose life and legend remains an integral part of Scot·ːh tourism.

The urban centres of the Burns industry are Dumfries ·d Ayr. **Dumfries**  is also "the Queen of the South", ·· ancient and important Border town whose character ·rvives the unsightly housing estates and factories on ·ɪ periphery, and which is within easy reach of the ·unting, history-rich Solway coast. Burns, the farmer·>et, took over Ellisland Farm some 6 miles (10 km) ·ɪtside the town in 1788, built the farmhouse and tried introduce new farming methods. His venture col·ɪsed and he moved to Dumfries to become an excise·an, but **Ellisland** (open Apr–Sept Mon–Fri and Sun ·ɪn; Oct–Mar Tues–Sat; tel: (01387) 740426; admis·ɪn charge), where he wrote *Tam o'Shanter* and *Auld ·ing Syne,* is now a museum – as is **Burns House** in ·ill Vennel (now Burns Street), Dumfries, where he ·ed in 1796 (open Apr–Sept Mon–Sat and Sun pm; ·ɪt–Mar Tues–Sat; tel: (01387) 255297; free).

To bring it all together, visit the stone mill on the ·ɪver Nith. This is home to the **Robert Burns Centre**

**TIP**

End your tour of Burns country with a drink at the Globe Inn (est. 1610) in Dumfries, where you can sit in the poet's favourite chair.

(open Apr–Sept Mon–Sat and Sun pm; Oct–Mar Tues–Sat; tel: (01387) 2648C admission charge), the major feature of VisitScotland's Burns Heritage Trail.

The handsome waterfront of the **River Nith,** with its 15th-century bridge, ai the red sandstone dignity of nearby **St Michael's Church**, in whose churchya Burns is buried, give Dumfries its distinctive character. Its environs have ju as much to offer. On opposing banks of the Nith estuary, where it debouch into the Solway, are **Caerlaverock Castle** (open daily Oct–Mar closed Sun a tel: (01387) 770244; admission charge), the **Wildfowl and Wetlands Tru Reserve** (open daily; tel: (01387) 770200) – a winter haunt of wildfowl – a **Sweetheart Abbey** (open Apr–Sept Mon–Sat and Sun pm; Oct–Mar clos Thur pm, Fri and Sun am; tel: (0131) 668 8800; admission charge).

The castle is strikingly well preserved, dates back to the 13th century and w the seat of the Maxwell family, later Earls of Nithsdale – one of the most po' erful local dynasties. It was besieged by Edward I during the Wars of Indepe dence and in 1640 fell to a 13-week siege mounted by the Covenanters. Tl graceful ruin of Sweetheart Abbey, in the pretty village of New Abbey, is a mo ument to the marital devotion of the noble Devorgilla Balliol, who not on founded this Cistercian abbey in 1273 but founded Balliol College, Oxford, memory of her husband. She also carried his heart around her until her own dea in 1290, when she and the heart were buried together in front of the high alta

The shallow estuary of the Solway is noted for the speed of its tidal race a the treachery of its sands, but the hazardous areas are well signposted, and you follow the coastal roads from River Nith to **Loch Ryan** you will find amiable succession of villages, yachting harbours, attractive small towns a good beaches, not to mention many secret coves and snug, deserted little ba

**BELOW:** sculptures by Rodin (left) and Henry Moore (right) gaze from Shawhead towards nearby Dumfries.

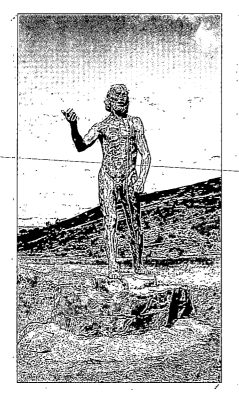

# Ancient Galloway

This is the ancient territory of Galloway, whose people once fraternised with Norse raiders and whose lords preserved a degree of independence from the Scottish crown until the 13th century. Many of Scotland's great names and great houses have seen action among these hills and bays. At **Dundrennan Abbey**  (open Apr–Sept Mon–Sun; tel: (01557) 500 262; admission charge), 7 miles (11 km) southeast of Kirkcudbright on the A711, Mary Queen of Scots is believed to have spent her last night in Scotland, on 15 May 1568, sheltering in this 12th-century Cistercian house on her final, fatal flight from the Battle of Langside to her long imprisonment in England.

**Kirkcudbright** ⓲ (pronounced *Kir-koo-bree*), at the mouth of the River Dee, has the reputation of being the most attractive of the Solway towns, with a colourful waterfront (much appreciated and colonised by artists) and an elegant Georgian town centre. Little remains of the Kirkcudbright which took its name from the vanished Kirk of Cuthbert, but it has a **Market Cross** of 1610 and a Tolbooth from the same period. **Broughton House** (open Easter–Oct daily pm; tel: (01557) 330437; admission charge) in Kirkcudbright was the home of E.A. Hornel, one of the Glasgow Boys, and has a major gallery of his paintings. Don't miss the wonderful Japanese-style garden, inspired by his visit to Japan in 1893.

Ten miles (16 km) northeast from Kirkcudbright is another neat and dignified little town, **Castle Douglas** ⓳, on the small loch of Carlingwark, where you will find a formidable tower stronghold. **Threave Castle** (open Apr–Sept: Mon–Sun; tel: (07711) 223101; admission charge) was built towards the end of the 14th century by the wonderfully named Archibald the Grim, third Earl of Douglas. It was the last Douglas castle to surrender to James II during the con-

*The Tolbooth at Kirkcudbright once entertained John Paul Jones, who was imprisoned for the manslaughter of his ship's carpenter. Jones restored his reputation in later life by laying the foundations of the American navy.*

**BELOW:**
Threave castle.

*Castle Douglas serves as market centre to a large tract of Galloway's rich hinterland, giving it some of the best food shops in the south of Scotland – particularly butchers.*

flict between the king and the maverick Border family. It also has associatio; with the Covenanters, who seized it in 1640 and vandalised the interior. **Threa' Garden** (open daily; tel: (01556) 502575; admission charge) has superb flow€ plant and tree displays all year.

## Villages of Galloway

In Galloway you will find villages unusually pretty for a country which isr famous for the aesthetics of its small communities. Their characteristic featu· is whitewashed walls with black-bordered doors and windows – as if they ha· taken their colour scheme from the black and white Belted Galloway cattle.

Many of the most pleasant villages – **New Galloway, Balmaclellan, Cros: michael** – are in the region of long, skinny **Loch Ken**, which feeds the Riv Dee; while to the west, shrouding the hills to the very shoulders of the isolat€ **Rhinns of Kells**, a tableland of hills around 2,600 ft (800 metres), is the massi• Galloway Forest Park, 150,000 acres (60,000 hectares) criss-crossed by Forest· Commission walking and mountain-biking trails and the Southern Upland W;

Amongst the trees you can find **Clatteringshaws Loch** , 12 miles (19 k)· northeast of Newton Stewart (a "planned town" built in the late 17th century i• a son of the Earl of Galloway) on the A712, which is the site of the **Clatterin▸ shaws Forest Wildlife Centre** (open Easter–Oct daily; tel: (01671) 40242 free) and a fascinating introduction to the range of the area's natural history.

Nearby, **Bruce's Stone** represents the site of the Battle of Rapploch Moss minor affair of 1307 but one in which the energetic Robert the Bruce routed t: English. There are, in fact, two Bruce's Stones in **Galloway Forest Park**, whi· creeps within reach of the coast at Turnberry, where he may have been born. T: second stone – reached only if one backtracks from Ne· ton Stewart and then travels northwest for 10 miles ( km) on the A714 before taking an unmarked road to t: east – is poised on a bluff above Loch Trool and reca▸ those hefted down the hill by the hero in another su▸ cessful wrangle with the English. About 4 miles (6.5 k)▸ away is a sombre landmark: the **Memorial Tomb** of ε Covenanters murdered at prayer. It is a simple sto· which records their names and the names of their kille:

## Saints and stones

Back on the coast, the A75 between benign **Gatehou▸ of Fleet** and **Creetown**, which hugs the sea below t' comely outriders of the distinctive hill **Cairnsmore Fleet**, was said by Thomas Carlyle to be the most bea▸ tiful road in Scotland. It has good views across **Wigtov Bay** to the flat green shelf which was the cradle of Sc( tish Christianity. The **Creetown Gem Rock Museu▸** (open Mar–Sept daily; tel: (01671) 820357; admissi• charge) has a wide range of precious stones on displa:

On the other side of the bay is the pleasant town **Wigtown** , whose **Martyrs' Monument** is one of ▸ most eloquent testaments to the Covenanters, who we heroically supported in the Southwest – the site of ▸ stake where in 1685 two women, one elderly and o· young, were left to drown on the estuary flats.

On the promontory south of Wigtown, the co; becomes harsher and the villages bleaker, as if it inde

pages
180-1

quired the gentling influence of Christianity. **Whithorn**  is the birthplace of ·ristianity in Scotland, and the **Whithorn Story Visitor Centre** (open Apr–Oct ·ily; tel: (01988) 500508; admission charge), in the town centre, is on the site of ·e first known Christian church in Britain, built by St Ninian around the year 400. ·ext to the Centre is the **Priory** where Mary Queen of Scots once stayed. Here ·u will find the Latinus Stone of 450, the earliest Christian memorial in Scot-nd, as well as a significant collection of early Christian crosses and stones.

Four miles (6 km) away is the misnamed **Isle of Whithorn**, a delightful town ·ilt around a busy yachting harbour and with more St Ninian connections: there the ruined **St Ninian's Chapel**, which dates from 1300 and may have been ·ed by overseas pilgrims, and along the coast is **St Ninian's Cave**, said to have ·en used by the saint as an oratory.

A little inland from the undistinguished shoreline of Luce Bay, playground the Ministry of Defence, are some relics of the Iron Age and Bronze Age, ·cluding **Torhouse Stone Circle**, a ring of 19 boulders standing on a low ·ound. The most impressive sight in this corner, however, is **Glenluce Abbey**  pen Apr–Sept Mon–Sat and Sun pm, Oct–Mar Sat, Sun pm; tel: 01581 ·0541; admission charge), a handsome vaulted ruin of the 12th century.

From Glenluce the traveller crosses the "handle" of that hammer of land called ·e **Rhinns of Galloway**, the southwest extremity of Scotland terminating in ·e 200-ft (60-metre) high cliffs of the Mull of Galloway, from which Ireland ·ems within touching distance. At the head of the deep cleft of **Loch Ryan** is the ·rt of **Stranraer** , market centre for the rich agricultural area, modest holi-·y resort and Scotland's main seaway to Northern Ireland. The Rhinns' other ·ain resort is **Portpatrick** , and among the somewhat limited attractions of

**TIP**

Portpatrick is the start of the Southern Upland Way, a coast-to-coast route across southern Scotland which runs for 212 miles (340 km) to Cockburnspath on the Berwickshire coast.

**BELOW:** cattle auction at Newton Stewart, a busy market town in Wigtownshire.

# The Ploughman Poet

Few poets could hope to have their birthday celebrated in the most unexpected parts of the world 200 years after their death. Yet the observance of Burns Night, on 25 January, goes from strength to strength. It marks the birth in 1759 of Scotland's national poet, Robert Burns, one of seven children born to a poor Ayrshire farmer. It was an unpromising beginning, yet today Burns's verses are familiar in every English-speaking country and are especially popular in Russia, where Burns Night is toasted with vodka. Millions who have never heard of Burns have joined hands and sung his words to the tune of that international anthem of good intentions, *Auld Lang Syne* (dialect for "old long ago"):

> *Should auld acquaintance be forgot,*
> *And never brought to mind?*
> *Should auld acquaintance be forgot,*
> *And days o' auld lang syne?*

This was one of many traditional Scottish songs which he collected and rewrote, in addition to his original poetry. He could and did write easily in 18th-century English as well as in traditional Scots dialect (which, even in those days, had to be accompanied by a glossary). His subjects ranged from love songs (*Oh, my luve's like a red, red rose*) and sympathy for a startled fieldmouse (*Wee, sleekit, cowrin', tim'rous beastie*) to a stirring sense of Scottishness (*Scots, wha hae wi' Wallace bled*) and a simple celebration of the common people (*A man's a man for a' that*).

The key to Burns's high standing in Scotland is that, like Sir Walter Scott, he promoted the idea of Scottish nationhood at a time when it was in danger of being obliterated by the English. His acceptance abroad, especially in Russia, stems from his championing of the rights of ordinary people and his satirical attack on double standards in Church and state.

An attractive and gregarious youth, Burns had a long series of amorous entanglements and, once famous, took full advantage of his acceptance into Edinburgh's high society. Finally, he married Jean Armour, from his own village, and settled on a poor farm at Ellisland, near Dumfries. No more able than his father to make a decent living from farming, he moved to Dumfries in 1791 to work as an excise officer. It was a secure job, and riding 200 miles (320 km) a week on horseback around the countryside on his duties gave him time and inspiration to compose prolifically. His affairs continued: the niece of a Dumfries innkeeper became pregnant, but died during childbirth. Four years later, in 1796, Burns too was dead, of rheumatic heart disease. He was 37.

The 612 copies of his first edition of 34 poems sold in Kilmarnock in 1786 for three shillings (15p); today each will fetch £10,000. Almost 100,000 people in over 20 countries belong to Burns clubs, and the poet's popularity embraces the unlikeliest locations. The story is told, for example, of a black gentleman who rose to propose a toast at a Burns Night supper in Fiji. "You may be surprised to learn that Scottish blood flows in my veins," he declared. "But it is true. One of my ancestors ate a Presbyterian missionary." ❏

**LEFT:** Burns, pictured at Alloway.

remote peninsula are two horticultural ones: the subtropical plants of **Logan Botanic Garden**  (open Mar–Oct: daily: tel: (01776) 860231) and the great monkey puzzle trees of **Castle Kennedy Gardens**, near Stranraer (open Apr–Sept daily; tel: (01776) 702024; admission charge).

Stranraer's trunk roads are the A75, infamous for the volume of heavy traffic disembarking from the ferries from Ireland, which strikes east to Dumfries and points south and blights Thomas Carlyle's "loveliest stretch" between Creetown and Gatehouse of Fleet; and the A77, which conducts you north past the cliffs of **Ballantrae** (*not* the Ballantrae of R.L. Stevenson's novel) to the mixed pleasures of Ayrshire and, ultimately, the edge of the Glasgow conurbation.

En route is the pleasant resort of **Girvan** ㉗, first of a series of resorts interspersed with ports and industrial towns, which stretches to the mouth of the Clyde. About 10 miles (16 km) offshore is a chunky granite monolith over 1,000 (300 metres) high – the uninhabited island of **Ailsa Craig**, sometimes called Paddy's Milestone for its central position between Belfast and Glasgow.

Here, too, you begin to see more clearly the mountains of Arran and the lower line of the Kintyre peninsula, while at **Turnberry**, a mecca for golfers and site of some fragments of castle which promotes itself as the birthplace of Robert the Bruce, there is a choice of roads to Ayr.

## Approaching Ayr

The coast road (A719) invites you to one of the non-Burnsian showpieces of Ayrshire – **Culzean Castle** ㉘ (castle open Mar–Oct daily; admission charge; country park daily all year; tel: (0870) 118 1945), magnificently designed by Robert Adam and built between 1772 and 1792 for the Kennedy family. Now owned by

*Transatlantic visitors are entertained at Culzean Castle by the Eisenhower Presentation, which recalls the flat given to the General for his private use.*

**BELOW:** Burns characters at Souter Johnnie's Cottage.

*According to Burns, Ayr was unsurpassed "for honest men and bonnie lasses".*

the National Trust for Scotland, it has a country park of 560 acres (226 hectar»
– the first in Scotland. A few miles beyond Culzean the road entertains driv
at the **Electric Brae**, where an optical illusion suggests you are going downl
rather than up.

The inland road (A77) takes you through **Kirkoswald** , where Burns w«
to school, and the first of the cluster of Burns shrines and museums: **Sou»
Johnnie's Cottage** (open Mar–Oct daily; tel: (01655) 760603; admissi»
charge), once the home of the cobbler who was the original Souter Johnnie
*Tam O'Shanter*. The B7024 then leads to the Mecca of Burns pilgrims, the ν
lage of **Alloway**, where he was born. Here, within the Burns National Herita
Park (tel: (01292) 443700), you can visit: **Burns Cottage** (open daily; admissi»
charge), **Alloway Kirk** (where his father is buried and which features in *Tε
O'Shanter*), the pretentious **Burns Monument** (a neoclassical temple) and »
13th-century **Brig o' Doon**, whose single span permitted Tam o' Shanter
escape from the witches. There's also the Burns Museum (open as cottage) a»
the audio-visual **Tam O'Shanter Experience** (open daily; admission char;
www.burnsheritagepark.com).

You are now on the doorstep of **Ayr** ⑳, a bustling resort associated not o»
with Burns but also with the warrior-patriot William Wallace, who is though»
have been born in **Elderslie**, near Paisley, and who was once imprisoned in A
Inland from Ayr, to the west and north, is another clutch of Burns associatio·
the village of **Mauchline** ⑳, where he married Jean Armour and where their c
tage is now yet another museum (open Easter–Oct Tues–Sat and Sun pm; »
(01290) 550045; admission charge), and **Poosie Nansie's Tavern** (still a p»
which inspired part of his cantata *The Jolly Beggars*. Nearby at **Failford** is Hi»
land Mary's Monument, which allegedly marks the s»
where Burns said farewell to his doomed fiancée M
Campbell; and then there is the sprawling town of **K·
marnock**, where the first edition of his poems was p»
lished in 1786. A hundred years later the town bui»
monument in his honour.

## Coasts and islands

The A77 from Kilmarnock – that road which began »
in Stranraer – takes you straight to the heart of Glasgc
But, if you are island or Highland bound, you shoι·
return to the coast. Between the industrial port and ·
shipbuilding town of Greenock, are various ferry poi»
for the Cowal peninsula and Clyde islands. **Irvine**
is the home of the **Scottish Maritime Museum** (oμ
daily; tel: (01294) 278283; admission charge;). Visit·
can board various lovingly restored vessels, includ;
the steam yacht *Carola*, tour a shipyard worker's ter
ment flat restored to its 1920s appearance, peruse »
exhibition and drink a coffee in the Puffer Bar. Nea»
is the **Magnum Centre**, one of Scotland's larg
leisure centres – south of Irvine are two golfing reso»
**Troon** and **Prestwick**.

**Ardrossan** serves the island of **Arran** ㉝, the ferr
disembarking passengers and cars at **Brodick**, the c;
ital. Arran is popular with walkers and climbers (»
sharp profile of the Arran ridge, which reaches 2,866·
874 metres at the rocky summit of Goatfell, provi«

**BELOW:** Brodick
Castle on Arran.

ining views). Yet the 2-mile (3-km) walk from Brodick's attractive harbour ·rodick Castle is congenial and effortless. The castle (open Easter–Oct daily; ntry park open daily all year; tel: (01770) 302202; admission charge), parts /hich date from the 14th century, is the ancient seat of the Dukes of Hamil- It contains various paintings and objets d'art from the collections of the es. There is an excellent tearoom serving traditional food.

rran's other main villages are **Lochranza, Blackwaterfoot, Whiting Bay** Lamlash, where a precipitous offshore island spans the mouth of Lamlash . **Holy Island** owes its name to St Molaise, who lived and meditated in a ₂ on its west coast. It is now a Buddhist retreat.

he other Clyde islands regularly served by ferry are **Bute** *(see box below)*, ₁ its attractive, ancient capital of **Rothesay**, once the premier destination for trippers on the Clyde paddle-steamers which took Glasgwegians "doon the ter" from the heart of their city, and **Great Cumbrae**, with the family resort **fillport**. The amiable little island of Great Cumbrae is reached from **Largs ㉞**, most handsome of the Clyde resorts and the scene, in 1263, of a battle which clusively repelled persistent Viking attempts to invade Scotland. The **ingar!** centre (open daily; tel: (01475) 689777; admission charge) dramat- ily traces the history of the Vikings in Scotland. The ferry crossing to Bute om **Wemyss Bay**, between Largs and Gourock. From Gourock you can also cd a ferry for Dunoon and the Cowal peninsula.

*The woodland garden of Brodick Castle is justly claimed to be one of the finest rhododendron gardens in Britain.*

## :aping the city

many people in West Central Scotland, the Cowal peninsula represents High- l escapism. It has a new population of second home-owners from the Glas-

**BELOW:** on Arran, a ruined 12th-century castle stands in picturesque Lochranza

## E ISLAND OF BUTE

ute is a comely island, especially at its northern end where the narrow Kyles of . almost close the gap with the Cowal insula (ferry). Rothesay, Bute's capital, is yal burgh which gives the title of duke e Prince of Wales. Its unusual moated ·:d castle with four round towers dates back to the early 13th ury, when it was stormed by Norsemen, soon to be routed at s. Its Winter Gardens and elegant promenade are especially ·/ in summer, despite the rise of package holidays to the ·terranean and further afield. It's worth spending a penny to he elegantly restored Victorian public toilets at the pierhead. **lount Stuart** (open May–Sept Sun–Fri and Sat until pm; tel: 01700 503877; admission charge) 3 miles (5 km) h of Rothesay, is an astonishing Gothic fantasy pile, with orous details. It reflects the 3rd Marquis of Bute's fascina- with astrology, mythology and religion. Its extensive nds are enchanting and boast a stylish visitors' centre. ne island's beaches and scenery still attract many visitors. ·lar areas are Ettrick Bay and Kilchattan Bay, two sandy hes on the east of the island. However, it's easy to leave rowd behind and escape to the green hills. The view from ada Hill once won the award for the best view in Britain.

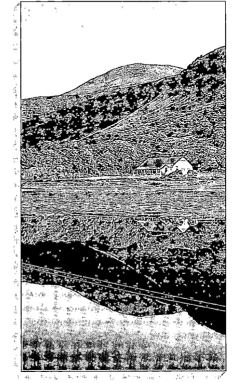

*The Grey Mare's Tail waterfall near Moffat drops 200 ft (60 metres) from a hanging valley.*

**BELOW:** looking out over Dalveen Pass.

gow conurbation, which makes it busy during weekends and holidays, des the time it takes to negotiate its long fissures of sea-lochs (**Loch Fyne** to west and **Loch Long** to the east, with several others in between). **Dunoon** is its capital, another ancient township turned holiday resort with another 1: century castle, of which only remnants remain on **Castle Hill**, where you again meet Highland Mary.

East of Gare Loch (not to be confused with Gairloch in the northwest), the Cl begins to be compressed between the once-great shipbuilding banks of **Cly side**, with the first of its resort towns on the north bank at **Helensburgh ㉞**, a stately dormitory for Glasgow. Those smitten with "Mackintoshismus" wish to visit here the **Hill House** (open Easter–Oct daily pm; restricted at p times; tel: (01436) 673900; admission charge), Charles Rennie Mackinto: finest domestic commission. Industrial **Dumbarton ㉟** is even closer to the and its name confirms it has been there since the days of the Britons. Its s[ tacular lump of rock was their fort, and supports a 13th-century castle wh has close connections with – inevitably – Mary Queen of Scots.

## Hidden treasures

The eastern edge of Southwest Scotland is dominated by the M74, the fren: highway which is Glasgow's access to the Borders and England. It car through some of the shapeliest hills in Scotland, with some lovely, lonely pl: and unexpected treasures tucked away in their folds.

A brief detour will bring you to **Moffat ㉟**, an elegant former spa town the broadest main street in Scotland. Northwest of Moffat is the **Devil's B Tub**, a vast, steep, natural vat in the hills where Border raiders used to hide st: cattle. Northeast of Moffat on the A708 is the specta lar **Grey Mare's Tail ㊱** waterfall. Further north is **1** **bie Sheil's Inn**, the meeting place of the circle of wr James Hogg (the "Ettrick Shepherd").

On either side of the M74, a few miles driving take you to the highest villages in Scotland: **Leadh** and **Wanlockhead**. Once centres of mining, an ide: their past can be seen at the **Wanlockhead Museum Lead Mining** (open Easter–Oct daily; tel: (016 74387; admission charge). Here, too, are Drumla: Castle, the historic market town of Lanark and the l orchards and dramatic falls of the River Clyde.

**Drumlanrig Castle and Country Park ㊵** (o] daily May–mid-Aug; tel: (01848) 330248; admiss charge) is reached by descending the precipit: **Dalveen Pass**, a natural stairway between the upla: of South Lanarkshire and the rolling pastures and wo land of Dumfriesshire. It is a palace of pink sandst: fashioned in late 17th-century Renaissance style on site of an earlier Douglas stronghold and near a Ror fort. Its rich collection of French furniture and Dt paintings (Holbein and Rembrandt are represent: includes interesting relics of Bonnie Prince Charlie

The A73 to **Lanark** skirts **Tinto Hill**, the high peak in Lanarkshire and the site of Druidic festival: is much climbed and much loved by Lanarksh schoolchildren who traditionally carry stones to ad its enormous cairn.

**Biggar ④** is a lively little town, with museums focusing on local history as if defiance of the greater celebrity of its big neighbour, **Lanark**. The high, handsome old Royal burgh was already important in the 10th century, when a parliament was held there, but is more closely identified with William Wallace. It is said that he hid in a cave in the Cartland Craigs, just below the town, after killing an English soldier in a brawl.

Lanark was also a Convenanting centre and is still a place of great character, much of it due to its weekly livestock market and the steep fall of the Clyde below the town at **New Lanark ④**, Scotland's most impressive memorial to the Industrial Revolution, which has been honoured as a World Heritage Site. Here, between 1821 and 1824, a cotton spinning village became the scene of a pioneering social and educational experiment of Robert Owen. The old, handsome buildings have been brought back to life and feature an imaginative **Visitor Centre** (open daily; tel: (01555) 661345; admission charge) and working models.

Nearby, the cataracts of the **Falls of Clyde Nature Reserve** are the preface to one of the river's prettiest passages, its last Arcadian fling among the orchards and market gardens of Kirkfieldbank, Hazlebank and Rosebank before it reaches the industrial heartland of North Lanarkshire.

Near one of those pastoral villages, **Crossford**, is one of Scotland's best-preserved medieval castles. **Craignethan Castle** (open Apr–Sept daily; tel: (01555) 860364; admission charge), was built between the 15th and 16th centuries on a site above a wooded pass 2 miles (3 km) from the Clyde, and was a stronghold of the Hamiltons, friends of Mary Queen of Scots. It has well authenticated claims to be the original Tillietudlem in Sir Walter Scott's *Old Mortality*. ❏

*The first Duke of Queensberry, for whom Drumlanrig Castle was built, was so horrified by its cost that he spent only one night in it.*

**BELOW:** New Lanark: memories of old industries.

# FORTH AND CLYDE

*Standing strategically as the gateway to the Highlands, the ancient town of Stirling is a focal point for any visit to Central Scotland and the waterways of the Forth and Clyde*

or centuries, Stirling's Old Bridge has given access to the north across the lowest bridging point of the River Forth, while the 250-ft (75-metre) volcanic plug which supports its castle was the natural fortress which made rling ⑬ significant from the 12th century onwards. The **Castle** (open daily; : (01786) 450000; admission charge) – every bit as impressive as Edinburgh stle – was the favourite residence of the Stuart monarchy and is one of Scot- d's renaissance glories. Nearby is the **Royal Burgh of Stirling Visitor Cen-** (open daily; tel: (01786) 479901; free), which vividly describes the long tory of the castle and town.

## roes of the past

achievements of both Wallace and Bruce are recalled around Stirling. On the k of **Abbey Craig**, above the site where Wallace camped, is the ostentatious **allace Monument** (open daily; tel: (01786) 472140), home of the hero's two- ided sword. From its elevation at the top of 246 spiral steps, you can see the ping ramparts of the **Ochil Hills**, while to the southeast the Forth spreads oss its flat plain to the spectacular flare-stacks of **Grangemouth**.

The site of the Battle of Bannockburn, a few miles south of Stirling, has been re or less consumed by a housing estate. No one is cisely sure where the battle was fought, but the inda beside the heroic bronze equestrian statue of ice is said to mark his command post. The **Ban- ckburn Heritage Centre** (open daily; tel: (01786) 2664; admission charge) gives an audio-visual ount of the matter. Also close to Stirling is the **Alloa wer** (open Apr–Oct daily pm; tel: (01259) 211701; nission charge), the superbly restored former home he Earls of Mar, built in the late 15th century with ngeon, medieval timber roof and an impressive ftop parapet walk with fine views.

**PRECEDING PAGES:**
New Lanark World
Heritage Village.
**LEFT:** the Forth
Railway Bridge.
**BELOW:** the Wallace
Monument, Stirling.

Stirling is almost equidistant from Edinburgh and isgow. If you take the M9 to Edinburgh, you stay ighly parallel to the broadening course of the Forth. ere are rewarding diversions to be made on this route. t outside Falkirk is the **Falkirk Wheel** (open daily 0am–6pm, tel: 08700 500 208; admission charge). ened in June 2002, this spectacular feat of engineering i unique rotating boatlift that carries boats between Forth & Clyde and Union canals *(see picture on ges 54–5)*. Visitors can see the lift in action and take ide on amphibious trip boats. Also near Falkirk are r good sections of the **Roman Antonine Wall** ⑭, ich the Emperor Antoninus Pius had built between the ths of Clyde and Forth around AD 140; while the torway itself has opened up a distracting view of the h and the late 15th-century **Linlithgow Palace** ⑮

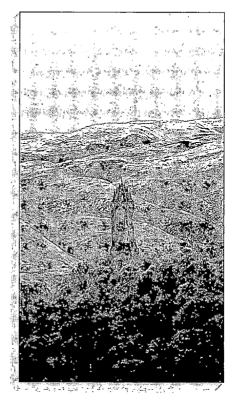

*Adjacent to the palace of Linlithgow is the Church of St Michael, Scotland's largest pre-Reformation parish church; the abstract golden crown was mounted on its tower in 1964.*

(open daily; tel: (01506) 842896; admission charge), the well-preserved ruins Scotland's most magnificent palace and birthplace of Mary Queen of Scots.

From the M9, you can also visit the village of **South Queensferry** on southern bank of one of the Forth's oldest crossings, where river becomes es ary. Until the **Forth Road Bridge** was built, ferries had plied between Sov and North Queensferry for 900 years. Today, South Queensferry hudd between and beneath the giant bridges which provide such a spectacular co trast in engineering design – the massive humped girders of the 1890 rail brid and the delicate, graceful span of the suspension bridge, opened in 1964.

At South Queensferry, you can take a boat excursion to the island of Inc **colm** in the Forth and visit the ruined abbey (open Mar–Sept Mon–Sat and S pm; tel: (0131) 668 8800), monastic buildings and gardens. Cross the Fo Road Bridge or take the train to North Queensferry to visit the huge aquariun **Deep Sea World** (open daily; tel: (01383) 411411; admission charge).

Near South Queensferry are **Hopetoun House** (open Easter–Oct daily; ▶ (0131) 331 2451; admission charge;), home of the Earls of Hopetoun, magn icently situated in parkland beside the Forth and splendidly extended by Willi; Adam and his son John between 1721 and 1754; and **Dalmeny House** (op July and Aug Mon, Tues and Sun pm; tel: (0131) 331 1888; admission charg home of the Earls of Rosebery and a fine collection of paintings.

## The Forth and Clyde

You can walk beside the Forth through the wooded Rosebery estate to the **Riv Almond,** where a little rowing-boat ferry transports you across this minor tr utary to the red pantiles and white crowstep gables of **Cramond** . Still v

## STIRLING CASTLE

The impressive bulk of Stirling Castle was a formidable cʜ lenge to any invaders. It had its most active moments d ing Scotland's Wars of Independence: surrendered to the Eng in 1296, it was recaptured by the warrior-patriot William Wall after the Battle of Stirling Bridge (not today's stone bridge, b around 1400, but a wooden structure). It became the last stro hold in Scotland to hold out against Edward I, the "Hamme the Scots". Eventually, it went back to the English for 10 yea until Robert the Bruce retook it in 1314 after the Battle of B nockburn, which decisively secured Scotland's independenc

The Stuarts favoured Stirling Castle as a royal resider James II and V were born in it, Mary Queen of Scots was crow there at the age of nine months, and its splendid collectio buildings reflects its history as palace and fortress. Perhaps most striking feature is the exterior façade, with ornate stonew which was largely cut by French craftsmen. The Great Hall Parliament House (so called because before 1707 this was on the seats of the Scottish Parliament), also has exquisite carv and tracery, which has recently been carefully reconstructe programme of major restoration has also included the kitchen the castle, which now recreate the preparations for a sumpti Renaissance banquet given by Mary Queen of Scots for the b tism of her son, the future James VI.

ıch its own 18th-century village, Cramond has a harbour which was used by ː Romans. Its **Roman Fort**, whose foundations have been exposed, was built ɔund AD 142, and may have been used by Septimius Severus.

Scotland's pre-eminent river, the **Clyde**, undergoes more personality changes ın any other in its progress to the western seaboard. The limpid little stream, ᴧich has its source 80 miles (130 km) southeast of Glasgow, moves prettily ᵊough the orchards and market gardens of Clydesdale before watering the lustries of North Lanarkshire and welcoming the ships and shipyards of Glas- w. The lower reaches of its valley have been colonised by the city's satellites, d by a clutter of hill towns: Wishaw, Motherwell and Hamilton.

ᴑOnce drab coal and steel towns, they are attempting to recover their dignity d vitality: witness the creation of **Strathclyde Country Park**, a huge recre- onal area with a 200-acre (80-hectare) loch, formed by diverting the Clyde, d subsuming part of the old estate of the Dukes of Hamilton. **Hamilton ㊽** s associations with Mary Queen of Scots, Cromwell and the Covenanters, ᴑo were defeated by Monmouth at nearby Bothwell Bridge in 1679. Immedi- ᴅly south of Hamilton is **Chatelherault** (visitor centre open daily; lodge closed ᵻ; tel: (01698) 426213; free), a glorious restored hunting lodge and kennels ᴧlt in 1732 for the Duke of Hamilton by William Adam.

*Most of the original 18th-century furni- ture and wall-cover- ings can still be seen at Hopetoun House.*

ᴮothwell Castle** (open Apr–Sept daily, Oct–Mar Sat–Wed 9.30am–5.30pm d Sun pm; tel: (01698) 816894; admission charge), perhaps the finest 13th- ntury castle in Scotland, was fought over by the Scots and English. Memories more recent times can be found in adjacent **Blantyre ㊾**, birthplace of explorer ːvid Livingstone, whose life is recalled at the **David Livingstone Centre** (open ɔn–Sat and Sun pm; tel: (01698) 823140; admission charge). ❑

**BELOW:** Bothwell Castle: Scotland's finest 13th-century stronghold.

# THE WEST COAST

*Mountain and moor, heather and stag, castle and loch – and a magical seaboard of isolated villages and small ports – are all to be found on the glorious west coast of Scotland*

Map page 220

From the long finger of Kintyre to the deep fissure of Loch Broom, the west coast is that part of Scotland which most perfectly conforms to its romantic image. Nowhere else in Scotland (outside Caithness and Sutherland) is physical sense of travelling more thrillingly experienced; and few other areas provide such opportunities for solitude and repose, as well as the slightly awesome impression that this dramatic landscape is not to be trifled with.

It all begins gently enough at the Clyde estuary, where the deep penetration of sea at **Loch Fyne** has created Scotland's longest peninsula, which is 54 miles (km) from Crinan to the Mull of Kintyre and never wider than 10 miles (16 ). This mighty arm is nearly bisected by West Loch Tarbert into the two ions of Knapdale and Kintyre, and its isolated character makes it almost as note as any of the islands.

Here there are rolling hills rather than mountains, rough moors and forests in apdale, grassy tops in Kintyre and a coast which is most interesting on its st side, with a close view of the island of Jura from **Kilberry Head**  (where u can also view a fine collection of medieval sculptured stones). **Tarbert** ❷ a popular port with yachties. Once a thriving herring fishing base, it's now annual host of dozens of yachts during May's Bell Laurie Scottish Sailing ries. There are several cosy pubs, and for accommodation, seek out the tourist office by the harbourside.

Further south is **Tayinloan** ❸, from where you can e the 20-minute ferry ride across to the tiny island of gha, noted for the fine **Achamore Gardens**, and ith again is the vast beach of **Machrihanish** ❹. Few ve kind words for the Kintyre "metropolis" of **Campltown**. However, from here it is only a short drive to tip of the peninsula, the **Mull of Kintyre** itself (now RSPB bird reserve). The Northern Ireland coast is only miles (19km) away, and legend has it that St lumba first set foot in Scotland at **Keil** ❺, near the liday village of Southend. You can see his "footnts" imprinted on a flat rock near a ruined chapel.

## enic drama

m the great lighthouse on the Mull, first built in 1788 d remodelled by Robert Stevenson, grandfather of bert Louis, there is nowhere else to go. You can reat back up the secondary road (B842) of Kintyre's t coast, which has its own scenic drama in the sandy eep of **Carradale Bay** and the view across the water the mountains of Arran, reached by car ferry from aonaig. The hump behind Carradale is **Beinn an irc**, Kintyre's highest hill (1,490 ft/447 metres). The ne means Mountain of the Boar, from a fearsome cimen said to have been killed by an ancestor of the mpbells. You can take in the ruined walls and sculp-

**PRECEDING PAGES:** Rannoch Moor. **LEFT:** Glenfinnan railway station. **BELOW:** in the cab of the Jacobite Steam Train.

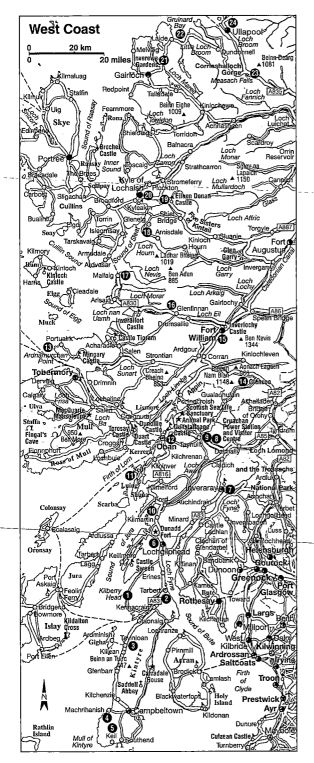

West Coast

tured tombstones of **Saddell Abbey**, 12th-century Cistercian house, and **Sk**ness Castle and Chapel.

From **Lochgilphead** ❻ – close where, at Ardrishaig, the 9-mile (15-k) Crinan Canal crosses the neck of peninsula and connects Loch Fyne to Atlantic Ocean – you have a choice of t main routes to the handsome port and resort of Oban. The longer route, up Lo Fyne by Inveraray to Loch Awe (A83 then A819) is the more dramatic, althou the shorter route (A816) keeps you close to the coast and its vistas of those lo lying islands, which are the floating o riders of the mountains of Jura and Mu

## Past communities

Both routes are punctuated by places interest. The most celebrated castle the area is **Inveraray** ❼ (Apr–O Mon–Sat and Sun pm; tel: (0149 302203; admission charge), the seat the chiefs of Clan Campbell, the Duk of Argyll, for centuries. The prese building – Gothic Revival, famous for magnificent interiors and art collection was started in 1743, when the 3rd Du also decided to rebuild the village Inveraray. The result is a dignified co munity with much of the orderly e gance of the 18th century. By means wax figures, commentary and imagin tive displays, **Inveraray Jail** (op daily; tel: (01499) 302381; admissi charge) brings to life a courtroom tr and life in the cells in the 19th century

Two very different museums call fo visit. Moored at the pier in Inveraray the 1910-built *Arctic Penguin*, a form lightship packed with seafaring exhib and now managed by the **Inverar Maritime Museum** (open dai Apr–Sept; admission charge). Som miles (8 km) south is **Auchindra Township Museum** (open Apr–Se daily; tel: (01499) 500235; admissi charge), whose dwellings and barns the 18th and 19th centuries were onc communal-tenancy Highland farm, pa ing rent to the Duke.

Between the two is the **Argyll WildN Park** (open Mar–Oct daily; tel (0149)

Map opposite

2264; admission charge), an extensive area of woodland, grassland and ponds h a wide variety of mammals and birdlife, and popular with children.

.och Awe, where the road takes you past the fallen house of the Breadalbane 1asty – the romantic ruin of **Kilchurn Castle** (contact Loch Awe boats; tel: 866) 833256) on a promontory on the water – is the longest freshwater loch 5cotland. At its northwest extremity, where it squeezes past the mighty moun- 1 of Ben Cruachan and drains into Loch Etive through the dark slit of the Pass Brander, it's as awesome as its name promises. Almost a mile inside Ben Cru- ▲an is the **Cruachan pumped storage generating station ❽**, an artificial ∕ern you can view on a bus trip from the lochside visitor centre (open r–Nov daily; tel: (01866) 822618; admission charge).

*The Pass of Brander is so steep and narrow that legend claims it was once held against an army by an old woman wielding a scythe.*

The road continues through **Taynuilt ❾**, a village of more than passing interest. e of the earliest monuments to Nelson was erected here when locals dragged an ;ient standing stone into the village and carved an inscription on it. It can still be ∙n, near the church. The main attraction, however, is the **Bonawe Iron Fur- ∙ce** (open Apr–Sept daily; tel (01866) 822432; admission charge). Founded in 53 by a North of England partnership, it is the most complete charcoal-fuelled ∩works in Britain. A little nearer to Oban, the road passes by the Connel Bridge, ler which are the foaming **Falls of Lora**, a remarkable waterfall which appears∙ ∟ series of dramatic cataracts as Loch Etive drains into the sea at ebb tide.

## ▶astal sights

∕ou take the A816 from Lochgilphead to Oban by the coast, you will pass one the ancient capitals of Dalriada, the kingdom of the early Scots. The striking inence of **Dunadd Fort** (*c.* AD 500–800) sets the mood for a spectacular

**BELOW:** Glen Tarbert: almost as remote as one of the Western Isles.

*The Tigh na Truish Inn on Seil, whose name means House of the Trousers, recalls the vindictive law which prohibited the wearing of the kilt after the 1745 Rising.*

group of prehistoric sites around the village of **Kilmartin** : standing ston burial cairns and cists are all accessible. Start with the collection of sculptu stones in the churchyard. As you drive north, the coast becomes more riv while the natural harbours of the sea lochs and the protective islands of **Shu Luing** (noted for its slate) and **Seil** attract the yachting fraternity.

Here, too, is **Arduaine Garden**, a 20-acre (8-hectare) promontory owned the National Trust for Scotland and renowned for superb rhododendrons, azal and magnolias (open daily; tel: (01852) 200366; admission charge). **Seil** and neighbours were supported by a vigorous slate industry until a great storm 1881 flooded the quarries deep below sea level and efforts to pump them failed. You can see vivid evidence of those days on Seil at the **Scottish Sl Islands Heritage Trust Centre** (open Apr–Oct: daily; tel: (01852) 3004 admission charge). Seil itself is so close to the mainland that it's reached by single stone arch of the 1791 Clachan Bridge, the "bridge over the Atlantic".

## Tourist capital

Every facility for visitors can be found in **Oban** , whose only beach, **Ganav Sands**, is 2 miles (3 km) north of the town. Whisky-making is explained at **Ob Distillery** (open Jan–Nov Mon–Fri, Easter–Oct also Sat, July–Sept also S pm; tel: (01631) 572004; admission charge) and there are castles to be visit the scant fragment of **Dunollie** on its precipitous rock and, at Connel, the f 13th-century fortress of **Dunstaffnage** (open Apr–Sept daily, Mar and C Sat–Wed; tel: (01631) 562465; admission charge). Three miles (5 km) east Oban is the **Rare Breeds Farm Park** (open Easter–Oct daily, Nov–Dec Sat a Sun; tel: (01631) 770608); admission charge).

**BELOW:** Oban, dominated by the folly of McCaig's Tower.

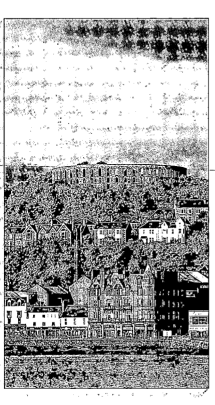

## SEAWAY TO THE HEBRIDES

Ringed by wooded hills and clasped within the sheltered Oban has the finest harbour on the Highland seaboard. H even a landlocked traveller feels the pull of the islands: there regular ferries to Mull, Barra, South Uist and Colonsay, as wel the nearby islands of Kerrera and Lismore. Oban is the focal p for tourists throughout the whole of Argyll, but also serves as shopping centre for the rural population of the region, so it's lik to be busy all year round. In August there's the added attractio the Argyllshire Highland Gathering, with displays of traditio dancing and folk music.

Hotels and boarding houses abound – a far cry from 1 when Dr Johnson had to content himself with a "tolerable i However, modern tourism hasn't been so kind to the dignity o high street; it lost the delightful Victorian buildings of its railw station in an act of institutionalised vandalism. But the town has atmosphere – mostly centred on the busy harbour. Pulpit is Oban's best viewpoint – and there is also the extraordinary of McCaig's Tower. John Stuart McCaig was an Oban banker financed this strange enterprise on a hill above the town centr give work to the unemployed and provide himself with a mem ial. The tower was raised between 1890 and 1900, but McCa grand plan was never completed. What remains looks like an a tere Scottish Colosseum.

Oban is a great place for island-hopping. **Mull** is just a 40-minute ferry ride way, as is the long fertile island of **Lismore**, whose name means "great garden". Oban Bay is pretty little **Kerrera**, reached by a small foot ferry. A walk round the island takes you past the dramatic ruin of **Gylen Castle** at its southern tip, commanding a spectacular view of sea, coastline and islands.

North from Oban, the A828 crosses the Connel Bridge to reach the lovely lands of Benderloch and Appin. Here is the **Scottish Sea Life Sanctuary** (open daily; tel: (01631) 720386; admission charge) with walk-through aquarium, touch tanks, seal pond and otter sanctuary with underwater viewing. At **Barcaldine** (tel: (01631) 720593) is found the **Black Castle**, now an upmarket accommodation option complete with secret stairs, bottle dungeon and resident ghost.

Continuing north leads you through **Appin**, a name which evokes romantic tragedy. In a historical incident made famous by Robert Louis Stevenson in *Kidnapped*, James Stewart of the Glens was wrongly hanged for the murder of Colin Campbell, the "Red Fox" and government land agent following the Jacobite rising of 1745. Further north still, at **Corran**, you can cross **Loch Linnhe** on a five-minute ferry ride to **Ardgour** and the tortuous drive to isolated **Ardnamurchan Point** , the most westerly point of the Scottish mainland.

## Mountain grandeur

Once across the Ballachulish Bridge, the full grandeur of the West Highlands lies before you. To the east is the sublime mountain scenery of perhaps the most famous glen in Scotland, though for the wrong reason: **Glencoe** ⑭, where in a savage winter dawn in February 1692, 40 members of the Clan Donald were

*The Scottish Sea Life Sanctuary near Barcaldine includes all kinds of marine life, from small crustaceans to seals and even sharks.*

**BELOW:**
Glencoe: even the unimaginative feel their spines tingle.

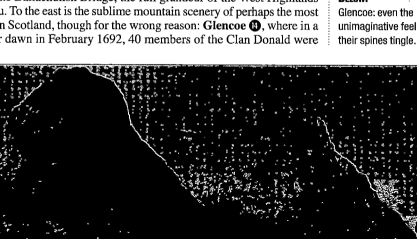

**BELOW:** the Glenfinnan Viaduct still carrying trains from Glasgow to Mallaig.

slaughtered by government soldiers to whom they had given shelter and hos[pi]tality. The power of the landscape here does not diminish and even the unim[ag]inative must feel a shiver of the spine as they follow the A82 between the d[ark] buttresses of **Buachaille Etive Mor**, **Bidean nam Bian** and the **Aona[ch] Eagach**. These mountains are notorious: they are among Britain's supre[me] mountaineering challenges, and nearly every winter they claim lives. T[he] National Trust for Scotland owns most of Glencoe and exhibitions at its **Gl[en]coe Visitor Centre** (open Mar–end Oct daily, Nov–Feb, Thur–Sun; tel: 08[45] 4932222; admission charge) near the foot of the glen tell its story.

## Big Ben

Some 15 miles (24 km) north of Ballachulish on the A82 is **Fort William ◆** The fort itself was demolished, not by the Jacobites but by the railway. A sec[ond] portrait of Bonnie Prince Charlie, and his bed, are among the Jacobite relic[s in] the **West Highland Museum** (open Mon–Sat, plus Sun pm July and Aug; [tel:] (01397) 702169; admission charge). Despite its fine position between the mou[n]tains and Loch Linnhe and proximity to world-class mountain-biking at Ne[vis] Range (www.nevisrange.co.uk), this busy town has little to commend it bey[ond] its proximity to **Ben Nevis** and glorious Glen Nevis. Britain's highest mount[ain] (4,406 ft/1,344 metres) looks a deceptively inoffensive lump from below, wh[en] you can't see its savage north face. But the volatile nature of the Scottish c[li]mate should never be underestimated when setting out on any hill-walk: [the] "Ben" is a long, tough day, and you should take advice from the visitor centre [at] its foot in Glen Nevis.

From Fort William, turn west on the A830, taking the "road to the Isles"

allaig, another ferry port for the Hebrides (particularly the "Small Isles" of nna, Rum, Eigg and Muck). At **Corpach** you will find **Treasures of the rth** (open Feb–Dec daily; tel: (01397) 772283; admission charge), an intrigu- ʒ geology-based exhibition of gemstones and rare minerals. In summer the ɔobite Steam Train runs through the spectacular scenery from Fort William Mallaig; for details, tel: (01463) 239026. This was the track that accommo- ted the Hogwart's Express in the movie version of *Harry Potter and the Cham- r of Secrets*.

The road continues past Loch Eil to **Glenfinnan** ⑯. In August 1745 Charles sed the white-and-crimson Stuart banner here to the cheers of 5,000 men who d rallied behind the charismatic young prince's impetuous adventure, which ʌs to cost the Highlands dear. A monument was raised on the spot in 1815; the tional Trust for Scotland's **Glenfinnan Visitor Centre** (open Easter–Oct ily; tel: (01397) 722250; admission charge) tells the story well.

The prince had landed from his French brig at **Loch nan Uamh**, a few miles ther west. Just over a year later, after the disaster of Culloden, he left from ʒ same place, having fled pursuing government troops for months around the ghlands and Islands: despite a price of £30,000 on his head – a fortune for the ɲe – he was never once betrayed. A memorial cairn on the shore of Loch nan ʌmh marks his final exit from Scotland.

From **Arisaig** the road passes between the silver sands of **Morar** and the deep ɔch Morar (said to be the home of Morag, another water monster) and comes an end at **Mallaig** ⑰, an important landing place for white fish and shellfish. ɔu can take a car ferry across the Sound of Sleat to **Armadale** on Skye or enjoy ʒruise to the great, roadless mountain wilderness of **Knoydart** with its two

*Contrary to popular belief, the figure at the top of the Glen- finnan monument is simply a Highlander, not Prince Charlie.*

**BELOW:** Mallaig fishermen splicing their ropes.

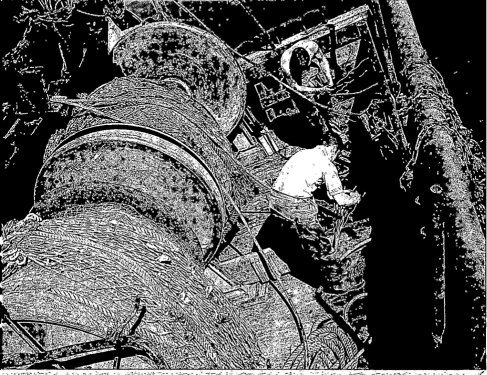

*A short diversion from Kyle of Lochalsh takes you to the popular holiday village of Plockton, where, because of its sheltered position, palm trees flourish.*

long sea lochs, **Hourn** and **Nevis** – said to be the lochs of Heaven and Hell. La at Inverie for a dram or pint at The Old Forge (tel: (01687) 462267), Britair remotest mainland pub.

## Peak district

The alternative from Fort William is to continue on the A82 and at **Invergar** turn west on the A87 to climb past a spectacular roadside viewpoint looki down Glen Garry and then drop to the head of Glen Shiel, with the famous pea of the **Five Sisters of Kintail** soaring above on your right. At Shiel Bridge minor road turns left over the Mam Ratagan pass to reach **Glenelg** , wortl visit not only for its beauty but also for **Dun Telve** and **Dun Troddan**, tv superb brochs – circular Iron Age towers with double walls which still sta over 30 ft (9 metres) high. Here, too, are the remains of **Bernera Barrack** quartered by Hanoverian troops during the 18th century.

Go back to Shiel Bridge and continue on A87 along lovely Loch Duich reach **Eilean Donan Castle** (open Apr–Oct daily; tel: (01599) 55520 admission charge), a restored Mackenzie stronghold on an islet reached by causeway and probably the most photographed castle in Scotland. The road ru on to **Kyle of Lochalsh** and the bridge across to Skye.

## Sublime scenery

From **Kyle of Lochalsh** , mainland travellers continue north by lovely **Lo Carron**, leaving Inverness-shire for the tremendous mountain massifs of **West Ross**. Here, on the isolated peninsula of **Applecross** and among the mighty pea of **Torridon** with their views to the Cuillin of Skye and the distant, drifting shap

' the Outer Hebrides, is some of Europe's most wild and spectacular scenery.
More gentle pursuits can be found at the village of **Poolewe**, where the road
rough Gairloch passes between Loch Ewe and **Loch Maree**, possibly the most
*blime inland loch in Scotland. The loch's particular features are the old Scots
nes which line its shores and the impressive presence of **Slioch**, the "mountain
' the spear", on its eastern shore.

**Inverewe Gardens** ㉑ (open daily; visitor centre open Easter–Oct daily; tel:
'1445) 781200; admission charge) provide a sumptuous international collection
' subtropical plants, growing – thanks to the mild climate created by the North
tlantic Drift – on the same latitude as Siberia. The gardens were begun in 1862
/ Osgood Mackenzie, further developed by his daughter Mrs Mairi Sawyer,
ıd given to the National Trust for Scotland in 1952.

A few miles further north is the glittering 4-mile (6-km) scoop of **Gruinard**
**ay** ㉒, with its coves of pink sand from the red Torridon sandstone, nearly 800
illion years old. The road then takes you round **Little Loch Broom**, below the
)werful shoulders of **An Teallach** ("The Forge": 3,483 ft/1,062 metres), high-
t of these mighty peaks and a mountain which, said W.H. Murray, made "most
⊀unros of the South and Central Highlands seem tame by comparison". (A
unro is a Scottish mountain of over 3,000 ft (900 metres), named for the man·
·ho collated them. There are 284 in all, of which nine rise higher than 4,000
'1,200 metres.) You are now within easy reach of **Loch Broom** itself, and the'
⊀bstantial fishing port and tourist centre of Ullapool *(see page 294)*. On your
ay, stop at the **Measach Falls** ㉓, 10 miles (16 km) before **Ullapool** ㉔, to
⊀mire the 120-ft (35-metre) drop into the spectacular **Corrieshalloch Gorge**,
ossed by a swaying Victorian suspension bridge.  ❑

**TIP**

From Glenelg you
can cross the water of
Loch Duich to Kylerhea
in Skye, as Dr Johnson
and Boswell did,
although the little
car ferry (tel: (01599)
522273) runs only in
summer. Alternatively,
use the Skye Bridge at
Kyle of Lochalsh.

**BELOW:** a pathway
through Inverewe
Gardens.

# SKYE

*Arguably the most magnificent of the dozens of Scottish islands, Skye is a romantic, misty isle of dramatic sea lochs, rocky peaks and breathtaking views*

**S**o deep are the incisions made by the sea lochs along the coast of Skye that, although the island is about 50 miles (80 km) long and 30 miles (50 km) wide, no part is more than 5 miles (8 km) from the sea. The population, unlike that of most Scottish islands, is on the increase – mainly due to immigrants, many of whom are from south of the border.

Dominating the "Misty Island" are the jagged **Cuillins**, on a sharp winter's day providing as thrilling a landscape as any in Nepal or New Zealand. Strangely, these, the greatest concentration of peaks in Britain, are referred to as "hills" rather than mountains; although they attain a height of not much more than 3,000 ft (900 metres), they spring dramatically from sea level.

Most visitors now reach Skye by driving over the road bridge which spans the **Kyleakin Narrows** between Kyle of Lochalsh and **Kyleakin ❶**. Alternative car-ferry routes are from Glenelg to Kylerhea and from Mallaig to Armadale. The former, a ferry (www.skyeferry.co.uk) accommodating a mere handful of cars, runs only during the summer – never on a Sunday – while the latter becomes a passenger-only ferry in the winter.

## Garden of Skye

Overlooking Kyleakin harbour are the scanty ruins of **Castle Moil**, once a stronghold of the Mackinnons and a lookout post and fortress against raids by Norsemen. Six miles (10 km) out of Kyleakin, turn south on the A851 and, after 17 miles (27 km), arrive at **Armadale ❷** and its ruined castle. **Armadale Castle Gardens and Museum of the Isles** (open Apr–Oct daily; gardens open daily; tel: (01471) 844305; admission charge) was formerly the home of the MacDonalds, who were once one of Scotland's most powerful clans and Lord of the Isles. The **Clan Donald Trust**, formed in the 1970s, which has members throughout the world, has turned one wing of the ruined castle into a museum with audio-visual presentations. The old stables house an excellent restaurant, a good bookshop, giftshop and luxurious self-catering accommodation. There's a ranger service and guided walks through the grounds with their mature trees and rhododendrons. Further exploration of this area, called **Sleat** (pronounced *Slate*), reveals why it bears the sobriquet "Garden of Skye".

Return north to reach **Broadford**, from where a diversion southwest on the B8083 leads, after 14 miles (22 km), to the scattered village of **Elgol ❸**. It was from here on 4 July 1746 that the Young Pretender, after being given a banquet by the Mackinnons in what is now called **Prince Charles's Cave**, finally bade farewell to the Hebrides. The view of the **Black Cuillins** from here is one of the most splendid views in all Britain.

*Many British moun-
taineers who have
challenged Everest
and other great
peaks of the world
did part of their
serious training on
the Cuillin Hills.*

**BELOW:** Skye's
romantic landscape.

In summer, motorboats go from Elgol across wide **Loch Scavaig**, past schoo-
of seals, to land passengers on the rocks from where they can scramble upwar-
to **Loch Coruisk** in the very heart of the Cuillins. The scene was much painted t
Turner and other Romantics and written about by Sir Walter Scott.

## Croft and castle

Backtrack once more to the A87 and, after 7 miles (11 km) with the Re
Cuillins to the left – they are much more rounded and much less dramatic tha
the Black Cuillins – you arrive at Luib and the thatched **Luib Croft Museun**
(open Easter–Oct daily; tel: (01471) 822427), the first of the Skye folk mus-
ums. Of particular interest is the collection of newspaper cuttings from the er
of the 19th century which deal with crofters' grievances. Skye was the scer
of some of the most intense fight-backs by crofters threatened with evictic
during the Clearances. The Battle of the Braes (1882) was the last such "battl-
fought in Britain.

The road continues through **Sligachan** ❹, a base for serious climbers of th
Black Cuillins, and then descends into **Portree** ❺, the island's capital, an attra-
tive town built round a natural harbour and with neat and brightly painted hous-
rising steeply from the water. In 1773, when they visited Portree, Dr Johnsc
and James Boswell dined in the Royal Hotel, then called McNab's Hostelr
believing it was "the only inn on the island". A quarter of a century before tha
Prince Charlie bade farewell to Flora MacDonald at MacNab's. Just south (
Portree is the **Aros Experience** (open daily; tel: (01478) 613649; admissic
charge for exhibition), where a multimedia presentation tells the story of th
island from 1700 to the present day. There are also attractive woodland walk:

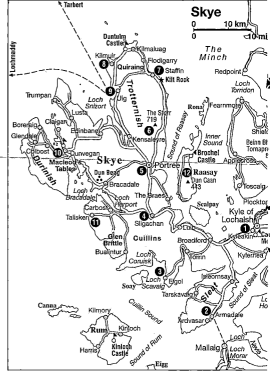

Magnificent rock scenery and breathtaking views can be enjoyed by driving ‎th from Portree on the **Trotternish Peninsula**. Seven miles (11 km) out along A855 is **The Storr** ❻, a 2,360-ft (719-metre) height which is shaped like a ‎wn and offers a stiff two-hour climb; to its east is the **Old Man of Storr**, an ‎lated 150-ft (45-metre) pinnacle of rock. Further north is **Kilt Rock**, a sea ‎ff which owes its name to columnar basalt strata overlying horizontal ones ‎eath, the result bearing only the most fanciful relationship to a kilt.

‎A further 2 miles (4 km) leads to **Staffin** ❼, immediately beyond which is ‎e **Quiraing**, so broken up with massive rock faces that it looks like a range in ‎niature rather than a single mountain. The various rock features of the ‎iraing – the castellated crags of **The Prison**, the slender, unclimbed 100-ft ‎-metre) **Needle** and **The Table**, a meadow as large as a football field – can be ‎reciated only on foot and can be reached readily by a path from a glorious ‎nor road which cuts across the peninsula from Staffin to Uig.

However, to take this road rather than to loop around Trotternish peninsula is ‎orego some historic encounters. The annexe of the **Flodigarry Hotel** was Flora ‎cDonald's first home after her marriage in 1750 to Captain Allan MacDonald. ‎arby is **Kilmuir churchyard** ❽, where Flora lies buried, wrapped in a sheet ‎m the bed in which the fugitive prince had slept. On a clear day there are fine ‎ws from here of the Outer Hebrides, from where Charlie and Flora fled to Skye. ‎Then, at the northwest tip of the peninsula, is the ruined **Duntulm Castle**, an ‎ient MacDonald stronghold commanding the sea route to the Outer Hebrides. ‎th of the castle is the **Skye Museum of Island Life** (open Apr–Oct Mon–Sat; ‎: (01470) 552206; admission charge), whose seven thatched cottages show ‎v the crofters lived. And so, after a few miles, to **Uig** ❾, from where the ferry

*A Celtic cross marks the spot where Flora MacDonald is buried in Kilmuir.*

**BELOW:**
the way we were:
the Skye Museum
of Island Life.

departs for Lochmaddy on North Uist and Tarbert on Harris. The A87 so▶
from Uig returns to Portree, but rather than continuing, turn right at the ju▶
tion with the A850 and travel westwards, across the base of the Trotterni▶
peninsula, to arrive after 19 miles (30 km) at Dunvegan.

Just before Dunvegan, look south to **Macleod's Tables,** which dominate t▶
**Duirinish peninsula.** Their flatness is attributed to the inhospitality sho▶
Columba when he preached to the local chief: in shame the mountains shed th▶
caps so that the saint might have a flat bed on which to lie.

## Legendary past

No other castle in Scotland boasts so long a record of continuous occupation▶
one family as **Dunvegan** ⑩ (castle and gardens open daily, gardens closed▶
winter; tel: (01470) 521206), which has been home to the MacLeods for the p▶
700 years. Set on a rocky platform overlooking Loch Dunvegan, its stucco▶
exterior lacks the splendour of at least a dozen other Scottish castles. Its in▶
rior, however, is another matter, with a wealth of paintings and memorabi▶
including a painting of Dr Johnson by Sir Joshua Reynolds and a lock of Bon▶
Prince Charlie's hair. Best known, though, is the "Fairy Flag", a torn and fad▶
fragment of yellow silk spotted with red. Some say a fairy mother laid it o▶
her half-mortal child when she had to return to her own people: others, m▶
prosaic, that it was woven on the island of Rhodes in the 7th century and tha▶
MacLeod captured it from a Saracen chief during the Crusades. Whatever ▶
origins, the Fairy Flag is said to have three magic properties: when raised in b▶
tle it ensures a MacLeod victory; when spread over the MacLeod marriage ▶
it guarantees a child; and when unfurled at Dunvegan it charms the herring

**BELOW:**
Dunvegan Castle.

: loch. The flag should be flown sparingly: its powerful properties will be exhausted when used three times. So far, it has twice been invoked.

Three miles (5 km) before Dunvegan, take the secondary B886 and travel northwards for 8 miles (13 km) to **Trumpan** where, in 1597, the "Fairy Flag" is unfurled. A raiding party of MacDonalds from the island of Uist landed and set fire to a church packed with worshipping MacLeods. The alarm was raised: the MacDonalds were unable to escape as a falling tide had left their longboats high and dry: they were decimated. The bodies of friend and foe alike were laid out on the sands below the sea wall, which was then toppled to cover the corpses. Primitive justice once practised on Skye is seen in the **Trumpan churchyard** in the shape of a standing stone pierced by a circular hole. The accused would be blindfolded and, if he could put his finger unerringly through the Trial Stone, was deemed innocent.

## cal flavour

*With a distinctive peaty flavour all of its own, the whisky from the Talisker Distillery has been described by one expert as having "all the uncertainties of the Skye weather".*

few miles west of Dunvegan are Colbost, then Glendale and Boreraig. The **Colbost Folk Museum** (open Easter–Oct daily; tel: (01470) 521296; admission charge) is very atmospheric, with a peat fire of the floor of the "black house" waiting to cook a stew and a box bed uncomfortable enough to be genuine. Behind the house an illicit whisky still is sadly no longer in use, but the restored 200-year-old watermill at **Glendale** is fully operational. A cairn at **Boreraig** marks the site of the piping school of the MacCrimmons, for 300 years the hereditary pipers to the MacLeods. Opposite is the **Boreraig Park Piping Centre** (open daily; tel: (01470) 511311; admission charge) which records the feats of the MacCrimmon family, exhibits and sells bagpipes and gives piping classes.

Heading south from Dunvegan, the A863 follows the shores of **Loch Bracadale**, one of the most magnificent fords of the west coast, with the black basalt wall of Wilisker Head away to the south. At **Dun Beag**, near Bracadale, is a well-preserved broch (circular Iron Age fortified building). A left turn onto the B885 before reaching Wilisker ⓫ leads back to **Portree**. Alternatively, remain on the A863 and either continue to Portree via Sligachan or on reaching the head of **Loch Harport**, go right on the B8009, and immediately cut back left into wooded **Glen little** and more glorious views of the Black Cuillins. Remaining on the B8009 would lead to **Carbost** and the **Talisker Distillery** (open Mon–Fri Nov–Mar, Easter–Oct Mon–Sat, plus Sun pm July–Aug; tel: (01478) 614308) where you can see how the "water of life" at Skye's sole whisky distillery is made.

**BELOW:** sunny day at Sligachan.

Some say that the sole purpose of Skye is to protect the small lush island of **Raasay** ⓬, just to the east. In the 18th century the English burned all Raasay's houses and boats because the laird had sheltered Bonnie Prince Charlie after Culloden. Today the island has a population of about 200. **Dun Caan**, an extinct volcano, dominates the centre of the island. Visitors can see the ruined Brochel Castle, home of the MacLeods of Skye and the grounds of Raasay House. When the exuberant Boswell stayed with Dr Johnson at Raasay House, now an outdoor pursuits centre, he danced a jig on top of the 1456-ft (443-metre) high Dun Caan ridge. ❏

# A CROFTER'S RUGGED LIFE

*The 17,000 crofts in the Scottish Highlands keep people on the land, but they function more as a traditional way of living than as a source of income*

The word "croft" derives from the Gaelic *croit*, meaning a small area of land. Often described as "a piece of land fenced around with regulations", the croft is both much cherished and highly frustrating. Its emotive power comes from its origins. In the aftermath of the Highland Clearances of the 19th century, groups of local men banded together to protect their families from being swept overseas to make way for sheep. At the time they were entirely at the whim of often absentee landowners.

By standing their ground despite all the odds – particularly at the so-called Battle of the Braes, in Skye – these men were rewarded in 1886 by an Act of Parliament which gave them security of tenure. It also regulated the rents they had to pay, and gave them a right to compensation for any improvements made to their properties. The croft had officially come into being.

## CROFTING TOWNSHIPS TODAY

A croft is usually a combination of a house and a handful of barren, boggy acres for the crofter to cultivate or on which to graze livestock. The crofting community – commonly called a township – acts together in such activities as fencing, dipping or hiring a bull. Very few crofters rely solely on their smallholding for an income.

Only 3,600 crofts are owner-occupied. The rest are tenanted, although the rental they pay to their landlord is minimal. It's estimated there are 17,725 crofts and 11,500 crofters in Scotland, with 33,000 people residing in crofting households.

In Assynt and on the island of Eigg, crofters banded together to become land-owners themselves, raising millions of pounds with appeals on the internet and the help of charities supporting traditional land use. There have been similar takeovers in the remote Knoydart peninsula and the Isle of Gigha. At Inverie, the main village of Knoydart, the Old Forge provides high-quality meals with fresh seafood and venison from the local red deer, which often wander freely in the single street.

△ **A VARIED LIVING**
Crofting is often more a way of life than a viable means of living. A modern crofter has to have several occupations and maybe even a couple of part-time jobs to make ends meet and support a family. The average crofting income is just £8,000 a year.

△ **FURNACE WORKSHOP**
Every crofting township us to have a blacksmith. Ever today, crofters have to be self-sufficient and able to mend practically everythin

◁ **A FAMILY AFFAIR**
When tenants get too old to work the croft themselves, have the right to assign the croft to the next generation Some 65 percent do just th

△ THE ELECTRONIC CROFT
Problems of remoteness are gradually being overcome by new technology. With the advent of computer networking and satellite communication, increasing numbers of crofters, particularly on the islands, are replacing the tweed loom in the shed with a keyboard in the living room.

△ NOT JUST A MAN'S WORLD
Despite the physical labour, some women are attracted to the crofting life, particularly as new housing replaces the poor conditions of the past.

◁ MOBILE MONEY
Modern services such as those provided by this mobile bank make life just a little easier in the more remote parts of the Highlands.

# A TRADITION THAT TIES UP THE LAND

The most common criticisms of crofting are that it ties up land in segments which are too small ever to be economically viable, that most crofters are too old to cope, and that too many crofts are left to run down by absentee tenants who have gone off in search of other, more rewarding ways of life.

These are all problems faced daily by the Crofters' Commission, the government body which was set up to oversee crofting affairs. Certainly, as far as agricultural production is concerned, crofting is a very small player. In fact, estimates suggest that some two-thirds of crofts are not actively farmed at all. However, crofting has lately been redefined to include any economic activity, so it can also cover such enterprises as running a Bed & Breakfast establishment.

The number of run-down crofts and older crofters is a sad fact of life today; younger Highlanders will inevitably move away to the cities in search of a career, only returning to the croft in later years. But any alternative agricultural projects have been shown to provide little in the way of employment, and they would radically alter the landscape.

Crofting has proven an effective stewardship of the land as it is. Without it, whole communities would simply pack up and leave.

# THE INNER HEBRIDES

*The Inner Hebrides have a variety of pleasures to explore: the .ractive landscape of Mull, the restored abbey on Iona and a host of smaller islands, some inhabited only by wildlife*

isitors come to the volcanic island of **Mull**  for the contrasting scenery, wooded and soft to bleak and bare; for fishing in the lochs; and for walking. Increasingly, it's an island renowned for its sightings of rare wildlife, luding the golden eagle. Visitors will find all types of terrain and weather; ll on a wet day past Loch Scridain, through the boggy desolation of the **Ross Mull**, or walk to the top of Mull's highest mountain, **Ben More**, a respectable 69 ft (950 metres).

he island is not large, only 25 by 26 miles (40 by 41 km), but don't be eived: a drive on the mainly single-track roads, running mostly round the imeter, is made even slower by Scotland's most feckless and fearless sheep, ich regard roads simply as grassless fields.

## tural charm

ll's trump card is **Tobermory**, the prettiest port in western Scotland, tucked ι wooded protected bay whose waters are almost invariably unruffled. Yet, 588, an explosion reverberated across the bay and the waters gurgled as the unish galleon *Florida* sank to the bottom. The exact spot, just 100 yards (90 tres) straight out from the pier, is well defined. And here, it is believed, a vast usure of gold awaits salvage. In 2007, yet another :mpt was made to retrieve it.

'he tall, brightly painted houses curving round the bour go back to the late 18th century, when the tish Fisheries Society planned a herring port. But the ι were fickle, and today Tobermory's sparkling harur bobs with pretty pleasure yachts. Be sure to stop it the small chocolate factory and shop, where the ciality is chocolate made with whisky.

'he other towns – **Craignure** in the east where the .an ferry docks, **Salen** in the narrow neck of the ınd, and **Dervaig** in the northwest – are neat, sereable little places. Drive through Glen More, the ient royal funeral route to Iona which bisects Mull ın east to west, for some of the best scenery on the ınd. These 20 roads form part of the popular annual ınocks Mull Rally, held in October.

'hen, on the west of the island, you will find **Cal- y**, the silver-sand beach where, after the Clearances, pairing emigrant ships set sail for the New World. e beach held happy memories for one émigré: lonel McLeod of the Northwest Mounted Police ned a new fort in Alberta after it.

'urther proof, if it be needed, that Scotland's two in exports are whisky and brains can be found south Calgary at **Loch Ba** near Salen. The **MacQuarie usoleum** houses the remains of Major-General chlan MacQuarie, the first Governor General of New

**PRECEDING PAGES:**
Tobermory on Mull.
**LEFT:** Iona Abbey.
**BELOW:** local
inhabitant on Iona.

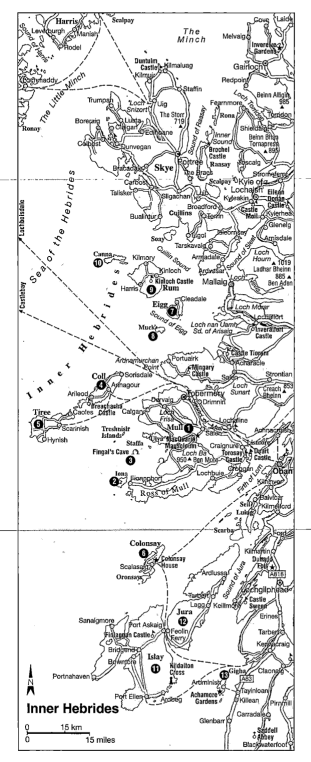

**Inner Hebrides**

South Wales, who is sometimes cal[led]
the "Father of Australia".

To understand what the 19th-cent[ury]
Clearances meant to all Hebride[ans]
and to grasp the harshness of a croft[er's]
life, see the tableaux, with sound co[m]-
mentary, at the **Old Byre Heritage C**[en]-
**tre** (open Easter–Oct daily; tel: (016[80]
400229) at Dervaig. They help expl[ain]
the islanders' fatalistic attitude to l[ife.]
Some charitable outsiders think this a[tti]-
tude stems from the trauma of the Cle[ar]-
ances, which still trouble the collect[ive]
consciousness. But cynical mainland[ers]
say the islanders are simply idle. Island[ers]
– when you find them, for many serv[ice]
jobs, particularly those which are co[n]-
nected with tourism, seem to be run [by]
incomers – say they work as hard as a[ny]-
one. Crofting and fishing, they argue, [just]
aren't understood by urbanised outsid[ers.]

Two castles are open to the pub[lic,]
both on the east. **Torosay** (open A[pr–]
mid-Oct: daily; gardens open all ye[ar;]
admission charge; tel: (01680) 81242[?],
with 19th-century Scottish baronial t[ur]-
rets and crenellations, is near Craign[ure]
and is reached from there on a 1½-m[ile]
(2-km) miniature steam railway. The c[as]-
tle is still lived in by the Guthrie-Ja[mes]
family and is a friendly, non-impos[ing]
house. On wet days (frequent), you [can]
leaf through old books in the draw[ing]-
room or visit the separately owned we[av]-
ing workshop in the grounds (open da[ily,]
free). There's shapely Italian statuary [in]
the large terraced grounds, fine clem[atis]
climbing on old brick walls and a swe[et]-
smelling rock garden.

The 13th-century **Duart Castle** (o[pen]
Apr Sun–Thur 11am–4pm, May–m[id-]
Oct 10.30am–5.30pm; tel: (01680) 8[12]
309; admission charge), on a drama[tic]
headland overlooking the Sound of M[ull,]
was the MacLeans' stronghold. M[ull]
belonged to the clan until it was forfei[ted]
when the MacLeans supported you[ng]
Prince Charles Edward, who [was]
defeated at Culloden in 1746. The ca[stle]
was deserted for almost 200 years, th[en]
restored by Sir Fitzroy MacLean earl[y in]
the 20th century. The tearoom in [the]
grounds serves homemade cake.

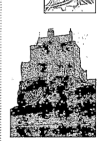

/Iull is the jumping-off point for several islands: Iona, Staffa, the Treshnish
·s, Coll and Tiree.

'ou feel a bit like a pilgrim as you board the serviceable little 10-minute shut-
for a day trip to **Iona ➋**. Near the ferry terminal at **Fionnphort**, on Mull's
ithwest tip,  the **Columba Centre** (open Easter–Oct daily; tel: (01681)
·'660; free) provides an introduction to Iona's saint. Cars and big coaches
n the mainland line the ferry road, for visitors must cross to the Holy Island
hout a vehicle. The main destination of visitors is the restored abbey (always
n; tel: (01828) 640411; free) but the general store near the ferry has added
ycle hire to its varied services, so in theory there's time  to see **Coracle Cove**
·re Columba landed in AD 563. From the abbey it is just 100 yards (90 metres)
he cemetery of **Reilig Oran** *(see below)*.

'ingal's Cave** on **Staffa ➌** is a big attraction; supposedly it inspired
ndelssohn to compose his overture. The experience of going into the cave, if
weather is good enough for landing, is well worth the 90-minute boat jour-
. The primeval crashing of the sea, the towering height of the cave and the
·nplete lack of colour in the sombre rocks make a powerful impression. Even
·ie little 47-ft (14-metre) partially covered passenger launch can't land, it's
·rth making the journey just to see the curious hexagonal basalt rocks with
gaping black hole of the cave. Birdwatchers, too, have plenty to enjoy.
·eyond Staffa are the uninhabited **Treshnish Islands** – a haven for puffins,
iwakes, razorbills, shags, fulmars, gannets and guillemots.

'rom Mull's northern flank, the Caledonian MacBrayne ferry can be seen
·ng from Oban to Coll and Tiree. There's the usual rivalry between these sister
·nds, most distant of the Inner Hebrides. People from Tiree can't understand

*Sir Fitzroy MacLean
of Duart Castle was
a Hussar in the Light
Brigade in the
Crimea in 1854: his
mementoes are dis-
played in the Grand
Banqueting Room.*

**BELOW:** the cloisters
of Iona Abbey.

## )LY **PILGRIMAGE**

'uriosity and a search for some intangible spiritual
·comfort draw well over half a million people from all
· the world each year to the tiny 3-mile (5-km) island of
·. Here St Columba and 12 companions landed from
·ind in the 6th century to set up the mission that turned
· into the Christian centre of Europe. In 1773 Dr Samuel
·nson was impressed with the piety of Iona. The abbey,
·ch had been suppressed at the Reformation, was still in
·s and there were not many visitors. In the 1930s the
·, sturdy building was restored by the Iona community,
· visitors have increased ever since. Some of the best
·oration is to be seen in the tiny cloister, especially the
·s and plants on the slender replacement sandstone
·imns, which were meticulously copied from the one
·aining medieval original.

·ntil the 11th century the Reilig Oran – or royal cemet-
·– was the burial place of Scottish kings, and there are
·· to be 48 Scottish rulers buried here, including Dun-
·. who was murdered by Macbeth in 1040. Here also lie
·bodies of eight Norwegian, four Irish and two French
·is. The cemetery is also the last resting place of John
·th, who was leader of Britain's Labour Party from 1992
· his untimely death in 1994.

why anyone wants to get off the ferry at Coll. The people of Coll maintain that inhabitants of Tiree are permanently bent by the island's ceaseless wind.

Purists, or those against progress, feel **Coll ❹** is too civilised. A young cyc. camping near the glorious west coast beaches, complained that the island's o hotel had gone suburban when it installed a sauna; while a 75-year-old resic of **Arinagour**, the island's only village, where most of the population of arot 150 live, spoke with astonishment of the local café's transformation into a bis

Families go to Coll for the simple holiday, pottering on uncrowded beach Much of the coast can be reached only on foot – although bicycles can be hir This isn't an island for antiquities, apart from the restored medieval castle **Breachacha**, and an 18th-century castle where Samuel Johnson and Jar Boswell spent most of their time when they were stranded on Coll for 10 d during their Highland Tour. Johnson commented on the island's garden fle ers but neither he nor Boswell climbed the giant dunes (100 ft/30 metres) s arating the beaches of Feall Bay and Crossapool Bay.

The Gaelic name for **Tiree ❺**, *Tir fo Thuinn*, means "land below the waves". a good description of this flat, sunny island whose two hills are only 400 ft h (120 metres). One of the islands' most eccentric visitors was Ada Goodrich Fr who claimed telepathic gifts and an ability to receive messages through sea she She spent three weeks on Tiree in 1894 investigating Highland second sight. spoke no Gaelic and was finally defeated, not by the language, but by the mo onous diet of tea, eggs, bread and jam provided by the Temperance Hotel.

Nowadays international windsurfers, who call Tiree the Hawaii of the No are attracted to the island by the great Atlantic rollers that break on the lc curving silver beaches.

*Dr Johnson was well aware of the bleaker side of the Hebrides: "Of these islands it must be confessed, that they have not many allurements, but to the mere lover of naked nature."*

**BELOW:** fascinating rock formations on Staffa.

Some people find **Colonsay** ❻, 40 miles (64 km) southwest of Oban, too ∎nd. But for others it is an antidote to the prettiness of Mull and the glowering ⁙illins of Skye. It has its antiquities – seven standing stones and six forts – as ∎ll as excellent wildlife – birds, otters and seals. It also has good white beaches ⁙ isn't over-mountainous. Visitors are few as there are no organised day trips, ⁙, because the ferry calls only three times a week, accommodation has to be ∎nd either at the one hotel or with families providing bed and breakfast.

The island, 8 miles (12 km) long and 3 miles (4 km) wide, has a population of ∎und 150 and is one of the largest British islands still in private hands. It is ⁙rmed by the North Atlantic Drift, and the gardens of **Colonsay House** have a ⁙iety of exotic plants.

At low tide it's possible to walk across muddy sands to tiny **Oronsay**, off the ∎thern tip of Colonsay; alternatively there are boat trips. Oronsay is about 2 ⁙es (3 km) square and has a population of six. Its fine 14th-century priory is the ⁙gest medieval monastic ruin in the islands, after Iona.

*It's said that the wild goats on Colonsay are descended from survivors of the Spanish Armada ships wrecked in 1588.*

## ⁙and-hopping

∎e small islands of Eigg, Muck, Rum and Canna can be reached from Mallaig ∎ the Sleat peninsula, the end of the "Road to the Isles". There's not a great ⁙al to do on the islands. Mostly people go for the wildlife, for a bit of esoteric ∎and-hopping or for superb walking, particularly on Rum.

The islands are all different, and, if you just want to see them without landing, ⁙e the little boat that makes the five- to seven-hour round-trip six times a week ⁙he summer, less often in winter. It's a service for islanders rather than a pleasure ∎at for visitors, and carries provisions, mail, newspapers and other essentials.

**BELOW:**
the calm before
the storm at Tiree.

Only those planning to stay are allowed to disembark. However, in summer, boating the *MV Shearwater* at Arisaig, 8 miles (13 km) before Mallaig, allows you stop for several hours at either Eigg or Rum.

**Eigg**  has had a chequered history in recent years. Owned first by Yorkshire businessman Keith Schellenberg and then by an eccentric German artist called Marum, it has now been bought by the Isle of Eigg Heritage Trust, a partnership between the islanders and the Scottish Wildlife Trust with a large contribution from public subscriptions. The famous rock prow known as The Sc (pronounced *Skoor*) can be climbed for magnificent views.

**Muck** is only 2 miles (3 km) long and has neither transport nor shops. Visitors must bring provisions and be landed by tender. Eighty breeds of birds n on Muck, whose name means "pig" (local porpoises were called sea-pigs).

There's an incongruous Greek temple on the rugged island of **Rum**: mausoleum of Sir George Bullough, the island's rich Edwardian proprietor. castellated **Kinloch Castle** was used as a convalescent home during the B War just after it was built, and was for a time a hotel. The island is owned Scottish Natural Heritage. There is fine birdwatching and hillwalking.

Graffiti adorn the rocks near the landing stage at **Canna**; they are at le 100 years old and record the names of visiting boats. The harbour's safe ha is one of the few deepwater harbours in the Hebrides. This sheltered island, most westerly of the four, is owned by the National Trust for Scotland an particularly interesting to botanists. No holiday accommodation exists.

**Islay** is the place to go if you enjoy malt whisky. There are over half dozen distilleries on this attractive little island, some with tours. Islay, wh Clan Donald started, was once the home of the Lord of the Isles. A fascinat sight into its medieval history is to be found at the archaeological site of **Fin-ggan** (visitor centre open; May–Sept daily pm; Apr and Oct Tues, Thur and ⊓n pm; tel: (01496) 810629); admission charge). Islay also has some good aches on the indented north coast.

Also on this side of the island is one of the best Celtic crosses in Scotland: the ⊓-century **Kildalton Cross** stands in the churchyard of a ruined, atmospheric ⊓le chapel. **Port Askaig**, where the ferry from the Kintyre peninsula docks, is ⊓retty little place with a hotel, once a 16th-century inn on the old drovers' road ew steps away from the ferry.

## ⊓ace and quiet

⊓ra ⑫, Islay's next-door neighbour, is so close you can nip over for a quick ⊓pection after dinner. Three shapely mountains, the Paps of Jura, 2,500 ft (750 ⊓tres) high, provide a striking skyline. Although palms and rhododendrons ⊐w on the sheltered east side, it's a wild island inhabited by sheep and red deer ⊓d is much favoured by sportsmen, birdwatchers and climbers. It was to the ⊓and of Jura that George Orwell came in 1947, seeking seclusion while work-⊓ on his novel *1984*.

⊓Gigha ⑬ has one of the nicest hotels in the islands – bright, spacious and ⊓autifully neat and simple. No need to take a car on the 3-mile (5-km) crossing ⊓m **Tayinloan** to this small green island popular with yachting people: no walk ⊓more than 3 miles from the attractive ferry terminal at **Ardminish** with its ⊓arkling white cottages. The formal attraction on Gigha is **Achamore Gar-⊓ns** (open daily; tel: (01583) 505254; admission charge). Seals, barking ami-⊓ly, cruise in the waters off the little used north pier.  ❑

Map, page 242

**TIP**

Tastings are available when you visit the distilleries of Laphroaig and Lagavulin at Port Ellen on Islay.

**BELOW:** mist over the Paps of Jura.

# THE OUTER HEBRIDES

*The dramatic islands of the Outer Hebrides are relentlesssly pounded by the cold Atlantic: visitors are either thrilled by their wild bleakness or find their remoteness disconcerting*

**PRECEDING PAGES:**
Hercules Irvine,
crofter.
**LEFT:** a corner of the
Outer Hebrides.
**BELOW:**
the port of Tarbert.

The Outer Hebrides, 40 miles (64 km) west of the mainland, are known locally as the Long Island. They stretch in a narrow 130-mile (208-km) arc from the Butt of Lewis in the north to Barra Head in the south. Each island gards itself as the fairest in the chain. The people live mainly by crofting and hing supplemented by tourism, with commercial fish farming – crabs and issels as well as salmon and trout – and teleworking growing fast.

There are enormous flat peat bogs on Lewis and North Uist, and the islanders t turf to burn rather than to export to the garden centres of England. The men t it during the summer and stack it *in situ*; when it has dried the women and ildren cart it home and stack it against the house for winter fires. A traditional essing on Lewis is: "Long may you live, with smoke from your house."

## erce loyalty

iese climatically hostile Western Isles of few trees and stark scenery are the idhealtachd, the land of the Gael. When their Gaelic-speaking inhabitants ange to English, as they politely do when visitors are present, they have vir- illy no accent and are among the easiest Scots for visitors to understand. They :re fiercely loyal to Bonnie Prince Charlie. When, after the Battle of Cullo- n in 1746, the young man, with a £30,000 price on ; head, dodged round the Outer Hebrides pursued by vernment forces, no one betrayed him.

**Harris** and the larger **Lewis** are really one island. wis is mostly flat moorland. Harris rises into high, :ky mountains culminating in North Harris in the ak of Clisham (2,622 ft/799 metres).

Turn north from the ferry terminal at **Tarbert ❶** for wis; south for Harris. Tarbert is in Harris, a land of re hills and fierce peaks. Ferries from Lochmaddy on rth Uist and Uig on Skye dock in this sheltered port ked into the hillside. There are a few shops selling irris tweed, the Harris Hotel, a tourist office, a bank d sheds.

A drive around South Harris (40 miles/64 km) is varding. As you head south on the A859 down the st coast, you pass many glorious beaches – **Lusken- e, Scarista** – before reaching **Leverburgh**, with the nains of the buildings erected by the industrialist Lord verhulme (of Sunlight soap fame) for a projected fish- ; port. The main road ends at **Rodel ❷** with the 16th- ntury **St Clement's Church**, one of the best examples ecclesiastical architecture in the Hebrides.

The single track road up the east coast offers superb iscapes and views across the Minch to Skye and tiny fts from where you hear – as you do throughout the ng Islands – the click-clack of crofters' looms pro- cing tweed.

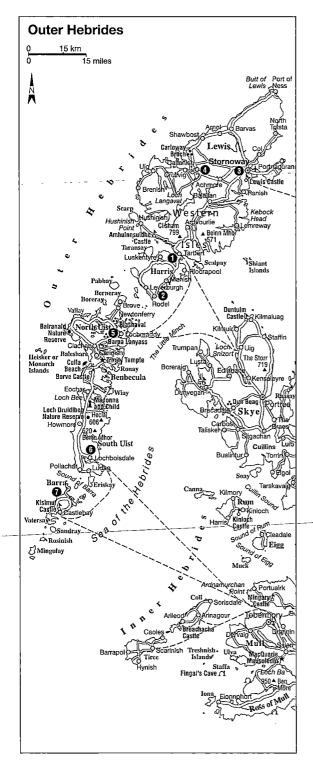

## Outer Hebrides

```
0        15 km
0              15 miles
```

N

Leave Tarbert for the north on t▪
A859 and after 4 miles (6 km) turn o▪
the B887, which clings to the shore ▪
**West Loch Tarbert**. The 16-mile (2▪
km) drive from Tarbert to gold▪
**Hushinish Point** is dramatic, partic▪
larly in the evening as the sun catches ▪
peaks of Beinn Dhubh on Harris acr▪
the water.

The road goes straight through the we▪
maintained grounds of **Amhuinnsuid▪
Castle** (pronounced *Avin-suey*), so cl▪
to the house you can almost see insi▪
This pale turreted castle, now a fishi▪
lodge, was built in 1868, and James B▪
rie began his novel *Mary Rose* here. ▪
stone's throw from the lodge, a salm▪
river runs into the sea.

From Hushinish, irregular ferries cr▪
to the small island of **Scarp**. In the 193▪
a new postal service was announc▪
here. A special stamp was issued; the fi▪
rocket was fired, but unfortunately ▪
exploded, destroying mail and projec▪

Backtrack to the A859, which twi▪
and turns past lochs and through mo▪
tains to arrive after 35 miles (56 km) ▪
**Stornoway ❸**, the capital of Lewis a▪
the only town in the Western Isles. M▪
activity in this solid town of 8,000 inha▪
itants is at the harbour, where seals ▪
nearly always be seen. They gi▪
Stornoway its nickname of Portrona (P▪
of Seals). Here, too, thousands of silv▪
fish, which will be turned into fertilis▪
can be seen sucked by giant vacu▪
hoses from boats' decks into waiting l▪
ries. This is also where the ferry fr▪
Ullapool, on the mainland, docks.

The best view of **Lews Castle** is fr▪
the harbour. Lord Leverhulme bought ▪
castle in 1918. In 1920 he purchased H▪
ris, becoming Britain's largest landow▪
His visions were admirable: to turn ▪
islanders into a viable community ▪
dependent on crofting but making th▪
living from the sea. He failed o▪
because of timing: today, fishing do▪
nates the island's economy.

To explore Lewis's many antiquiti▪
leave Stornoway on the A859 and, a▪
a couple of miles, bear right onto ▪
A858. **Callanish** (Calanais) ❹ and

agnificent standing stones are 16 miles (26 km) from Stornoway. The 13 rit-
·l stones, some 12 ft (3 metres) high, are set in a circle like Stonehenge. The
**allanish Visitor Centre** (open Apr–Sept Mon–Sat, Mar and Oct Wed–Sat;
·l: (01851) 621422) is close by.

Keeping to the A858, you soon reach the upstanding remains of the 2,000-
·ar old **Carloway Broch**; the folk museum at **Shawbost** (open Apr–Sept
·on–Sat; tel: (01851) 710212; admission charge) and **Arnol** with its **Black-
·use Museum** (open Mon–Sat; tel: (01851) 710395; admission charge), which
·ows how the people of Lewis used to live. A different world unfolds if, just
·fore Callanish, you take the B8011: it leads to **Uig** and its wondrous beaches.

Map, opposite

## 1e Uist archipelago

·chmaddy ❺, where the ferry from Uig in Skye docks, is the only village on
·orth Uist, and you're almost through it before you realise it's there. But to
·ow its status it has a hotel and a bank.

The Uist archipelago of low bright islands dominated by the glittering sea is
·4 miles long and only 8 miles at its widest (80 by 13 km) and is so peppered
·th lochs that on the map the east coast round Benbecula looks like a sieve.

Rather than setting south on the A865, which runs for 45 miles (72 km) and
·nich, because of causeway and bridge, virtually makes North Uist, Benbec-
·a and South Uist one island, travel around North Uist anticlockwise on the
·367 and A865. On a 45-mile (72-km) trip, you will pass superb beaches and
·tiquarian treasures.

Three miles (5 km) north from Lochmaddy are the standing stones of
·ashaval. Three miles further on, a turn-off on the right (B893) leads to **New-**

*Nobody knows why
the Callanish stones
are there. Once
known as Nu Fir
Breige – the false
men – they have
been claimed as a
Viking parliament,
a landing base for
UFOs and a site for
predicting eclipses.*

**BELOW:**
the Callanish
standing stones.

## 1NDING OUR WAY

·he official tourist map of the
Outer Hebrides is essential
the Uists. Even though only
·e main road links the three
·nds of North Uist, Benbecula and South Uist, most sign-
·sts are in Gaelic; the map gives them in English too. The
·chmaddy tourist office has a free sheet of English/Gaelic
·mes put out by the Western Isles Islands Council. To help
·serve one of Europe's oldest languages, the council has
·t up Gaelic-only place names and signposts in the Outer
·brides. In English-speaking Benbecula and in Stornoway
·Lewis, the signs are also in English. Gaelic is a living lan-
·age on these islands: local people often speak Gaelic
·ong themselves and in the schools the children are
·ght in both English and Gaelic. And church services –
·both the Protestant islands in the north and the Catholic
·nds in the south – are also usually held in Gaelic.

There are other problems to waylay the unsuspecting
·tor: locals warn that roads in North Uist may be different
·m the map because the constant movement of the bog
·kes them change direction. Certainly at times the cause-
·y road feels as springy as a dance floor.

Rare species to be
spied at the Balranald
sanctuary include the
corncrake, lapwing
and barnacle geese.
The Visitor Centre
is open all year
(tel: (01463) 715000).

**BELOW:**
sheep shearers at
work on South Uist.

tonferry and the new causeway to the island of **Berneray**, where Prince Charl
occasionally recharges his batteries. Back on Uist, in the middle of the no
shore, is the rocky islet of **Eilean-an-Tighe**, the oldest pottery "factory" in We
ern Europe: it produced quality items in Stone Age times.

Still on the north coast is the superb beach of **Vallay** (actually an isla
reached on foot: beware tides). Round on the west coast, green and whiter th
in the east, is **Baleshare**, another island with a great beach joined to Uist by
causeway. Before reaching here, you pass the **Balranald Nature Reserv**
which was created to protect the breeding habitat of the red-necked phalaro

At **Clachan** the A865 turns south while the A867 runs northeast to return
Lochmaddy. Five miles (8 km) along the latter is **Barpa Lanyass**, a 5,000-ye
old squashed beehive tomb. Nearby is the **Pobull Fhinn** standing stone circ
Backtrack to the A865; just before the causeway is **Carinish**, where Scotlan
last battle with swords and bows and arrows took place. Close by is the ruin
12th-century **Trinity Temple**.

Cross the North Ford by the 5-mile (8-km) causeway to reach tiny **Benbecu**
whose eastern part is so pitted with lochs that most people live on the west coa
The traveller now has the choice of proceeding due south for 5 miles (8 km)
the southern tip of Benbecula or turning right onto the B892, which makes a l
mile (16-km) loop around the west of the island before rejoining the A865.

The loop road first passes the small airport and a Royal Artillery base bef
reaching **Culla Beach** – the best of many great beaches – and the ruins of **Bor**
**Castle** with 10-foot (3-metre) thick walls. The castle, one of the most impo
tant medieval ruins in the Outer Hebrides, was built in the 14th century and w
the home of the MacDonalds of Clanranald, who once ruled Benbecula.

The South Ford, separating Benbecula and **South Uist**, is crossed by a half-mile (800-metre) long single-track bridge. Immediately on entering South Uist turn right and drive for 1 mile (1.6 km) along the loch-lined road to **Eochar** and the shell-covered school bus in Flora Johnstone's garden. Flora so enjoyed sticking on shells that, in the 1960s, she then started on her cottage walls. Beyond this is **Loch Bee**, with its hundreds of mute swans.

## Beach beauty

Return to the main road (A865), which runs down the west of the island for 22 miles (35 km). All the time, to the west, are seascapes with yet more splendid beaches and, to the east, mountains and peat bogs dominated by **Beinn Mhor** (2,034 feet/620 metres) and **Hecla** (1,988 feet/606 metres). These names, Celtic and Norse, reveal the dual main stream in the island's population.

First encountered to the east, after 4 miles (6 km), atop **Rueval Hill**, "hill of miracles", is the modern pencil-like statue of **Madonna and Child**, which was paid for by worldwide donations. Just beyond this, still to the east, is the **Loch Druidibeg Nature Reserve**, with its corncrakes and greylag geese.

Next, to the west, is **Howmore**. Little here indicates that this was the ancient ecclesiastical centre of the island: now, protected whitewashed cottages, one a youth hostel, stand in flowery meadows. Continue beyond Howmore to reach a superb beach. A little further to the south is the renovated **Kildonan Museum** with local history displays, crafts shops and a tearoom. Nearby, before the turn-off to **Milton**, is a bronze cairn and plaque honouring the birthplace of Flora MacDonald. Two miles (3 km) further south, the A865 turns left to run for 4 miles (6 km) to tiny **Lochboisdale** ⑥, the main village in the south of the island and the terminal for the Oban ferry.

*Flights to Barra have to work to a flexible timetable: the runway disappears twice a day under the incoming tide.*

**BELOW:** coming out of her shell: Flora Johnstone of Eochar, South Uist.

At **Pollachar**, at the southwest tip, is a 3,000-year-old standing stone surrounded by wild orchids and clover from where you can gaze across to Eriskay and Barra. From **Ludag**, 1 mile (1.6 km) to the east, a car ferry (tides willing) crosses the 1½-mile (2-km) stretch to **Eriskay**. The island, the subject of the hauntingly beautiful "Eriskay Love Lilt", is disappointing, though for a fishing island only 2 by 3 miles (3 by 5 km) with a population of around 200, it has had much fame. Bonnie Prince Charlie landed on the long silver beach on the west side on 23 July 1745. Two hundred years later the *Politician*, a cargo ship laden with whisky, sank in the Eriskay Sound. Compton Mackenzie's *Whisky Galore* (known in America as *Tight Little Island*) was a hilarious retelling of the redistribution of the cargo.

Fishing dominates **Barra** ⑦, as it always has. In the 1880s, choice Barra cockles were eaten in London. By the 1920s Barra herring were so important that girls came from as far away as Yarmouth in England to work 15 hours a day in **Castlebay**, the capital, gutting the silver darlings. In the past 20 years, lobster fishing has become important, with about 40 boats operating.

The **Barra Heritage Centre** (open Easter–Sept daily; tel: (01871) 810413; admission charge) tells the island's story. Also worth visiting is **Kisimul Castle**, the home of the MacNeils of Barra (open Apr–Sept Mon–Sat; tel: (01871) 810313; admission charge). ❑

# CENTRAL SCOTLAND

*Perth is a superb centre for exploring the Central Highlands – the ochs of the Trossachs, the ancient city of St Andrews and romantic castles nestling in the hills*

Georgian terraces and imposing civic buildings line the riverside in the genteel city of **Perth** , but principal streets are uncompromisingly Victorian. No dullness, though. "All things bright and beautiful" on the 36 bells of the handsome 15th-century **St John's Kirk** heralds the hour strike – a contrast to John Knox's iconoclastic preaching here in the mid-16th century.

Behind the imposing portico and dome of the **Museum and Art Gallery** (open Mon–Sat; tel: (01738) 632488; free) is drama in Sir David Young Cameron's landscape *Shadows of Glencoe*, in the stuffed but still snarling wildcat, its bushy tail black-tipped, and in Perth's link with space, the Strathmore Meteorite of 1917. More art can be enjoyed in the roundhouse of the old waterworks, now the delightful **Fergusson Gallery** (open Mon–Sat; tel: (01738) 441944; free) devoted to the life and works of the Perthshire painter J. D. Fergusson, one of the Scottish Colourists. *The Fair Maid of Perth*, Sir Walter Scott's virginal heroine, lived in **Fair Maid's House**, the setting for his novel of the scene of the battle of Clans on the meadow of the North Inch nearby.

Those with presents to buy are catered for at **Caithness Glass** at Inveralmond (open daily; tel: (01738) 492320; free), where the mysteries of glass-blowing are revealed (Mon–Fri) and there's a shop. For exercise you can walk round the **Bells Cherrybank Gardens** (open May–Sept Mon–Sat and Sun pm; tel: (01738) 627330; admission charge) with the National Heather Collection, or go for something more energetic at **Bells Sports Centre** (open daily; tel: (01738) 622301), both on Glasgow Road. History and tradition take the stage in the **Perth Theatre**, the longest established theatre in Scotland.

## Beyond the city

Splendid views over the city and River Tay can be enjoyed from the top of **Kinnoull Hill** on the outskirts of the city, while **Branklyn Garden** (open daily; admission charge; tel: (01738) 625535) has been described as "the finest two acres of private garden in the country".

Perth is ringed with castles, some family homes, others romantic ruins like **Huntingtower Castle**, 3 miles (5 km) west (open Apr–Sept daily, Oct–Mar closed Thur and Fri; tel: (01738) 627231; admission charge). An intriguing rooftop walk gives glimpses of hidden stairs and dark voids that must have struck terror into James I during his year's imprisonment here.

**Scone Palace** (open Easter–Oct daily; tel: (01738) 552300; admission charge), 2 miles (3 km) north of Perth, was Scotland's Camelot and home to the much travelled Stone on which 40 kings of Scotland were crowned. Brought here in the 9th century and taken to London in 1296 by Edward I, it was stolen in 1950 from beneath the Coronation Chair in Westminster Abbey and

**PRECEDING PAGES:**
St Andrews
cathedral and
graveyard.
**LEFT:** Scone Palace.
**BELOW:** a race on
the River Tay.

recovered from Arbroath. (It is now in Edinburgh Castle.) The Earl of Mansfield
home offers such diverse charms as six generations of family photographs, High
land cattle, ornamental fowls and giant trees, as well as period furniture, elega
porcelain and paintings.

A lake for all seasons, **Loch Leven ②** is heaven for trout anglers and the ch
sen wintering ground for wild geese and other waterfowl. On an island a
reached by ferry from the lochside is the ruined **Loch Leven Castle** (op
Apr–Sept daily; tel: (07778) 040483 and (07767) 651566; admission charge
once prison to the notorious Wolf of Badenoch and Mary Queen of Scots.

**Falkland Palace ③** (open Easter–Oct Mon–Sat and Sun pm; tel: (0133
857397; admission charge), sitting cosily in the main street of its old Roy
Burgh, was the favourite retreat of the Stuart kings. Stone lintels that top ma
doors carry the incised initials of the couples the houses were built for in t
1600s, the date and a heart. Loving care is evident everywhere in the many lau
dered green spaces and carefully conserved weavers' houses.

**Castle Campbell ④** (open Apr–Sept daily, Oct–Mar closed Thur and F
tel:(01259) 742408; admission charge) is rather impressively situated at the he
of Dollar Glen, southwest of Perth. **Menstrie Castle** (open Easter and May–Se
Wed and Sun pm; tel: (01259) 211701; free), near Stirling, the birthplace of S
William Alexander, James VI's lieutenant, links Scotland with Nova Scotia.

## The kingdom of Fife

The M90 motorway that links Perth to Edinburgh does more than bypass Fi
thrust out into the North Sea between the Firth of Forth and the Tay. It bypass
an area rich in history, architecture and scenery. The kingdom's harbours nud

*A guided tour of
Falkland Palace
includes an explan-
ation of Royal
Tennis, the game of
kings (quite unlike
modern tennis) that
has been played on
the court here since
1539.*

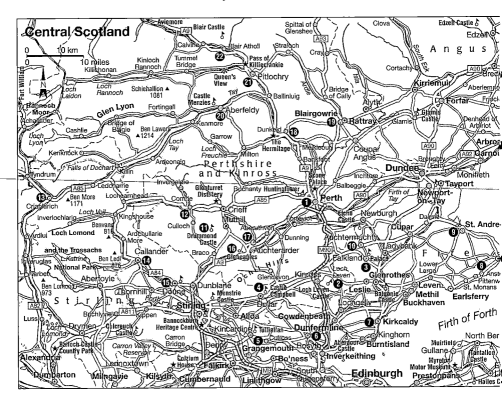

Map opposite

ie another on a coast tilted towards Scandinavia, buildings reflecting the thriv-
g trade it had in the 17th century with the Baltic and the Low Countries.

**Culross** ❺, where the Firth of Forth narrows, is a unique survival: a 17th-
id 18th-century town that looks like a film set, and often is. Then it was a
noky, industrial town with coal mines and salt pans, manufacturing griddles
id baking plates for oatcakes. Sir George Bruce, who took over where the min-
g monks left off in 1575, went on to such success that James VI made Culross
Royal Burgh. Today, the town's wealth of old buildings, with crow-stepped
ibles and red pantiled roofs, make it one of Scotland's finest showplaces. The
ıwn House's clock tower dominates the waterfront (house open June–Aug
iily, Mar–May, Sept and Oct daily pm only; tel: (01383) 880359; admission
iarge) and the **Mercat Cross**, the tiny market place and oldest house (1577).

Wynds, or pathways, lead past the **Palace** (open as Town House; closed Oct),
hich is probably the finest gentleman's house of its period in Scotland, the
itudy" (open as Town House), with a 17th-century Norwegian painted ceil-
g, and **Snuff Cottage** (1673). Past the house with the Evil Eyes are the church,
e ruined abbey and the magnificent Abbey House.

Although **Dunfermline** ❻ was for 600 years capital of Scotland, burial place
kings, with a fine church and abbey (open daily Oct–Mar closed Thur pm,
:i and Sun am; tel: (01383) 739026; admission charge), it owes its interna-
ınal fame to its humblest son, Andrew Carnegie. The great philanthropist
)ened the first of 3,000 free libraries here in 1881. The tiny cottage where he
as born (open Apr–Oct Mon–Sat and Sun pm; tel: (01383) 724302; admission
iarge) contrasts vividly with **Pittencrieff House**, the mansion he left to the
wn on his death, which is now a museum with changing exhibitions on local

*An inscription on
Snuff Cottage reads
"Wha wad ha thocht
it". "Noses wad ha
bought it" is the sec-
ond line, which is on
a house in Edin-
burgh owned by the
same snuff merchant.*

**BELOW:** the gardens
at Falkland Palace,
a favourite retreat
of the Stuarts.

history, costume and other period themes (open daily; tel: (01383) 722935; free
The cut-out words "King Robert the Bruce" on the church tower advertise h
burial here in 1329. At **Leven**, behind the esplanade and the parked oil rigs, a
marvellous shell gardens. Begun in 1914, walls, walks, menagerie and avia
are patterned with shells, broken china and Staffordshire figures.

**Kirkcaldy's** ❼ association with coal and floor coverings may not appeal, b
the Lang Town, as it is often called, made important contributions to architectur
economics and literature. Robert Adam and Adam Smith were born here an
the **Kirkcaldy Museum** (open Mon–Sat and Sun pm; tel: (01592) 412860; fre
has a superb collection of paintings by the Scottish Colourists, Sir Henry Ra
burn and Sir David Wilkie, and also the distinctive Wemyss Ware pottery ca
be viewed. Lower Largo, its tiny harbour and inn stage-set beneath a viaduc
gave birth in 1676 to Alexander Selkirk, Daniel Defoe's "Robinson Crusoe
The original "Fifie" fishing boats were built at **St Monans**, but the shipya
now builds only pleasure craft. A path leads from the harbour to the 14th-centu
church, its feet on the rocky shore.

**Pittenweem** bustles with the business of fish. Nearby, **Anstruther** ❽, wi
the **Scottish Fisheries Museum** (open daily; tel: (01333) 310628; admissic
charge), and **Crail** end the run of picturesque harbours before Fife Ness
reached. The oldest Royal Burgh in East Neuk, Crail's crow-stepped gables a
red-tiled roofs ensure that artists outnumber fishermen.

There is a nice contrast in leaving the simplicities of Crail for the concentr
tion of learning, religious importance and historical significance that is
**Andrews** ❾. Best known as the home of golf, by 2008 it will have seven cours
to offer players and a collection of memorabilia on display at the **British Go**

*BELOW: gutting fish in Crail harbour.*

## ANCIENT AND ROYAL

The Scots are so obsessed with golf that it is said that Mary Queen of Scots went off to play when her husband had just been assassinated. Wherever you are in Scotland there will be a golf course nearby. There are over 500 courses to choose from, and even tiny Highland villages have their own 9-hole courses. The game was developed as far back as the 16th century on the coastal courses known as "links", and you can still pl on some of the world's oldest courses along the east coa of Scotland – though for a cheaper round it's advisable avoid the Championship courses.

At St Andrews, golf qualifies as "ancient" as well a "royal": its Old Course was laid out in the 15th century an the Royal and Ancient Golf Club formed in 1754. There a no fewer than six courses here. The Old Course is flanke by the New on the seaward and by the Eden on the inla side. Tucked between the New and the whitecaps of t North Sea is the shorter Jubilee Course. The Strathtyru is an 18-hole course of modest length, while the Balgro is a 9-hole beginners' layout. In 2008, the 18-hole Cas Course will also open (www.standrews.org.uk).

Map, page 260

**Iuseum** (open Nov–Mar Mon–Sat; tel: (01334) 460046; admission charge) ımediately opposite the "Old" starters' hut.

The damage to the cathedral following John Knox's impassioned sermons arted neglect that reduced it to ruins. **St Rule** nearby survives as a tower, and **t Andrews Castle** (open daily; tel: (01334) 477196; admission charge) fared ttle better, though it has a wonderful dungeon that children find irresistible. Isewhere, the **West Port** spans a main street and steeples abound, but not for imbing, as Dr Johnson found. At the **Aquarium** (open daily; tel: (01334) 74786; admission charge) all kinds of marine life can be seen settings that semble their natural surroundings. The **University**, whose buildings line North treet, is the oldest in Scotland.

Off the road back to Perth is **Hill of Tarvit** (open Apr–May and Sept, hur–Mon 1–5pm; June–Aug, daily 1–5pm; tel: (0844) 4932185; admission ıarge), a superb mansion house remodelled by Sir Robert Lorimer with mag-ıficent garden and grounds (open daily all year). Further on, **Auchtermuchty** ) has surviving thatched cottages once used by weavers. The tea shop keeps ւe key to the Pictish, chimney-like church tower. At the base of the tower is an ıcised Pictish stone.

## ·ochs, rivers and mountains

/estward from Perth, roads follow rivers in the ascent to the lochs and watershed ʄ the Grampians. At **Crieff** you can visit **Glenturret**, the oldest distillery in ːotland (open daily; tel: (01764) 656565; admission charge), and glass, pot-·ry and textile workshops. The romance of the **Drummond Arms** as the scene ʄ Prince Charles Edward's council of war in 1746 endures though it has been

*Innerpeffray Library has a Treacle Bible, so called because "Is there no balm in Gilead?" is translated into "Is there no treacle in Gilead?"*

**BELOW:** students celebrating Raisin Day at St Andrews University.

*The cathedral and town of Dunkeld were fought over and the Highlanders defeated in 1689. Only the choir of the cathedral was restored and the main building is still roofless.*

**BELOW:** climbing up the Black Watch Monument near Aberfeldy.

rebuilt. Five miles (8 km) southeast of Crieff is the oldest public library in Scotland, the **Innerpeffray Library** (Mar–Oct, Wed–Sat and Sun pm; tel: (0176 652819; admission charge), founded in 1680. Also near Crieff, **Drummond Castle** ⑪ opens only its Italianate gardens (open Easter and May–Oct daily pm; te (01764) 681433; admission charge).

**Comrie's** ⑫ situation on the River Earn where two glens meet makes it ᵃ attractive walking centre. The town is on the Highland Boundary Fault and known as "Scotland's Earthquake Centre". From Comrie the road passes Loᴄ Earn with magnificent mountain scenery until **Lochearnhead** is reache Beyond here the high peaks have it – **Ben More**, **Ben Lui** and **Ben Bhuidhe** until the lochs reach in like fingers from the coast of the Western Isles.

**Crianlarich** ⑬ is a popular centre with climbers and walkers. For those ᴏ wheels, **Ardlui** is a beautiful introduction to **Loch Lomond**. The largest body ᴏ water in Britain, full of fish and islands, it is best known through the song whiᴄ one of Prince Charles Edward's followers wrote on the eve of his execution. ᴀ the south end of the loch is the **Balloch Castle Country Park** (castle visitᴏ centre open Easter–Oct daily; garden open daily all year; tel: (01389) 75821ᴇ Also in Balloch is the National Park Gateway Centre, the visitor centre for tʰ **Loch Lomond and the Trossachs National Park**. Opened in July 2002, encompasses 720 sq miles (1,865 sq km) of wonderful scenery.

The road back to **Aberfoyle** traverses the Queen Elizabeth Forest Park and leaᴅ to the splendid wooded scenery of the **Trossachs**, best viewed on foot or from tʰ summer steamer on **Loch Katrine**. Scott's *Lady of the Lake* and *Rob Roy* attractᴇ flocks of Victorian visitors. **Callander** ⑭ found fame as the "Tannochbrae" of tʰ BBC TV series *Dr Finlay's Casebook*. In Callander the **Toy Museum** (open daiᴸ Apr–Oct; tel: (01877) 330004) is crammed with toys froᴹ the past 100 years including Victorian-era tin soldiers.

**Doune's** 15th-century castle ⑮ (open Apr–Sept dailʸ Oct–Mar closed Thur and Fri; tel: (01786) 84174: admission charge) is remarkably complete with tw great towers and hall between. Close by is **Dunblan** the west front of its 13th-century cathedral was describᴇ by the Victorian writer Ruskin as a perfect example ᴏ Scotland's church architecture. Eleven miles (18 kmᵐ east of Dunblane, the famous moorland courses ᴏ **Gleneagles** ⑯ are a golfer's paradise.

**Auchterarder's** ⑰ situation to the north of the Ochᵉ Hills is a convenient point at which to hit the Mill Traiᴸ Thanks to good grazing and soft water, Scotland's worlᵈ famous tweeds, tartans and knitwear have been producᴇ here in the Hillfoots villages since the 16th century. Tʰ trail leads from the Heritage Centre in Auchterarder, wiᵗ the only surviving steam textile engine and Tillicoultry handsome Clock Mill powered by waterwheel, to tʰ most modern mills in Alloa and Sauchie.

## Moving north

From Perth, the road north bypasses **Bankfoot's** raspᵇ berry canes and motor museum. At **Dunkeld** ⑱, crosᵗ Telford's fine bridge over the Tay's rocky bed for tʰ charm and character of this old ecclesiastical capital ᴏ Scotland. A delightful museum in the cathedral's **Chapᵗ ter House** introduces Niel Gow, the celebrated fiddler.

Romantics will feel at home at **The Hermitage**, west of the town. Built in 1758, ˑis is the centrepiece of a woodland trail beside the River Braan, a folly poised ˑer a waterfall. At the foot of the Highlands is **Blairgowrie** . which reserves ˑ charm for anglers and lovers of raspberries and strawberries. At **Meikleour** ˑe road to Perth is bordered by a beech hedge, over 120 ft (36 metres) high and ˑ804 ft (550 metres) long and planted in 1746.

**Aberfeldy** ⓴, easily reached from Dunkeld, is noted for the fine Wade Bridge ˑross the Tay, built in 1733. A beautiful walk is through the **Birks of Aberfeldy** the Moness Falls. To the west of Aberfeldy is **Castle Menzies** (open Apr–mid-ˑct Mon–Sat and Sun pm; tel: (01887) 820982; admission charge), a good exam-ˑe of a 16th-century Z-plan tower house. Beyond is glorious **Glen Lyon**, the ˑngest and one of the most beautiful glens in Scotland, with the village of **Fortin-ˑll**, where you can find Scotland's oldest tree, a yew over 3,000 years old. ˑearby, **Loch Tay**, a centre for salmon fisheries, has **Ben Lawers** 3,984 ft (1,214 ˑetres) towering above it.

Seek out **Pitlochry** ㉑ for spectacle. The Festival Theatre, magnificently situ-ˑed overlooking the River Tummel, has an excellent summer programme of ˑama and music. But it's upstaged by the dam at the hydroelectric power station ˑhere in spring and summer thousands of migrating salmon can be seen through ˑindows in a fish ladder (open Apr–Oct daily; tel: (01796) 473152). The Queen's ˑiew, 8 miles (13 km) northwest of Pitlochry, is a truly royal vista up Loch Tum-ˑel, dominated by the cone-shaped Schiehallion (3,547 ft/1,081 metres).

Beyond the **Pass of Killiecrankie** where Soldier's Leap recalls the battle of ˑ89, is **Blair Atholl** ㉒, key to the Central Highlands, and Blair Castle (open ˑr–Oct: daily; tel: (01796) 481207; admission charge). ❑

*Blair Castle is home to the Duke of Atholl, the only person in Britain permitted to have a private army.*

**BELOW:** the Pitlochry Valley.

# THE EAST COAST

*he coast and countryside between the Firth of Tay and the sandy
ɔray Firth is a region of rare and subtle loveliness: here the scale
is human and the the history dense*

Map. pages 270-1

cotland's east coast and its hinterland are often neglected by indolent
tourists, but reward industrious ones. This is, after all, probably the most
industrious (but not industrial) region of the country. Its ports and coastal
lages have given Scotland its fishing industry. Its agriculture, from the rich
·plands of Angus to the famous beef farms of Aberdeenshire – the largest
ɜtch of uninterrupted farmland in Britain – has been hard won and hard
rked. "Our ancestors imposed their will on Buchan," says the writer John R.
lan of that flinty outcrop buffeted by the North Sea, "an idea imposed on
·ure at great expense of labour and endurance, of weariness and suffering."
t is, therefore, the east coast of Scotland which most physically and visibly
ɜmplifies that which is most dogged and determined (and perhaps dour) in
Scottish character; and which best knows how to exploit its assets. The north-
t port of Peterhead, for example, already Europe's busiest fishing harbour,
ɩed itself into a major berth for North Sea oil-supply vessels; while the gen-
, wooded valley of the River Spey is not only the centre of malt whisky pro-
ɔtion but with its "Malt Whisky Trail" has made tourist capital out of its
ebrated local industry.

Along this coast you can learn to live without the majestic wilderness and
thic melodrama of the West Highlands and their
·hipelago – although you will find echoes of their
·⍺osphere in the Grampian glens of Angus and the out-
·ers of the Cairngorms which reach into Aberdeen-
·re – and explore the versatility of man's dealings with
land and the sea.

## ⍰e of two cities

ɜ east coast cities are **Dundee** and **Aberdeen**, of
·⍺parable size (about 200,000) and separated only by
·miles (110 km). In recent years, Dundee, which long
ɩ the feel of a city down on its luck, has capitalised
its vigorous industrial past – rooted in textiles, ship-
·lding and jute – and has transformed itself into a pop-
·⍰ destination and a vibrant centre of arts, culture and
·covery. On the other hand, Aberdeen, the "Granite
y", is as solid and unyielding as its nickname, a town
;uch accustomed prosperity and self-confidence that
ɩssumed its new title of oil capital of Europe as
ugh doing the multinationals a favour.

Topographically, **Dundee** ❶ promises more than it
ɩills. It has a magnificent position on the Tay estuary.
; dominated by an extinct volcano called the Law, and
·ɩas been fancifully called the Naples of the North.
·m the south side of the estuary, from the spectacular
·roaches of its road and rail bridges, you might be per-
·ded that its setting merits the comparison. There are
·er points of similarity. Like Naples, Dundee has had

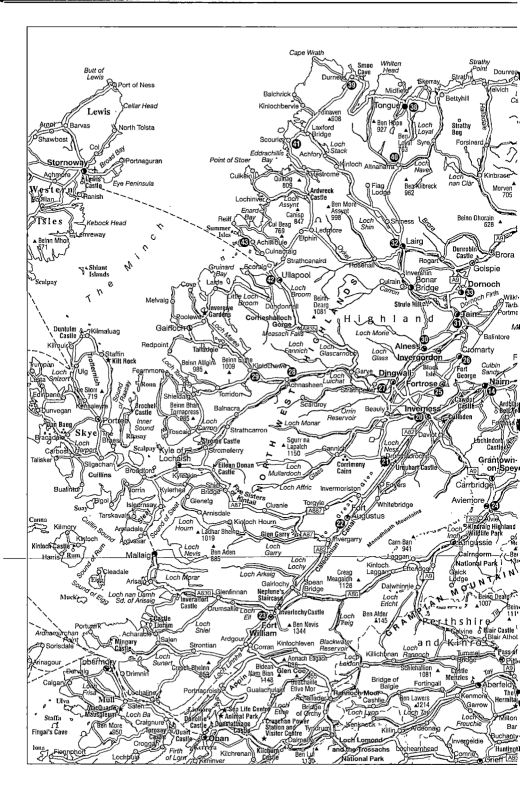

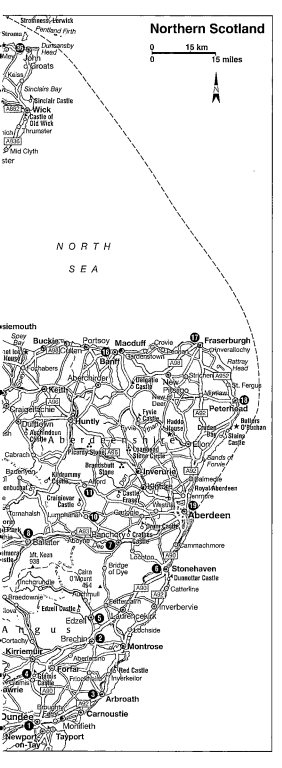

**Northern Scotland**

0          15 km
0                  15 miles

N

NORTH

SEA

its share of slums and deprivation; like Naples, it is a port with a long maritime history (it was once the centre of the Scottish wine trade, and a leading importer of French claret). Unlike Naples, it has dealt its own history a mortal blow by destroying its past in a series of insensitive and sometimes shady developments.

"Perhaps no town in Scotland has been oftener sacked, pillaged and destroyed than Dundee," wrote an 18th-century historian, commenting on the fact that since the 11th century Dundee had the habit of picking the losing side in the various internecine and international conflicts which plagued Scotland. The city's own fathers – and the **University of Dundee** – completed the process in the 20th century. A distinguished Scottish newspaper editor refused to set foot in Dundee after a graceful 17th-century town house was demolished to make way for the building of the **Caird Hall** (concerts and civic events) in the 1930s. Less controversial is the purpose-built **Dundee Contemporary Arts Centre** by the River Tay (open daily; tel: (01382) 909900).

## Building on the past

Little is left of antiquity for the history-conscious tourist: the 15th-century **Old Steeple**; the venerable **Howff graveyard**, which occupies land given to the city by Mary Queen of Scots; the **East Port**, remnant of Dundee's fortified wall. But showing new initiative – and in the spirit of enterprise which is revitalising its economy through sunrise industries – Dundee is now capitalising on its maritime past.

The major attraction is **Discovery Point** (open daily; tel: (01382) 201245; admission charge), which tells the story of Antarctic discovery and has displays on the "last wilderness" of Antarctica. Captain Scott's ship *Discovery*, built in Dundee, is moored here and may be boarded. In Victoria Dock is the restored HMS *Unicorn* (open Apr–Oct daily, Nov–Mar Sat and Sun, Wed–Fri pm; tel: (01382) 200900; admission charge), the oldest British warship still afloat and one of only four frigates left in the world. Dundee had a high reputation for building clippers and whalers

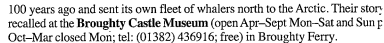

*The flagstaff of the Signal Tower once signalled personal messages to the Bellrock Lighthouse. If a keeper's wife gave birth to a child, trousers or a petticoat would be hoisted to tell him whether the baby was a boy or girl.*

**BELOW:** service with a smile in Dundee.

100 years ago and sent its own fleet of whalers north to the Arctic. Their story recalled at the **Broughty Castle Museum** (open Apr–Sept Mon–Sat and Sun p Oct–Mar closed Mon; tel: (01382) 436916; free) in Broughty Ferry.

Another reminder of past glories is to be found at the award-winning **V dant Works** (open Nov–Mar Wed–Sun; tel: (01382) 225282; admission charg a former jute mill in which an imaginative range of displays now tell the h tory of Dundee's important jute and textiles industries. Looking forward, **S sation Dundee** (open daily; tel: (01382) 228800; admission charge) is innovative hands-on science centre that focuses on the five senses.

Outside of Dundee, the county of Angus is an eloquent fusion of hill, gl farmland, beaches and cliffs, and its towns and villages reach back into the da of Scottish history. **Brechin ❷** has a 12th-century cathedral and one of the o two Celtic round towers remaining on the Scottish mainland. Set in the Brec Castle Centre Country Park, **Pictavia** (open daily Apr–Oct; tel: (01356) 6262 admission charge) visitor centre tells the story of the Picts, the first known inh itants of Scotland. The twin Caterthun Hills near Brechin are ringed with c centric Iron Age ramparts and there are Pictish sculptured stones in churchyard of **Aberlemno**, off the A90, while the former Royal Burgh **Arbroath ❸**, a fishing port and holiday resort moving into light industry, v once a Pictish settlement.

**Arbroath Abbey** (open daily; tel: (01241) 878756; admission charge), no handsome ruin, dates back to 1178 and was the scene, in 1320, of a key event in troubled history of Scotland: the signing of the Declaration of Arbroath. The the Scottish nobles reaffirmed their determination to resist the persistent invasi of the English and to preserve the liberty and independence of their country.

Arbroath's red cliffs and harbour at the Fit o' the T (foot of the town) remain atmospheric, with its lo cottage industry of smoking haddock to produce celebrated Smokies. The **Signal Tower** complex, b in 1813 to serve the families of the keepers of the lon Bellrock Lighthouse, now houses a museum (o Mon–Sat, July–Aug also Sun pm, Sept–June clo Sun; tel: (01241) 875598; free) telling the story of lighthouse and its keepers and the Arbroath people.

### Royal setting

Between Arbroath and Dundee is the resort **Carnoustie**, which has a famous golf course and a lo sand, while 13 miles (22 km) to the north is the eleg town of **Montrose**, built at the mouth of a vast ti basin which is the winter home of pink-footed Ar geese. Inland, the country town of **Forfar** (where K Malcolm Canmore held his first parliament in 1057 a striking point for the gloriously underused and so how secretive glens of Angus and lies close to w must be considered the county's star attraction: **Gla Castle ❹** (open Mar–Dec daily; tel: (01307) 8403 admission charge), the exquisite fairy-tale home of Earls of Strathmore and Kinghorne and the childh home of the late Queen Mother. It was claimed Shakespeare for the legendary setting of *Macbe* ("Hail Macbeth, Thane of Glamis!")

A group of 17th-century cottages in the village

.mis have now been turned by the National Trust for Scotland into the **Angus lk Museum** (open Apr–June and Sept weekends only, July–Aug Mon–Sat ⋆ Sun pm; tel: (01307) 840288; admission charge), illustrating the nature of ⋆nestic and agricultural life over the past 200 years.

⋆ visit to Glamis can be combined with a visit to **Kirriemuir,** birthplace of the ⋆ter J.M. Barrie and the "Thrums" of his novels. The house in which the author *ᵖeter Pan* was born is a museum (open Mar–Oct Sat–Wed pm; tel: (01575) ⋆646; admission charge) where you can see Barrie's very first theatre.

⋆irriemuir is also the gateway to **Glen Prosen** and **Glen Clova,** from where committed walker can penetrate deep into the heart of the Grampians to **Glen** ⋆l and pick up the old drove roads over to Deeside. These routes were once ⋆d by armies, rebels and whisky smugglers, as well as cattle drovers. They ⋆k easy walking on the Ordnance Survey map, but can be treacherous.

⋆o the southwest is **Glen Isla** and to the north **Glen Lethnot** (route of a ⋆hisky road" formerly used by smugglers to outwit Revenue men). Here too is graceful, meandering **Glen Esk,** which is reached through the pretty village ⋆dzell ❺, where **Edzell Castle** (open Apr–Sept daily, Oct–Mar closed Thur ⋆ Fri; tel: (01356) 648631; admission charge), the ancestral home of the Lind-⋆ family, has a magnificent walled Renaissance garden.

### e challenge of the northeast

⋆zell lies on the Angus boundary with Aberdeenshire, and here the country-⋆ begins to alter subtly. It lies, too, on the western edge of the **Howe of the** ⋆arns, which means something special to lovers of Scottish literature. This ⋆he howe, or vale, which nurtured Lewis Grassic Gibbon, whose brilliant tril-

**TIP**

The Scottish Wildlife Trust has an informative Visitor Centre (open daily; tel: (01674) 676336) on the south side of the tidal basin at Montrose, from which many birds can be viewed.

**BELOW:** Glamis Castle: exterior grandeur and interior splendour.

ogy *A Scots Quair* gave the 20th-century Scottish novel and the Scots langu its most distinctive voice: *Sunset Song, Cloud Howe, Grey Granite.* The **Gı sic Gibbon Centre** at Arbuthnott (open Mar–Oct daily; tel: (01561) 3616 admission charge) tells his life story. His lilting, limpid prose sings in your e as you cross these rolling fields of rich red earth and granite boulders to a co that becomes ever more riven and rugged as you near **Stonehaven**  and the skies, luminous light, spare landscape and chilly challenge of the northeast

"The Highland Fault meets the sea at Stonehaven, and when you cross it ' say goodbye to ease and amplitude," writes John R. Allan, the northeast's m eloquent advocate. The A90 to Aberdeen bypasses Stonehaven, but this li fishing port-turned-seaside resort is worth a visit for the drama of its cliffs . **Dunnottar Castle** (open Mon–Sat and Sun pm, Nov–Mar Fri–Mon; tel: (015 762173), standing on its own giant rock south of the town. In the dungeon; these spectral ruins Covenanters were left to rot, and the Scottish Regalia – "Honours of Scotland" – were concealed in the 17th century from Cromwe Roundheads. Today's brave souls may wish to take a dip in Stonehaven's deco heated outdoor swimming pool (open June–Aug).

From Stonehaven to Aberdeen is a clear, high, exhilarating run of 15 m: (24 km) along the cliffs. But why not let the Granite City and the coast be climax to your northeast tour and take, instead, the A957 to the lower Dee ` ley? Called the Slug Road from the Gaelic for a narrow passage, it deposits ` near the little town of **Banchory** , where you can watch salmon leaping at **Bridge of Feugh** and visit the late 16th-century tower house of **Crathes** and renowned gardens (house open Easter–Oct: daily; gardens open daily all ye tel: (01330) 844525; admission charge).

## ·yal haunts

: **Dee Valley** is justly celebrated for its expansive beauty and the pellucid, ·t-brown grace of its salmon river, and at the handsome village of **Aboyne**, ,ween Banchory and Ballater, you begin to tread on the rougher hem of the .tern Highlands. Deeside's royal associations make it the tourist honeypot Aberdeenshire. **Ballater** ❽ is where the family pops down to the shops >k for the "By Appointment" signs) while staying at **Balmoral** (grounds ·. exhibitions open Apr–July daily; tel: (013397) 42534; admission charge). ·ce 1852 Balmoral has been a private royal residence, and in midsummer Queen shares her gardens with the public and her prayers with her sub- .s at nearby **Crathie** church. Eight miles (13 km) west of Balmoral on the 3 is the village of **Braemar** ❾, much loved by Queen Victoria, and best >yed in September when the Highland Gathering brings people from all ·r the world. Fairy-tale **Braemar Castle**'s surprising charm and intimacy n from being lived in (open Apr–Oct Sat–Thur, July–Aug also Fri; tel: 3397) 41219; admission charge).

'rom Banchory you can strike over to Donside (the valley of Aberdeen's sec- l, lesser-known river), taking the A980 through the village of **Lumphanan** ❿, ·ged to be the burial place of the doomed King Macbeth whose history has >ften been confused with Shakespeare's fiction. But **Macbeth's Cairn** does- ·mark the grave of the king – it is a prehistoric cairn. (It has now been estab- ·ued that Macbeth, like so many of the early Scottish kings, was buried on ·a.) You can see at Lumphanan, however, one of Scotland's earliest medieval ·chworks, the **Peel Ring of Lumphanan.**

·lear the explosively-named village of Echt is the magnificent **Castle Fraser** ·en Apr–June and Sept–Oct Wed–Sun, July–Aug ·ly; tel: (01330) 833463; admission charge). Com- ·ted in 1636, it has been the home of the Fraser chiefs ·r since. Extensive walks can be taken in the grounds. ·Jonside's metropolis is the little country town of ·ord ⓫, now promoting itself as a tourist centre. It ·. offer the **Alford Valley Railway**, a narrow-gauge ·senger steam railway which does afternoon tourist ·.s (open Apr–May and Sept Sat and Sun pm, ·ue–Aug daily; tel: (07879) 293934; admission ·rge), **Grampian Transport Museum** (open ·t–Oct daily; tel: (01975) 562292; admission charge) · nearby **Kildrummy Castle** (open Apr–Sept daily; · (01975) 571331) a romantic and extensive 13th- ·tury ruin which featured prominently in the Jacobite ·vellion of 1715.

·Ilder history can be found at the **Archaeolink** at Oyne ·en Apr–Oct daily; tel: (01464) 851500; admission ·rge) a "pre-history park" which takes you on a jour- ·' back in time.

## ·urney through the hills

·e lonely, savage massif of the **Cairngorms**, which ·ame Britain's biggest national park in 2003, domi- ·es the Eastern Highlands. There is no direct route ·ough its lofty bulk, but from Deeside and Donside ·u can pick up the road which circles round it and give ·urself a thrilling journey.

*Highlight of the Donside summer is the Lonach Highland Gathering, trad- itional games of a kind more authentic than the glitzy gath- ering at Braemar.*

**BELOW:** Balmoral Castle, the Queen's holiday home.

*You can view Strath-spey in comfort and style from the Strath-spey Railway: the steam train runs through the valley during the summer months.*

**BELOW:** blooms in the prosperous heartland of Aberdeenshire.

At the hamlet of **Cock Bridge**, 32 miles (52 km) west of Alford, beside the a tere, curtain-walled **Corgarff Castle** (open Apr–Sept daily, Oct–Mar Sat and S pm; tel: (01975) 651460), the A939 becomes the **Lecht Road**, which rises p cipitously to some 2,000 ft (600 metres) before careering giddily down into village of Tomintoul. In winter, the Lecht is almost always the first main roa Scotland to be blocked with snow, encouraging an optimistic ski developmen its summit. A mile or so to the north of that summit, look out for the **Well of Lecht**. Above a small natural spring, a white stone plaque, dated 1745, reco that five companies of the 33rd Regiment built the road from here to the Spey

**Tomintoul** ⑫, at 1,600 ft (500 metres), is one of the highest villages in Sc land and a pickup point for the "Malt Whisky Trail" which can take you mean ing (or perhaps reeling) through seven famous malt whisky distilleries in a around the Spey Valley. The **Glenlivet Distillery** (open mid-Mar–Oct: daily; (01542) 783220) was the first in Scotland to be licensed. From Glenlivet you also enjoy the extensive walks and cycleway network on the Crown Estate.

**Strathspey** – *strath* means valley – is one of the loveliest valleys in Scotland much celebrated for the excellence of its angling as for its malt whisky indus When you descend from the dark uplands of the Lecht passage through Tomint to the handsome granite town of **Grantown-on-Spey** ⑬, you see a land gradu tamed and gentled by natural woodland, open pastures and the clear, com waters of the River Spey itself. This pretty town is the focal point of the 935-mile (2,420-sq-km) **Cairngorms National Park**, Britain's biggest national p

Grantown, like so many of the small towns and large villages in this area, an 18th-century "new town", planned and built by its local laird. It makes a g centre for exploring Strathspey and it's also within easy reach of the Mo

Map, pages 270–1

rth, and the leading resort and former spa town of Nairn. The route from antown (the A939) takes you past the island castle of **Lochindorb** – once : lair of the Wolf of Badenoch – Alexander Stuart, the notorious outlawed son Robert II, who sacked the town of Forres and destroyed Elgin Cathedral.

**Nairn ⓮**, when the sun shines – and the Moray Firth claims to have the biggest are of sunshine on the Scottish mainland – is a splendid place, even elegant, with ie hotels and golf courses, glorious beaches and big blue vistas to the distant hills the north side of the firth. Look out for the resident bottlenose dolphins; boat ps are available, and the best time to see them is between June and August.

On Nairn's doorstep is **Cawdor Castle** (open May–mid-Oct daily; tel: (01667) 4615; admission charge), 14th-century home of the Thanes of Cawdor (more acbeth associations); eastwards up the coast are the ghostly **Culbin Sands**; and the Ardersier peninsula to the west is the awesome and still occupied **Fort eorge** (open daily; tel: (01667) 460232; admission charge) built to control and imidate the Highlands after the 1745 Rebellion.

*In a great sandstorm of 1695 the Culbin Sands finally over-whelmed the village of Culbin, which now lies buried beneath them.*

## asted heath

ie most poignant and atmospheric reminder of Charles Edward Stuart's costly venture, however, is **Culloden Moor**, which lies between Nairn and Inver-ss. Culloden was the last battle fought on Britain's mainland, and here in April 46 the Jacobite cause was finally lost to internal conflicts and the superior rces of the Hanoverian Army. Now owned by the National Trust for Scotland, is a melancholy, blasted place – in effect, a war graveyard where the High-iders buried their dead in communal graves marked by rough stones bearing e names of each clan. The new **Visitor Centre** (open daily; tel: (01463)

**BELOW:** a bottlenose dolphin in the Moray Forth.

*Aberdeenshire is said to have more castles, both standing and ruined, than any other county in Britain.*

**BELOW:** rough seas can confine fishing boats to port for between three weeks and three months a year.

790607; admission charge), complete with a "Battle Immersion Theatre", te the gruesome story of how in only 40 minutes the Prince's army lost 1,200 m to the King's 310. "Butcher" Cumberland's Redcoats even slaughtered some the bystanders who had come out from Inverness to watch.

The coast and countryside to the east of Nairn is worth attention – a com nation of fishing villages like **Burghead** and **Findhorn** (now famous for t Findhorn Foundation, an international "alternative" community whose life a work, based on meditation and spiritual practice, have turned the sand dun into flourishing vegetable gardens). And there are pleasing, dignified inla towns built of golden sandstone, like **Forres**, **Elgin** ⓯ and **Fochabers**, t ancient capital of Moray. Elgin's graceful cathedral, now in ruins, dates back 1224 (open Apr–Sept daily, Oct–Mar closed Thur and Fri; tel: (01343) 54717 admission charge). With its medieval street plan still well preserved, Elgin one of the loveliest towns in Scotland.

Monks clad in coarse white habits add a medieval touch to the giant **Plu carden Abbey** (open daily; tel: (01343) 890257; free), hidden in a sheltered va ley 5 miles (8 km) southwest of Elgin. The abbey, founded in 1230, fell in disrepair until, in 1948, an order of converted Benedictines started to rebuild

### Decision time

The **River Spey** debouches at Spey Bay, which is the site of the **Tugnet Ice Hou** run by the Whale and Dolphin Conservation Society (WDCS; tel: (01343) 82033 a thick-walled house with a turf roof, built in 1830 to store ice for packing salm and now housing an exhibition dedicated to the salmon fishing industry a wildlife of the Spey estuary. The Spey marks something of a boundary between t

:ile, wooded country and sandy coast of the Moray Firth and that plainer, harsher d which pushes out into the North Sea.

Iere the motoring tourist, with Aberdeen in sight, is faced with a choice. u can either cut the coastal corner by driving straight through the prosper- s heartland of Aberdeenshire by way of **Keith, Huntly, Inverurie** and yet ›re Aberdeenshire castles (Huntly, Fyvie and Castle Fraser, to name but ee); or you can hug the forbidding littoral of Banffshire and Buchan and ; for yourself John R. Allan's "stony fields and diffident trees", the work- nlike ports of **Buckie, Fraserburgh** and **Peterhead**, and that whole chain ‹ough-hewn fishing villages and harbours which has harnessed this trucu- ‹t coast into something productive. Here you will find spectacular ‹scapes, rich birdlife and the enduring fascination of working harbours, ‹h markets and museums dedicated to the maritime history. One of these, Fraserburgh, is the **Scottish Lighthouses Museum** (open Mon–Sat and ‹n pm; tel: (01346) 511022; admission charge), which tells the story of the ‹hts and keepers who manned them.

**3anff ⓰** is a town of some elegant substance with a Georgian centre, while ; 16th-century merchants' houses around **Portsoy** harbour have been agree- ly restored. This village is also distinguished for the production and working Portsoy marble, and a pottery and marble workshop are installed in one of ‹ harbour buildings, while there is beauty and drama to be found in **Cullen**, ‹h its striking 19th-century railway viaducts and its sweep of sand.

Between Macduff and **Fraserburgh ⓱**, where the coast begins to take a right- ¡le bend, tortuous minor roads link the precipitous villages of **Gardenstown,** 'ovie and **Pennan**, stuck like limpets to the bottom of cliffs, and south of

**BELOW:** Macduff: the safest haven for fishing boats on the Moray Firth.

# The Impact of North Sea Oil

The SNP would argue otherwise, but the days when it was assumed that the North Sea's "black gold" would cure all Scotland's social and industrial ailments may be long gone. The huge oil revenues have disappeared into the maw of the British Treasury, and little has come back across the border. As one Scottish nationalist put it: "Scotland must be the only country on Earth to discover oil and become worse off".

Even after devolution, Scotland still has no access to the revenues, but it has acquired a mature, technologically advanced industry that employs thousands of people and underwrites a great many other jobs all over the country. The birth of the offshore oil industry partly compensated for the jobs lost in traditional heavy industries like coal, shipbuilding and steel.

Oil was discovered in the North Sea in the 1960s, and development proceeded rapidly.

The early days between 1972 and 1979 were astonishing. Every week new schemes were announced for supply bases, refineries and petrochemical works. Scotland was galvanised. The Scottish National Party (SNP) startled Britain by getting 11 members elected to parliament in 1974 on the crude but effective slogan "It's Scotland's Oil". Heady days, but they didn't last. When the price of oil slumped in 1985–6 from $40 to less than $10 a barrel, recession struck the east coast. Nevertheless, recovery followed, and production reached a new peak of 2.95 million barrels per day in 1999. In 2007, North Sea crude oil was selling at over $60 a barrel.

Minimal government regulation and free competition make the area attractive to the oil companies. The high quality of the oil, political stability and proximity to large European markets have made the area a major world player despite relatively high production costs.

Oil and gas flow from over 100 oilfields off the east coast of Scotland. Though the UK is Europe's largest producer of oil and natural gas, the government estimates it will become a net importer of oil within a decade. Many oil platforms are in the deep, stormy waters of the East Shetland Basin, while others lie under the shallower seas east of Edinburgh. The oil comes ashore in Scotland at three points: on the island of Flotta in Orkney, at St Fergus north of Aberdeen, and at Sullom Voe in Shetland. This last is Europe's largest oil and gas terminal, processing over 500,000 barrels of crude oil per day. Its impact on the local environment is closely monitored by the Shetland Oil Terminal Environmental Advisory Group (SOTEAG) based at Aberdeen University. Aberdeen is the oil capital, where every oil company, exploration firm, oil-tool manufacturer and diving company has a foothold.

Whilst the SNP continues to fight for Scotland's share of oil revenues, major oil companies are reapproving their North Sea oil activity as older fields become less productive. Nevertheless, the days of North Sea oil production are far from over, with recent estimates suggesting in 2006 the UK produced over 1.5 million barrels of oil per day from the area, or 34 percent of overall North Sea oil production. ❑

**LEFT:** North Sea oil rig.

eterhead ⓫ the sea boils into the **Bullers O'Buchan**, a high circular basin of ιcky cliff which in spring and summer is home to untold thousands of seabirds. Close by are the gaunt clifftop ruins of **Slains Castle**, said to have ignited e imagination of Bram Stoker and inspired his novel *Dracula*. It is certain-true that Stoker spent holidays at the golfing resort of Cruden Bay, where e craggy shore begins to yield to sand until, at the village of Newburgh and e mouth of the River Ythan, you find the dramatic dune system of the **Sands Forvie** nature reserve. South from here, an uninterrupted stretch of dune ιd marram grass reaches all the way to Aberdeen.

*Writing in 1929,
H.V. Morton was
uncompromising in
his description of
Aberdeen: "a city of
granite palaces,
inhabited by people
as definite as their
building material.
Even their preju-
dices are of the same
hard character."*

## ranite city

f all Britain's cities, **Aberdeen** ⓭ is the most isolated. It comes as a shock to ive through miles of empty countryside from the south and, breasting a hill, find vealed below you the great grey settlement clasped between the arms of Dee and on, as if it were the simple, organic extension of rock and heath and shore instead a complex human artifice. On the sea's horizon you might see a semi-submersible l rig on the move; in the harbour, trawlers jostle with supply vessels; and there e raw new ribbon developments of housing and warehousing to the north and uth of the city. But otherwise Aberdeen, in its splendid self-sufficiency and glo-ιus solitude, remains curiously untouched by the coming of the oil industry.
Aberdeen is largely indifferent to the mixed reception it receives from out-ιers. Its infuriating complacency, however, has been its strength, and will almost rtainly be its salvation when the North Sea oil wells run dry and the city re-cuses on its own considerable resources of sea, land and light industry.
Much of historic Aberdeen remains, although most of its imposing city centre

**BELOW:** the graceful crown tower of· King's College.

## TONY FAÇADE

ιe city of Aberdeen inspires strong ιotions. You are either convinced at its own conceit of itself is well ·served — the city's Book of ιmembrance contains the senti-ent, "Aberdeen to Heaven — nae a ιeat step" — or you find its exposed ιerface with the North Sea and its granite austerity wintry ·aspect and chilly of soul. Even those who affect to dislike ιo so with ambivalence. The northeast's most famous ·iter, Lewis Grassic Gibbon, wrote: "It has a flinty shine ιen new — a grey glimmer like a morning North Sea, a cold ·eliness that chills the heart... Even with weathering it ιuires no gracious softness, it is merely starkly grim and compromising.... One detests Aberdeen with the detest-on of a thwarted lover. It is the one haunting and exas-ιratingly lovable city in Scotland."
To counteract its critics, the city's tourist board has tried ιrd to change the image of Aberdeen from Granite City to ·se City, lavishing attention on every flower bed in the city. efforts have been rewarded by regular victories in the ·ritain in Bloom" award (after 10 wins the city was ιbarred from entering to give other places a chance).

*Marischal College is the second-largest granite building in the world – the largest is the Escorial near Madrid.*

dates only from the 19th century, with the building of **Union Street**, its ma thoroughfare, in the early 1800s and the rebuilding of **Marischal College**, part the ancient University of Aberdeen, in 1891. The façade of Marischal Colleg which stands just off Union Street in Broad Street, is an extraordinary fretwork pinnacles and gilt flags in which the unyielding substance of white granite made to seem delicate. Occupying part of the college is an **archaeology and h tory museum** (open Mon–Fri and Sun pm; tel: (01224) 274301; free).

Union Street's die-straight mile (1.6 km) from Holborn Junction skirts t arboreal churchyard of St Nicholas, Aberdeen's "mither kirk", and terminat in the **Castlegate**, which is virtually the same square which has occupied th space since the 13th century. Its centrepiece is the 17th-century **Mercat Cros** with its sculptured portrait gallery of the Stuart monarchs.

The cross is the focus of Aberdeen's long history as a major market town a import-export centre. For centuries fishwives from **Fittie**, the fishing village the foot of the Dee, and farmers from the expansive hinterland brought the produce to sell round the cross, while more exotic products from Europe a the New World were hefted up the hill from the harbour by porters from t Shore Porters' Society, Britain's oldest company.

## Historic sights

Aberdeen's oldest quarter and civic origins, however, lie to the northwest of t city centre on the banks of the River Don, whose narrow, sandy estuary w never developed as harbour and port in the manner of its larger twin, the De Although Aberdeen was already a busy port when it was granted a royal chart in the 12th century by King William the Lion, its earliest settlement was to

...und clustered around **St Machar's Cathedral** in Old Aberdeen, once an inde-
...ndent burgh. The cathedral, founded in the 6th century, is one of the oldest
...ranite buildings in the city (although it has a red sandstone arch which is a rem-
...ant of an earlier building) and has colourful, jewel-like stained-glass windows.
...he cobbled streets and lamplit academic houses surrounding it are atmospheric
...d peaceful. Here, too, is Aberdeen's first university, **King's College** (founded
... 1495 by Bishop Elphinstone).

Aberdeen's history has often been self-protective; the city gave the Duke of
...umberland, later to become infamous as "Butcher" Cumberland, a civic recep-
...on as he led his Hanoverian army north to confront Prince Charles Edward
...tuart's Jacobites at Culloden. But it is to its credit that it offered protection to
...obert the Bruce during Scotland's Wars of Independence in the 14th century. In
...turn, Bruce gave the "Freedom Lands" to the city (which still bring it an
...come) and ordered the completion of the **Brig o' Balgownie** (bridge), whose
...uilding had been interrupted by the wars.

*Brig o' Balgownie, near St Machar's Cathedral, is the oldest Gothic bridge in Scotland.*

## ...resent attractions

...he vigorous **Art Gallery** on Schoolhill (open Mon–Sat and Sun pm; tel: (01224)
...23700; free) has an impressive collection of European paintings mainly from the
...8th to the 20th century, as well as works by contemporary Scottish artists and a
...culpture court. For anyone with a military bent, the **Gordon Highlanders**
**...useum** (open Apr–Oct Tues–Sat and Sun pm; tel: (01224) 311200; admission
...arge) is a must. This unique collection tells the story of one of the most cele-
...ated fighting units in the British Army. There is also an award-winning **Mar-**
**...ime Museum** (open Mon–Sat and Sun pm; tel: (01224) 337700; free) that recalls
...berdeen's long and fascinating relationship with the sea.

**BELOW:** Aberdeen Art Gallery.

A lively theatre, a succession of festivals and games –
...u could go on listing the more obvious attractions of
...berdeen. Today, besides all its other activities, Aberdeen
...nfidently promotes itself as a holiday resort. Children
...all ages make a beeline for **Satrosphere** (open daily;
...l: (01224) 640340; admission charge), a "hands-on"
...teractive science and technology centre.

And between the mouths of the two rivers the sands
...e authentically golden, though don't expect to sunbathe
...ten or comfortably on them: the northeast gets a major
...hare of Scotland's sunshine, but Aberdeen's beach is
...en-backed and exposed to every bitter breeze from the
...orth Sea. Its parks, however, are glorious, wonderfully
...ell kept and celebrated, like many of the other open
...aces, for their roses. The **Cruickshank Botanic Gar-**
**...n** (open Mon–Fri; free) in the university area also has
...plendid variety of plants from many parts of the world.

Further afield, **Hazelhead**, on the city's western edge,
**...uthie Park**, with extensive winter gardens, and
...aton Park on the River Don are probably the best
...en spaces, but all have good play areas and special
...tractions for children in summer. There is also a per-
...anent funfair at the beach and, a few miles inland at
...aryculter in the Dee Valley, one of the country's most
...tractive small "theme parks": **Storybook Glen** (open
...ily; tel: (01224) 732941; admission charge), with
...ant tableaux of favourite childhood characters. ❑

# THE NORTHERN HIGHLANDS

*Favourite haunt of royalty – past and present – the Highlands
is a place of many colours: faded industrial glory, wild northern
coastline and the beauty of glen and mountain*

Nowhere in Britain is the bloodied hand of the past so heavily laid as it is the Highlands. The pages of its history read like a film script – and has often served as one. There are starring roles for Bonnie Prince Charl Flora MacDonald, Mary Queen of Scots, Rob Roy, the Wolf of Badenoch a Macbeth, with a supporting cast of clansmen and crofters, miners and fish folk, businessmen and sportsmen.

The cameras could find no better point at which to start turning than **Invern** , the natural "capital" of the Highlands. It is assured of that title by its eas fortified situation on the River Ness where the roads through the glens conver Shakespeare sadly maligned the man who was its king for 17 years, Macbe His castle has disappeared, but from **Castlehill** a successor dominates the ci a pink cardboard cut-out, like a Victorian doll's house, that makes Flora M. Donald in bronze shield her eyes and her dog lift a paw.

In the nearby **Museum** (open Mon–Sat; tel: (01463) 237114; free), the de mask of Flora's Bonnie Prince shares cases with Mr Punch in his "red Gariba coat", and Duncan Morrison's puppet figure that once delighted local childr Traditions are strongly represented in silversmithing, taxidermy, bagpipes and f dles, and even a 7th-century Pictish stone depicting a wolf. Preserved in front of

**Town House**, on busy High Street, uphill from the riv is the **Clach-na-Cuddain**, a stone on which wom rested their tubs of washing. **Abertarff House**, Church Street, is the city's oldest secular building, d ing from 1593. It has one of the few remaining exa ples of the old turnpike stair and is home these days small art galleries.

Dolphin-watching cruises run from Inverness h bour, out under the handsome Kessock Bridge, ope in 1982 to ease traffic from the North Sea oil firms Easter Ross. The bridge replaced the ancient Kesso ferry between the city and the Black Isle.

## Loch Ness

From an area of Inverness rich in industrial archaeolo the **Caledonian Canal** climbs through six locks lik flight of stairs to the "Hill of Yew Trees", **Tomnahuri** This highland waterway, which joins the North Sea a the Atlantic Ocean through the Great Glen, was predic by a local seer a century before it was built: "Full-rigg ships will be seen sailing at the back of Tomnahuric Now you can set sail here in summer for a trip on **Lo Ness**, and enjoy "a wee dram in the lingering twiligh The dram may assist you in spotting the Monster, lake's supposed ancient occupant. You can take a va ety of combined bus and boat tours from Inverness, year round (tel: (01463) 233999; www.jacobite.co.uk; Lo Ness Express, tel: (0800) 3286426).

Urquhart Castle ㉑ (open daily; tel: (01456) 450551; admission charge) is a
cturesque ruin on the loch's edge (15 miles/24 km south of Inverness on the
82) which bears the scars of having been fought over for two centuries.

At **Fort Augustus** ㉒ (29 miles/48 km further south), the canal descends in
other flight of locks near the **Clansmen Centre** (open Apr–Oct daily; tel:
1320) 366444; admission charge), which illustrates the glen's history from
ctish to modern times. The garrison, set up after the 1715 Jacobite Rising,
ter became a Benedictine abbey.

Turn right at **Invergarry** onto the A87 for the beauty of glen and mountain
the road to Kyle of Lochalsh and Skye. Or, continuing south on the A82, stop
the "Well of the Heads" monument, which records the murder of a 17th-
ntury chieftain's two sons and, as reprisal, the deaths of seven brothers, whose
ads were washed in the well, then presented to the chief.

The A82 now crosses to the east bank of **Loch Lochy**. Six miles (10 km)
fore Fort William is **Nevis Range**, where gondolas whisk you in 12 minutes
2,150 ft (645 metres), giving stunning views of Scotland's highest mountains.
the outskirts of **Fort William** ㉓ *(see page 224)*, take the A830 and you'll
mediately reach "Neptune's Staircase", where eight locks lead the Caledon-
Canal into the sea and from where there are grand views of Ben Nevis.

## viemore's attractions

om Inverness you can also head southeast towards **Aviemore** ㉔ and the mag-
ficent scenery of the Cairngorms. Aviemore barely existed before the railway
me here on its way to Inverness in the 1880s. Today, and after a slump in
rtunes in the 1990s, Aviemore is a thriving magnet for outdoor types and hol-

**TIP**

If you fail to spot the
real Loch Ness
monster, you can
always visit the two
visitor centres at
Drumnadrochit, where
multimedia shows
invite you to separate
fact from fiction.

**BELOW:** Loch Ness:
inspiration for
monster fantasies.

idaymakers. The centrepiece of the revamped centre is the impressive **Macdo-ald Aviemore Highland Resort** complete with golf course and spa (tel: (0147 815300; www.aviemorehighlandresort.com).

Nearby, at Carrbridge, is the **Landmark Centre** (open daily; tel: (0147 841613; admission charge). The attractions at this heritage park include a treet trail through the forest, an adventure playground and horse-logging.

Six miles (10 km) southwest of Aviemore at Kincraig is the **Highland Wildl Park** (open daily; tel: (01540) 651270; admission charge), an outpost of the Roy Zoological Society of Scotland. Here once indigenous animals, including wolve boar and bison, run free. Part of the park is drive-through, part walk-through.

Further south at **Kingussie** is the **Highland Folk Museum** (open Apr–Se Mon–Sat, Oct Mon–Fri; tel: (01540) 661307; admission charge). The museu has a whole replica "township" of Highland blackhouses from about 1700, fai fully reproduced from excavations throughout the north. Craftsmen keepi alive the ancient skills in building, furnishing and various types of thatching a on hand to explain and instruct in their secrets.

Only a few miles from Kingussie, on the A86, is the village of **Laggan** a the enchanted countryside that inspired the BBC television series *Monarch the Glen*, chronicling the ups and downs of an impecunious young laird a his struggles to keep a Highland estate alive.

### Moving north

Back at the northern end of the Great Glen the A9 crosses the neck of the **Bla Isle,** which is neither island nor black but forest and fertile farmland, and bisected by roads serving the oil centres on the north shore of the Cromarty Fir

*Real-life Highland folk recall days gone by at the Highland Folk Museum.*

**BELOW:** a resident of the Highland Wildlife Park.

## AVIEMORE'S EXPANSION

It's doubtful if the Clan Grant, whose war cry was "Sta Fast Craigellachie", could have resisted the forces at w in Aviemore, below their rallying place. The quiet Speysi halt has been transformed into a year-round resort by opening of roads into the Cairngorms and chairlifts for skiers. In the 1960s, Brewers built the Aviemore Cen recently extensively revamped to form the impressive M donald Aviemore Highland Resort at its centre. Shops alo the main street cater for the mass of visitors, selling o door equiment for skiing and mountaineering.

The beginnings of Aviemore's expansion date back the 1880s when the railway arrived here on its way Inverness. Once an important junction, Aviemore ha branch line to Grantown-on-Spey and Forres. Tod Aviemore is still a central base from which to explore spectacular mountains and moors: a relaxing way to en the scenery can be had by wining and dining on a Highl Railway steam train which runs in the summer months route from Aviemore to Boat of Garten; for details, (01479) 810725. A year-round funicular railway carr skiers and sightseers to the summit of Cairn Gorm, wh provides some breathtaking views of Rothiemurchus a Strathspey; for details, tel: (01479) 861336.

Just before you reach Fortrose, the one-time fishing village of **Avoch**, still ·ith its pretty harbour, was a focal point during the Scottish Wars of Indepen-·nce. Half a mile west along the coast stands the great mound of Ormond Cas- ·e with only the slightest remains of its one-time bastion still visible. This was ·e base of a largely unsung Highland hero Andrew De Moray, who raised a ·ighland army which cleared the north of the English invaders in a brilliant ·uerrilla campaign which drove them back through the Southern Highlands. ·aving disposed thus far of the Auld Enemy, he joined William Wallace to form ·credible force for the notable victory at the Battle of Stirling Bridge. In May ·ich year there is a procession of villagers to the top of the castle hill to com- ·emorate the Highland Gathering, as it is known.

On the golf links at **Fortrose ㉕**, on the east shore, a plaque marks the spot ·here, in the 17th century, the Brahan Seer, accused of being a witch, was put to ·ath in an oil barrel – but not before he had foretold the building of the Cale- ·nian Canal, the demise of crofting and much more. The annual St Boniface's ·air is held in the square adjacent to the magnificent ruins of a 14th-century cathe- ·al; the fair's traders and entertainers wear medieval costume.

Nearby, at Rosemarkie, is **Groam House Museum** (open May–Sept Mon– ·t and Sun pm, Oct–Apr Sat and Sun pm; tel: (01381) 620961; admission ·arge), a Pictish interpretive centre with a superb collection of sculptured ·ones, audio-visual displays and rubbings.

**Cromarty ㉖**, at the extreme tip of the Isle, lost face as a Royal Burgh through ·clining fortunes as a seaport and trading community, but has earned rightful ·pularity as a place where visitors can literally step back into history in the ·spoilt old town. Taped tours point out some of the most beautiful late 18th- ·ntury buildings in Britain: the **Courthouse**, now a ·izewinning museum (open Apr–Oct daily, Mar, ·ov–Dec daily pm; tel: (01381) 600418; admission ·arge); the thatched cottage where early geologist ·ugh Miller, Cromarty's most famous scholarly son, ·ved (open May–Sept daily pm; tel: (01381) 600245; ·lmission charge) and the **East Kirk**, with its three ·ooden lofts.

A road leads to **South Sutor**, one of two precipitous ·adlands guarding the narrow entrance to the Firth of ·romarty, where numerous oil rigs are moored. Around ·e rigs swim the North Sea's only resident group of ·ttlenose dolphins, plus innumerable grey and com- ·on seals.

Though Scots had long known the local sulphur and ·alybeate springs at **Strathpeffer ㉗**, it took a doctor ·ho had himself benefited to give substance to "mir- ·le" recoveries and, incidentally, recognise their prof- ·ble potential. Dr Morrison opened his pump room ·ound 1820, and the new railway brought thousands to ·l the hotels and, if they felt inclined, enjoy "low- ·essure subthermal reclining manipulation douche". A ·uple of wars intervened and the spa declined, but, like ·l things Victorian, this elegant town is enjoying some- ·ng of a revival as a resort of character. The old rail- ·ay station is now a visitor centre.

On leaving Strathpeffer, join the A835, which, after ·arve, winds through Strath Ben and **Achnasheen ㉘**.

**TIP**

If you want a taste of the Strathpeffer waters, call in at the town's Water Sampling Pavilion.

**BELOW:** cross- country skiing near Loch Morlich.

*Beinn Eighe*
*is a fascinating*
*geological*
*"pudding" of old red*
*sandstone topped*
*with white quartzite.*

From here the southern leg (A890) through Glen Carron is the stuff of photom
rals, with Kyle of Lochalsh at the end of the rainbow that leads across the sea
Skye. Achnasheen's northern leg (A832) leads to **Kinlochewe** at the head
**Loch Maree** and close to the National Nature Reserve of **Beinn Eighe**. In t
pine forests there is a good chance of seeing rare and protected wildlife; natu
trails begin in the car park.

## Changing times

Alternatively, from **Dingwall** – was Macbeth really born here? – road (A9) a
rail cling to the east coast. **Evanton** has an abundance of accommodation, a
there's a good chance of seeing seals on the shore walk. Near **Alness** , or
hill, is a replica of the Gate of Negapatam in India, which General Sir Hect
Munro, hero of its capture, had built by local men. Today Alness is dormito
to **Invergordon** on Cromarty Firth, which offered shelter to Britain's na
through two world wars and suffered the closure of its naval base in 1956. T
area has also seen dramatic changes since the choice of Nigg Bay for the co
struction of oil-rig platforms.

Memories at **Tain** are older, going back to 1066, when it became a Roy
Burgh. Though St Duthac was born and buried here, it didn't save the tv
chapels dedicated to him from disastrous fires – or guarantee sanctuary. Tod
visitors can call in at the **Glenmorangie Distillery** (open Mon–Fri, June–A
daily; tel: (01862) 892477; admission charge) to see how the famous m
whisky is made and to try a sample.

From Tain, the A836 leads to **Bonar Bridge**, and motorists have to adjust
negotiate single-track roads and the sheep that share them. This is Viking cou

**BELOW:** Lairg
sheep sales.

Map, pages 270-1

', more Scandinavian than Scottish, with spectacular views of heather-
vered moor and loch. At **Invershin** is a superbly situated castle without a bur-
n of history. Retainers, some heavy-laden, come and go beneath the towers
d battlements with which it is over endowed. Carbisdale Castle was built as
e as 1914 for the Duchess of Sutherland and is now a youth hostel.

The nearby **Falls of Shin** offer glimpses of salmon ascending the cataracts
they migrate, while the visitor centre has educational wildlife events for
ildren. The centre also accommodates the "Harrods of the North", as it is
own locally, with products from the prestigious London store set up by its
ntroversial owner Mohamed Al Fayed, who is also the laird of the 65,000-
re (26,000-hectare) Balnagown Estate in Easter Ross. It sells mainly tourist
uvenirs, but has a range of fine foodstuffs plus a restaurant and tearoom.

## rofting country

Ill roads meet at Lairg," it's said. Sometimes in August it seems all the sheep
Scotland do as well. **Lairg** ❸ is in the heart of Sutherland crofting country,
d the lamb sales identify it as a major market-place. Mirrored in the quiet
aters of Loch Shin is an Iron Age hut circle on the hill above the village.

The eastern spoke (A839) from Lairg's hub reaches the coast at Loch Fleet and
ornoch ❸, where some regard Royal Dornoch, opened in 1616, as offering bet-
r golf than the Old Course at St Andrews. Dornoch Castle's surviving tower suf-
ed the indignities of use as a garrison, courthouse, jail, school and private
sidence. Now it's a hotel. The lovely cathedral is also a survivor: badly dam-
ed in a 17th-century fire, it was largely restored in the 1920s. The last witch to
burned in Scotland, Janet Horne, was condemned to death in Dornoch in 1727,

**TIP**

There are a lot of
single-track roads in
this part of Scotland.
Cautious drivers
should use the passing
places not only to let
oncoming vehicles
pass but also to allow
faster traffic from
behind to overtake.
Beware of sheep on
the road!

**BELOW:** crofting is
still a way of life in
remote areas of the
Highlands.

*Dunrobin Castle
is the Scottish home
of the Dukes of
Sutherland, who
played a leading role
in the Highland
Clearances.*

**BELOW:** spectacular
cliffs carved out
by the sea at
Duncansby Head.

though her commemoration stone reads 1722. More happily, the Dunfermline born industrialist and philanthropist Andrew Carnegie, who made his money in the United States, bought nearby Skibo Castle (now a country club) in the 1890 and lived there until he died in 1919; he funded the town's Carnegie Library.

To the north is **Golspie**, which lives in the shadow of the Sutherlands. A oversize statue of the controversial 1st Duke looks down from the mountain; stone in the old bridge is the clan's rallying point; and nearby is the Duchess **Dunrobin Castle** (open Apr–Oct Mon–Sat and Sun pm; tel: (01408) 63317 admission charge), an improbable confection of pinnacles and turrets trying be a schloss or a château. Formal gardens are a riot of colour in summer. The prehistoric fort at Carn Liath a little further along the coast is a nice antidote.

The gold rush that brought prospectors to the burns of **Helmsdale ③** in th 1860s was short-lived. The town's main attraction today is the **Timespan Heritage Centre** (open Apr–Oct Mon–Sat and Sun pm; tel: (01431) 821327; admission charge), which brings the history of the Highlands to life; there is also large garden with a unique collection of medicinal and herbal plants. Intrep visitors keep going north to **Caithness**, for centuries so remote from the centre of Scottish power that it was ruled by the Vikings. Trade links were entirely b sea, and in the boom years of the fishing industry scores of harbours were buil The fleets have gone; the harbours remain.

The A9 to **Berriedale** twists spectacularly past the ravines of the Ord of Cait ness and on to **Dunbeath**, where a few lobster boats are a reminder of past glo ies. Here, too, is the **Laidhay Croft Museum** (open Easter–Oct daily; te (01593) 731370; admission charge), a restored longhouse with stable, hou and byre all under one roof. **Lybster ③** offers more bustle, but at **Mid Cly**

Map pages 270-1

ave the road at a sign, "Hill o' Many Stanes", for a mystery tour. On a hillside are 2 rows, each with an average of eight small stones, thought to be Bronze Age.

Herring were the backbone of **Wick**'s prosperity and come to life again in the **Wick Heritage Centre** (open June–Sept Mon–Sat; tel: (01955) 605393; admission charge). More than 1,000 boats once set sail to catch the "silver darlings". Now the near-deserted quays give the harbour a wistful charm.

## Natural attractions

or cross-country record-breakers, **John o' Groats** ⑯, at the end of the A99, has natural attraction – although, contrary to popular belief, it is not the northernost point in Britain. A Dutchman, Jan de Groot, came here in 1500 under orders rom James IV to set up a ferry service to Orkney to consolidate his domination ver this former Scandinavian territory. A mound and a flagstaff commemorate ne site of his house. Boat trips run from the harbour to Orkney and to **Dunansby Head**, 2 miles (4 km) to the east, where many species of birds nest on the dramatic towering stacks. From here a road runs to the lighthouse. West of John ' Groats, on the A836, is the **Castle of Mey**, the late Queen Mother's home. urther on is **Dunnet Head**, the British mainland's most northerly point.

The approaches to **Thurso** ⑰ are heralded by the Caithness "hedges" that line ne fields, the flagstones that were once shipped from local quarries to every corner of the old Empire. The streets of Calcutta were paved by Caithness. **Fisheriggins**, the fishermen's old quarter, is a facsimile reproduction from 1940, but lsewhere there is pleasant Victorian town-planning. **Scrabster** is Thurso's outort, with a ferry to Orkney. The site of Scotland's first nuclear power research tation, now defunct, at **Dounreay** was partly chosen for its remoteness.

*Jan de Groot's response to requests from his eight sons as to who should succeed him was to build an octagonal house with eight doors and with an octagonal table in the middle so that each sat at the "head".*

**BELOW:** surfing off the north coast.

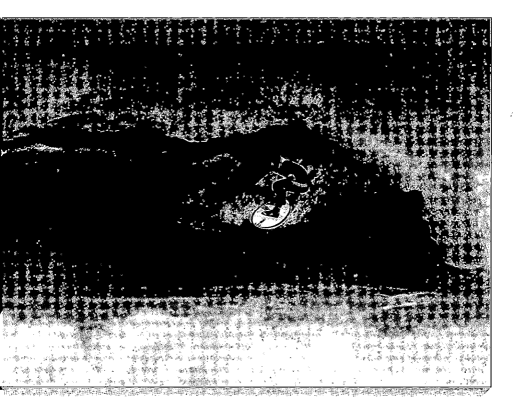

## The furthest point

It's an odd feeling: nothing between you and the North Pole except magnificent cliff scenery. At **Tongue** the sea loch pokes deep into the bleak moorland and near **Durness** , which has some huge expanses of wonderful beach, the Alt Smoo River drops from the cliff into the Caves of Smoo. From Durness, a combined ferry and bus service travels to **Cape Wrath**. From here, the top left hand corner of Britain, Orkney and the Outer Hebrides can be seen. Look out for cooties, sea cockies, tammies and tommienoories (puffins by another name).

The return to Lairg can be made south from Tongue on the lovely A836 through **Altnaharra** , where crosses, hut circles and Pictish brochs abound. From Durness the A838 joins the western coast at **Scourie** , where mermaids are mistaken for seals and palm trees grow.

**Ullapool** , 52 miles (83 km) south of Scourie, is a resort for all seasons, beautifully situated on Loch Broom facing the sunset. The **Ullapool Museum and Visitor Centre** (open Mar–Oct Mon–Sat, Nov–Feb Thur and Sat; tel: (01854) 612987; admission charge) has displays on the history and people of the area. Today, a car ferry serves Stornoway in Lewis and trippers leave for the almost deserted but delightfully named **Summer Isles**. And smoking is good for you at **Achiltibuie** , where fish and game are cured in spicy aromatic brines.

Another route south is through **Bettyhill**, where the 18th-century kirk is now a museum of the Clan MacKay and the 19th-century Highland Clearances. **Strathnaver**, to the south, was the centre of this once-powerful clan which raised thousands of fierce mercenaries for campaigns throughout Europe. A testimony to their warlike history is reflected in the fact that Strathnaver has the remains of no less than 10 brochs (fortified towers).

*The rich supplies of herring inspired the British Fisheries Society in 1788 to build fisher cottages at Ullapool and improve the harbour.*

**BELOW:** the sands of Sandwood Bay.

# Peatland versus Profit

Travel through the far north of Scotland and one is struck by the dearth of population. It's hard to imagine that from Neolithic times until the controversial Highland Clearances of the 17th and 18th centuries, much of the wild landscape of Caithness and Sutherland was populated by scores of crofters and thriving coastal settlements.

Indeed, even the Flow Country, a rugged "wilderness" that encompasses almost 400,000 hectares (1 millions acres) of habitat-rich peatland, once supported settlers. Today, this fragile ecosystem and site of the world's largest bogland, is owned or managed by an array of private shooting estates and national conservation and land-management agencies including the Royal Society for the Protection of Birds (RSPB), Forestry Commission Scotland, Scottish Natural Heritage and the Deer Commission for Scotland.

Incorporating over 20 Sites of Special Scientific Interest, few doubt the ecological importance of the Flow Country, beloved by fishermen, walkers and twitchers alike. Indeed, ornithologists estimate over 60 percent of Europe's greenshanks annually breed in the Flow Country, while the peatland's startling diversity of fauna and flora also supports rare mosses, short-eared owls, golden eagles, plovers and hen harriers.

However, until very recently the Flow Country was a watchword for controversy. Until common sense prevailed (and generous tax concessions for wealthy investors were removed) conservation bodies struggled throughout the 1980s to counter the excesses of misguided commercial forestry projects designed to maximise revenue by planting and selling for timber huge swathes of (non-indigenous) conifer trees. To the dismay of the "green lobby", these ill-advised "job and profit" motivated ventures threatened to unbalance a fragile ecosystem that had existed on the peatland for thousands of years.

Fortunately, today's forestry masters have ensured a more enlightened approach has been adopted by overzealous landowners. With over 8 percent of Scotland's total land area under its control, Forestry Commission Scotland (FCS) is now actively involved in helping reverse some of the worst excesses of commercial land management that for decades blighted the Flow Country.

According to Tim Cockerill, Forest District Manager for Dornoch: "We are now trying to find a balance [between sustainable forestry and conservation]. We accept that the process of afforestation in the past was a step too far and we are working with agencies such as the RSPB to identify forested areas where natural habitats can best be restored."

With over 10,000 hectares (25,000 acres) of peatland and grassland under the RSPB's ownership, initiatives include helping to reintroduce waterfowl by restoring watercourses to over 2,000 hectares (5,000 acres) of bog previously drained for forestry.

Though the scars of the Clearances remain, it could be argued that the Flow Country will slowly recover from this more recent folly to befall the landscape. ❑

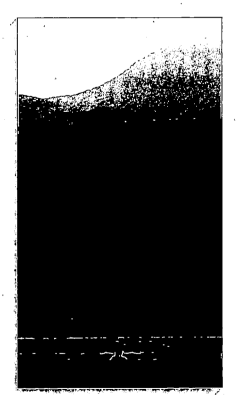

**RIGHT:** the unspoilt Highlands.

# HIGHLAND FLORA AND FAUNA

*The wilderness of northern Scotland may appear to be older than living memory, but humans have actually had a big impact on its natural history*

The symbol of Scotland – the thistle – is not tough enough for the Highlands. Heather, bilberry *(left)*, bog cotton, asphodel and sphagnum moss (a springy, water-retaining plant that eventually rots down into peat) are the plant survivors here.

But ranging across this unrelentingly bony land are a couple of other particularly resilient symbols of Scotland – golden eagles and red deer.

Red deer in the Highlands are thought to number 330,000, a population which is barely restrained by the huge deerstalking industry. In the summer the herds are almost invisible to all but the hardiest walkers, but in the winter they descend into river valleys in search of food. The golden eagle is virtually invisible all year round, although the population is relatively stable in the mountains. Recent moves have re-established pairs of white-tailed sea-eagles on the island of Rum, though breeding hasn't yet been particularly successful.

Causing concern is the capercaillie, a turkey-sized game bird with the mating call of a brass band. Although it is no longer hunted, it has never learned to cope with modern deer fences: flying low through woodland, it crashes straight into them at speed.

Another distinctive Highland bird is also vanishing fast. The corncrake's unmistakable rasping call is only heard in remote corners of the outer Hebridean islands.

## CURSED WEE BEASTIE

One thriving specimen of Highland natural history is often omitted from the brochures: the biting midge. There are some 34 species of midge in Scotland. Only two or three attack humans, and *Culicoides impunctatus* (with distinctive speckled wings) does the lion's share. In the end, you have to laugh, or they'd drive you crazy. After all, as they say, midges are compassionate creatures: kill one, and a couple of thousand arrive for the funeral.

▷ **GOLDEN EAGLE**
Eagle pairs mate for life. A young eagle will stay with its parents for up to a year before setting off in search of new territory and a mate of its own.

▽ **WATER MAMMALS**
Seals are more timid than they used to be, thanks to aggressive fish farmers. Otters survive in wilder areas, and there are efforts to reintroduce beavers to a couple of rivers.

▷ **HERD INSTINCT**
The idea that deer are nomadic and range for great distances in search of food is a romantic misconception. A study project on the island of Rum proved that most animals remained "hefted" to the couple of square miles where they were born.

◁ **RED GROUSE**
The red grouse, a game bird tough enough to nest on open moorland, has suffered heavily from over-hunting by humans and by birds of prey. Intensive studies have so far failed to come up with a solution which will bring the numbers back up again. It is now officially an endangered species.

## RETURN OF THE LONESOME PINE

△ **PINE MARTEN**
There are only 3,000 of these small nocturnal mammals left in Great Britain, all in Scotland, where they nest in hollow trees. Their numbers were drastically reduced by the fur trade in the early 20th century.

◁ **YELLOW SAXIFRAGE**
The saxifrage is common in the Arctic, but it regularly adds a splash of colour to Scottish moorlands. The most colourful season in the Highlands is autumn, when the heather is in bloom.

Long ago, most of the now desolate areas of the Highlands were forested. Over the centuries the trees were felled for timber and to accommodate livestock. Deer and sheep are very effective grazers, and tree shoots don't stand a chance. Stop at a loch to compare the growth onshore with that on offshore islands and you will see how destructive grazing animals can be.

Several decades ago the Forestry Commission, a government body, set about fencing off areas of moorland for reforestation. To make the initiative economically viable they chose the fast-growing sitka spruce, which they planted in marching rows. The result is not particularly pleasing on the eye, and there has been controversy over the use of public money. There are also worries about the damage coniferisation causes to the unique habitats in many areas – like the areas of bogland in parts of Caithness.

Recently several initiatives to reforest large areas with native Scots pine *(above)* and deciduous trees have been started on privately purchased land by charitable organisations such as the Royal Society for the Protection of Birds, John Muir Trust and Scottish Woodlands Trust. It will be many years before these large-scale plantings start to show themselves on the landscape.

# ORKNEY

*In few places in the world is the marriage of landscape
and seascape so harmonious, or is there such a profusion
of archaeological wonders and variety of wildlife*

S ix miles (12 km) of sea separate the northeast corner of Scotland from an
archipelago of 70 islands, 20 of which are inhabited. This is Orkney (the
word means "seal islands" in old Icelandic), which extends over 1,200 sq.
iiles (3,100 sq. km). If you believe there are more islands it may be because
ou have drunk too well of the products of Orkney's two distilleries or are count-
ig seals – both common and grey – which abound in these waters.

The "ey" is Old Norse for islands, and so one should refer to Orkney and not
the Orkneys" or "the Orkney Islands". It also announces an ancient affiliation
vith Norway, an affiliation historical rather than geographical, for Norway lies
00 miles (480 km) to the east. Orkney was a Norwegian appendage until the
nd of the 15th century, and the true Orcadian is more Norse than Scot. With a
ch tradition of sagas, it's no surprise that 20th-century Orkney produced such
distinguished literati as Edwin Muir, Eric Linklater and George Mackay Brown.

To Orcadians, Scotland is the "sooth" (south) and never the "mainland", for
that is the name of the group's principal island: when inhabitants of the smaller
dands visit the largest, therefore, they journey to **Mainland**, and when they
avel to the UK they are off "sooth" to Scotland. Not that there are many of
iem to travel: the population is about 19,500, of whom one-quarter live in the
apital, Kirkwall. Travel within the archipelago is by
rries and more often by planes. The Loganair flight
etween Westray and Papa Westray is the shortest com-
nercial flight in the world. In perfect weather condi-
·ons it takes only two minutes.

## Ancient and modern

o wander these islands is, for the dedicated lover of
rchaeology, a taste of paradise. Orkney offers an unin-
:rrupted continuum of mute stones from Neolithic
.mes (about 4500 BC) through the Bronze and Iron Ages
) about AD 700, followed by remains from the days
·hen the islands were occupied successively by the
'elts and the Vikings.

**Kirkwall** ❶ is dominated by the 12th-century **St
Magnus Cathedral** (open Mon–Sat; free). Construc-
·on began in the Norman style, but its many Gothic fea-
·ures attest to more than 300 years of building. Facing it
. the ruined **Bishop's Palace** (open Apr–Sept daily; tel:
)1856) 871918; admission charge), a massive struc-
·ure with a round tower reminiscent of a castle. In the
3th century the great Norwegian king, Haakon
iaakonsson, lay dying here while Norse sagas were
:ad aloud to him. Nearby is a third ancient building,
he **Earl Patrick's Palace** (open as Bishop's Palace), a
)mantic gem of Renaissance architecture. It is roof-
·ss: in the 17th century its slates were removed to build
he town hall.

Other Kirkwall attractions are the **Tankerness House Museum** (open Mon–Sat and Sun pm, Oct–Apr closed Sun; tel: (01856) 873191; free), which presents the complete story of Orkney from prehistory to the present; the **Orkney Library**, one of the oldest public libraries in Scotland; a golf course and a sports and leisure centre.

## War and peace

South of Kirkwall is the great natural harbour of **Scapa Flow**. Here, the captured German fleet was anchored after World War I and eventually scuttled. Only six of the 74 ships remain on the bed of this deep, spacious bay, which is bliss for the scuba-diver, a peaceful cornucopia for the deep-sea angler.

The island of **Flotta**, at the south of Scapa Flow, is a North Sea oil terminal through which 12 percent of Britain's oil passes. This is the Orcadians' only concession to black gold.

Fifteen miles (24 km) west of Kirkwall is picturesque **Stromness ❷**, Orkney's second town. A well on the main street testifies that, in the 17th century, Stromness was developed by the Hudson Bay Company, whose ships made this their last port of call before crossing the Atlantic. The **Pier Arts Centre** (open Tues–Sat; free) houses a collection of 20th-century paintings and sculpture, and the museum (open May–Sept daily; tel: (01856) 850025; admission charge) has natural history exhibits, model ships and a display on the scuttling of the German Fleet at Scapa Flow. There is also a golf course and indoor pool here.

Most of Mainland's major archaeological sites are to the north of Stromness. Crawl into awesome **Maeshowe ❸** (open Apr–Sept daily, Oct–Mar closed Thu pm, Fri and Sun am; tel: (01856) 761606; admission charge), the most magni-

**BELOW:** One in six of all seabirds that breed in Britain nests in Orkney.

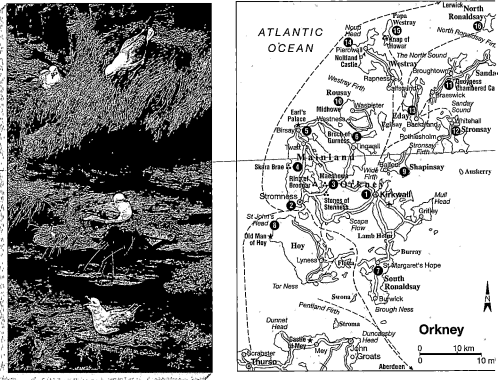

Orkney

ent chambered tomb in Britain, which dates from 3500 BC. Within is a spa-
ous burial chamber built with enormous megaliths; on some of these
e incised the world's largest collection of 12th-century Viking runes.
Near Maeshowe are the **Ring of Brodgar** and the **Standing Stones of Sten-**
**ss**, the remains of two of Britain's most spectacular stone circles. When the
rmer (whose name means "Circle of the Sun") was completed, about 1200
C, it consisted of 60 standing stones set along the circumference of a circle
out 340 ft (103 metres) in diameter. Today, 27 stones, the tallest at 14 ft
metres), still stand. The four giant monoliths of Stenness are all that remain of
at particular circle of 12 stones, erected about 2300 BC.
**Skara Brae** ❹ (visitor centre and replica house open Mon–Sun daily; tel:
1856) 841815; admission charge), Britain's Pompeii, sits on the Atlantic coast
ongside a superb sandy beach. The settlement, remarkably well preserved,
nsists of several dwelling houses and connecting passages and was engulfed
sand 4,500 years ago after having been occupied for 500 years. Skara Brae is
quintessential Stone Age site; no metal of any kind was found.
Five miles (8 km) north is **Birsay** ❺ with its 16th-century **Earl's Palace**.
pposite is the **Brough of Birsay**, a tiny tidal island (avoid being stranded); it
covered with rich remains of Norse and Christian settlements. A further 8
les (13 km) east, and guarding Eynhallow Sound, is the **Broch of Gurness** ❻
pen Apr–Sept daily; tel: (01856) 751414; admission charge).
The principal southern islands are South Ronaldsay, Burray, Lamb Holm,
oy and Flotta. Technically, the first three are no longer islands, being joined
Mainland by the **Churchill Barriers**. These were built by Italian prisoners
ring World War II after a German submarine penetrated Scapa Flow and sank

*One stone in Maes-howe is surely the forerunner of today's graffiti. It says simply: "Ingigerd is the sweetest woman there is."*

**BELOW:** Ring of Brodgar: 3,000 years ago there were 60 stones.

*Brochs are Iron Age (100 BC to AD 300) strongholds built by the Picts. Unique to Scotland and ubiqui- tous in Orkney, they were circular at their base and their mas- sive walls tapered gently inwards to a height of about 60 ft (18 metres).*

the battleship *Royal Oak*. On **Lamb Holm** enter some Nissen huts and be asto
ished at the beautiful chapel built with scrap metal by these prisoners. T
**Orkney Wireless Museum** (open Apr–Sept: Mon–Sat and Sun pm; tel: (0185
874272; admission charge) at **St Margaret's Hope ❼** on **South Ronalds**
displays communications equipment from World War II.

**Hoy**, the second-largest island of the archipelago, is spectacularly differe
The southern part is low-lying, but at the north stand the heather-covered Cuila
(1,420 ft/426 metres), from where all Orkney, except Little Rysa, can be viewe
A stroll along the 1,140-ft (367-metre) high **St John's Head ❽**, which tee
with seabirds (beware the swooping great skuas) and boasts some rare plan
is sheer delight for the geologist, ornithologist and botanist, or for those w
just like to ramble. Immediately south of St John's Head is Orkney's most ve
erable inhabitant, the **Old Man of Hoy**, who, sad to say, appears to be cracki
up. This 450-ft (135-metre) perpendicular sandstone column continues to ch
lenge the world's leading rock-climbers.

## Northward-bound

And so to the northern islands. Fertile **Shapinsay ❾** is so near Mainland tha
is called suburbia. Also near Mainland, but further west and readily reached
local ferry are **Rousay ❿** and **Egilsay**. Rich archaeological finds have earn
the former the sobriquet "Egypt of the North". Visit the remarkable 76-ft (2
metre) long Neolithic **Midhowe Chambered Cairn** (open Apr–Oct: Mon–S
and Sun pm), aptly named the "Great Ship of Death", which has 12 burial co
partments each side of a central passage. Nearby is the magnificent **Midhov**
**Broch,** Rousay's finest archaeological site. Ascend Mansemass Hill and str

**BELOW:** the chapel built in Orkney by Italian prisoners during World War II.

Ward Hill for superb views of **Eynhallow**, medieval Orkney's Holy Island,
tween Rousay and Mainland.

On **Egilsay** an unusual round church, which has affinities with similar build-
gs in Ireland, marks the 12th-century site of the martyrdom of St Magnus.

Low-lying **Sanday**, with its white beaches, has room for a golf course but not
the exclusion of archaeological remains. Most important is the **Quoyness
hambered Cairn ⓫** (open Apr–Oct: Mon–Sat and Sun pm), standing 13 ft
metres) high and dating from about 2900 BC. It is similar to, but even larger
an, Maeshowe. **Stronsay ⓬**, another low-lying island with sandy beaches,
s formerly the hub of the prosperous Orkney herring industry. **Eday ⓭** may
bleak and barren, yet it is paradise for birdwatchers and has the customary
mplement of archaeological edifices.

**Westray**, the largest northern island, is unique in that its population is increas-
g. This is largely because of a successful fishing fleet which contradicts the
sertion that the Orcadian is "a farmer with a boat". **Noup Head ⓮** is Westray's
d reserve and splendid viewpoint. The island also has a golf course and the
ined renaissance **Notland Castle**. **North Hill Nature Reserve** on **Papa
estray ⓯** is home to Arctic terns and skuas. At **Knap of Howar** (open
r–Oct; tel: (01856) 872044) there are considerable remains of the earliest
nding dwelling houses in northwest Europe (approximately 3000 BC). Their
cupants, archaeologists have found, had "a strong preference for oysters".

On the most northerly island, **North Ronaldsay ⓰**, a dyke around the island
nfines sheep to the shore, leaving better inland pastures for cattle. Seaweed,
e sole diet of these sheep, results in dark meat with an unusually rich flavour:
acquired taste. ❑

**BELOW:** at home
with an Orkney
islander.

# SHETLAND

*Remote and mysterious, the Shetland Islands are a geologist's*
*·d birdwatcher's paradise, withstanding the pounding of the sea*
*and – more recently – the invasion of oil companies*

Map page 308

he writer Jan Morris called them "inset islands". In those two words she
succinctly defined the mystery of the **Shetland Islands,** whose remoteness (200 miles/320 km to the north of Aberdeen) means that, in maps of
:ain, they are usually relegated to a box in the corner of a page.
he 15 inhabited islands – 85 or so more are uninhabited – are dotted over 70
es (112 km) of swelling seas and scarcely seem part of Britain at all. The tiny
ulation of less than 22,000 doesn't regard itself as British, or even as Scottish,
as Norse. The nearest mainland town is Bergen in Norway. Norwegian is
ght in the schools. The heroes of myths have names like Harald Hardrada
King Haakon Haakonsson.
pring comes late, with plant growth speeding up only in June. Rainfall is
vy, mists are frequent and gales (record gust: 177 miles/285 km an hour)
:p the islands virtually treeless. However, it's never very cold, even in mid-
·ter, thanks to the North Atlantic Drift; and in midsummer (the "Simmer
1") it never quite gets dark.
'he late January festival of Up-Helly-Aa is loosely based on a pagan fire fes-
·l intended to herald the impending return of the sun. A procession of *guizers*
·n dressed in winged helmets and shining armour) parades through the streets
·ying burning torches with which they set fire to a
·lica of a Viking longship. It is an authentic fiesta pri-
·ily for islanders, but at other times the Shetlander is
·eptionally hospitable and talkative. When he says,
·u'll have a dram," it's an instruction, not an enquiry.

**PRECEDING PAGES:**
Lerwick, Shetland's
capital.
**LEFT:** Britain's most
northerly lighthouse.
**BELOW:** Shetland
knitting.

## ·d and new settlements

·) check-in counters confront passengers at **Sumburgh**
**·port** on the main island, **Mainland:** one is for fixed-
·g aircraft, the other for helicopters. North Sea oil gen-
·es the traffic, and at one time threatened to overwhelm
·islands. But the oil companies, pushed by a determined
·al council, made conspicuous efforts to lessen the
·act on the environment and, although almost half of
·ain's oil flows through the 1,000-acre (400-hectare)
·lom Voe terminal on a strip of land at the northern end
·Mainland, they seem to have succeeded beyond most
·nders' expectations. The 16 crude oil tanks, each hold-
·21 million gallons (95 million litres) were painted
·tletoe-green, 124 species of birds have been logged
·in the terminal boundary, and outside the main gates
·ıffic sign gives priority to otters.
·A concentrated anthropological history of the islands
·cated at **Jarlshof ❶**, a jumble of buildings near the
·port. Waves of settlers from the Stone, Bronze and
·ı Ages built dwellings here, each on the ruins of its
·decessor. The Vikings built on top of that, and
·lieval farmsteads later buried the Viking traces. At

*It's worth attending a folk concert in Shetland, as the islands are full of astonishingly accomplished fiddlers.*

the end of the 19th century the site was just a grassy mound, topped wi医 medieval ruin. Then a wild storm laid bare massive stones in a bank above beach, and archaeologists moved in. Hearths were found where peat fires bui 3,000 years ago. Today old wheelhouses (so called because of their radial wa have been revealed, and an **exhibition area** (open Apr–Sept daily; tel: (01S 460112; admission charge) fleshes out Jarlshof's history.

En route to the capital, Lerwick, 27 miles (43 km) to the north, the offsh island of **Mousa** is home to sheep and ponies, and also to a spectacularly w preserved broch, a round drystone tower more than 40 ft (13 metres) high.

**Lerwick** ❷ looks no more planned than Jarlshof. The old town has cha with intimate stone-paved alleys leading off the main street of granite how and dignified shops (no chainstores here). The windows of the baronial-lc ing **town hall** were presented to the town by Norway, Holland and German thanks for Shetland's kindness to seamen.

The sea and rural landscape dominates the **Shetland Museum** (tel: (015 695057), sited above the library in Hillhead. Its theme is the history of lif Shetland from prehistory to the present. It has a collection of 5,000-year beads, pots and pumice stones found when excavating Sumburgh airport.' new museum reopened in 2007 at Hay's Dock after a £4.9 million revamp.

Six miles (10 km) from Lerwick is the old fishing port of **Scalloway** ❸, o Shetland's capital. Its main feature is the gaunt ruins of an early 17th-cent castle built for Earl Patrick Stewart, a nephew of Mary Queen of Scots (c Mon–Sat; key from Shetland Woollens next door).

Deep voes (inlets) poke into the Shetland Islands like long fingers so tha part of the watery landscape is more than 3 miles (5 km) from the sea. As

## LOCAL POPULATIONS

**S**heep outnumber people on Shetland by more than 10 to one. "They eat everything," says one islander. Shetland ponies are more loved. They were carefully bred to keep their legs short so that they could pull carts through Britain's coal mines, but these days they graze freely. But it's birds that dominate Shetland. Because of the lack of woodlands there are fewer than 50 breeding species, but no lack of numbers. Filling the sky and cliff ledges are 30,000 gannets, 140,000 guillemots and 300,000 fulmars. Shetland supports more than 50 percent of the world's population of great skuas (bonxies). Puffins *(above)* begin to arrive in May, and before long there are 250,000 of them. Take a small boat round the islands and, as well as the birds, you can find seal colonies, porpoises and dolphins.

**Shetland**

0 ___ 10 km
0 ___ 10 miles

N

ATLANTIC OCEAN

The Faither

Esha Ness

Shetland Islands

Muckle
Hermaness
Unst ❻
Haroldswick
Baltas

Belmont
Muness
Castle

Gutcher

Mid Yell
Yell ❺
Fetlar
Fu

Isbister
Yell Sound

Colgrave Sound

Uist

Hillswick
Sullom
Voe
Toft

St. Magnus Bay
Brae
Voe

Out
Skerries

Voe

Muckle Roe

Symbister
Whalsay

Papa Stour
Melby

Shetland Mainland
Heglibister
Girlsta

Lax

Walls

Vaila
Tingwall
Weisdale
Scalloway ❸
Hamnavoe

Lerwick ❷
Isle of Noss
Bressay
Easter Quarff

Foula
Ham ❼

West Burra
Cunningsburgh

Mousa
Broch
Leverwick

Boddam
Sumburgh

Jarlshof ❶
Fair Isle ❽

Stromness,
Aberdeen

NOR
SE

e across Mainland's moors, meadows and hills, dramatic sea views abruptly
erialise. Arguably, Shetlanders were always more sailors than landlubbers,
clearly "matters of state" were held on dry land. It is said that a Norse par-
ment once stood by the loch of Tingwall .

## mote places

all ferries connect a handful of smaller islands to Mainland. **Yell** ⑤, a peaty
ce, has the **Old Haa Visitor Centre** (open May–Sept Tues–Thurs, Sat, and
pm; tel: (01957) 722339; donations) which includes a display of the story of
wrecking of the German sail ship, the *Bohus*, in 1924, and a craft centre sell-
genuine rather than generic Shetland garments. **Unst** ⑥, the UK's most
therly island, has an important nature reserve at **Hermaness** with a visitor
tre (open Apr–mid-Sept: daily; tel: (01957) 711278; free). From the cliffs at
maness gaze out on rocky **Muckle Flugga**, the last land before the Arctic
cle. **Fetlar**'s name means "fat island", a reference to its fertile soil. **Whal-**
is prosperous, thanks to its notably energetic fishermen. The **Out Skerries**,
attered archipelago, has a thriving fishing fleet. The peacefulness and abun-
t wild flowers of **Papa Stour**, a mile of turbulent sea west of Mainland, once
acted a transient hippy colony.

oula ⑦, 14 miles (23 km) to the west of Scalloway, must be Britain's
otest inhabited island and, most winters, is cut off for several weeks by awe-
e seas. The spectacular 1,200-ft (370-metre) cliffs are home to storm petrels,
at skuas and a host of other seabirds. **Fair Isle** ⑧, 20 miles (32 km) to the
thwest, is the home of Fair Isle sweaters, whose distinctive geometric pat-
s can be dated back 2,000 years to Balkan nomads.               ❑

**TIP**

Keen ornithologists
make for the Bird
Observatory on Fair
Isle, a major European
centre set up to moni-
tor birds all year round
(open Apr–Oct; tel:
(01595) 760258).

**BELOW:** the
Viking festival,
Up-Helly-Aa.

# TRAVEL TIPS

# **T** RANSPORT

# GETTING THERE
# AND GETTING AROUND

## GETTING THERE

### By Air

There are excellent services from London (Heathrow, London City, Gatwick, Luton and Stansted airports) and several English regional airports to Edinburgh, Glasgow, Aberdeen and Inverness. You will get the cheapest fare by booking well in advance. Airlines flying these routes include **British Airways** and **British Midland**.

Flying time from London to Edinburgh or Glasgow is about 70 minutes, and under two hours from London to Aberdeen or Inverness.

Ryanair and easyJet have very low-price, no-frills flights into Scotland. **EasyJet** flies from London (Gatwick, Luton and Stansted) to Edinburgh and Glasgow, to Inverness (from Gatwick and Luton) and to Aberdeen (Luton only), while **Ryanair** flies from London (Stansted) to Glasgow Prestwick, and also from Dublin to Aberdeen and Edinburgh. **Aer Lingus** flies from Dublin to Glasgow and Edinburgh.

Glasgow International Airport is Scotland's busiest airport with over 40 airlines serving 80 worldwide destinations. Over 1 million passengers go through the airport during peak summer months. Glasgow receives non-stop flights from New York (**Continental**), Philadelphia (**US Airways**), Las Vegas (**My Travel**), Orlando and Boston (**FlyGlobespan**), Toronto (**Zoom, Air Transat, FlyGlobespan**), Ottawa, Vancouver and the Dominican Republic (**Zoom**). It also receives non-stop flights from Amsterdam (**KLM and easyJet**), Barcelona (**FlyGlobespan**), Berlin and Geneva (**easyJet**), Copenhagen (**BMI**), Dubai (**Emirates**), Lahore (**Pakistan International Airlines**), Reykjavik (**Icelandair**) and Stockholm (**SAS**).

Direct Ryanir flights from Oslo, Riga, Shannon, Dublin, Frankfurt, Dusseldorf, Brussels, Paris, Stockholm, Gothenburg, Wrocklaw, Krakow, Milan, Rome, Pisa, Grenoble, Marseille and Barcelona all land at Glasgow Prestwick. Edinburgh airport handles non-stop flights from destinations including Atlanta (**Delta Airlines**), New York (**Continental Airlines**), Toronto (**FlyGlobespan**), Dublin (**Aer Lingus** and **Ryanair**), Faro (**Monarch**), Shannon (**Ryanair**), Milan (**easyJet**), Dortmund (**easyJet**), Amsterdam (**easyJet, KLM**), Barcelona (**FlyGlobespan**), Brussels (**BMI**), Chambery (**British Airways**), Copenhagen (**BMI**), Dalaman (**Monarch**), Bergen (**Wideroe**), Bodrum (**Onur Air**), Frankfurt (**Lufthansa**), Geneva (**easyJet, FlyGlobespan, BMI, British Airways**), Oslo (**Norwegian.No**), Paris (**Air France, flybe**), Alicante (**easyJet, FlyGlobespan**), Arrecife (**LCE International**), Madrid (**easyJet**) and Zurich (**Swiss International, BMI**).

Direct flights into Aberdeen include from Amsterdam (**KLM, BMI**), Bergen (**Wideroe**), Brussels (**BMI**), Copenhagen (**SAS**), Dublin (**Ryanair**) and Stavanger (**SAS**). Direct flights into Inverness airport include from Dublin (**Aer Arann**) and Belfast (**easyJet**).

### By Rail

There are frequent InterCity services to Scotland from many mainline stations in England. On most trains the journey time from London (Euston or King's Cross) to Edinburgh is just over four hours and to Glasgow about 5½ hours.

Sleeper services run between London (Euston) and Edinburgh, Glasgow, Aberdeen, Inverness and Fort William. Try to avoid travel on Sundays when services are often curtailed, and engineering works mean that journeys can take much longer. A limited number of cheap fares, known as Apex fares, are available for those booking at least seven days in advance. For current fares and timetables, call National Rail Enquiries on (08457) 484950; www.nationalrail.co.uk.

## Airports

● **Edinburgh Airport** (tel: (0870) 040 0007) is 8 miles (13 km) west of the city centre with good road access and a useful Airlink bus service to the heart of town. A taxi will take approximately 20 minutes.
● **Glasgow International Airport** (tel: (0870) 040 0008) is 8 miles (13 km) west of the city centre alongside the M8 motorway at Junction 28. A coach service runs between the airport and Buchanan Street bus station, in the city centre, and takes about 25 minutes.

● **Glasgow Prestwick Airport** (tel: (0871) 223 0700) is 30 miles (48 km) south of the city centre and easily reached by road or a 45-minute rail link to Central Station.
● **Aberdeen Airport** (tel: (0870) 040 0006) is 7 miles (11 km) west of the city centre with excellent road access (A96). A coach service runs between airport and city centre.
● **Inverness Airport** (tel: (01667) 464000) is about 10 miles (16 km) east of the town. A bus link runs into the city centre.

## By Road

There are good motorway connections from England and Wales. The M1/M6/A74 and M74 is the quickest route, though heavily congested at the southern end. The A1(M), a more easterly approach, is longer but may be a better bet if you plan to make one or two stopovers. Edinburgh and Glasgow are about 400 miles (650 km) from London.

### Bus Services

Scottish Citylink (tel: (08705) 505050) and National Express (tel: (08705) 808080) operate daytime and overnight coaches from England to Scotland. The journey takes about 9 hours from London to Edinburgh or to Glasgow. Coach travel may not be as comfortable or as fast as the trains, but it is a good deal cheaper, unless you can get an Apex fare on the train.

## By Sea

Every evening one of the Super Fast Ferries leaves Zeebrugge in Belgium to make the 17-hour crossing to Rosyth which is about 30 minutes by road from Edinburgh. In Scotland tel: (0870) 410 6040; www.superfast.com.

# GETTING AROUND

## By Air

There is a network of regular air services which is especially valuable if going to the islands. Barra, Benbecula, Campbeltown, Islay, Kirkwall (Orkney), Stornoway (Lewis), Sumburgh (Shetland) and Tiree are all serviced by Glasgow International airport. Some of these destinations can also be reached from Inverness, Aberdeen and Edinburgh airports. Flying to these destinations saves a lot of time and can also give a different perspective on the countryside. The major carrier is Loganair (which holds a British Airways franchise). British Airways, central booking number for all services is (0845) 850 9850, or log on to www.loganair.co.uk.

## By Rail

First ScotRail offers a wide variety of tickets which permit unlimited travel throughout Scotland. The Freedom of Scotland Travel Pass permits unlimited travel on eight or 15 consecutive days or on four out of eight or 10 out of 15 consecutive days. Two other rover

**ABOVE:** travel back in time on one of the many steam-train excursions.

passes are available: a Central Scotland Rover ticket offers 3 days' unlimited travel out of 7; and the Highland Rover is valid for 4 out of 8 consecutive days.

Scottish Travelpasses permit unlimited travel for eight or 15 consecutive days on Scotrail and most of the Caledonian MacBrayne west-coast ferries. Together with discounts on the P&O ferries and many buses and postbuses, these are truly comprehensive Scottish travel tickets. Details can be obtained from First ScotRail, tel: (08457) 550033, www.firstscotrail.co.uk.

A few routes to try are:
**Glasgow to Fort William and Mallaig** (164 miles/265 km). Train enthusiasts head for the West Highland line, which operates regular trains from Fort William to the fishing port of Mallaig, from which a ferry departs for Skye. From Glasgow, the route passes alongside Loch Lomond, across the wild Rannoch Moor and, after Fort William, over the majestic Glenfinnan Viaduct and hillsides dotted with deer.
**Glasgow to Oban** (101 miles/163 km). The train branches off the Fort William route at Crianlarich and heads past ruined Kilchurn Castle and the fjord-like scenery of the Pass of Brander to Oban, "gateway to the Inner Hebrides".
**Perth to Inverness** (118 miles/190 km). The route, through forested glens and across the roof of Scotland, takes in Pitlochry, Blair Atholl and Aviemore. As well as being a ski centre, Aviemore is the departure point for steam trains on the 5-mile (8-km) Strathspey Railway line.
**Inverness to Kyle of Lochalsh** (82 miles/132 km). This twisting line with breathtaking scenery takes in lochs, glens and mountains from

the North Sea to the Atlantic Ocean, and is especially dramatic towards Kyle of Lochalsh, from where the bridge leads over the water to the Isle of Skye.
**Inverness to Wick or Thurso** (161 miles/260 km). Passes by castles, across moorland and on to Britain's most northerly rail terminals.

## Steam Trains

Railway preservation societies are alive and thriving in Scotland. Over half a dozen other lines operate steam trains of one sort or another.

The **Northern Belle**, a luxury touring train operated by Orient-Express, offers day excursions and short breaks in Scotland. These trips include all meals served at seat, accommodation in hotels and off-train visits. Information from Northern Belle, 20 Upper Ground, London SE1 9PF, tel: (0845) 077 2222; www.orient-express.com

The **Caledonian Railway** (Brechin), Angus, runs steam-train rides every Sat from July–August and every Sunday from May to September, from Brechin to Bridge of Don. Brechin station is also open on Saturdays. Enquiries to Brechin Station, 2 Park Road, Brechin, Angus DD9 7AF. Tel: (01356) 622922; www.caledonianrailway.co.uk.

The **Bo'ness & Kinneil Railway**, West Lothian, runs steam-hauled trains on most weekends April–August, daily in July, and Tuesday in June on a 3-mile (5-km) branch line to Birkhill for a visit to the Avon Gorge and the Fireclay Mine. Historic Scottish locomotives, rolling stock and railway buildings. Enquiries to Bo'ness Station, Union Street, Bo'ness EH51 9AQ. Tel: (01506) 822298, www.srps.org.uk.

TRANSPORT

ACCOMMODATION

EATING OUT

ACTIVITIES

A–Z

## Caledonian MacBrayne Ferries

An essential item for any visitor who intends to explore the island-studded west coast – the Hebrides and the islands of the Clyde – is the Caledonian MacBrayne timetable, which can be obtained from:
Ferry Terminal,
Gourock, PA19 1QP
Tel: (01475) 650100
Reservations: (08705) 650000
www.calmac.co.uk.
Faced with a myriad of island destinations, the uninitiated may find CalMac's timetable daunting, though locals whip through it with ease. Summer booking is vital to avoid the nerve-racking, time-consuming "standby" queue.

Caledonian MacBrayne, a fusion of two companies, grew out of the 19th-century passenger steamers and now has a near-monopoly on west-coast routes. Calling into over 30 ports throughout the west coast, its 31 vessels service 24 routes, from the Isle of Arran in the south to Lewis in the Outer Hebrides. They sell island hopscotch tickets and, best value for visitors with cars, bicyles and motorhomes, rover tickets, giving 8 or 15 days' unlimited travel on most routes.

**Strathspey Railway** runs during the summer months and Christmas for 5 miles (8 km) from Aviemore (Speyside) to Boat of Garten, providing good views of the Cairngorm Mountains. It is hoped to extend the line to Grantown-on-Spey. Enquiries to Aviemore Station, Dalfaber Road, Aviemore, Inverness-shire PH22 1PY. Tel: (01479) 810725, www.strathspeyrailway.co.uk.

The **Mull & West Highland Railway** has steam and diesel trains running April–mid-October on a narrow-gauge track for 1¼ miles (2 km) through superb mountain and woodland scenery from the ferry terminal at Craignure to Torosoy Castle and Gardens on Mull. Enquiries to tel: (01680) 812494. Fax: (01680) 300595, www.mullrail.com.

At the top end of the market is the **Royal Scotsman**, one of the world's most exclusive trains. This mobile hotel for just 32 passengers combines spectacular scenery with superb food and wine and impeccable service. A variety of two- and seven-night tours are available; highlights include Glamis Castle and the islands of Bute and Syke. Tours operate between April and October, departing from and returning to Edinburgh. Enquiries to The Royal Scotsman, 46a Constitution Street, Edinburgh EH6 6RS, tel: (0845) 077 2222, www.royalscotsman.com

The **Jacobite Steam Train** chugs its way from Fort William to the fishing port of Mallaig; its picturesque route, including crossing of the Glenfinnan Viaduct appears in the fictional Harry Potter novels of the celebrated Scottish writer, J.K. Rowling.

The train runs from June to mid-October (Mon–Fri) and daily throughout July and August. Contact the West Coast Railway Company on tel: (01524) 737751; www.steamtrain.info.

## Ferries

Scottish ferries are great. On long routes, like the five-hour Oban to Barra ferry, there are car decks, cabins, comfortable chairs, a restaurant and self-service cafeteria. On others, such as the 7-hour round trip to the tiny islands of Eigg, Muck, Rum and Canna, ferries are basic with wooden seats and minimal refreshments. These working boats, carrying goods and mail as well as passengers, are mainly used by islanders, with some birdwatchers and occasional curious visitors. Take note that unless you specify beforehand, disembarking for sightseeing is not allowed.

There is plenty of small private enterprise on the west coast. There are cruises from Arisaig on the mainland to Skye and Mull as well as to Eigg, Muck, Rum and Canna. Day trips to the National Trust for Scotland island of Staffa with Fingal's Cave, to the bird island of Lunga and the uninhabited Treshnish Islands, start from the Ulva, Dervaig and Fionnphort, all of which are on Mull, while Staffa can also be reached from Iona. There is a 10-minute shuttle service from Fionnphort on the southwest tip of Mull to Iona. These trips allow some time ashore, and there is no dificulty in finding out about such services when you arrive. Tourist information centres and many hotels have brochures.

If voyaging to the Outer Hebrides feels like sailing to the edge of the world, taking a ferry to the ancient isles of Orkney and Shetland (the Northern Isles) is equally exhilarating. Two major ferry companies ply these routes, and in summer it's essential to book ahead.

### Orkney

**Northlink Orkney & Shetland Ferries** run roll-on/roll-off car ferry services from Aberdeen (8 hours) or Scrabster (1 hour 45 minutes) on the mainland to Stromness, and also services from Lerwick in Shetland.

A passenger ferry runs from May to September from Gill's Bay, near

**BELOW:** the Caledonian MacBrayne ferry heads out from Oban harbour.

John o'Groats, to Burwick on South Ronaldsay (tel: (01955) 611353). The crossing takes around 40 minutes. Connecting buses can be boarded on Orkney, and there are cars for hire.

Once on Orkney, a dozen or so smaller islands can be visited by local ferries. The Kirkwall tourist office has more details.

### Shetland

The **P&O** service, which takes 14 hours between Aberdeen and Lerwick, Shetland's main port, is on modern roll-on/roll-off vessels with cabins, shops, restaurants and cafeterias.

Once again, local ferries ply between the small islands. **Northlink Orkney & Shetland Ferries Ltd:** routes, timetables and fares may be obtained from Ferry Terminal, Stromness, Orkney, KW16; tel: (0845) 600 0449; www.northlinkferries.co.uk

### Pleasure Cruises

On Loch Katrine, which has supplied Glasgow with water since 1859, the **SS Sir Walter Scott**, Scotland's only screw steamer in regular passenger service, makes two daily round-trip voyages between the Trossachs and Stronachlachar piers from April until the end of October. The morning trip permits a 15-minute landing at Stronachlachar, while the two one-hour afternoon trips are non-landing. Enquiries to Trossachs Pier Complex, Loch Katrine, Callander FK17 8HZ; tel: (01877) 376316; www.lochkatrine.co.uk.

The Argyll Forest Park ferry service runs from May–October (daily July–Aug; Mon–Fri all other months). There are four different cruises available, with morning and afternoon sailings from Greenock and Helensburgh respectively. Both departure points offer the chance to cruise along Loch Long and pop into

**ABOVE:** several companies run cruises from Ullapool to the Summer Isles.

the picturesque village of Blairmore, observe marine life including dolphins, and the option to visit the famous Benmore Botanic Gardens on Cowal. For further information contact: Clyde Marine Cruises, Victoria Harbour, Greenock, tel: 01475-721281; www.clydecruiser.co.uk. Similar cruises from Gourock, with longer time ashore, can be enjoyed from the end of April to the end of September on Caledonian MacBrayne craft (see box on page 316).

**PS Waverley**, the world's last sea-going paddle steamer, sails on the Clyde (day trips) from Waverley Terminal, Anderston Quay, Glasgow, from June until August. Tel: (0845) 130 4647; www.waverleyexcursions.co.uk.

From April to October the **Maid of the Forth** sails from South Queensferry, just outside Edinburgh, to Inchcolm Island with its ruined medieval abbey; seals are often spotted during the voyage. Trips last about 3 hours, with 1½ hours spent ashore. Contact: Maid of the Forth, Hawes Pier, South Queensferry; tel: (0131) 331 5000; www.maidoftheforth.co.uk.

At Easter and from May to September the 130-passenger **MV Shearwater** sails each morning from Arisaig for a full day to the small islands (Rum, Eigg, Muck) of the Inner Hebrides. Several hours are spent ashore. Contact: Murdo Grant, Arisaig Harbour, Inverness-shire PH39 4NH. Tel: (01687) 450224; www.arisaig.co.uk.

During the summer months the **TSMV Western Isles** makes half- and full-day cruises from Mallaig past dramatic scenery to surrounding lochs, or to the islands of Rum and Canna, or to Skye with landings. Contact: Bruce Watt Sea Cruises, Mallaig; tel: (01687) 462320; www.knoydart-ferry.co.uk.

From May to September daily sailings (weather permitting) are made from Anstruther to the Isle of May aboard the **May Princess**. The trip lasts about 5 hours, with 3 hours ashore to explore the island, whose cliffs, at least until July, are covered with breeding kittiwakes, razorbills, guillemots and shags. Scotland's oldest lighthouse and the ruins of a 12th-century chapel can also be visited. Contact: Anstruther Pleasure Trips, Pittenweem Road, Anstruther, Fife KY10 3DS; tel: (01333) 310103; www.isleofmayferry.com.

From Easter until mid-October **Anne of Etive** departs from Taynuilt on 1½- and 3-hour cruises into Loch Etive. The route covered is inaccessible except by boat. If you are lucky you'll spot seals on the rocks, the golden eagle of Ben Starav and deer on the crags. Morning and afternoon departures from Sunday–Friday. Contact: Donald Kennedy, Taynuilt; tel: (01866) 822430; e-mail: lochetive@aol.com.

Several companies run 2- to 4-hour cruises from Ullapool to the Summer Isles. Some are nature cruises, some

### The Hebridean Princess

The **Hebridean Princess**, more a stately country-house hotel on water than the usual run-of-the-mill luxury liner and accommodating only 49 passengers in elegant cabins, makes a series of cruises from Oban from March until October. The region covered is the northwest coast of Scotland, Inner and Outer Hebrides, the Orkney and Shetland Islands and even St Kilda. The route varies from cruise to cruise, with voyages lasting 4–8

nights, and the printed schedule may be altered to avoid bad weather. Cars can roll-on and roll-off the ship, thus enabling travellers to explore independently at the various ports of call.

Bookings can be made through: Hebridean International Cruises, Kintail House, Carleton New Road, Skipton, N Yorkshire, BD23 3AN. Tel: (01756) 704 704. Fax: (01756) 704 794; www.hebridean.co.uk

are sunset cruises and some permit landing on the islands. (Try Summer Queen Cruises; tel: (01854) 612472; www.summerqueen.co.uk.)

Summer Isles cruises also depart from Achiltibuie aboard the **Hectoria** from May to September. These last about 4 hours and permit landing on the islands. Contact; Achiltibuie Post Office; tel: (01854) 622200.

## Public Transport

### By Bus

Major towns have their own bus services. For timetable information on all public transport services in Scotland contact **Traveline** tel: (0870) 608 2608; www.travelinescotland.com. In addition, there are bus services serving rural communities and linking the various towns. The national bus network is run by **Scottish Citylink**; tel: (0870) 550 5050; www.citylink.co.uk. The visitor who intends to make frequent use of buses should investigate the various tickets which allow unlimited use of buses for specific periods. Contact Scottish Citylink or the tourist board for more details.

An unusual delight and a superb way to meet the people and learn something of their customs is to board one of the sadly diminishing Royal Mail Postbuses, which provide an essential post-and-passenger service in isolated parts of the country. To people in rural communities the familiar red Postbus is both a welcome friend and a lifeline to the world outside. The buses cover over 100 routes stretching from the Borders to the Outer Hebrides, and you can hail a Postbus at any point along its route. Contact: **Royal Mail Postbuses**; tel: 0845 7740740; www.postbus.royalmail.com.

## By Taxi

The major cities have sufficient taxi stands. Outside the cities, you will probably need to phone for a taxi.

## Private Transport

Scotland has an excellent network of roads which, away from the central belt, are usually not congested. Driving on the left is the rule and passengers must wear seat belts. In urban areas, the speed limit is either 30 or 40 mph (48 or 64 km/h), the limit on country roads is 60 mph (97 km/h), and on motorways and dual carriageways 70 mph (113 km/h).

In some parts of the Highlands and on many of the islands, roads are single track with passing places. The behaviour of drivers on these roads tends to show that good old-fashioned courtesy is not dead. On these narrow roads, please use the "passing places" to let oncoming vehicles pass, or to let others behind you overtake.

Radio Scotland (FM 92.4–94.7/ MW 810) broadcasts details of road conditions throughout the day, with details of particular problems, accidents or emergencies. The broadcast travel information includes details of ferry, rail or air travel hold-ups or changes. Local radio stations also broadcast travel and road information.

Even today you can travel many miles in the Highlands and on the islands without seeing a petrol station. If you see a fuel stop – fill up. If you are planning to drive on a Sunday in the Outer Hebrides, fill up your tank on the Saturday. This is because, in some places, strict Sunday observance means that filling stations will be closed.

## Car Rentals

Self-drive rental costs £30–£70 a day, depending on the type of car and the duration of the rental. The rates are reduced in the October–April off-season. For more detailed information, apply directly to the car rental companies *(see below)*.

### Edinburgh

*(Area code: 0131)*
**Arnold Clark**
Seafield Road
Tel: 657 9120
**Enterprise Rent-a-Car**
12 Annandale Street
Tel: 557 0000
**Europcar**
24 East London Street
Tel: 557 3456
**W.L. Sleigh Ltd** (chauffeur-driven)
6 Devon Place
Tel: 337 3171

**Edinburgh Airport**
**Alamo & National**
Tel: 331 1922
**Avis** Tel: 344 3900
**Budget** Tel: 333 1926
**Hertz** Tel: 0870 846 0009
**Enterprise** Tel: 348 4000

### Glasgow

*(Area code: 0141)*
**Alamo & National Car Rental**
76 Lancefield Quay
Tel: 204 1051
**Avis**
70 Lancefield Street
Tel: 221 2827
**Enterprise Rent-a-Car**
45 Finnieston Street
Tel: 221 2124.
**Hertz**
138 Hyde Park Street
Tel: 0870 850 2657.
**Little's Chauffeur Drive**
1282 Paisley Road West
Tel: 883 2111

**Glasgow Airport**
**Avis** Tel: 0870 608 6338
**Arnold Clark** Tel: 847 8602
**Europcar** Tel: 887 4281
**Hertz** Tel: 0870 846 0007

### The Southwest

**Ayr**
**Arnold Clark**
196 Prestwick Road
Tel: (01292) 270037
**Enterprise**
Whitfield Drive
Tel: 01292 619123

**Prestwick Airport**
**Avis**
Terminal Building
Tel: (0870) 608 6359

**BELOW:** the Postbus is always a welcome sight on the Isle of Skye.

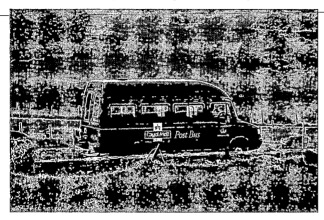

**ABOVE:** you can drive for miles without seeing another motorist.

**Northern Vehicle Hire (Europcar)**
Terminal Building
Tel: (01292) 678198

### Forth & Clyde

**Stirling**
**Alamo & National Car Rental**
124 Glasgow Road
Tel: (01786) 812828
**Budget**
Kerse Road
Tel: (01786) 441165

### The West Coast
**Fort William**
**Easydrive**
Lochybridge
Tel: (01397) 701616
**Slipway Autos**
Annat Point
Corpach
Tel: (01397) 772404

**Oban**
**Flit**
Glencruitten Road
Tel: (01631) 566553

### Inner Hebrides
**Skye**
**Ewen MacRae**
West End Garage, Portree
Tel: (01478) 612554
**Sutherland's Garage**
Broadford
Tel: (01471) 822225

### Outer Hebrides
**Lewis**
**Lewis Car Rentals**
52 Bayhead Street
Stornoway
Tel: (01851) 703760
**Arnol Motors**
Arnol
Tel: (01851) 710548

**Stornoway Car Hire** (Airport)
Tel: (01851) 702658
**Benbecula**
**Ask Car Hire**
Linicleat
Tel: (01870) 602818
**Maclennan Bros. Motors Ltd.**
Balivanich
Tel: (01870) 602191

**South Uist**
**Laing Motors**
Lochboisdale
Tel: (01878) 700267

### Central Scotland
**Perth**
**Arnold Clark**
St. Leonard's Bank

### Bikers Welcome

Every summer, scores of
motorcyclists don their leathers to
tour Scotland's winding roads on
two-wheels. Glencoe, the Isle of
Skye and the remote Applecross
Peninsula are among the more
popular routes. Furthermore, as
increasing numbers of Scotland's
forty and fifty year olds seek to
rediscover their youth astride a
growling Harley Davidson, B&B's
and many pubs have positively
responded by displaying "Bikers
Welcome" signs on their premises.
   **Scotland by Bike** is a new
venture offering 5–10 day tours
and customised accompanied/
unaccompanied tours of the
countries Highlands and islands on
two-wheels. Top of the range bikes
can also be hired. For details see
www.scotlandbybike.com or tel: 01224-
330640 or 07796 170999.

Tel: (01738) 442202
**Hertz**
405 High Street
Tel: (01738) 624108
**National**
Glasgow Road
Tel: (01738) 631531

### The East Coast
**Aberdeen**
**Arnold Clark**
Girdleness Road
Tel: (01224) 249159
**Avis**
Dyce Airport
Tel: (0870) 6986315
**Europcar**
121 Causewayend
Tel: (01224) 631199

**Dundee**
**Arnold Clark,**
East Dock Street
Tel: (01382) 225382
**Avis**
Old Glamis Road
Tel: (01382) 818313
**Enterprise Rent-a-Car**
131 Seagate
Tel: (01382) 205040
**Europcar**
Clepington Road
Tel: (01382) 455505
**Alamo & National Car Rental**
45–53 Gellalty Street
Tel: (01382) 22403

### The Northern Highlands
**Aviemore**
**Northern Vehicle Hire**
Tel: (01479) 811463

**Inverness**
**Budget**
Railway Terrace
Tel: (01463) 713333
**Europcar**
Harbour Road
Tel: (01463) 235337

**Inverness Airport**
**Hertz** Dalcross
Tel: (0870) 850 2661
**Europcar** Dalcross Industrial Estate
Tel: (01667) 460000

### Orkney
**Kirkwall**
**W.R. Tulloch & Sons Ltd**
Castle Garage, Castle Street
Tel: (01856) 872125

### Shetland
**Lerwick**
**Bolt's Car Hire**
26 North Road
Tel: (01595) 693636
**John Leask & Son**
Esplanade
Tel: (01595) 69316

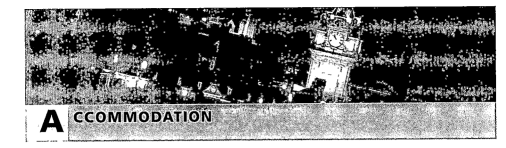

# A CCOMMODATION

# HOTELS, YOUTH HOSTELS AND BED & BREAKFASTS

## Types of Accommodation

A wide range of accommodation is available in Scotland, from hotels of international standard to simple Bed & Breakfast (B&B) accommodation. Prices vary from under £25 a night for Bed & Breakfast to well over £200 at the most luxurious hotels.

VisitScotland (www.visitscotland.com) operates a system of grading accommodation concentrating on assessment of quality (although symbols still indicate services available). Star gradings range from one star (fair and acceptable) to five stars (exceptional/world-class). These are applied to all types of accommodation, including hotels, Bed & Breakfasts and self-catering.

If you are planning a caravan or camping holiday, look out for the Thistle logo. The "Thistle Award" is bestowed by the industry and VisitScotland to parks which meet standards of excellence in environment, facilities and caravans.

Staying in Bed & Breakfast accommodation is not only economical, it is also a flexible and potentially interesting way to see the country. Local tourist offices operate a convenient booking service (for which there is usually a small charge) and, except at the height of the tourist season in July and August, it is not necessary to reserve in advance. Bed & Breakfasts in VisitScotland's scheme will, at a minimum, be clean and comfortable. With luck you may find the proprietor friendly and a mine of local information on local routes and things to see and do. Most of the better Bed & Breakfast establishments serve dinner on request, which is usually excellent and modestly priced.

Particularly good value are Campus Hotels, the name given to Bed & Breakfasts and self-catering facilities offered by the Scottish universities in Aberdeen, St Andrews, Dundee, Edinburgh, Glasgow and Stirling. These are available during vacations. In addition to accommodation, they offer the use of university facilities such as tennis courts and swimming pools (see below).

There is also a vast choice of self-catering accommodation in chalets, flats, cottages and castles. A few websites to try include:
www.aboutscotland.com
www.assc.co.uk
www.cottages-and-castles.co.uk
www.scottish-holiday-cottages.co.uk
www.unique-cottages.co.uk.
In addition, the regional tourist boards have listings of self-catering accommodation.

Information on all types of accommodation is available from VisitScotland and local tourist information centres (see page 359), or log on to their website, www.visitscotland.com, where you can find comprehensive listings, sorted by area, and refine your search to your specific requirements.

Except for the more expensive city hotels, prices quoted include breakfast. Approximate guides to prices per person per night in high season in a double room are:

£ = below £30
££ = £30–50
£££ = £50–80
££££ = more than £80

Note that, especially for the hotel chains, room rates vary widely according to demand, and weekend rates in city business hotels are often much lower than weekdays. It's always worth enquiring about special offers: many hotels offer good-value short breaks outside the main holiday periods.

On occasions, the distinction between Bed & Breakfast establishments, guest houses and private hotels becomes blurred, especially when the former have en suite facilities and serve dinner. All rooms in the following establishments have an en suite bath/shower unless otherwise stated.

## Campus Hotels

Excellent accommodation is available during summer and Easter vacations and, on several campuses, throughout the year, at Scottish universities. Both B&B accommodation (some rooms en suite; no single supplement) and self-catering units are offered on a nightly or weekly basis. Access to the university's sports facilities is usually permitted.

The standard of accommodation is high, but so is the demand, so it's advisable to reserve a few months in advance.

Prices are usually between £20–30 per person per night.
Contact numbers are:
● Aberdeen – (01224) 262134
● Dundee – (01382) 344039 (B&B); (01382) 573111 (self-catering)
● Edinburgh – (0131) 651 2055
● Glasgow – (0141) 330 4116/330 2318
● Heriot-Watt – (0131) 451 3669
● St Andrews – (01334) 476161
● Stirling – (01786) 467141/2
● Strathclyde – (0141) 553 4148
● Napier (Edinburgh) – (0131) 455 3738

# EDINBURGH

## Hotels

*(If phoning from outside area, use code: 0131)*

### ££££

**Prestonfield House Hotel**
Prestonfield
Tel: 225 7800
www.prestonfield.com
This beautiful 17th-century mansion is a celebrity hideaway hotel. 21 bedrooms combine antiquity with modernity. 2 miles south of the Scottish Parliament. Excellent restaurant.

**Balmoral Hotel**
1 Princes Street
Tel: 556 2414
Fax: 557 3747
www.roccofortehotels.com
188 rooms. Edinburgh's premier hotel, built in 1862 and reopened in 1991. All rooms recently underwent a tasteful £7 million refurbishment. Many rooms have a view of the castle.

**Caledonian Hilton Hotel**
Princes Street
Tel: 222 8888
Fax: 222 8889
www.hilton.com/caledonian
249 rooms. The grande dame of Edinburgh hotels is constantly being upgraded. Many rooms with view of the castle.

**Channings**
15 South Learmonth Gardens
Tel: 332 3232
Fax: 332 9631
www.channings.co.uk
41 rooms. A series of splendid Edwardian adjoining houses, minutes from city centre. Comfortable reception area and lounges. Bedrooms individually furnished.

**Dalhousie Castle Hotel**
Bonnyrigg
Tel: (01875) 82015
Fax: (01875) 821936
www.dalhousiecastle.com
34 rooms. A truly imposing 13th-century castle standing in parkland and forest through which flows the South Esk River. James VI, Queen Victoria and Sir

**ABOVE:** the Balmoral Hotel, the elegant Edinburgh landmark in Princes Street.

Walter Scott all stayed here. The restaurant is in an atmospheric dungeon, and there is a chapel in the hotel.

**George Hotel**
19–21 George Street
Tel: 225 1251
Fax: 226 5644
www.principal-hotels.com
195 en suite rooms. Very central, well-established, grand old hotel.

**The Glasshouse Hotel**
2 Greenside Place
Tel: 525 8200
Fax: 525 8205
www.theetoncollection.com
65 rooms. Situated near the east end of Princes Street, this is a state-of-the-art building with the rooms surrounding a 2-acre roof garden. The exterior rooms have splendid views to the New Town or across the Firth of Forth. Breakfast available on request, but the hotel has no restaurants: though there are many just minutes away.

**Radisson SAS Hotel**
80 High Street
Tel: 557 9797
Fax: 557 9789
www.sas.radisson.com

238 rooms. A modern hotel situated on the Royal Mile. Well-equipped leisure centre.

**Howard Hotel**
34 Great King Street
Tel: 315 2220
Fax: 557 6515
www.thehoward.com
18 rooms. Three interconnected 18th-century town houses in the New Town result in a magnificent classical hotel.

**Norton House Hotel**
Ingliston
Tel: 333 1275
Fax: 333 3752
www.handpicked.co.uk
47 rooms. Baronial country house hotel in wooded grounds. Close to airport. Excellent restaurant and informal bistro.

**The Scotsman**
20 North Bridge
Tel: 556 5565
Fax: 652 3625
www.thescotsmanhotelgroup.co.uk.
68 rooms. A boutique hotel produced from a remarkably successful make-over of *The Scotsman* newspaper offices. Comfortable rooms have all mod cons and

health club with pool.

**Sheraton Grand Hotel & Spa**
1 Festival Square
Tel: 229 9131
Fax: 228 4510
www.sheraton.com/grandedinburgh
265 rooms. Set back from busy Lothian Road and close to city centre. Complete leisure club.

### £££

**Best Western Bruntsfield Hotel**
69 Bruntsfield Place
Tel: 229 1393
Fax: 229 5634
www.bw-bruntsfieldhotel.co.uk
75 rooms. Well-established hotel 1 mile (1.5 km) from Princes Street.

**Malmaison**
1 Tower Place, Leith
Tel: 468 5000
Fax: 468 5002

ACCOMMODATION

EATING OUT

ACTIVITIES

A – Z

**ABOVE:** the Glasshouse Hotel.

www.malmaison.com
100 rooms with cable TV. A former seamen's mission, the Malmaison is an award-winning contemporary hotel with stylishly designed rooms, situated on the waterfront of Leith. Haunted turret room.

**Royal Terrace Hotel**
18 Royal Terrace
Tel: (0870) 850 2608
Fax: 557 5334
www.royalterracehotel.co.uk
107 rooms. Georgian terrace building on a cobbled street, minutes from east end of Princes Street. Leisure club and large private garden.

**Point Hotel**
34 Bread Street
Tel: 221 5555
Fax: 221 9929
www.point-hotel.co.uk.
Cutting-edge minimalist hotel with colour-themed floors close to Castle. Jacuzzis in suites. Attractive bar and restaurants.

**££**

**Ailsa Craig Hotel**
24 Royal Terrace
Tel: 556 6055
Fax: 556 1022
www.townhousehotels.co.uk
18 rooms. Elegant, recently refurbished hotel with stunning views over the Forth and Calton Hill.

**Bank Hotel**
1 South Bridge
Tel: 622 6800
Fax: 622 6822
www.festival-inns.co.uk
9 rooms. Former bank in midst of Royal Mile, now converted into café-bar with bedrooms.

**Edinburgh City Premier Travel Inn**
1 Morrison Link
Tel: (0870) 238 3319
Fax: 228 9836
www.travelinn.co.uk
281 rooms. Interesting bid to provide economical, comfortable, no-frills accommodation in city centre.

**Holiday Inn Edinburgh North**
107 Queensferry Road
Tel: 0870 400 9025
Fax: 332 3408
www.holiday-inn.co.uk
Friendly hotel with 101 rooms. 1½ miles (2.5 km) west of city centre.

**Travelodge Central**
33 St Mary's Street
Tel: (0870) 191 1637
Fax: 557 3681
www.travelodge.co.uk
193 rooms. Standard no-frills hostelry adjacent to Holyrood end of Royal Mile.

**Guest Houses**

(If phoning from outside area, use code: 0131)

**££**

**Stuart House**
12 East Claremont Street
Tel: 557 9030
Fax: 557 0563
www.stuartguesthouse.com
6 rooms (5 en suite).

Refurbished Georgian house close to city centre. Non-smoking.

**£**

**Ashlyn Guest House**
42 Inverleith Row
Tel/Fax: 552 2954
7 rooms (5 en suite). Listed Georgian house. Close to the Botanic Gardens; five minutes' drive from the city centre.

**Balquhidder Guest House**
94 Pilrig Street
Tel: 554 3377
www.ohwy.com
6 rooms (5 en suite). A former church manse, built in 1857, this centrally located detached house offers a warm family welcome.

**Joppa Turrets**
1 Lower Joppa
Tel/fax: 669 5806
www.joppaturrets.co.uk
7 rooms (5 en suite). On the beach at Joppa but close to bus routes and 5 miles (8 km) from city centre.

**Salisbury Guest House**
45 Salisbury Road
Tel/Fax: 667 1264
www.salisburyguesthouse.co.uk
8 rooms (7 en suite). Georgian listed building, near Holyrood Palace, Scottish Parliament and Royal Mile.

Your best bet for low-priced accommodation in Edinburgh is a **B&B**. The Edinburgh and Lothians Tourist Board will help find one for you.
Tel: 473 3855
www.edinburgh.org/accommodation;
www.visitscotland.com

# GLASGOW

**Hotels**

(If phoning from outside area, use code: 0141)

**££££**

**One Devonshire Gardens**
1 Devonshire Gardens
Tel: 339 2001
Fax: 337 1663
www.onedevonshiregardens.com
35 rooms. Exquisite, luxury boutique hotel on a tree-lined Victorian terrace in the

residential area of West End. Each room different, impeccable service.

**Glasgow Hilton**
1 William Street
Tel: 204 5555
Fax: 204 5004
www.hilton.com
317 rooms. Modern 20-floor tower in the centre of the city, just off the motorway. Health and leisure club. Excellent restaurant.

**Malmaison**
278 West George Street
Tel: 572 1000
Fax: 572 1002
www.malmaison.com
Stylish 72-room hotel in former Greek Orthodox church in city centre. Chic and comfortable.

**£££**

**ABode Glasgow**
129 Bath Street
Tel: 221 6789

www.abodehotels.co.uk
Trendsetting hotel combines luxurious rooms with stunning traditional architecture throughout. The restaurant is equally stylish.

**Best Western Ewington Hotel**
132 Queens Drive
Tel: 423 1152
Fax: 422 2030
www.mckeverhotels.co.uk
43 rooms. Well-appointed

terrace hotel in leafy street beside Queen's Park.

**City Inn**
Finnieston Quay
Tel: 240 1002
Fax: 248 2754
www.cityinn.com/glasgow
164 rooms. Pleasant property on the north side of the river with great deck. Close to Conference Centre and to Science Centre.

**Crowne Plaza**
Congress Road
Tel: 0870 4431 691
Fax: 221 2022
www.crownplaza.com
289 rooms. Sited on the River Clyde next to the Scottish Exhibition Centre.

**Hilton Glasgow Grosvenor**
Grosvenor Terrace
Tel: 339 8811
Fax: 334 0710
www.hilton.co.uk
96 rooms. Hotel with striking façade near the Botanic Gardens, university and trendy Byres Road.

**Langs Hotel**
2 Port Dundas Place
Tel: 333 1500
Fax: 352 2456
www.langshotels.co.uk.
100 well-equipped rooms. Ideally situated next to bus terminal, concert hall and 17-screen cinema. Duplexes available. PlayStations in all rooms, health club (no pool).

**Menzies Glasgow**
27 Washington Street
Tel: 222 2929
www.menzies-hotels.co.uk
128 feng shui rooms and 12 suite apartments. 10 minutes from Central Station.

**Millennium Hotel**
George Square
Tel: 332 6711
Fax: 332 4264
www.millenniumhotels.com
117 rooms. Situated in the heart of George Square next to Queen Street Station.

**Radisson SAS Hotel**
301 Argyle Street
Tel: 204 3333
Fax: 204 3344
www.sas.radisson.com
247 rooms. One of the city's newest hotels. Adjacent to Central Station.

**Thistle Glasgow**
36 Cambridge Street
Tel: (0870) 333 9154

Fax: 333 9254.
www.thistlehotels.com/glasgow
300 rooms. Good hotel in the heart of the city.

## ££

**Babbity Bowster**
16–18 Blackfriars Street
Tel: 552 5055.
Fax: 552 7774.
E-mail: babbitybowster@ gofornet.co.uk
6 rooms. This place is better-known for its food and atmosphere and its great folk music sessions. But it's a handy base in the Merchant City and close to the shopping and nightlife.

**Holiday Inn Glasgow**
161 West Nile Street
Tel: 352 8300
Fax: 352 8311
www.higlasgow.com
113 rooms. Ideally situated next to bus terminal, concert hall and 17-screen cinema. Duplexes available.

**Jurys Glasgow Hotel**
Great Western Road
Tel: 334 8161
Fax: 334 3846
www.jurysdoyle.com
136 rooms. Budget hotel in the West End complete with pool.

**Kirklee Hotel**
11 Kensington Gate
Tel: 334 5555
Fax: 339 3828
www.kirkleehotel.co.uk
9 rooms. An Edwardian town house in an almost original condition in the West End conservation area. The extensive collection of paintings and drawings adds to the atmosphere of a bygone age. One of the hidden gems of Glasgow.

**Novotel Hotel**
181 Pitt Street
Tel: 222 2775
Fax: 204 5438
www.novotel.com
139 rooms. One of the city's newer hotels, and in touching distance of trendy bars and restaurants. A neighbour is the headquarters of the city police.

**The Pipers Tryst**
30–34 McPhater Street
Tel: 353 5551
Fax: 353 1570
www.thepipingcentre.co.uk
8 rooms. This very small

**ABOVE:** the Grecian temple frontage of the Malmaison Hotel.

hotel is part of the Glasgow Piping Centre and is very close to the Royal Concert Hall and the city centre – and no, the sound of bagpipes won't keep you awake at night.

**Quality Hotel Central**
99 Gordon Street
Tel: 221 9680
Fax: 226 3948
www.choicehotelseurope.com
222 rooms. The city's oldest hotel is part of Central Station. Leisure centre.

**Saint Jude's**
190 Bath Street
Tel: 352 8800
Fax: 352 8801
www.saintjudes.com
6 rooms. A superb small hotel furnished in modern designer mode, attached to a smashing restaurant in the fashionable Merchant City. Fitness suite, jacuzzi and sunbed.

**Sherbrooke Castle**
11 Sherbrooke Avenue
Tel: 427 4227
Fax: 427 5685
www.sherbrooke.co.uk
21 rooms. Scottish

baronial castle in own grounds on south side, about 3 miles (5 km) from city centre. Handy for the Burrell Collection and Pollok Country Park.

## £

**Argyll Guest House**
970 Sauchiehall Street
Tel: 357 5155
Fax: 337 3283
www.argyllguesthouseglasgow.co.uk
20 rooms. Private hotel in Georgian terrace by Kelvingrove Park and a few minutes' walk from the art galleries, university and Museum of Transport.

**Express by Holiday Inn**
122 Stockwell Street
Tel: 548 5000
Fax: 548 5048

| PRICE CATEGORIES |

Approximate prices per person per night in a double room in high season:
**£** = less than £30
**££** = £30–50
**£££** = £50–80
**££££** = more than £80

www.hiexpress.co.uk
128 rooms. On north side of river, a tad away from the heart of the city. Close to the Glasgow mosque and the Citizens Theatre.
**Hillhead Hotel**
32 Cecil Stree
Tel: 339 7733
Fax: 339 1770
www.hillhead-hotel.co.uk
11 rooms. Close to Byres Road and the busy West End, this small, warm and friendly hotel also offers free car parking.
**Ibis Hotel**
220 West Regent Street
Tel: 225 6000
Fax: 225 6010
www.ibishotel.com
141 rooms. Don't be put off by the psychedelic appearance of this efficient modern hotel in a quiet part of the city centre. Compact rooms with workstation and computer points. Close to motorway.
**Kelvin Hotel**
15 Buckingham Terrace
Tel: 339 7143
Fax: 339 5215
www.thekelvinhotel.com
9 rooms. Family-run hotel in one of the Victorian terraces just off Great Western Road and very close to the Botanic Gardens and Byres Road.
**Greek Thomson Hotel**
Elderslie Street
Tel: (0870) 240 7060
www.activehotels.com
A 17-bedroom, simply furnished town house close

**ABOVE:** the conservatory of the Millennium Hotel.

to West End and city centre restaurants.

## Guest Houses

*(If phoning from outside area, use code: 0141)*

### ££

**The Town House**
4 Hughenden Terrace
Tel: 357 0862
Fax: 339 9605
www.thetownhouseglasgow.com
10 rooms. Elegantly

refurbished Victorian town house in quiet conservation area in West End. Very well established.

### £–££

**Alamo Guest House**
46 Gray Street
Tel: 339 2395
www.alamoguesthouse.com
10 rooms (4 en suite). Situated on pleasant, quiet road alongside Kelvingrove Park. Good value and comfortable.

**Euro Hostels**
318 Clyde Street
Tel: 222 2828
www.euro-hostels.co.uk
Basic clean (and en suite) accommodation ideal for those seeking central location on a budget. Safe and friendly.
**The Flower House Bed & Breakfast**
33 St Vincent Crescent
Tel: 204 2846
www.scotland2000.com/flowerhouse
4 rooms. The flowers crowding round the front of the building explain the name. A warm, friendly, lovely guest house.
**Glasgow Youth Hostel**
7–8 Park Terrace
Tel (0870) 004 1119
www.syha.org.uk
Charming dorms sleep four to six. All rooms en suite. One of Scotland's best hostels, extensively refurbished following a fire.
**McLays Guest House**
268 Renfrew Street
Tel: 332 4796
Fax: 353 0422
www.mclaysgh.co.uk
62 rooms (39 en suite). Lots of singles. Well-appointed, comfortable guest house only a few minutes from the city centre.
**Number 36**
36 St Vincent Street
Tel: 248 2086
www.no36.co.uk
Located in Finnieston in a Victorian town house. Within close proximity of the SECC and Kelvingrove.

# THE BORDERS

## Hawick

**Mansfield House Hotel**
Weensland Road
Tel: (01450) 360400
Fax: (01450) 372007
www.mansfield-house.com
12 rooms. Victorian country house hotel in 10 well established acres
(4 hectares). Glorious public rooms. ££–£££

## Innerleithen

**Traquair Arms**
Traquair Road
Tel: (01896) 830229

Fax: (01896) 830260
www.traquair-arms-hotel.co.uk
15 rooms. Charming country house hotel with excellent food, close to historic Traquair House.
££–£££

## Jedburgh

**Jedforest Hotel**
Jedburgh, Roxburghshire TD8 6PJ
Tel: (01835) 840222
Fax: (01835) 84226
www.jedforesthotel.com
The first and last hotel in Scotland. Stands in 35 acres (15 hectares) of a

private estate on the banks of Jedwater River. ££

## Kelso

**Cross Keys**
The Square
Tel: (01573) 223303
Fax: (01573) 225792
www.cross-keys-hotel.co.uk
28 rooms. Old coaching inn set in town centre square with French character. ££
**The Roxburghe Hotel & Golf Course**
Heiton
Tel: (01573) 450331

Fax: (01573) 450611
www.roxburghe.net
22 bedrooms. 18th-century house, 3 miles (5 km) south of Kelso and nestling on the banks of the River Teviot. Superb public rooms and beautiful grounds. Fishing, clay pigeon shooting, croquet, tennis, championship golf course.
£££–££££

## Kircudbright

**Toadhall**
16 Castle Street.
Tel/Fax: (01557) 330204

Central location, big breakfasts and good sized rooms, including one with a four poster bed. **££**
**Best Western Selkirk Arms**
High Street
Tel: (01557) 330402
Fax: (01557) 331639
www.bw-selkirkarmshotel.co.uk
16 rooms. Pleasant hotel with garden. Will attract lovers of Robert Burns as the scene of the *Selkirk Grace*. **££–£££**.

## Melrose

**Burts Hotel**
Market Square
Tel: (01896) 822285
Fax: (01896) 822870
www.burtshotel.co.uk
20 rooms. Tastefully modernised old town house in main square, close to magnificent ruined abbey. **££**

## Peebles

**Castle Venlaw Hotel**
Edinburgh Road, Peebles
Tel: (01721) 720384
Fax: (01721) 724066
www.venlaw.co.uk
12 rooms. A wide variety of rooms in this pleasantly situated 200-year-old castle on the outskirts of Peebles. **££££**
**Cringletie House Hotel**
Edinburgh Road
Tel: (01721) 725750
Fax: (01721) 720244.
www.cringletie.com
12 rooms. Elegantly furnished hotel in its own grounds 2 miles (3 km) from Peebles. Renowned restaurant. **£££–££££**
**Peebles Hotel Hydro**
Innerleithen Road
Tel: (01721) 720602
Fax: (01721) 722999
www.peebleshotelhydro.co.uk
129 rooms. Large,

imposing château-style hotel set in 34 acres (14 hectares) overlooking the River Tweed Valley and Border Hills. Leisure centre, excellent tennis, walking and riding. Families with children welcome. **££££**
**Tontine Hotel**
High Street
Tel: (01721) 720892
Fax: (01721) 729732
www.tontinehotel.com
36 rooms. 1808-established coaching inn on graceful main street, with views from rooms at back to the River Tweed. **££**

## St Boswells

**Dryburgh Abbey Hotel**
Tel: (01835) 822261
Fax: (01835) 823945
www.dryburgh.co.uk
38 rooms. This hotel is

beautifully situated next to Dryburgh Abbey and the River Tweed. **£££–££££**

## Selkirk

**Glen Hotel**
Yarrow Terrace
Tel/Fax: (01750) 20259
www.glenhotel.co.uk
8 rooms. Small, friendly hotel close to Ettrick Water, good food. Traditional hearty Borders breakfasts. Fishing and horse riding can be arranged. **££**
**Philipburn Country House Hotel**
Linglie Road
Tel: (01750) 20747
Fax: (01750) 724188
www.philipburnhousehotel.co.uk
14 beautifully decorated rooms, some with balconies overlooking the gardens. Jacuzzi and steam showers. **£££**

# THE SOUTHWEST

## Arran

**Auchrannie Country House Hotel and Spa**
Brodick
Tel: (01770) 302234
Fax: (01770) 302812
www.auchrannie.co.uk
28 rooms. Mansion in 10 acres (4 hectares) of grounds near bay and castle. 36-bedroom leisure, health and spa resort nearby. **££–£££**
**Kilmichael House Hotel**
Glen Cloy, by Brodick
Tel: (01770) 302219
Fax: (01770) 302068
www.kilmichael.com
This is the place to stay on Arran. Set in acres of mature garden, this luxurious country house with award-winning restaurant offers four individually style bedrooms, three suites and a "wee dram" on your arrival. **£££–££££**

## Ayr

**Ramada Jarvis Caledonian Hotel**
Dalblair Road
Tel: (01292) 269331

Fax: (01292) 610722
www.ramadajarvis.co.uk
118 rooms. Town-centre hotel close to all facilities and beach: many rooms with fine views. Leisure club. **££**

## Dumfries

**Cairndale Hotel and Leisure Club**
English Street
Tel: (01387) 254111
Fax: (01387) 240288
www.cairndalehotel.co.uk
91 rooms. Regular live entertainment (*ceilidhs* in summer), full leisure club; activities include golf, walking and fishing. **££–£££**

## Gatehouse of Fleet

**Cally Palace**
Tel: (01557) 814341
Fax: (01557) 814522
www.callypalace.co.uk
56 rooms. Magnificent public rooms and comfortable bedrooms in this Georgian mansion set in extensive forest and parkland. Exclusive use of 18-hole golf course. **£££**

**Murray Arms Inn**
Ann Street
Tel: (01557) 814207
Fax: (01557) 814370
www.murrayarmshotel.co.uk
13 rooms. Attractive 18th-century posting inn where Robert Burns wrote *Scots Wha Hae*. **££**

## Girvan

**Westin Turnberry Resort**
Turnberry
Tel: (01655) 331000
Fax: (01655) 331706
www.westin.com/turnberry
221 rooms. Luxury country club and spa. Elegance and gracious service, especially in the restaurants, which provide superb views and food. Activities include horse-riding, squash, tennis and golf, including Colin Montgomerie Links Golf Academy. **£££–££££**

## Moffat

**Auchen Castle Hotel**
Beattock
Tel: (01683) 300407
Fax: (01683) 300727
www.auchencastle.com
25 rooms of which 15 in

castle and 10 in modern wing. Set in 28 acres (12 hectares) of grounds with spectacular views. **££££**
**Buchan Guest House**
Beechgrove
Tel: (01683) 220378
www.buchanguesthouse.co.uk
Pretty guest house a short walk north of the city centre. **£–££**
**Moffat House Hotel**
High Street
Tel: (01683) 220039
Fax: (01683) 221288
www.moffathouse.co.uk
20 rooms. An 18th-century Adam mansion set in own grounds. **££–£££**

## Newton Stewart

**Kirroughtree House Hotel**
Tel: (01671) 402141
Fax: (01671) 402425
www.kirroughtreehouse.co.uk

### PRICE CATEGORIES

Approximate prices per person per night in a double room in high season:
**£** = less than £30
**££** = £30–50
**£££** = £50–80
**££££** = more than £80

TRANSPORT

ACCOMMODATION

EATING OUT

ACTIVITIES

A–Z

**ABOVE:** the Corsewall Lighthouse Hotel in Stranraer.

17 rooms. Cheerful and colourful Georgian mansion in large established landscaped gardens (with croquet and pitch and putt in the grounds). Strong Burns associations. Renowned for traditional Scottish food. **£££–££££**

### Stranraer

**Corsewall Lighthouse Hotel**
Kircolm
Tel: (01776) 853220
Fax: (01776) 854231
www.lighthousehotel.co.uk
9 rooms and 3 suites.

This warm and friendly hotel is set in the old lighthouse keeper's quarters. Located on a wild and windy headland miles from anywhere, this is a beautiful spot right off the beaten track. Excellent five-course dinners. Advance booking recommended. **££££** (includes dinner)

**North West Castle Hotel**
Tel: (01776) 704413
Fax: (01776) 702646
www.northwestcastle.co.uk
71 rooms. Comfortable hotel on seafront. Facilities include curling rink, gym, and indoor pool. **£££**

### Troon

**Marine Hotel**
Crosbie Road
Tel: (01292) 314444
Fax: (01292) 316922
www.paramount-hotels.co.uk
89 rooms. Traditional hotel with some rooms overlooking the famous golf course. Health and fitness club. **£££–££££**

**Piersland House Hotel**
Craigend Road
Tel: (01292) 314747
Fax: (01292) 315613
www.piersland.co.uk
30 rooms. Built for Sir Alexander Walker of whisky fame. Renovated in traditional style. Good restaurant. **££–£££**

# FORTH AND CLYDE

### Airth

**Airth Castle Hotel**
Tel: (01324) 831411
Fax: (01324) 831419
www.airthcastlehotel.com
23 rooms in castle, plus 99 in adjoining country club. Historic castle, now converted into a fine hotel set admist 17 acres (7 hectares) of grounds. **£££–££££**

### Falkirk

**Best Western Park Hotel**
Camelon Road
Tel: (01324) 628331
Fax: (01324) 611593
www.bestwestern.com
55 rooms. Modern hotel close to Dollar Park and

Mariner Leisure Centre. **£**
**Macdonald Inchyra Hotel**
Grange Road, Polmont
Tel: (0870) 1942115
Fax: (01324) 71716134
Central reservations:
Tel: (0870) 400 9191 (UK)
www.macdonald-hotels.co.uk
98 rooms. Fine country house hotel with beauty-and-fitness centre, tennis courts. **£££**

### Fintry

**Culcreuch Castle Hotel**
Fintry, nr Stirling G63 0LW
Tel: (01360) 860228
Fax: (01360) 860555
www.culcreuch.com
14 rooms. This 14th-century castle with pleasant modern rooms claims to be the oldest inhabited castle in Scotland. It stands in 1,600 acres (670 hectares) of glorious parkland and features an ornamental loch. Free fishing is available to guests. Such a wonderful setting makes it a very

popular location for wedding parties. **££–£££**.

### Stirling

**Garfield Guest House**
12 Victoria Square
Tel: (01786) 473730
6 rooms. Large Victorian house in quiet square, close to town centre. B&B only. **£**

**Number 10**
10 Gladstone Place
Tel: (01786) 472681
www.cameron-10.co.uk.
Very central 3-bedroom guest house in friendly house built in Victorian era. Within walking distance of castle and the Old Town. Quiet residential area. **££**

**Park Lodge Country House Hotel**
32 Park Terrace
Tel: (01786) 474862
Fax: (01786) 449748
www.parklodge.net
9 rooms. Part-Victorian, part-Georgian hotel in heart of town, filled with antiques. Some rooms with four-poster beds. **££**

**Stirling Highland Hotel**
Spittal Street
Tel: (01786) 272727
Fax: (01786) 272829
www.paramount-hotels.co.uk
96 rooms. Restored, listed former school in centre of town with observatory on roof. Good food in Scholar's Restaurant. Health and leisure club. **££**

**Stirling Management Centre**
Stirling University campus
Tel: (01786) 451712
Fax: (01786) 450472
www.smc.stir.ac.uk
75 rooms (all en suite). Purpose-built conference centre/hotel on bucolic university campus 3 miles (5 km) from Stirling. Use of university's pool and gym. **£££**

**Terraces Hotel**
4 Melville Terrace
Tel: (01786) 472268
Fax: (01786) 45031
www.terraceshotel.co.uk
Georgian house, extensively revamped and close to the town centre. Good food. **££**

# THE WEST COAST

### Arisaig

**Garramore House**
South Morar
Tel: (01687) 450268
E-mail: garramorehouse@aol.com
Old hunting lodge converted into a comfortable guest house. Children and pets are welcome. Set in beautiful woodland gardens with great views of islands. Sandy beaches nearby. **£**

### Arrochar

**Lochside Guest House**
Main Street
Tel: (01301) 702467
This 6-bedroom guest house on the shores of Loch Long is handy for the popular ascent of "The Cobbler" behind the village. Great base for birdwatching, fishing and mountains. Newly built conservatory. **£–££**

### Crinan

**Crinan Hotel**
Tel: (01546) 830261
Fax: (01546) 830292
www.crinanhotel.com
22 rooms. Some rooms have private balconies; all have stunning sea views of the Sound of Jura. Dine in Lock 16, the rooftop seafood restaurant and eat the "catch of the day". From here, admire the seascapes and the activity on the canal below. **££££**

### Eriska

**Isle of Eriska**
Ledaig by Oban
Tel: (01631) 720371
Fax: (01631) 720531
www.eriska-hotel.co.uk
19 rooms. Welcoming hotel on private island joined to the mainland by a short bridge. Bedrooms vary in size and each has its own character. Terrific spa. Lovely grounds with tennis, croquet and 6-hole golf course, driving range, golf academy. **££££**

### Fort William

**Crolinnhe**
Grange Road
Tel: (01397) 702709
www.crolinnhe.co.uk
Excellent guesthouse behind town centre, very friendly, good food and jacuzzi. **££**

**Inverlochy Castle Hotel**
Torlundy
Tel: (01397) 702177
Fax: (01397) 702953
www.inverlochycastle.com
17 rooms. One of Europe's best stone-walled (castle) hotels. Imposing public rooms. Set in glorious grounds with views of Ben Nevis. Wonderful cuisine and wine list. Snooker, tennis and game fishing. **££££**

**Moorings Hotel**
Banavie
Tel: (01397) 772797

Fax: (01397) 772441
www.moorings-fortwilliam.co.uk
28 rooms. 3 miles (5 km) from town at Neptune's Staircase at the start of the Caledonian Canal with superb views of Ben Nevis. **££–£££**

### Gigha

**Gigha Hotel**
Isle of Gigha
Tel: (01583) 505254
www.gigha.org.uk
11 en suite rooms. Pleasant, cosy hotel on this community-owned island and 10 minutes' walk from pierhead. Good food, especially fresh fish. **££**

### Glenelg

**Glenelg Inn**
Tel: (01599) 522273
Fax: (01599) 522283
www.glenelg-inn.com
7 rooms. Lively pub with restaurant is the focal point of this waterfront inn. Bedrooms, which are individually and tastefully decorated, have grand views of Skye. **££–£££**

### Glenshiel

**Cluanie Inn**
Tel: (01320) 340238
Fax: (01320) 340293
www.cluanieinn.com
10 rooms. Traditional Scottish inn, fully modernised, far away from it all between Loch Ness

and Skye. Inviting roaring fires in public rooms. **££–£££**

### Inveraray

**George Hotel**
Main Street East
Tel: (01499) 302111
Fax: (01499) 302098
www.thegeorgehotel.co.uk
Atmospheric, friendly hotel serving delicious traditional food in centre of town. Real ales on tap while resident ghost and a double jacuzzi to be found among 27 rooms. **£££**

### Kyle of Lochalsh

**Lochalsh Hotel**
Ferry Road
Tel: (01599) 534202
Fax: (01599) 534881
www.lochalshhotel.com
38 rooms. Magnificently situated, comfortable hotel on the water's edge with superb views of Skye and the Cuillins. **££**

### Loch Awe

**Ardanaiseig Hotel**
Kilchrenan, by Taynuilt
Tel: (01866) 833333
Fax: (01866) 833222
www.ardanaiseig.com
16 rooms plus 2-bedroom cottage. Elegant country house hotel far away from it all. Beautiful furnished rooms. Woodland garden. Hotel boats for fishing; tennis, snooker. **£££–££££**

**BELOW:** Inverlochy Castle in Fort William.

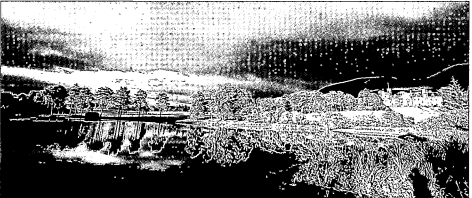

**Taychreggan Hotel**
By Taynuilt
Tel: (01866) 833211
Fax: (01866) 833244
www.taychregganhotel.co.uk
20 rooms. Old hotel around a cobbled courtyard on a secluded part of Loch Awe. Game and coarse fishing, boating, snooker.
**£££–££££**

### Loch Lomond

**Ardlui Hotel**
Ardlui
Tel: (01301) 704243
Fax: (01301) 704268
www.ardlui.co.uk
10 rooms. Friendly country house hotel on loch shore, good atmosphere, fine food, excellent walking. **££**
**De Vere Cameron House Hotel**
Tel/fax: (01389) 755565
www.devere.co.uk.
96 rooms. A handsome mansion house standing in 100 acres (40 hectares) by the side of Loch Lomond. Excellent leisure facilities include a 9-hole golf course and a bustling marina for sailing and windsurfing.
**££££**
**The Lodge on Loch Lomond**
Luss
Tel: (01436) 860201
Fax: (01436) 860203
www.loch-lomond.co.uk.
29 rooms. Luxurious modern lochside hotel with magnificent views. Each bedroom has sauna en suite. **£££–££££**

### Loch Melfort

**Loch Melfort Hotel**
Arduaine
Tel: (01852) 200233
Fax: (01852) 200214
www.lochmelfort.co.uk
23 rooms. A relaxed atmosphere prevails in this splendid hotel, which looks out on magnificent scenery, about 20 miles (32 km) south of Oban. Sample the fricassée of local shellfish with herb pasta ribbons and homemade puddings from the restaurant. **££££**

### Oban

**Columba Hotel**
Esplanade
Tel: (01631) 562183
Fax: (01631) 564683
www.obanhotels.com
50 rooms. Well-established hotel on waterfront. **££**
**Knipoch Hotel**
6 miles (10 km) south of Oban on the A816
Tel: (01852) 316251
Fax: (01852) 316249
www.knipochhotel.co.uk
22 rooms. Peaceful, elegant family-run hotel with well-appointed bedrooms. **££££**
**Manor House Hotel**
Gallanach Road
Tel: (01631) 562087
Fax: (01631) 563053
www.manorhouseoban.com
11 rooms. Built in 1780 and situated in own grounds on commanding promontory with fine view of Oban Bay. Good restaurant. **£££** (includes dinner)

### Talladale

**The Old Mill**
Talladale
Tel: (01445) 760271
www.theoldmillhighlandlodge.co.uk
6 en suite rooms form part of a lodge built on a former horse mill. Spectacular views towards Torridon.
**£££**

### Tarbert (Loch Fyne)

**Stonefield Castle Hotel**
Tel: (01880) 820836
Fax: (01880) 820929
www.stonefieldcastle.co.uk.
33 rooms. Baronial mansion set in 60 acres (24 hectares) of glorious gardens and woodlands.
**££££** (includes dinner)

# SKYE

**ABOVE:** a thatched stone cottage on the Isle of Skye.

### Portree

**Cuillin Hills Hotel**
Tel: (01478) 612003
Fax: (01478) 613092
www.cuillinhills-hotel-skye.co.uk
28 rooms. A 19th-century former hunting lodge in large grounds just outside Portree, with views over Portree Bay to the Cuillins.
**££££**
**Rosedale Hotel**
Beaumont Crescent
Tel: (01478) 613131
Fax: (01478) 612531
www.rosedaleshotelskye.co.uk
19 rooms. Comfortable waterfront hotel converted from former fishermen's houses. Some bedrooms are very small. **££**
**Skeabost House Hotel**
Skeabost Bridge
Tel: (01470) 532202
Fax: (01470) 532454
www.skeabostcountryhouse.co.uk
19 rooms. Former hunting lodge in 12 acres (5 hectares) of secluded woodlands and garden on the shore of Loch Snizort. Famous Sunday buffet lunch is served in sunny conservatory. Salmon fishing, 9-hole golf course.
**££–£££**
**Viewfield House**
Tel: (01478) 612217
Fax: (01478) 613517
www.viewfieldhouse.com
12 rooms. Idiosyncratic country house hotel in extensive wooded grounds overlooking the bay. Open mid April–mid-October. Each room different: all large. Something of a time warp, although the bathrooms are modern. An experience. **£££** (includes dinner)

### Staffin

**Flodigarry Country House Hotel**
Tel: (01470) 552203
Fax: (01470) 552301
www.flodigarry.co.uk
19 rooms. Historic mansion beneath the Quiraing Mountains offering glorious views. Ceilidhs held on Saturday night. Separate house where Flora MacDonald once lived has been tastefully converted into rooms. **£££**

## Sleat

**Ardvasar Hotel**
Tel: (01471) 844223
Fax: (01471) 844495
www.ardvasarhotel.com
10 rooms. Traditional white-washed hotel overlooks Sound of Sleat and Mallaig. 1 mile (1.5 km) from Mallaig–Armdale ferry. **£££**
**Eilean Iarmain (Isle of Ornsay) Hotel**
Tel: (01471) 833332
Fax: (01471) 833275
www.eilean-iarmain.co.uk
12 rooms plus 4 suites in converted stables. Friendly 19th-century inn by the sea featuring Gaelic

hospitality. Spectacular views. Renowned for its seafood. **£££**

## Dunvegan

**Atholl House Hotel**
Tel: (01470) 521219
Fax: (01470) 521481
www.athollhotel.co.uk
9 rooms. Former manse on outskirts of the village with superb views of Loch Dunvegan. **££**
**Roskhill House**
Tel: (01470) 521317
www.www.roskhillhouse.co.uk
Built in 1890, the lounge was once the village post office. All five bedrooms

have en suite bath/shower. Evening meals by prior arrangement. Pets welcome. **££**

## Sligachan

**Sligachan Hotel**
Tel: (01478) 650204
Fax: (01478) 650207
www.sligachan.co.uk
22 rooms. Famous climbers' hotel, fully modernised, with magnificent views of the Cuillins and Loch Sligachin. Full of atmosphere. Range of real ales from Cuillen Brewery, and malts. Golf and fishing nearby. **££**

## Broadford

**Tir Alainn**
by Broadford
Tel: (01471) 822366
www.visitskye.com
Terrific views and a warm welcome are provided by the hosts of the cosy three room B&B. **£–££**

# THE INNER HEBRIDES

## Iona

**Argyll Hotel**
Tel: (01681) 700334
Fax: (01681) 700510
www.argyllhoteliona.co.uk
The oldest inn on the island has 16 en suite rooms. Restaurant serves traditional food using the finest local produce. Open Feb–Oct. **££**
**St Columba Hotel**
Tel: (01681) 700304
Fax: (01681) 700688
www.stcolumba-hotel.co.uk
27 rooms. Situated close to the famous abbey, this tranquil hotel enjoys fine views across the water to Mull. **££**

## Mull

**Druimard Country House Hotel**
Dervaig
Tel/Fax: (01688) 400345
www.druimard.co.uk
7 rooms. Beautifully restored Victorian country house widely known for its interesting cuisine. Pleasant conservatory and informal atmosphere. **£££** (includes dinner)
**Western Isles Hotel**
Tobermory
Tel: (01688) 302012
Fax: (01688) 302297
www.mullhotel.com
28 rooms. Gothic-style building magnificently

situated above Tobermory Bay. **£££–££££**

## Raasay

**Isle of Raasay Hotel**
Tel/Fax: (01478) 660222
www.isleofraasayhotel.co.uk
12 rooms. Take the ferry from Sconser on Skye to the smaller island of Raasay for escapism in beautiful natural surroundings. Superb walking and birdlife. **£**

## Tiree

**Glebe House**
By Scarinish
Tel: (01879) 220758

www.glebehousetiree.co.uk
4 rooms. This former manse is tastefully furnished throughout. Through your window enjoy views of sandy, pristine beaches and Gott Bay. Lovely dinners. **£££**
**Scarinish Hotel**
Scarinish
Tel: (01879) 220308
Fax: (01879) 220410
www.tireescarinishhotel.com
Refurbished hotel. 6 en suite rooms. Dinner served in the Old Harbour Restaurant. The Lean To Bar, serving beer and whisky, is a friendly meeting place. Dogs welcome. **££**

# THE OUTER HEBRIDES

## Barra

**Castlebay Hotel**
Castlebay
Tel: (01871) 810223
Fax: (01871) 810455
www.castlebay-hotel.co.uk
12 rooms. Overlooks the bay with its castle. Easy access to ferry. **££**
**Dunard Hostel**
Castlebay
Tel: (01871) 810443
www.dunardhostel.co.uk
Small friendly family-run hostel, a few minutes from the ferry terminal, bank and shops. **£–££**

## Harris

**Scarista House,**
Scarista
Tel: (01859) 550238
Fax: (01859) 550277
www.scaristahouse.com
5 rooms. Former manse run by very friendly couple. Superb views of sea, and bedrooms are comfortable; excellent restaurant using local produce. **£££**

## Lewis

**The Cabarfeidh**
Manor Park, Stornoway

Tel: (01851) 702604
Fax: (01851) 705572
www.cabarfeidh-hotel.co.uk
Comfortable, recently refurbished hotel conveniently located close to ferry terminal and town centre. **£££**

## North Uist

**Lochmaddy Hotel**
Lochmaddy
Tel: (01876) 500331
Fax: (01876) 500210
www.lochmaddyhotel.co.uk
Traditional white-washed Highland building.

15 rooms with en suite facilities. Conveniently placed close to the ferry terminal, and with lovely sea views. Good restaurant serving game and local seafood and a good selection of malts. **££**
**Tigh Dearg Hotel**
Lochmaddy
Tel: (01876) 500700
www.tighdearghotel.co.uk
Stylish hotel with 8 designer rooms. Guests have use of gym, sauna and steam room. Superb restaurant, views of the harbour. **££££**

# CENTRAL SCOTLAND AND FIFE

## Anstruther

**The Spindrift**
Pittenweem Road
Tel/Fax: (01333) 310573
www.thespindrift.co.uk
8 rooms (7 en suite). Non-smoking B&B in Victorian house 10 minutes by car from St Andrews. **£**

## Auchterarder

**Gleneagles Hotel**
Tel: (0800) 389 3737 (UK)
Tel: (1-866) 881 9525 (US)
Fax: (01764) 662134
www.gleneagles.com
275 rooms. Unbridled luxury is the name of the game at the "Palace in the Glen". Public rooms are very grand; bedrooms are tastefully furnished and comfortable. Health spa and leisure centre with three swimming pools. Activities include tennis, croquet, squash, clay pigeon shooting, fishing, horse riding, falconry, off-road driving and, of course, golf. **££££**

## Auchtermuchty

**Ardchoille Farm Guest House**
Dunshalt
Tel/Fax: (01337) 828414
3 rooms. Elegant, modern farmhouse with superb views of Lomond Hills. Attractive dining room with fine china and crystal; excellent food. **£–££**

## Blair Atholl

**Dalgreine**
Bridge of Tilt
Tel/fax: (01796) 481276
www.dalgreine-guest-house.co.uk
6 rooms (2 en suite). Charming large house close to Blair Castle, superb walking, secluded garden. **£**

## PRICE CATEGORIES

Approximate prices per person per night in a double room in high season:
**£** = less than £30
**££** = £30–50
**£££** = £50–80
**££££** = more than £80

## Blairgowrie

**Altamount House Hotel**
Coupar Angus Road
Tel: (01250) 873512
Fax: (01250) 876200
www.altamounthouse.co.uk
7 rooms. Lovely country house, close to town centre, set in 7 acres (3 hectares) of gardens and wooded grounds. Excellent food. **££**

## Callander

**Arden House**
Bracklinn Road
Tel/fax: (01877) 330235
www.ardenhouse.org.uk
6 rooms. This non-smoking house with superb views of the Trossachs was the setting for the vintage BBC TV series Dr Finlay's Casebook. **£–££**
**Bridgend House Hotel**
Bridgend
Tel: (01877) 330130
Fax: (01877) 331512
www.bridgendhotel.co.uk
5 en suite rooms. 17th-century family-run hotel with magnificent views of Ben Ledi. **£**
**Callander Meadows**
Main Street
Tel: (01877) 330181
www.callandermeadows.co.uk
Seek out this 3-bedroomed den of tranquillity and you'll be rewarded with delicious fare in the restaurant and a great nights sleep. **£**
**Roman Camp Country House Hotel**
Callander
Tel: (01877) 330003
Fax: (01877) 331533
www.roman-camp-hotel.co.uk
14 rooms. Very plush hotel in converted 17th-century hunting lodge set in beautiful gardens that sweep down to the River Teith, in which fishing is available. Renowned for its cuisine. **£££**

## Carnoustie

**Station Hotel**
Station Road
Tel: (01241) 852447
Fax: (01241) 855605
www.stationhotel.co.uk
12 rooms. A family-run

hotel from which it is but a giant step to the championship golf course and a small step to the station platforms. **£–££**

## Crieff

**Crieff Hydro Hotel**
Tel: (01764) 655555
Fax: (01764) 653087
www.crieffhydro.com
213 rooms. Magnificent Victorian building, in 900 acres (360 hectares) of grounds. Superb accommodation, food and leisure facilities. **££££**

## Dunblane

**Cromlix House**
Kinbuck
Tel: (01786) 822125.
Fax: (01786) 825450
www.cromlixhouse.com
14 rooms. One of Scotland's great country house hotels. All rooms are large and splendid, and antiques abound. Magnificent conservatory. Noted for its superb food and extensive wine list. Trout and salmon fishing, clay pigeon shooting, tennis and croquet all available. **££££**
**Dunblane Hydro Hotel**
Perth Road
Tel: (01786) 822551
Fax: (01786) 825403
www.dunblanehydrohotel.com
206 rooms. Hotel with Victorian façade in 44 acres (18 hectares) of grounds. Excellent sports and leisure facilities. **££–£££**

## Dunkeld

**Kinnaird Estate**
Dalguise
Tel: (01796) 482440.
Fax: (01796) 482289.
www.kinneardestate.com
9 rooms. Be pampered in elegant surroundings in this country house hotel 4 miles (6 km) northwest of Dunkeld. Renowned for its cuisine and service. **££££**
**Hilton Dunkeld House**
Tel: (01350) 727771
Fax: (01350) 728924
www.dunkeld.hilton.com
97 rooms. Splendid hotel,

former home of the Duke of Atholl, on the banks of the River Tay in 280 acres (112 hectares) of woodland. Extensive leisure facilities, including clay pigeon shooting and tennis. **££££**

## Falkland

**Covenanter Hotel**
Tel: (01337) 857224
Fax: (01337) 857163
www.convenanterhotel.co.uk
9 rooms plus 2 suites. 17th-century coaching inn in conservation village, close to magnificent Falkland Palace. **£–££**

## Glenisla

**Glenisla Hotel**
Kirkton of Glenisla
Tel: (01575) 582223
Fax: (01575) 582203
www.glenisla-hotel.com
6 rooms. Friendly, comfortable hotel in magnificent setting. **££**

## Glenshee

**Spittal of Glenshee Hotel**
Tel: (01250) 885215
Fax: (01250) 885223
www.spittalofglenshee.co.uk
48 rooms. Slightly eccentric but very friendly and lively hotel in wonderful setting. Regular live entertainment. **££**

## Killin

**Ardeonaig House Hotel**
By Killin
Tel: (01567) 820400
Fax: (01567) 820282
www.ardeonaighotel.co.uk
An award-winning, small country house exuding warmth and a personal touch with a South African wine list. 10 acres of own grounds by south shore of the Tay. **£££–££££**

## Kinloch Rannoch

**Macdonald Loch Rannoch Hotel**
Tel: (01882) 632201/(0870) 194 2112
Fax: (01882) 632203
www.loch-rannoch.com
47 rooms. Converted

shooting lodge in magnificent surroundings; excellent food, lively entertainment, wide range of leisure activities. **£££**

## Perth

**Ballathie House Hotel**
Kinclaven by Stanley
Tel: (01250) 883268
Fax: (01250) 883396
www.ballathiehousehotel.com
43 rooms. Relaxing and civilised former shooting lodge on River Tay. Graciously proportioned public rooms. Comfortable bedrooms. **£££**

**Best Western Queens Hotel**
Leonard Street
Tel: (01738) 442222
Fax: (01738) 638496
www.bestwestern.co.uk
50 rooms. Comfortable hotel with good leisure complex. Situated close to the city centre. **£££**

**Huntingtower Hotel**
Crieff Road
Tel: (01738) 583771
Fax: (01738) 583777
www.huntingtowerhotel.co.uk
34 rooms. Country house hotel 3 miles (5 km) west of Perth, standing in its own beautiful grounds. **££–£££**

**Iona Guest House**
2 Pitcullen Crescent
Tel/Fax: (01738) 627261
www.ionaperth.co.uk
5 rooms. Comfortable semi-detached house with private parking. **£**

**Kinnaird Guest House,**
5 Marshall Place.
Tel: (01738) 628021.
Fax: (01738) 444056.
www.kinneard-guesthouse.co.uk
7 rooms. Comfortable, friendly guest house, part of a Georgian terrace overlooking South Inch Park. Private parking. **£–££**

**Murrayshall House Hotel**
Scone
Tel: (01738) 551171
Fax: (01738) 552595
www.murrayshall.com
41 rooms. Sumptuously appointed, elegant country house in 300 acres (120 hectares) of parkland, 4 miles (7 km) north of Perth. Superb food and wine served in luxurious dining room. Has two

challenging 18-hole golf courses. **£££–££££**

**Parklands**
St Leonards Bank
Tel: (01738) 622451
Fax: (01738) 622046
www.theparklandshotel.com
14 rooms. Classical Georgian town house, refurbished, overlooking the South Inch Park. **££–£££**

**Ramada Jarvis Perth**
West Mill Street
Tel: (01738) 628281
Fax: (01738) 643423
www.ramadajarvis.co.uk
76 rooms. This is a comfortable hotel converted from a 15th-century watermill, situated in the city centre. **££–£££**

**Salutation Hotel**
34 South Street
Tel: (01738) 630066
Fax: (01738) 633598
www.strathmorehotels.com
84 rooms. One of Scotland's oldest hotels, where Bonnie Prince Charlie is said to have stayed. **££–£££**

## Pitlochry

**Atholl Palace Hotel**
Atholl Road
Tel: (01796) 472400
Fax: (01796) 473036
www.athollpalace.co.uk
90 rooms, including turret suites. This majestic building is set in 50 acres (20 hectares) of grounds. Has health and sports facilities. **£££**

**Dunfallandy House Hotel**
Logierait Road
Tel: (01796) 472648
Fax: (01796) 472017
www.dunfallandy-house.com
8 rooms. Georgian mansion set above the town, with glorious views of Tummel Valley. **££**

**Killiecrankie Hotel**
Tel: (01796) 473220
Fax: (01796) 472451
www.killiecranklehotel.co.uk
10 rooms. Good country house hotel in beautiful setting overlooking the Pass of Killiecrankie, 3 miles (5 km) north of Pitlochry. **£££**

**Knockendarroch House Hotel**
Higher Oakfield
Tel: (01796) 473473
Fax: (01796) 474068

**ABOVE:** Atholl Palace Hotel, Pitlochry.

www.knockendarroch.co.uk
12 rooms. Victorian mansion overlooking the town and Tummel Valley. Two rooms have four-poster beds. **££**

## St Andrews

**Cleveden House**
3 Murray Place
Tel/Fax: (01334) 474212
www.clevedenhouse.co.uk
7 rooms (5 en suite). Five minutes' walk from Old Course, beach and town centre. **££**

**The Inn on North Street**
127 North Street
Tel: (01334) 473387
Fax: (01334) 474664
www.theinnonnorthstreet.com
13 rooms. Late Victorian building close to the Old Course and beaches. **£££**

**Rusacks Hotel**
Pilmour Links
Tel: (0870) 400 8128
Fax: (01334) 477896
www.macdonaldhotels.com
68 rooms. Grand, refurbished Victorian hotel remodelled on golfing

theme and overlooking the legendary 18th hole of the Old Course. **££££**

**St Andrews Old Course Hotel**
Tel: (01334) 474371
Fax: (01334) 477668
www.oldcoursehotel.co.uk
134 rooms. Large luxury hotel overlooking the famous 17th "Road" Hole of Old Course. Well-equipped health club. **££££**

**West Park House**
5 St Mary's Place
Tel: (01334) 475933
Fax: (01334) 476634
www.westpark-standrews.co.uk
3 en suite rooms. Listed Georgian house close to all activities. **£**

## St Fillans

**Achray House Hotel**
Tel: (01764) 685231
Fax: (01764) 685230
www.achray-house.co.uk
9 rooms. Welcoming small hotel with superb views across Loch Earn (fishing possible). Mountain bikes for guests' use. **££**

TRANSPORT
ACCOMMODATION
EATING OUT
ACTIVITIES
A – Z

# THE EAST COAST

## Aberdeen

**Aberdeen Marriott**
Overton Circle, Dyce
Tel: (01224) 770011
Fax: (01224) 722347
www.marriotthotels.com
155 rooms. Luxurious hotel with full leisure facilities, close to airport. **£££**

**Atholl Hotel**
54 Kings Gate
Tel: (01224) 323505
Fax: (01224) 321555
www.atholl-aberdeen.co.uk
34 rooms. Elegant granite Victorian hotel in the West End. **£££**

**Brentwood Hotel**
101 Crown Street
Tel: (01224) 595440
www.brentwood-hotel.co.uk
63 rooms. Situated in a pretty granite town house this is one of the most comfortable small hotels in the area. Offers good rates at the weekend. **££**

**Caledonian Thistle Hotel**
10–14 Union Terrace
Tel: (0870) 333 9151
Fax: (0870) 333 9251
www.thistlehotels.com
77 rooms. Business-oriented hotel in city centre, close to railway station, just off Union Street. **££££**

**Marcliffe at Pitfodels**
North Deeside Road, Cults
Tel: (01224) 861000
Fax: (01224) 868860
www.marcliffe.com
42 rooms. Sprawling country house hotel set in large grounds in western suburbs. Very well appointed, excellent food. **££££**

**Strathisla Guest House**
408 Great Western Road
Tel: (01224) 321026
www.strathisla-guesthouse.co.uk
Set in a spacious terraced house with five cosy en suite rooms, this is a home-from-home experience. **£**

## Alford

**Kildrummy Castle Hotel**
Kildrummy
Tel: (01975) 571288
Fax: (01975) 571345
www.kildrummycastlehotel.co.uk
16 rooms. Baronial mansion with lots of wood panelling, tapestries and grand staircase overlooking ruined 13th-century castle. Glorious gardens. Excellent food accompanied by splendid wine list. **£££**

## Ballater

**Glen Lui Hotel**
Invercauld Road
Tel: (013397) 55402
Fax: (013397) 55545
www.glen-lui-hotel.co.uk
19 rooms. This is a friendly country house hotel with superb views towards Lochnagar. Fishing, golf, and skiing available nearby. Good wine list. **£**

**Hilton Craigendarroch**
Braemar Road
Tel: (013397) 55858.
Fax: (013397) 55447.
www.craigendarroch.hilton.com
45 rooms. Excellent modern hotel with full leisure facilities, golf, fishing and shooting. **£££**

**Netherley Guest House**
2 Netherley Place.
Tel/Fax: (013397) 55792
9 rooms (4 en suite). Family-run guest house in centre of village, high standards of service. **£**

## Banchory

**Banchory Lodge**
Dee Street
Tel: (01330) 822625
Fax: (01330) 825019
www.banchorylodge.co.uk
22 rooms. Large, well-furnished rooms, log fires and Victorian furnishings. On the banks of River Dee with private fishing; bicycles available for guests; 2 golf courses nearby. **££££**

## Carrbridge

**Dalrachney Lodge Hotel**
7 miles (11 km) north of Aviemore
Tel: (01479) 841252
www.dalrachney.co.uk
This beautiful Victorian hunting lodge will delight with delicious dinners, roaring fires, and views to die for. **£££**

## Braemar

**Invercauld Arms Hotel**
Tel: (013397) 41605
Fax: (013397) 41428
www.shearingsholidays.com
68 rooms. Historic building now offering high standards of accommodation and food. Minimum stay two nights. **££**

**Moorfield House**
Tel: (013397) 41244
6 rooms (2 en suite). Very welcoming and friendly family-run hotel at edge of famous Braemar Highland Games Park. **£**

## Dundee

**Discovery Quay Travel Inn**
Riverside Drive
Tel: (0870) 197 7079
Fax: (01382) 203237
www.travelinn.co.uk
40 rooms. Informal family-friendly hotel overlooking River Tay; indoor play area; close to Discovery Centre. **££**

**Hilton Dundee**
Earl Grey Place
Tel: (01382) 229271
Fax: (01382) 200072
www.hilton.com/dundee
129 rooms. Modern hotel with good leisure facilities. Situated on the banks of the River Tay with views across to Fife. **£££**

**Shaftesbury Hotel**
1 Hyndford Street
Tel: (01382) 669216
Fax: (01382) 641598
www.shaftesbury-hotel.co.uk
12 rooms. Refurbished Victorian mansion in peaceful residential area yet close to city and university. **£–££**

**Swallow Hotel**
Kingsway West
Tel: (01382) 641122
www.swallowhotels.com
103 rooms. Victorian mansion in large grounds. Swimming pool and a conservatory restaurant. Good for families. **££–£££**

## Elgin

**Mansion House Hotel**
The Haugh
Tel: (01343) 548811
Fax: (01343) 547916
www.mansionhousehotel.co.uk
23 rooms. Tastefully restored baronial mansion with castellated tower in woodland setting

**BELOW:** the old harbour at Portsoy.

overlooking River Lossie. Many rooms have four-poster beds. Leisure centre with indoor swimming pool and beauty salon. **£££**

## Grantown-on-Spey

**Culdearn House**
Woodlands Terrace
Tel: (01479) 872106
Fax: (01479) 873641
www.culdearn.com
9 rooms. Elegant Victorian house. Great selection of malt whiskies and good wine list. **££££** (includes dinner)
**Tigh na Sgiath Country House Hotel**
Dulnain Bridge
Tel: (01479) 851345
Fax: (01479) 821173
www.tigh-na-sgiath.co.uk
8 rooms. Lovely old refurbished house in secluded grounds. Good food and wine. **££**

## Inverurie

**Macdonald Pittodrie House**
By Inverurie
Tel: (0870) 194 2111

Fax: (01467) 681648
www.macdonaldhotels.co.uk
27 rooms. 17th-century family house exudes character and luxury. Seek out the billiard room and snug bar. **£££–££££**

## Macduff

**The Highland Haven**
Shore Street
Tel: (01261) 832408
Fax: (01261) 833652
E-mail: bill.alcock@btopenworld.com
40 rooms. Harbour-side hotel with great views. Spa bath, sauna, Turkish steam room. Golf and fishing available. **£**

## Montrose

**Woodston Fishing Station**
St Cyrus
Tel: (01674) 850226
Fax: (01674) 850343
www.woodstonfishingstation.co.uk
A family run B&B (and self-catering guest house) nestled above coastline on the St Cyrus Nature Reserve. Perfect for walking and fishing. **££–£££**

## Nairn

**Golf View Hotel**
Seabank Road
Tel: (01667) 452301
Fax: (01667) 455267
www.swallow-hotels.com
42 rooms. Victorian hotel overlooking the sea and the Black Isle. Leisure centre, tennis and near golf course. **£££**
**Links Hotel**
1 Seafield Street
Tel: (01667) 453321
Fax: (01667) 456092
10 rooms. Elegant Victorian building with sea views. Log fires. Inclusive golf packages utilising hotel's two courses plus 20 others nearby. **££**

## Newburgh

**Udny Arms Hotel**
Main Street
Tel: (01358) 789444
www.udny.co.uk
26 rooms. Riverside inn with great food and character. Rooms tastefully furnished with period furniture. Close to

Cruden Bay golf course. **££–£££**

## Peterhead

**Waterside Inn**
Fraserburgh Road
Tel: (01779) 471121
www.swallow-hotels.com
105 rooms. On banks of River Ugie and not far from the sea. Full leisure facilities. **££**

## Portsoy

**Boyne Hotel**
2 North High Street
Tel/Fax: (01261) 842242
www.boynehotel.co.uk
12 rooms. Charming building in beautiful fishing village. Golf, fishing, whisky trail close by. **£–££**
**The Station Hotel**
Seafield Street, Portsoy
Tel: (01261) 842327
www.stationhotelportsoy.co.uk
Golfers, walkers and wildlife enthusiasts will enjoy this handy base that includes 14 en suite rooms and a restaurant serving great food. **£££**

# THE NORTHERN HIGHLANDS

## Alchiltibuie

**Summer Isles Hotel**
Tel: (01854) 622282
Fax: (01854) 622251
www.summerisleshotel.co.uk
Delightful hotel with suites and log cabins in tiny village at the end of a 15-mile (24-km) track with glorious views over the Summer Isles. Open Easter–Oct. **£££–££££**

## Aviemore

**Aviemore Highland Resort**
Tel: (0845) 608 3734
www.aviemorehighlandresort.com
Four hotels catering for every budget, luxury self-catering lodges, a range of leisure amenities including golf and spa and several restaurants are all part of this striking development in the heart of Aviemore. **££–£££**
**Hilton Coylumbridge**
Tel: (01479) 810661

Fax: (01479) 811309
www.hilton.com
175 rooms. In the heart of the Grampians and an ideal centre for outdoor leisure. Good for families: large wooded grounds and play area for kids. Leisure centre with pool and spa. **£££**

## Beauly

**Lovat Arms Hotel**
High Street
Tel: (01463) 782313
Fax: (01463) 782862
www.lovatarms.com
22 rooms. All rooms feature a clan tartan and many have canopied or half-tester beds. Produce from family farm served in dining room. **£££**
**Priory Hotel**
The Square
Tel: (01463) 782309
Fax: (01463) 782531
www.priory-hotel.com
36 rooms. Comfortable privately owned hotel in an

attractive village square next to priory ruins. Scrumptious afternoon tea. **££££**

## Cromarty

**Royal Hotel**
Marine Terrace
Tel: (01381) 600217
Fax: (01381) 600813
www.royal-hotel.activehotels.com
20 rooms. Comfortable, welcoming family hotel with great view of the Cromarty Firth where dolphins swim among parked oil rigs. **£–££**

## Dingwall

**Tulloch Castle Hotel**
Tulloch Castle Drive
Tel: (01349) 861325
Fax: (01349) 863993
www.tullochcastle.co.uk
19 rooms. Elegant country house hotel dating back to 12th century in superb surroundings, ideal for a relaxing break. **£££**

## Dornoch

**2 Quail Restaurant and Rooms**
Castle Street, Dornoch
Tel: (01862) 811811
This 3-bedroom Victorian house prides itself on a home-from-home ambience and excellent cuisine. Your hosts will be more than happy to advise on the best fairways in the area. **££–£££**

## Drumnadrochit (on Loch Ness)

**Drumnadrochit Hotel**
Tel: (01456) 450218

### PRICE CATEGORIES

Approximate prices per person per night in a double room in high season:
**£** = less than £30
**££** = £30–50
**£££** = £50–80
**££££** = more than £80

Fax: (01456) 450793
www.drumnadrochithotel.co.uk
29 rooms. Modern hotel close to Loch Ness and the visitor centres for "monster watchers". **£–££**

## Fort Augustus

**Lovat Arms Hotel**
Tel: (01320) 366206
Fax: (01320) 366677
www.lovatarms-hotel.com
25 rooms. Long-established friendly hotel near centre of village, close to loch and Caledonian Canal. Large selection of malt whiskies. **££–£££**

## Gairloch

**The Old Inn**
Tel: (0800) 542 5444
Fax: (01445) 712445
www.theoldinn.co.uk
14 rooms. Charming hotel in mountain and sea setting. Excellent food and real ale ("Taste of Scotland" accredited). Good for wildlife-watching. **£–££**

## Invermoriston

**Glenmoriston Arms Hotel**
Tel: (01320) 351206
Fax: (01320) 351308
www.glenmoriston-arms-hotel.co.uk
8 rooms. This 200-year-old coaching inn nestles in a lovely glen close to Loch Ness. **£££**

## Inverness

**Glenmoriston Town House Hotel**
Ness Bank, Inverness
Tel: (01463) 223777
www.glenmoristontownhouse.com
An award-winning, 30-room boutique hotel that oozes style and class; and that's before you dine in the award-winning restaurant. **£££–££££**
**Bunchrew House Hotel**
Bunchrew

### PRICE CATEGORIES

Approximate prices per person per night in a double room in high season:
£ = less than £30
££ = £30–50
£££ = £50–80
££££ = more than £80

Tel: (01463) 234917
Fax: (01463) 710620
www.bunchrew-inverness.co.uk
14 rooms. Every inch a 17th-century Scottish baronial home, yet comfortable and relaxed. Stands in 20 acres (8 hectares) of shores on the Beauly Firth, 3 miles (5 km) west of Inverness. Afternoon tea on the lawn a delight. **£££–££££**
**Columba Hotel**
Ness Walk
Tel: (01463) 231391
Fax: (01463) 715526
www.british-trust-hotels.com
76 rooms. Refurbished hotel on banks of River Ness. Close to town centre. **££–£££**
**Culduthel Lodge**
14 Culduthel Road
Tel/Fax: (01463) 240089
www.culduthel.com
11 rooms. Splendid 19th-century house overlooking the Moray Firth, Inverness and the Black Isle. **££**
**Culloden House Hotel**
Culloden
Tel: (01463) 790461
Fax: (01463) 792181
www.cullodenhouse.co.uk
28 rooms. An architectural gem 3 miles (5 km) east of Inverness, associated with Bonnie Prince Charlie and the Battle of Culloden. Magnificent public rooms, four-poster curtain-framed beds. Dine in the Adam Room on local produce cooked in the French manner. 40 acres (16 hectares) of lovely grounds. Tennis, sauna, solarium, snooker. **££££**
**Dunain Park Hotel**
Tel: (01463) 230512
Fax: (01463) 224532
www.dunainparkhotel.co.uk
11 rooms. Georgian country house, 4 miles (6 km) from Inverness on A82, set in 6 acres (2.5 hectares) of gardens and grounds. Wide variety of bedrooms, some with four-poster beds. Auld Alliance (marriage of French and Scottish produce and skills) is served accompanied by a fair selection of wines. Indoor swimming pool, sauna, croquet. **£££–££££**
**Ramada Jarvis Inverness**
33 Church Street

Tel: (01463) 235181
Fax: (01463) 711206
www.ramadajarvis.co.uk
106 rooms. Elegant city hotel alongside the River Ness with all facilities. **£££**
**Whinpark Guest House**
17 Ardross Street
Tel/Fax: (01463) 232549
www.whinparkhotel.com
10 rooms. Victorian house situated in quiet area close to River Ness. **£**

## Kincraig

**Ossian Hotel**
Tel: (01540) 651242
Fax: (01540) 651633
www.ossian@kincraig.com
9 rooms. Pleasant, small Highland hotel just off the main road providing friendly service. Vegetarian meals and lovely dinners. **££**

## Kingussie

**Scot House Hotel**
Newtonmore Road
Tel: (01540) 661351
Fax: (01540) 661111
www.scothouse.com
9 rooms. Friendly, welcoming hotel in centre of village. **££**

## Lochinver

**Albannach Hotel**
Baddidarroch
Tel: (01571) 844407
www.thealbannach.co.uk
5 rooms. Delightful 19th-century house set in a walled garden. All comforts for those who enjoy the outdoors. Excellent home cooking and vegetarians welcome. **££££** (includes dinner)
**Inver Lodge Hotel**
Iolaire Road
Tel: (01571) 844496
Fax: (01571) 844395
www.inverlodge.com
20 rooms. A modern hotel with superb loch views. **£££–££££**

## Newtonmore

**Balavil Sport Hotel**
Tel: (01540) 673220
Fax: (01540) 673773
www.balavil.mckeverhotels.co.uk
50 rooms. Refurbished building on main street with excellent leisure facilities. **££**

**The Pines Guesthouse**
Station Road
Tel: (01540) 673271
Fax: (01540) 673882
5 rooms. Beautiful building set in wooded grounds providing peaceful accommodation. **£**

## Scourie

**Eddrachilles Hotel**
Badcall Bay
Tel: (01971) 502080
Fax: (01971) 502477
www.eddrachilles.com
11 rooms. Beautifully maintained hotel on 320 acres (130 hectares) of waterfront property with stunning sea views. Close to Handa Island bird sanctuary. Open Mar–Oct. **££**

## Strathpeffer

**Dunraven Lodge**
Golf Course Road
Tel: (01997) 421210
3 rooms. Beautiful Victorian villa in extensive grounds overlooking the village; peaceful and relaxing. **££**
**Ben Wyvis Hotel**
Strathpeffer
Tel: (0870) 950 6264
With its commanding views over the town and lying in the shadow of Ben Wyvis, this is a comfortable hotel with its own 32-seat cinema. **£££**

## Ullapool

**Ceilidh Place**
14 West Argyle Street
Tel: (01854) 612103
Fax: (01854) 612886
www.theceilidhplace.com
24 rooms (10 en suite). With bookshop, café, restaurant and concert hall, this is not only a good hotel but is also the cultural centre of Ullapool. Bunk House with 9 cheaper rooms is spartan but immaculate and great value for families. **£–£££**
**Harbour Lights Hotel**
Garve Road
Tel: (01854) 612222
www.harbour-lights.co.uk
19 en suite rooms. Comfortable hotel close to the picturesque shores of Loch Broom. A short walk from the village. **££**

# ORKNEY

**Albert Hotel**
Kirkwall
Tel: (01856) 876000
Fax: (01856) 875397
19 rooms. Newly
refurbished hotel in the
centre of town. Orkney ales
and whiskies. **££**
**Barony Hotel**
Birsay
Tel: (01856) 721327

Fax: (01856) 721302
www.baronyhotel.com
Panoramic views to
Boardhouse Loch and
Brough of Birsay. Ideal for
birdwatching and trout
fishing. **££**
**Foveran Hotel**
St Ola, Kirkwall
Tel: (01856) 872389
Fax: (01856) 876430

www.foveranhotel.com
8 rooms. Family-run hotel
set in 35 acres (14
hectares) overlooking
Scapa Flow. **£££**
**Lynnfield Hotel**
Holm Road, Kirkwall
Tel: (01856) 872505
Fax: (01856) 870038
www.lynnfieldhotel.com
10 rooms. Formerly the

home of the distillery
manager: you can taste the
"guid stuff" – and it's free.
Good local cooking. **££**
**Thira Guest House**
Stromness
Tel: (01856) 851181
www.thiraorkney.co.uk
Purpose-built and roomy
guest house with views over
Hoy Sound. **£–££**

# SHETLAND

**Broch House Guest House**
Upper Scalloway
Tel: (01595) 880051
Fax: (01595) 880731
3 rooms. Modern house in
elevated position with view
over Scalloway. **£**
**Buness House**
Baltasound, Unst
Tel: (01957) 711315
Fax: (01957) 711815
E-mail: buness@zetnet.co.uk
4 rooms. 17th-century
building on island of Unst,
most northerly isle in

Britain. Close to
Hermaness nature reserve
and fine cliff scenery.
**££–£££**
**Busta House Hotel**
Busta, North Mainland
Tel: (01806) 522506
Fax: (01806) 522588
www.bustahouse.com
22 rooms. Country house
hotel 23 miles (37 km)
north of Lerwick, dating
from 1588 and with private
harbour and slipway.
**££–£££**

**Grand Hotel**
Commercial Street, Lerwick
Tel: (01595) 692826
Fax: (01595) 694048
www.kgqhotels.co.uk
24 rooms. Oldest purpose-
built hotel in Shetland, fully
refurbished. Convenient
location close to harbour
and town centre. **££**
**Shetland Hotel**
Holmsgarth Road, Lerwick
Tel: (01595) 695515
Fax: (01595) 695828
www.shetlandhotels.com

65 rooms. Modern hotel
with leisure complex. Views
of the harbour and Isle of
Bressay. **££**
**Sumburgh Hotel**
South Mainland
Tel: (01950) 460201
Fax: (01950) 460394
www.sumburgh-hotel.shetland.co.uk
32 rooms. Former laird's
house, close to airport and
Jarlshof ancient monument.
Two bars serving local Auld
Rock ale. Superb beaches
nearby. **££**

# HOSTELS AND CAMPING

## Youth Hostels

There are about 60 YHF
hostels in Scotland, many of
them in the Highlands. The
hostels provide low-cost
accommodation, usually with
dormitory-type bedrooms,
although these days there
are some twin and double
rooms and even en suite
facilities. The hostels are
open to members of the
International Youth Hostel
Federation (IYHF), or you can
join the SYHA at any hostel.
They admit children from five
years and up; there is no
upper age limit. You can stay
in a hostel for one night
without becoming a member.
To join the Youth Hostels
Association is free for
five–17 year-olds and £8
for adults. Accommodation
costs between £9 and £19
a night depending on the
time of year and the
facilities at the hostel.
    For details contact the
Scottish Youth Hostels

Association (SYHA),
7 Glebe Crescent,
Stirling, FK8 2JA.
Tel: (01786) 891400
Central info and
reservations line: (08701)
553255, www.syha.org.uk

## Independent Hostels

Scotland has a growing
network of excellent
independent hostels which
provide similar
accommodation to the SYHA
hostels but with the
advantage that you don't
have to join any
organisation to use them.
Prices are very reasonable
and the facilities are often
surprisingly good; large
dormitories are gradually
being replaced by two- and
four-bed rooms. Moreover,
many of these hostels are
in remote locations.
For more details, contact
Independent Backpackers
Hostels Scotland,

The Secretary
SIM, PO Box 7024,
Fort William
PH33 6YX.

## Camping

There are many campsites
around Scotland and these
are normally open
April–October. Expect to pay
up to £10 to pitch a tent.

Many hostels allow
camping. For detailed
information on Scottish
campsites contact;
ScottishCamping.com Ltd,
Blairs College, South
Deeside Rd., Aberdeen
AB12 5LF; tel: (01224)
860347; www.scottish-
camping.com. They will also
answer any camping
queries.

**BELOW:** camping on the edge, with wonderful views.

# E ATING OUT

# RECOMMENDED RESTAURANTS, CAFÉS & BARS

### Scottish Cuisine

More than 50 years have elapsed since that distinguished travel writer H.V. Morton wrote: "Scotland is the best place in the world to take an appetite." The country is renowned for its produce from river and sea, from farm and moor. Fish is something of a speciality, with salmon being particularly good: kippers and Arbroath Smokies (haddock smoked over wood) are delicious, too. Shellfish are excellent and exported all over the world, while Aberdeen Angus beef and Border lamb are both renowned. Various dishes are distinctly Scottish, such as haggis – which is probably more enjoyable if you don't know what should be in it (the heart, lungs and liver of a sheep, suet, oatmeal and onion).

Over the past decade culinary skills have come to match the quality of the produce, and today it is possible to enjoy superb meals in Scotland served in the most elegant of restaurants as well as in simple small spaces with scarcely more than half a dozen tables. The hours at which restaurants, especially smaller ones away from the main cities, serve meals tend to be less flexible than in many other countries. High tea, usually served from 5 to 7pm, usually consists of fish and chips or an egg dish followed by lashings of scones and pancakes, all accompanied by gallons of tea.

Dr Samuel Johnson remarked, "If an epicure could remove by a wish, in quest of sensual gratifications, wherever he had supped he would breakfast in Scotland." No doubt he would say the same today. There is surely no better way to start the day than a

**ABOVE:** a platter of fresh seafood, including langoustines, oysters and mussels.

bowl of porridge followed by Loch Fyne kippers and Scottish oatcakes. On a more mundane level, there is no shortage of fast-food outlets of one sort or another throughout Scotland. For a cheap and enjoyable takeaway meal, you could do a lot worse than try the humble "chippie" (fish and chip shop).

Lunch is almost invariably considerably less expensive than dinner, and nearly all restaurants have set menus, which are about half the price of an à la carte dinner.

### Taste of Scotland

The *Taste of Scotland* scheme invites eating places to apply for membership. Its original and continuing objective is to promote restaurants and producers which are believed to offer the very best of

Scottish cuisine. All members are inspected before being admitted to the scheme; over 400 restaurants, bistros and cafés are listed on its website where quality, service and in many cases considerable innovation can be guaranteed. Visit www.taste-of-scotland.com.

However, it's not only the above which offers an insight into the best of Scotland's culinary treats. VisitScotland runs a nationwide quality-assurance scheme called "Eat Scotland", providing visitors with a handy reference for quality eateries. Visitors to Glasgow and Edinburgh can discover the latest gossip on cafés and restaurants in *The List's Eating and Drinking Guide*, while the wonderful Outer Hebrides now have their very own "Speciality Food Trail" (www.outerhebridesfoodtrail.com).

# EDINBURGH

*(If phoning from outside area, use code: 0131)*

## Scottish

**Abstract**
33–35 Castle Street
Tel: 229 1222
This new dining experience by Edinburgh Castle exudes culinary confidence. Scallops, poached Scottish oysters and fine cuts of beef all appear on the menu, while the tasting menu aims to confound creations such as vanilla mustard ice cream with scrambled egg. This is a reassuringly expensive dining experience. **£££+**

**Restaurant at the Bonham**
35 Drumsheugh Gardens
Tel: 274 7444
A blend of classic and contemporary cuisine served in the dining room of an elegant upmarket, boutique hotel. Organic Scottish produce with modern flavours. Leave room for stunning desserts. Light bites served in the lounge. "Aficionados Wine List" offers rare bottles. **£££**

**Restaurant Martin Wishart**
54 The Shore, Leith
Tel: 553 3557
One of the best restaurants in the city (one of three with a Michelin star), opened in 1999. Imaginative and dynamic cooking. Menu changes daily. **£££**

**A Room In The West End**
26 William Street
Tel: 226 1036
The simplicity of the decor belies a talent for producing unusual culinary dishes with a distinctly modern Scottish theme. **£££**

**Sweet Melindas**
11 Roseneath Street
Tel: 229 7953
Excellent food and wine at reasonable prices in a joyous atmosphere in a south neighbourhood restaurant. Daily changing menu. Booking advisable, especially for Tuesday dinner when customers pay what they think the food is worth. **££**

## Contemporary/ International

**The Balmoral Hotel Number One Restaurant**
1 Princes Street
Tel: 556 2414
This Michelin-starred restaurant oozes style and panache without being pompous. Culinary treats such as baby spinach soup with salt-cod ravioli; sirloin with smoked mash and gingerbread soufflé. Eat at lunchtime to safeguard your budget or splash out on an evening tasting menu. **£££**

**Martin's**
70 Rose St North Lane
Tel: 225 3106
Difficult to find, this small, well-established restaurant is well worth the trouble. Limited but confident contemporary menu with best cheeseboard in town. Excellent, discreet service. **£££**

**Oloroso**
33 Castle Street
Tel: 226 7614
Stunning setting in a penthouse space with glass walls and a roof terrace. Excellent food cooked to precision. Bar snacks also available. **£££**

**The Witchery by the Castle**
352 Castlehill, Royal Mile
Tel: 225 5613
Imaginative Scottish cuisine. Two restaurants, each with unusual atmosphere. Upstairs is dark and atmospheric – while downstairs is bright with a small outdoor terrace for fine weather. Excellent wine list. **£££**

## Fish and Seafood

**Café Royal Oyster Bar**
17a West Register Street
Tel: 556 4124
An Edinburgh institution where the ambience is everything. Stained glass and polished wood; always bustling and seafood is the house speciality. **£££**

**Creelers**
3 Hunter Square
Tel: 220 4447
Like its sister establishment on the Isle of Arran, specialises in imaginative cooking of fresh seafood, plus game and vegetarian dishes. **£££**

**Fishers**
1 The Shore, Leith
Tel: 554 5666
58 Thistle Street
Tel: 225 5109
A compact, homely seafood restaurant looking out over the water of Leith. Crab cakes are delicious or tuck into the seared tuna. Lunch or dinner. **£££**

**The Shore Bar & Restaurant**
3–4 The Shore, Leith
Tel: 553 5080
Fresh Scottish fish and shellfish at an 18th-century inn with traditional dining and a changing blackboard menu in the bar. **£££**

**Skippers Bistro**
1a Dock Place, Leith
Tel: 554 1018
Intimate, cosy restaurant with wood-panelled booths. Friendly service and some of the best seafood in town. **££–£££**

## Chinese

**Rendezvous**
10a Queensferry Street
Tel: 225 2023
Edinburgh's oldest Chinese restaurant (over 50 years) continues to thrill the palate with its reasonably priced a la carte and buffet menu. **££**

### PRICE CATEGORIES

Average cost of a three-course evening meal per person, excluding wine:
**£** = below £15
**££** = £15–25
**£££** = above £25

ACCOMMODATION

EATING OUT

ACTIVITIES

A – Z

**BELOW:** enjoying a drink on the outdoor terrace of Oloroso, with views of Edinburgh Castle.

**ABOVE:** the tempting interior of Glass & Thompson.

## Kweilin
19 Dundas Street
Tel: 557 1875
Large space serving authentic Cantonese dishes, especially strong on seafood. One of the best Chinese in town. ££

**Duck's at Le Marché Noir**
2–4 Eyre Place
Tel: 558 1608
Scottish/French menus served along with excellent wines in restful ambience in a quiet corner of the New Town. £££

**Jacques**
8 Gillespie Place
Tel: 229 6080
Uncomplicated, quality food in authentic surroundings, with the feel of a French rural town. Close to the Theatre Royal. ££

**Le Sept**
5 Hunter Square
Tel: 225 5428
This long-established restaurant specialises in fish and crêpes. Simple, pub-style tables (a few outdoors). ££–£££

### Indian

**The Himalaya**
171 Bruntsfield Place

Tel: 229 8216
The interior is a little cramped, but the simple yet tasty tandoori dishes definitely won't disappoint. Be warned... the naan breads are huge. ££

**Indian Cavalry Club**
3 Atholl Place
Tel: 228 3282
Don't be put off by the paramilitary uniforms of the staff – this upmarket Indian restaurant with an emphasis on steaming attempts, with a fair amount of success, to blend brasserie and Indian restaurant. ££

**Kalpna**
2 St Patricks Square
Tel: 667 9890
Gujarati and southern Indian vegetarian food in a non-smoking restaurant. Moderately priced wine list. £–££

**Lancers Brasserie**
5 Hamilton Place
Tel: 332 3444
Modest interior, with three rooms serving Bengali and northern Indian cuisine. Renowned for curries. Modest wine list. ££

### Italian

**Vittorias**
113 Brunswick Street
Tel: 556 6171
A terrific atmosphere and great food assured in this family-run Edinburgh institution. Book ahead for a weekend table. £–££

**Ristorante Tinelli**
139 Easter Road
Tel: 652 1932

Small and unpretentious, with a limited menu of superb northern Italian food. Fine cheese selection. ££

### Mexican

**Blue Parrot Cantina**
49 St Stephen Street
Tel: 225 2941
This basement restaurant in Stockbridge is small, with a Moroccan blue and wood interior. The menu's not bad either, and the food is authentically spicy. Good range of tequilas and cocktails. ££

**Viva Mexico**
41 Cockburn Street
Tel: 226 5145
Cosy restaurant that transports you back to atmosphere of old Mexico. Food (for some) on spicy side. Good selection for veggies. Great margaritas. ££

### Thai

**Thai Lemongrass**
40–1 Bruntsfield Place
Tel: 229 2225
The 20-minute walk (5 minutes taxi) south up Lothian Road will whet your appetite for this authentic Thai cuisine bursting with flavour and attentive staff. More than competes with the many Thai eateries emerging in the city. ££

### Vegetarian

**David Bann's Vegetarian Restaurant**
56 St Mary's Street
Tel: 556 5888

An extensive and varied well prepared global menu from a very experienced vegetarian chef. Open all hours. ££

**Henderson's Salad Table**
94 Hanover Street
Tel: 225 2131
Basement self-service eatery that gets busy, especially at lunchtime. Excellent vegetarian choice and low-key live music played in the evenings. ££

### Bistros

**Centotre**
103 George Street
Tel: 225 1550
Northern Italian flavours abound in this classy, tiled former bank turned bistro-bar slap bang in the city centre. For balsamic on bread, a bowl of olives and a glass of white wine, here's your answer. ££

**Olive Branch**
91 Broughton Street
Tel: 557 8589
(Also Holy Corner, Bruntsfield)
Wicker chairs, an airy ambience and a wide-ranging menu of salads, classic burgers and even soup in a mug won't disappoint. Great for Sunday brunch. £

**Waterfront Wine Bar & Grill**
1c Dock Place
Tel: 554 7427
Moderately priced fish dishes and good choice of vegetarian dishes served in a conservatory on the dock. Excellent wine selection on blackboards. £££

### Cafés

**Elephant House**
21 George IV Bridge
Tel: 220 5355
Popular coffee house serving a huge range of exotic teas and coffees, plus great cakes and pastries.

**Favorit**
19 Teviot Place
Tel: 220 6880
New York deli meets Italian café. Two stylish eateries serving filling wraps, breakfasts and luscious fruit drinks. Open early morning until late.

**Filmhouse**
Lothian Road
Tel: 228 2688
This is no ordinary cinema, showing a rash of cutting-edge European films. It's also a convivial place for all ages to meet. Sampling simple fare like baked potatoes, sandwiches or a few Czech beers.

**Glass & Thompson**
2 Dundas Street
Tel: 557 0909
Café cum bistro serving Mediterranean-style goodies. Excellent cakes, pastriesand buttery shortbread.

**Valvona and Crolla**
19 Elm Row
Tel: 556 6066
Multrees Walk
Tel: 557 0088
Most wonderful Italian restaurant, at the rear of a fabled deli. Breakfast and lunch only, and queues not infrequent. Closed Sunday. ££

### Pubs and Bars

Good areas to try include the Royal Mile, Grassmarket, Rose Street, Haymarket, George Street and West Register Street.

The Living Room and the Opal Lounge on George Street will appeal to the hip and trendy.

### Near Edinburgh

Some top restaurants on the outskirts of Edinburgh are:

**Champany Inn**
Linlithgow, Lothian EH49 7LU
17 miles (25 km) from Edinburgh
Tel: (01506) 834532
lAberdeen Angus is the speciality, and from the grill come entrecôte, pope's

eye, porterhouse, sirloin and rib eye. The seafood is just as excellent. £££

**Rhubarb Restaurant**
Prestonfield House Hotel
Tel: 225 7800
Deep reds and plush, elegant surroundings greet the discerning diner within this period building Scottish and international cuisine. £££

**Open Arms Hotel**
Dirleton, near Edinburgh
Tel: (01620) 850241
Pleasant restaurant overlooking village green and 16th-century castle ruin. £££

# GLASGOW

*(If phoning from outside area, use code: 0141)*

### Scottish

(These restaurants do not serve *only* Scottish food.)

**Babbity Bowster**
16 Blackfriars Street
Tel: 552 5055
Friendly upstairs restaurant serving Scottish food. Renowned for its Burns Night supper. ££

**Michael Caines at ABode**
129 Bath Street
Tel: 572 6011
This restaurant continues to win awards and praise among foodies seeking fine Scottish/French cuisine and Mediterranean flavours. This is a slightly formal though convivial dining experience with the renowned ABode Hotel. ££

**No. Sixteen**
16 Byres Road
Tel: 339 2254
An unassuming, even off-putting, shopfront belies an excellent cuisine prepared with the best Scottish ingredients combined with flavours from here, there, everywhere. Imaginative wine list. ££

### International

**The Bistro**
1 Devonshire Gardens
Great Western Road
Tel: 387 3434
Set in the classy West End

hotel, guests feast on Scottish-influenced cuisine with a twist. £££

**Bluu**
60 Trongate, Merchant City
Tel: 548 1350
English and European-style cuisine converges under the roof of this chic eatery that also offers a lounge-style bar. £££

**City Merchant**
97 Candleriggs
Tel: 553 1577.
West coast seafood a speciality. £££

**Cafe Francais**
4 Byres Road
Tel: 334 5959
This faux-Parisien bistro in the heart of the West End delivers scallops, coq au vin and crêpes in a cosy ambience and style. ££

**Nairns**
13 Woodside Crescent
Tel: 353 0707
Established by celebrity chef Nick Nairn, this highly rated restaurant serves wonderful complementary Scottish cuisine with flair. Closed Sun and Mon. £££

**Stravaigin**
28–30 Gibson Street
Tel: 334 2665
*Stravaigin* is a Scots word for "wandering about", which this restaurant's "Global Twist" menu does – and with great success. Attractive, inexpensive wine list. Bar/café on ground floor serves just as excellent but less expensive

food. Open late. £££

**Stravaigin 2**
8 Ruthven Lane
Tel: 334 7165
Offshoot of Stravaigin *(see above)* but more a brasserie than a restaurant. Innovative fusion dishes. Pre-theatre menu good value. ££

**Two Fat Ladies**
88 Dumbarton Road
Tel: 339 1944
Small and gets very busy, so book in advance if you want to sample the excellent contemporary food, usually fish and game. Closed Sundays. ££–£££

**The Ubiquitous Chip**
12 Ashton Lane
Tel: 334 5007

The Chip is much more than a Glasgow institution. Beloved by media types, it also attracts more than its fair share of celebrities, for both the food and the ambience. £££

### Fish and Seafood

**Harry Ramsden's**
251 Paisley Road
Tel: 429 3700
Over 10 years on the south bank of the Clyde and still the best fish and chips in town. £

**Mussel Inn**
157 Hope Street
Tel: 572 1405
Mussels, scallops and oysters are the stars of this restaurant opened by a

**BELOW:** mussels at the Mussel Inn.

collective of west coast shellfish producers. **££**

**Rogano**
11 Exchange Place
Tel: 248 4055
A glamorous Art Deco institution where oysters and fish soup are specialities. Very expensive, although the downstairs casual Café Rogano is more affordable. **£££**

## Chinese

**Amber Regent**
50 West Regent Street
Tel: 331 1655
Upmarket, with a wide selection of Cantonese dishes and Szechuan dishes. Booking essential. Closed Sundays. **££**

**Peking Inn**
191 Hope Street
Tel: 332 7120
Delightful Cantonese/ Pekinese restaurant serving tasty seafood. Booking essential, particularly at the weekend, when long queues are likely. **££**

## French

**Brian Maule at Chardon d'Or**
176 West Regent Street
Tel: 248 3801
Brian Maule was head chef at the renowned Le Gavroche restaurant in London. Here he produces a refined marriage of the Auld Alliance (Scottish and French) cuisine served in a dining room decorated with Post-Impressionist art. **£££**

## Greek

**Konaki**
920 Sauchiehall Street
Tel: 342 4010
No-nonsense, pleasant Greek restaurant whose owners are from Crete and so serve excellent Greek

food. Good choice for vegetarians. **£–££**

## Indian

**Ashoka**
108 Elderslie Street
Tel: 221 1761
This is the original Ashoka, located near the Mitchell Library and the best of several Indian restaurants in the vicinity. **££**

**Mother India**
28 Westminster Terrace
Tel: 221 1663
Beautiful Indian home cooking in relaxed atmosphere. Especially pleasing for vegetarians. Licensed but also BYOB. **££**

**Shish Mahal**
66–68 Park Road
Tel: 339 8256
Established in 1964 as one of the original curry houses and still run by the same family. **££**

**The Wee Curry Shop**
7 Buccleuch Street
Tel: 353 0777
also Ashton Lane
Tel: 357 5280
This child of Mother India serves delightful no-nonsense food chosen from a concise menu at half a dozen tables within view of the chef. **£–££**

## Italian

**L'Ariosto**
92–94 Mitchell Street
Tel: 221 0971
This place looks tiny from the front, but inside it opens out onto a traditional Italian courtyard, although this one is indoors. Tuscan cuisine at its very best. **£££**

**The Battlefield Rest**
56 Battlefield Road
Tel: 636 6955
This was a former tram stop, complete with waiting room and ticket office. Now it is a popular eating spot; the lunchtime menu and pre-theatre menu are good value. Closed Sunday. **£–££**

**Ristorante La Fiorentina**
2 Paisley Road West
Paisley Road Toll
Tel: 420 1585
Upmarket Italian restaurant south of the river but pretty

**ABOVE:** the Mackintosh-inspired Willow Tea Rooms.

near the city. Classic Tuscan cooking meets modern Mediterranean with a classy wine list and excellent seafood. **£££**

**Fratelli Sarti** has two venues:
121 Bath Street/133 Wellington Street
Tel: 204 0440/572 7000
Enter an informal café (closed Sundays) on Wellington Street or enter from Bath Street into a basement restaurant-deli. Both are warm, friendly Italian eateries with a traditional menu – and wild boar pizza – and a long wine list. **£–££**
42 Renfield Street.
Tel: 572 7000.
A more serious and distinguished restaurant in a former bank serving a traditional Italian menu. Leave room for the *torte della mamma*. **££**

**La Lanterna**
35 Hope Street
Tel: 221 9160
Basement restaurant opposite Central Station much frequented by Glasgow's Italian community. **££**

**Di Maggio's**
21 Royal Exchange Square
Tel: 248 2111
61 Ruthven Lane
Tel: 334 6000
1038 Pollokshaws Road
Tel: 632 4194
West Nile Street
Tel: 333 4999
Straightforward, no-nonsense Italian cooking at an affordable price. A favourite with students. **£**

**La Parmigiana**
447 Great Western Road
Tel: 0141-334 0686

Many Glaswegians consider this to be the best Italian restaurant in the city (est. 1978) with its predominantly Milano cuisine and splendid wine list. Closed Sundays. **££–£££**

## Thai

**Thai Fountain**
2 Woodside Crescent
Tel: 332 2599
Excellent Thai cuisine in elegant setting. Closed Sundays. **££–£££**

## Miscellaneous

**Air Organic**
36 Kelvingrove Street
Tel: 564 5200
Pacific Rim-influenced cuisine with a wide selection of dishes. **££**

**The Arches Café Bar**
253 Argyle Street
Tel: 565 1035
The Arches is an arts venue under the main railway bridge at Central Station. This café-bar is in the cellar underneath and it has been set up like a minimalist jazz bar. Small menu but superb and very cheap. **£**

**Café Gandolfi**
64 Albion Street
Tel: 552 6813
The grandfather of modern Glasgow café life. Fresh Scottish ingredients with a slight Mediterranean twist is the staple of this Merchant City eatery. **££**

**Corinthian**
191 Ingram Street
Tel: 552 1101
This fine Victorian building is now a gathering spot for

the smart and trendy. It has several bars and a nightclub as well as a restaurant, making it a one-stop shop for a night out. Reasonable food. **££–£££**

**étain**
The Glass House, Springfield Court
Tel: 225 5630
This is now part of the "Individual Restaurant Company", and it certainly retains the highly individualistic style brought to Glasgow by predecessor Sir Terence Conran. Emerge from the private lift behind Princes Square into a whorl of designer sophistication. The international food excites – at a price. **£££**

**Kember and Jones**
134 Byres Road
Tel: 337 3851
Once in a while a delicatessen/café opens that truly excites. Here, plates arrive groaning under the weight of the club sandwich or huge platters that are a speciality. Italian, Spanish and French influences are all to be found in a convivial atmosphere. **£–££**

**The Living Room**
150 St Vincents Street
Tel: (0870) 220 3028
Relaxed, informal dining is offered in an airy atmosphere. Great selection of food including old favourites, such as bangers and mash or the more refined roasted lamb cutlets. **££**

**Pancho Villas,**
26 Bell Street.
Tel: 552 7737.
Owned and run by a Mexican, this is about as good as Mexican eating gets in the UK. With the quality of its food and its Merchant City location, it attracts a wide mix of people and can get busy. **£–££**

**Uisge Beatha**
232–246 Woodlands Road
Tel: 564 1596
The translation of the pub name "water of life" hints that this is where to enjoy a few drams of fine malt and meet kilt-wearing staff. Let's be honest, it's more a pub than an eatery, but there are reasonable toasties, and a lovely,

cheery atmosphere.
**Willow Tea Rooms**
217 Sauchiehall Street
Tel: 332 0521
Most tourist attractions have a tearoom. In this case it's the tearoom that is the attraction. Charles Rennie Mackintosh designed the interior of this for tearoom baroness Kate Cranston, and it's still possible to take lunch here or enjoy afternoon tea. **£**

### Vegetarian

**Grassroots Café**
97 St Georges Road
Tel: 333 0534
Cosy Charing Cross establishment. As well as vegetarian food, they also cater for vegans and people on gluten- and wheat-free diets. **£**

**The 13th Note**
50–60 King Street
Tel: 553 1638
Strictly vegetarian and vegan, based mainly on Greek dishes, but with other influences as wide-ranging as Italy and the Far East. **£**

### Pubs and Bars

The city centre offers a bewildering choice – try the Merchant City area, George Square, Argyle Street, Hope Street and Sauchiehall Street for starters. The suburbs (particularly Byres Road and Shawlands) and surrounding towns are also very well supplied with excellent pubs, many providing very good food as well.

## NEAR GLASGOW

An outstanding restaurant on the outskirts of Glasgow:
**Gleddoch House Hotel**
Langbank, Renfrewshire (near Glasgow airport)
Tel: (01475) 540711
Elegant restaurant featuring Scottish dishes in a small hotel which has a first-class 18-hole golf course and a host of other facilities. Booking essential. **£££**
Hotel has 39 bedrooms.

# THE BORDERS

**Cringletie House Hotel**
Edinburgh Road, Peebles
Tel: (01721) 730233
The restaurant of this gracious country house hotel has had a good reputation for many years. The south of France is the main inspiration. Fixed-price evening menu. Reservations advisable. **£££**

**Kailzie Garden Restaurant**
Kailzie, Peebles
Tel: (01721) 722807
An unpretentious restaurant housed in the old stable square and carefully converted to retain as many original features as possible. Limited menu of good home cooking and baking

using local produce. Special evening dinners on last Friday of every month. Homely atmosphere. **£–££**
**Simply Scottish**
6–8 High Street, Jedburgh
Tel: (01835) 864696
Bistro-style café using good local produce to create imaginative, tasty meals. Traditional Scottish food. **££**

**Wheatsheaf Hotel**
Main Street, Swinton
Tel: (01890) 860257
A small Berwickshire village yields this genuine country, award-winning inn with a surprisingly extensive and imaginative menu specialising in Scottish game and seafood. 7 bedrooms. **££–£££**

# THE SOUTHWEST

**Creebridge House Hotel**
Minigaff, Newton Stewart
Tel: (01671) 402121
Imaginative cuisine served in the brasserie, and the chance to sample real ales. The main restaurant, serving an a la carte menu, overlooks the landscaped gardens. **££–£££**
**Enterkine House**
Annbank by Ayr
Tel: (01292) 521608

Traditional Scottish food and exquisite wines served in elegant dining room (no jeans) in a recently restored country house hotel in 310 acres (130 hectares) of green fields, rivers and woodland. 6 Rooms. **£££**
**Fouters' Bistro**
2a Academy Street, Ayr
Tel: (01292) 261391
An attractive cellar bistro

which for aeons has been serving good creative Scottish dishes cooked with local products in a pleasant atmosphere. **££**
**Kilmichael House**
Brodick Arran
Tel: (01770) 302 219
The four-course evening meal complete with canapés in this beautiful retreat will make your island stay memorable. **£££**

**MacCallums of Troon Oyster Bar**
The Harbour, Troon
Tel: (01292) 319339
A somewhat eclectic and sometimes surprising seafood menu served in an unpretentious high-roof stone shed right next to fish market on the harbour. Great atmosphere. Try the grilled lobster and chips. **££**

TRANSPORT

ACCOMMODATION

EATING OUT

ACTIVITIES

A–Z

# FORTH AND CLYDE

**Chambo**
Mine Road, Bridge of Allan
(near Stirling)
Tel: (01786) 833617
An old Victorian building
which was the pump room
when Bridge of Allan was a
spa. Offering an
imaginative menu of
seasonal specialities
including Scottish crab and
Perthshire lamb served in a
tastefully furnished semi-
circular dining room. **££**
**The Drovers Inn**
Inverarnan-by-Ardlui

Tel: (01301) 704 234
The Drovers Howff, The
Poachers Den and The
Laird's Bothy; each a
drinking and eating area of
this 300 year-old pub exude
real character. Forget
"theme' bar". The kilts real
ale, stuffed animals and
cock-a-leekie soup are the
real thing – even 17th-
century outlaw Rob Roy
drank here. **£–££**
**Hermann's Restaurant**
58 Broad Street, Stirling
Tel: (01786) 450 632

Very close to Stirling
Castle, the Tirolean owner
will tempt you with a fusion
of Austrian and Scottish
flavours in his cosy
restaurant. **££–£££**
**Macdonald Houstoun
House**
Uphall
Tel: (0870) 194 2107
The Tower Restaurant
serves excellent Scottish
food from local produce
served in the handsome
dining room of a 16th-
century house. A prodigious

wine list with labels from
around the world and a
splendid selection of malts.
**££–£££**. The hotel has 71
en suite rooms, some with
four-posters, and stands in
20 acres (8 hectares) of
grounds next to a golf
course.
**Olivia's**
5 Baker Street, Stirling
Tel: (01786) 446277
Modern Scottish and Thai
cooking. Daily changing
menu using local produce.
**££**

# THE WEST COAST

**Airds Hotel**
Port Appin
Tel: (01631) 730236
An inviting old inn on the
edge of Loch Linnhe.

Serves beautifully
presented, delicious, first
class cuisine. Excellent
wine list. 12 comfortable
and chintzy bedrooms for

those who wish to stay
over. **£££+**
**Coast**
104 George Street, Oban
Tel: (01631) 569900
Loch Melfort mussels and
West Coast crab tart are
just a few of the delicious
dishes on offer. **£££**
**Loch Fyne Oyster Bar**
Clachan Farm, Cairndow
Tel: (01499) 600264
Increasingly popular – with
the finest of oysters served
in this café-cum-restaurant,
smokehouse and produce
shop at the head of Loch
Fyne. Those who can tear
themselves away from the
oysters will enjoy the
langoustines and food from
the smokehouse – eel,
mussels, etc. Leave room
for excellent Scottish
cheeseboard. Good,
inexpensive wine list.
Booking advisable. **££**
**Lock 16-Rooftop Seafood
Restaurant**
Crinan Hotel, Crinan

Tel: (01546) 830261
(This must be distinguished
from the hotel's equally
excellent main dining room
on the ground floor.) A
simple room with
spectacular views,
especially when the sunset
puts on a show. A closer
view is of the locks at the
end of the Crinan Canal
and the fishing fleet
unloading its catch prior to
it becoming the hotel's five-
course dinner (time of
delivery noted on menu).
Booking essential. **£££**
**The Waterfront**
The Pier, Oban
Tel: (01631) 563110.
This is an excellent seafood
restaurant close to the ferry
terminal (**££–£££**) but for a
simple inexpensive taste of
the sea you can't beat **John
Ogden**'s tiny green shack at
the ferry terminal, serving
takeaway crab, mussels
and all manner of pickled
delights. **£**

**BELOW:** tucking in at the Loch Fyne Oyster Bar.

# SKYE

**Kinloch Lodge**
Sleat
Tel: (01471) 833214
Lady Claire Macdonald, one
of Scotland's best-known
cookery writers, presides
over the dining room, which
offers a full five-course
menu each night, with
variety and imagination to
the fore. Individually styled

bedrooms complete the
wonderful experience.
**£££+**
**Lochbay Seafood
Restaurant**
Stein, Waternish
Tel: (01470) 592235
Halibut, shark, skate and
ling may well be the
specials in the atmospheric
informal restaurant, which

consists of two cottages
built in 1740. If this is too
esoteric, then there are
always lobster, crab,
scallops and oyster.
Booking advisable. **££**
**Three Chimneys
Restaurant**
Colbost, by Dunvegan
Tel: (01470) 511258
Seafood platter and lobster

feast are two of many
mouth-watering creations
served during a candlelit
dinner in this atmospheric
restaurant in what was
formerly a croft. But do
leave room for the
scrumptious desserts. No
smoking. There are 6
bedrooms in The House
Over-By. **£££+**

**ABOVE:** shrimp pots piled high.

# THE INNER HEBRIDES

**Cafe Fish**
Main Street, Tobermory, Isle of Mull
Tel: (01688) 301 253
Seafood such as squat
lobster is the speciality.
Though Tobermory isn't
lacking in eateries, this
cosy restaurant has the
edge over many. **££**

**The Chip Van**
Fisherman's PierTobermory,
Isle of Mull
Tel: (01688) 302 390
Enjoy an al freso meal on
the seafront from the §Les
Routiers award-winning
team. **£**

**The Glassary**
Sandaig, Isle of Tiree
Tel: (01879) 220684
Unquestionably the best
place to eat on the island.
Simplicity is the key, with a
regularly changing menu
drawing on Tiree's renowned

reputation for beef, lamb
and seafood. Book ahead. If
you over-indulge, there are
six en suite rooms. **££**

**Mediterranea**
Salen, Isle of Mull
Tel: (01680) 300200
In the midst of the
Hebrides, visitors will
discover this authentic
Sicilian restaurant staffed
by Italians. Colourful, airy
interior, delicious food and
a wonderful welcome. Book
ahead. **££–£££**

**The Water's Edge
Restaurant**
Tobermory Hotel, Main Street,
Tobermory
Tel: (01688) 302091
A platter of Ulva Bay crab,
Sound of Mull mackerel and
Tobermory Bay mussels is
just one of the tempting
dishes on offer. **£££**

# THE OUTER HEBRIDES

**Scarista House**
Scarista, Isle of Harris
Tel: (01859) 550 238
This three-bedroomed,
18th-century former
manse, packed with
character and affording
views over Scarista Sands,
is an impressive, delightful
retreat in itself. Add the
opportunity to dine in style
on carefully selected locally

reared meats and
wonderful desserts and
you'll be loathe to leave
this hidden Hebridean gem.
Advance booking essential.
**££–£££**

**Langass Lodge**
Locheport, Isle of North Uist
Tel: (01876) 580 285
Nature abounds outside
this fascinating former
sporting lodge complete

with its own Neolithic stone
circle. The cuisine is as
inspirational as the
scenery, with generous
servings of fresh from-the-
sea crab, lobster, crayfish
and sea and brown trout,
complemented by tempting
locally reared game and a
tasty Drambuie crème
brûlée. Booking essential.
**££–£££**

**Skoon Art Cafe**
Geocrab, Isle of Harris
Tel: (01859) 530 268
For a warm welcome,
delicious home-baking,
hearty soups and views of
the Hebrides (and excellent
local paintings), this is a
recommended stop in your
journey through the land of
Harris tweed. Mon–Sat
only. **£**

# CENTRAL SCOTLAND AND FIFE

**Andrew Fairlie at
Gleneagles**
Gleneagles Hotel, Auchterarder
Tel: (01764) 694267
Two-Michelin-starred
restaurant set in an
exclusive resort hotel.
Andrew Fairlie is Scottish
Chef of the Year, and this is
definitely one of Scotland's
best restaurants. Superb
French food confidently
served in opulent
surroundings. Dinner only,
but never on a Sunday.
**£££+**

**The Cellar**
24 East Green, Anstruther
Tel: (01333) 310378
Just off the harbour,

a walled courtyard leads to
an atmospheric restaurant
serving splendid seafood.
Excellent wine list – French
and New World bins –
complements the food.
Booking essential. **£££**

**Dean's at Let's Eat**
77 Kinnoull Street, Perth
Tel: (01738) 643377
Exceptional, award-winning
bistro-style restaurant in
city centre that has a
pleasant, relaxed
atmosphere. **££–£££**

**Kind Kyttock's Kitchen**
Cross Wynd, Falkland
Tel: (01337) 857477
Just opposite the palace,
this small tearoom serves

home-cured ham, free-
range eggs, freshly baked
bread and scones. **£**

**Monachyle Mhor**
Balquhidder
Tel: (01877) 384 622
A gourmet's delight and
five-star hidden gem. Lunch
and dinner served in the
hotel's conservatory. **£££+**

**Peat Inn**
Peat Inn by Cupar, Fife
Tel: (01334) 840206
An 18th-century village inn
with an international
reputation, only 6 miles (10
km) from St Andrews. A
limited menu lists the very
best of Scottish produce
cooked imaginatively and

served stylishly in
beautifully furnished dining
rooms. Superb wine list
includes many half-bottles.
Booking essential. **£££+**

**Redrooms/Perth Theatre**
High Street, Perth
Tel: (01738) 472709
A lively place for lunch and
pre-theatre dinner. Good
coffee bar. **£**

---

**PRICE CATEGORIES**

Average cost of a three-
course evening meal per
person, excluding wine:
**£** = below £15
**££** = £15–25
**£££** = above £25

# THE EAST COAST

**Agacan**
113 Perth Road, Dundee
Tel: (01382) 644227
Lively, popular Turkish restaurant. Enjoy the mezze, kebabs and stuffed pittas. Takeaways an option. Closed lunchtimes. **£**

**Ashvale Fish Restaurant**
44–48 Great Western Road
Aberdeen
Tel: (01224) 596981
A chance to visit an award-winning sit-down "chippie" serving not only great fish and chips but other fresh local dishes. **££**

**But'n'Ben**
Auchmithie, near Arbroath
Tel: (01241) 877223
Lunch, high tea and dinner are served in a traditional cottage with quarry tile floors and open fires in this out-of-the-way coastal village. The produce is local, cooking is traditional, and you can sample the famous Arbroath Smokie (fish). **££**

**Cafe Society**
9 Queen's Road, Aberdeen
Tel: (01224) 208 494
After more than 15 years dishing out contemporary/fusion cuisine to the locals, this busy restaurant continues to appeal with tasty salads, staple special burgers and a spirited staff. **£–££**

**Cornerstone Coffee House**
118 Nethergate, Dundee.
Tel: (01382) 202121
Plain cooking with no pretensions. Clean, pleasant café where a good, inexpensive meal can be enjoyed. Mon–Sat, 9am–4pm. **£**

**Foyer Restaurant & Gallery**
Trinity Church, 82a Crown Street
Aberdeen
Tel: (01224) 582277
Enjoy good contemporary British cuisine in an architecturally altered church which also houses an art gallery and is part of an organised charity for young homeless and disadvantaged people. Child-friendly. Closed Sun and Mon. **£–££**

**Green Inn**
9 Victoria Road, Ballater
Tel: (013397) 55701
In a village well served with excellent, yet expensive, restaurants, this inn on the village green serves imaginative tasty dishes prepared with local produce. The inn has three bedrooms. **£££**

**Old Monastery**
Drybridge, Buckie
Tel: (01542) 832660
A setting fit for the gods, with the bar in the cloisters and the restaurant in the chapel, with original pitch pine ceiling and monk stencils. Scottish/French cuisine is accompanied by extensive wine list. **£££**

**Rama Thai**
32 Dock Street, Dundee
Tel: (01382) 223 366
The food isn't the first thing associated with the City of Discovery, but judging by the packed tables feasting on steamed king prawns and excellent green curry, this is where to spice up your Dundee dining. Imaginative menu. **£–££**

**Rocpool Reserve**
Culduthel Road, Inverness
Tel: (01463) 240 089
Located in the centre of Inverness, this elegant boutique hotel has a fine restaurant. The menu is seasonal Italian. Excellent wine list. **£££**

**The Seafood Restaurant**
Bruce Embankment, St Andrews
Tel: (01334) 479 475
A classy destination beside the sea that offers evening diners succulent plates of lobster, prawns, halibut and scallops while you relax and gaze out to sea. **£££**

**Silver Darling**
Pocra Quay
North Pier, Aberdeen
Tel: (01224) 576229
The name derives from the local term for herring. Wonderful ambience, just across from the fleet landing its catch. Soon it will be on your table, often sumptuously cooked in Provençal style. **£££+**

**Twin City Café**
4 City Square, Dundee
Tel: (01382) 223 662
Get your latte and cappuccino here. Wide-ranging daytime menu with a Middle Eastern influence. Friendly service. **£**

**BELOW:** a welcoming bowl of Scotch broth.

# NORTHERN HIGHLANDS

**Achin's Bookshop**
Inverkirkaig, Lochinver
Tel: (01571) 844262
Simple, excellent home-cooking in Scotland's

immaculate and well-stocked, most remote northerly bookshop. Hearty soups and toasties. Open Easter–Oct. Quality craft goods also on sale. **£**

**Badachro Inn**
by Gairloch
Tel: (01445) 741255
Popular pub on a sheltered bay with a garden by the sea. Wonderful prawns and a variety of other seafood dishes. **££**

**Bayview Hotel**
Russell Street, Lybster
Tel: (01593) 721346
A cosy bar and dining room popular with locals. Nearly 100 malt whiskies. Very friendly. **£**

**Café 1**
75 Castle Street, Inverness
Tel: (01463) 226200
Popular bistro serving ultra-fresh contemporary Scottish dishes. Good wines. Closed Sunday. **££**

**The Cross**
Tweed Mill Brae, Kingussie
Tel: (01540) 661166
Superb Scottish cuisine served in an old tweed mill converted into a delightful eating space. Superb wine list – clarets, half-bottles, dessert wines. Great cheeseboard. Also good accommodation in nine bedrooms. **£££**

**Culloden House Hotel**
Culloden, nr Inverness

Tel: (01463) 700461
Dine in the exquisite Adam Room on local produce prepared French-style in this architectural gem 3 miles (5 kms) south of Inverness. **£££**

**Dower House**
Muir of Ord
Tel: (01463) 870090
18th-century cottage with an ornate dining room. Modern style fusion cusine. five bedrooms. **£££**

**Dunain Park Hotel**
Fort William Road nr. Inverness
Tel: (01463) 230512
Scots-French cuisine in a Georgian country house set in lovely gardens. Excellent wines and malt list. Just outside Inverness on road to Loch Ness. **£££**

**Glen Mhor Hotel**
9–12 Ness Bank, Inverness
Tel: (01463) 234308
Pleasant Scottish Riverview Restaurant serves imaginatively cooked local produce – salmon, beef, game. Nico's Bistro at the rear serves similar but less expensive food. **££**

**Kishorn Seafood and Snack Bar**
Kishorn, Strathcarron
Tel: (01520) 733240
An immaculate roadside snack shack which serves the freshest of shellfish prepared while you wait. Eat in or takeaway. Open Easter–Oct. **£**

**Kylesku Hotel**
Kylesku
Tel: (01971) 502231
Beautifully situated small restaurant with own smokery serves delicious moderately priced meals. The hotel also has nine rooms. Closed Oct–Mar. **££**

**Seafood Restaurant**
Tarbet, Scourie
Tel: (01971) 502251
As the name suggests, seafood including hot smoked mackerel dominates the menu, using produce caught from the restaurant's own boat in Loch Laxford. Open Easter–Aug. **££**

**Tea Store**
Argyll Street, Ullapool
Tel: (01845) 612 122
This is the place for your breakfast with the locals. **£**

**Tigh-an-Eilean**
Shieldaig
Tel: (01520) 755251
Excellent, traditional country cooking in a small restaurant in a small hotel on the shores of beautiful Loch Carron. **££–£££**

# ORKNEY

**Creel Restaurant**
St Margaret's Hope
South Ronaldsay
Tel: (01856) 831311
Historic seafront house offering innovative modern cooking with strong Orcadian influence and fresh ingredients including prime Orkney beef, and seaweed-fed lamb from North Ronaldsay. **£££**

**Foveran Hotel**
St Ola, Kirkwall
Tel: (01856) 872389
Scandinavian-style building offering outstanding seafood and wide variety of other dishes. Advance booking essential. eight en suite bedrooms. **£££**

**Hamnavoe Restaurant**
35 Graham Place, Stromness
Tel: (01856) 850606
Small family-run restaurant using fresh ingredients. Seafood is the speciality and there are vegetarian options, too. Evenings only. **££**

**Kirkwall Hotel**
Harbour Street, Kirkwall
Tel: (01856) 872232
A prime example of Scottish cuisine at its best. Homemade beef pie topped with flaky pastry and Orkney fudge cheesecake laced with whisky are just a few dishes on offer. **££**

**The Watersound Restaurant**
The Sands Hotel, Burray
Tel: (01856) 731298
Full a la carte menu using local produce. The hotel was originally built as a fish store in 1860. **££**

# SHETLAND

**Braewick Café**
Eshaness, North Mainland
Tel: (01806) 503345
From this clifftop location enjoy simple, local fare in a child-friendly environment. **£**

**Burrastow House**
Walls
Tel: (01595) 809307
The 18th-century Burrastow Guest House has excellent home-cooking, with, as you would expect, an abundance of fish and fine organic, local lamb. Menus change daily. Booking required for non-residents. **£££**

**Busta House Hotel**
Busta
Tel: (01806) 522506
Restaurant specialises in Shetland lamb and fish dishes. Good choice of vegetarian dishes and fine selection of malts. Open every day. Bar meals also available. **£££**

**Peerie Shop Café**
Esplanade, Lerwick
Tel: (01595) 692816
Freshly made soups, toasties, smoothies, scones and muffins, and a whole range of lattes are served up in a stylish atmosphere. **£**

**Queen's Hotel**
24 Commercial Street, Lerwick
Tel: (01595) 692826
The seafood is modestly priced and tasty, and if you're lucky, diners may spot a whale out of the window. **££**

**Wind Dog Café**
Gutcher, Yell
Tel: (01957) 744321
Opposite the post office. In the summer open every night for evening meals and Sunday lunch. Internet access. Bookings preferred. **££**

**BELOW:** lobster salad at the Busta House Hotel.

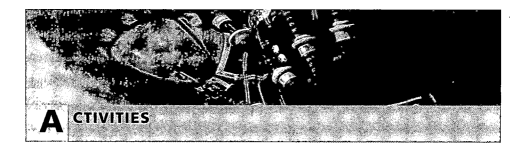

# ACTIVITIES

# THE ARTS, FESTIVALS, NIGHTLIFE, SHOPPING AND SPECTATOR SPORTS

## THE ARTS

### Museums, Galleries and Places of Interest

From its Neolithic standing stones to the clan system and a string of philosophers, inventors and architects at the forefront of the 17th-and 18th-century Enlightenment. Scotland's innumerable museums and galleries offer the visitor a fascinating insight to its history and culture.

### Edinburgh

**The National Gallery and Royal Scottish Academy**
The Mound
www.nationalgalleries.org
The impressive **National Gallery** is one of five National Galleries of Scotland and Edinburgh's second most visited attraction. Extensively refurbished in recent years, within its impressive stone walls at the foot of the Mound visitors will find Scotland's greatest collection of fine art, spanning from the early Renaissance to the 19th century. Among the masterpieces are works by Rembrandt, Raphael and Monet, and *The Skating Minister* painted by the Scottish artist Raeburn.

Reopened in 2003, the **Royal Scottish Academy** building is also to be found here with various temporary exhibitions showcased over two floors. The new **Weston Link** beneath the two galleries exhibits works by Monet and includes a café and a 200-seat lecture theatre.

**The Scottish National Portrait Gallery**
1 Queen Street
The first such purpose-built gallery in the world, its portraits offer a visual history of those who have shaped the nation, including royals, poets, philosophers and heroes.

**The Scottish National Gallery of Modern Art and the Dean Gallery**
75 Belford Road
These huge buildings sit in extensive grounds about 15 minutes' walk west of Princes Street. The Modern Art Gallery exhibits both contemporary works and those from the 19th century, while Dada and Surrealist art sits alongside works by Paolozzi in the Dean.

All of the above are free and open daily 10am–5pm. Tel: (0131) 624 6200. See also www.natgalscot.ac.uk
**The Fruitmarket Gallery**
45 Market Street
Tel: (0131) 225 2383
www.fruitmarket.co.uk
Open Mon–Sat 11am–6pm,
Sun 12–5pm
A not-for-profit gallery, offering visitors inspirational contemporary art.
**National Museums Scotland**
Chambers Street
Tel: (0131) 247 4422
www.nms.ac.uk
Open daily 10am–5pm, free.
From steam engines and mummies of ancient Egypt to the history of Scotland's sporting greats and the influence of the Picts, Romans and Vikings, the **National Museum** and adjoining **Royal Museum** house thousands of fascinating exhibits, including natural history specimens.
**National War Museum**
Edinburgh Castle
Tel: (0131) 247 4413
www.nms.ac.uk
Open Apr–Oct daily 9.45am–5.45pm, until 4.45pm Nov–March; admission charge.
**National Museum of Flight**
East Fortune Airfield, East Lothian
Tel: (01620) 897240
Open Apr–Oct daily 10am–5pm, March, weekends only; admission charge.

**BELOW:** the sandstone, cylindrical exterior of the Museum of Scotland.

## The Borders

**Paxton House,**
by Berwick-upon-Tweed
Tel: (01289) 386291
www.paxtonhouse.co.uk
Open Apr–Oct daily 11am–5pm;
admission charge.
Housed within one of the UK's finest
examples of an 18th-century
Palladian country house, Paxton
House contains paintings from
1760–1840, including works by
Scottish artists Raeburn and Wilkie.

## Glasgow

Entry to all Glasgow museums is free.
**Kelvingrove Art Gallery and Museum**
Argyle Street
Tel: (0141) 287 2699
www.glasgowmuseums.com
Open daily 9am–5pm
Spread across 13 museums, the city
of Glasgow owns one of the richest
collections in Europe. Reopened in
2006 following a three-year, £28
million refurbishment, Kelvingrove is
arguably the city's masterpiece, with
its sprawling space containing over
8,000 exhibits, including a WWII
Spitfire plane hanging from its ceiling
and paintings by Monet and Van Gogh.
**Museum of Transport**
Bunhouse Road
Tel: (0141) 287 2720
www.glasgowmuseums.com
Open daily Mon–Thur and Sat
10am–5pm, Fri and Sun 11am–5pm
A wonderful world of old Glasgow
tramcars, the world's oldest pedal
cycle, steam locomotives and famous
Scottish-builts cars such as Argyll,
and Johnson and Albion.
**The Burrell Collection**
Pollokshaws Road
Tel: (0141) 287 2550
www.glasgowmuseums.com
Open daily Mon–Thur and Sat
10am–5pm, Fri and Sun 11am–5pm.
Over 9,000 works of art from around
the world.
**National Museum of Rural Life**
East Kilbride
Tel: (0131) 247 4377
www.nms.ac.uk
Open daily 10am–5pm; admission
charge.

## Ayrshire

**Burns National Heritage Park**
Murdoch's Lone, Alloway
Tel: (01292) 443 700
www.burnsheritagepark.com
Open daily; admission charge
Discover the area that inspired
Scotland's most famous poet.

## Aberdeen

**Duff House**
by Banff
Tel: (01261) 818181

www.duffhouse.org.uk
Open Apr–Oct daily 11am–5pm,
Nov–Mar Thur–Sun 11am–4pm;
admission charge
Designed by William Adam in 1735,
this baroque mansion house
contains the Dunimarle Library (open
by appointment only), a rare
collection of over 4,000 volumes and
works by Boucher and El Greco.

## Inverness

**Inverness Museum and Art Gallery**
Castle Wynd
Tel: (01463) 237114
www.invernessmuseum.com
Open Mon–Sat 9am–5pm
Reopened in 2006 following a multi-
million pound refurbishment, here's
where to discover the history of the
Highlands, including the impact of
the infamous Clearances.

## Shetland Islands

**Shetland Museum and Archive**
Hays Dock, Lerwick
Tel: 01595 695057.
www.shetland-museum.org.uk
Following a multi-million pound refit,
the new Shetland Museum and
Archive has recently opened.

## Outer Hebrides

**Taigh Chearsabhagh Museum and
Arts Centre**
Lock Maddy, Isle-of-North-Uist
www.taigh-chearsabhagh.org
Open Mon–Sat 10am–5pm
Museum and gallery with changing
displays of local life and history.

## Inner Hebrides

**The Old Byre Heritage Centre**
Dervaig, Isle of Mull
Tel: (01688) 400229
www.old-byre.co.uk
Open Apr–Oct Wed–Sun
10.30am–6.30pm
This small museum offers an
excellent insight into the history and
wildlife of Mull and Iona.

### Music

Although hardly a swinging country –
other than when dancing the
Highland Fling – Scotland has its fair
share of after-dark activities.
    The Royal Scottish National
Orchestra and the Scottish Chamber
Orchestra are excellent and give
regular concerts in both Glasgow and
Edinburgh, as well as travelling to
other parts of the country. The
Scottish Opera and Scottish Ballet
operate similar schedules.
    Folk music abounds, with clubs in
every town. Information is available
locally and through newspaper
advertisements.

## Ceilidhs

In the Highlands and Islands,
especially in isolated villages, the
inhabitants hold occasional ceilidhs,
which might be defined as informal
social gatherings with folk music and
formation dancing. There is always
an experienced caller to ensure that
all dancers keep in step during the
energetic reels. A useful resource for
the latest ceilidhs and folk music
locations can be found at
www.footstompin.com; tel: (0131) 441
3135. Details of events can often be
obtained from local tourist boards.
Arguably, Hootenanny pub in
Inverness is one of the most lively
locations to experience a ceilidh.
    Some regular and more
commercial ceilidhs, which are
tailored for tourists (see also www.hi-
arts.co.uk), are:

## Edinburgh

**King James Thistle Hotel**
Leith Street
Tel: (0131) 556 0111
www.thistlehotels.com
Dinner and show, Apr–Oct. Nightly at
7pm.
**Prestonfield House**
Priestfield Road
Tel: (0131) 662 2300
"Taste of Scotland" show, including
meal.
Mid-Apr–Oct, Sun–Fri at 7pm.

## Inverness

**Hootenanny**
64 Church St
Tel (01463) 233 651
www.hootenanny.co.uk
The place for hearing traditional
music. Ceilidhs most nights,
June–mid-Sept, Mon–Thur.

## Lerags/Oban

**The Barn**
Cologins, Lerags (3 miles/5 km)
south of Oban
Tel: (01631) 564501.
Folk band every Sun afternoon.
**MacTavish's Kitchens**
George Street, Oban
Tel: (01631) 563064
Mid-May–Sept, daily 8–10pm.

## Glasgow

**The Riverside**
Fox Street (off Clyde Street)
Tel: (0141) 248 3144
Every Friday and Saturday from 8pm.
The place that started the ceilidh
revival in Glasgow. Dance classes
Monday evenings.

## Skye

**Flodigarry Country House Hotel**
Staffin, Skye
Tel: (01470) 552203

Most Saturdays throughout the summer until 11.30pm (officially – in reality often later).

## Theatre

Theatre flourishes, with audiences responding to innovation. Glasgow's Citizens Theatre and Edinburgh's Traverse Theatre are both internationally renowned for mounting new plays and experimental works. Aberdeen, Dundee, Perth and Inverness are all home to first-class repertory theatres, while during the summer months the Pitlochry Festival Theatre puts on professional performances.

Commercial theatre, too, is still alive and kicking in the major cities. Its main venues are the Lyceum and Festival Theatre in Edinburgh and the King's in Glasgow.

### Aberdeen

**Aberdeen Arts Centre**
33 King Street
Tel: (01224) 635208

### Dundee

**Dundee Rep Theatre**
Tay Square
Tel: (01382) 223530

### Edinburgh

**Edinburgh Playhouse**
18–22 Greenside Place
Tel: (0131) 557 2692
**Festival Theatre**
13–29 Nicholson Street
Tel: (0131) 529 6000

**King's Theatre**
2 Leven Street
Tel: (0131) 529 6000
**Royal Lyceum**
30B Grindlay Street
Tel: (0131) 248 4848
**Theatre Workshop**
34 Hamilton Place
Tel: (0131) 226 5425
**Traverse Theatre**
Cambridge Street
Tel: (0131) 228 1404

### Glasgow

**Centre for Contemporary Arts**
350 Sauchiehall Street
Tel: (0141) 352 4900
**Citizens Theatre**
119 Gorbals Street
Tel: (0141) 429 0022
**The King's Glasgow**
297 Bath Street
Tel: (0141) 287 7000
**Tron Theatre**
63 Trongate
Tel: (0141) 552 4267
**Tramway Theatre**
25 Albert Drive
Tel: (0141) 422 2023

### Inverness

**Eden Court Theatre**
Bishops Road
www.eden-court.co.uk
This flagship theatre project is expected to reopen after major refurbishment in 2008.

### Mull

**Oruimfin**
Tel: (01688) 302 673

Mull Theatre is one of Scotland's foremost touring theatre companies. Following the closure of its "Little Theatre" in Dervaig, a new production centre is being built outside Tobermory.

### Perth

**Perth Theatre**
185 High Street
Tel: (01738) 621031

### Pitlochry

**Pitlochry Festival Theatre**
Tel: (01796) 484626

### Stirling

**MacRobert Arts Centre**
University of Stirling
Tel: (01786) 461081

## Arts Festivals

### Edinburgh

During the annual Edinburgh International Festival in August – and the concurrent Fringe, Jazz, Film and Book festivals – there is a vast choice of quality cultural events in the city every night, ranging from opera and experimental theatre to soon-to-be-famous comedy talents *(see also page 157)*.
**Edinburgh International Festival**, tel: (0131) 473 2000; www.eif.co.uk
**Edinburgh Fringe Festival**, tel: (0131) 226 0026; www.edfringe.com
**Military Tattoo**, tel: (08707) 555 118; www.edintattoo.co.uk
**Edinburgh International Film Festival**, tel: (0131) 228 4051; www.edfilmfest.org.uk
**Edinburgh International Jazz Festival**,

**BELOW:** an impromptu street performance at the Edinburgh Festival Fringe.

## Festival Tips

- **Programmes** can be obtained from the festival offices, the tourist information office or city bookshops.
- **For online information** about all of Edinburgh's festivals visit www.edinburghfestivals.co.uk.
- **Advance bookings** are taken for International Festival performances from April and for Military Tattoo performances from December the previous year. Demand for seats at the latter, particularly, is very high, and early booking is recommended. For Fringe events, it is often only necessary to book in advance for big-name or short-duration shows. Bookings are taken from around mid-June.
- **The Hub** on Castlehill is open year-round. You can book here for all the main festivals.
- **The Guide** magazine is published every day during the summer festivals, with full up-to-date listings; look also in the Scottish newspapers and *The List* magazine for reviews.
- **To avoid queues** at the venue and telephone booking fees, visit one of the Fringe sales points at the Festival Fringe office or The Hub.
- **Spontaneous festival-goers** should head for one of the top Fringe venues, such as the Pleasance (60 The Pleasance), Assembly Rooms (54 George Street) or Gilded Balloon at Teviot Row House in Bristo Square.

tel: (0131) 467 5200;
www.jazzmusic.co.uk
**Edinburgh International Book Festival,** tel: (0131) 228 5444;
www.edbookfest.co.uk.
**Childrens International Theatre Festival,** tel: (0131) 225 8050;
www.imaginate.org.uk

### Glasgow

**Celtic Connections,** 2–3 weeks in January. International Celtic music festival. Tel: (0141) 353 8000;
www.celticconnections.com
**Glasgow International Jazz Festival,** July. Tel: (0141) 552 3552;
www.jazzfest.co.uk
**World Pipe Band Championships,** August. Tel: (0141) 221 5414;
www.rspba.org.

### Ayr and Ayrshire

**Burns an' a' that!** Festival for two weeks at end of May and beginning of

June in celebration of Robert Burns. Held mainly in Ayr but also throughout Ayrshire. Poetry, theatre and music. Tel: (01292) 678100; www.ayrshire-arran.com and www.visitscotland.com

### Dumfries

**Dumfries & Galloway Festival of Arts,** 10 days end of May to beginning of June. Tel: (01387) 260447;
www.dgartsfestival.org.uk

### Perth

**Perth Arts Festival,** 10 days end of Mary to beginning of June.
Tel: (01738) 475295;
www.perthfestival.co.uk

## Other Festivals

### Edinburgh

**International Science Festival**
(Two weeks in April)
Tel: (0131) 220 1882
www.sciencefestival.co.uk
**Edinburgh Hogmanay**
(29 Dec – 1 Jan).
www.edinburghshogmanay.org. A festival to see out the old and to bring in the New Year. Frenetic celebrations culminate in the largest New Year's Eve (Hogmanay) street party in Europe (great fireworks).

## Calendar of Events

In addition to the festivals above, the following cultural and sports events are annually staged in Scotland. For a small country, Scotland's villages, towns and cities host a staggering number events. Since 2003, over 162 international events have collectively generated over £300m for the national economy. From the Shetland Island Games to the Open Golf Championships in St Andrews and Edinburgh's international cultural festivals, events are both hugely popular and big business for the country.

However, while contemporary blockbusters such as Edinburgh and Glasgow's Hogmanay (New Year's Eve) parties, the musical extravaganza "T in the Park" (Kinross) and Edinburgh's cultural festivals annually attract tens of thousands of revellers, Scots also continue to hold dear national and local celebrations of historical dates and figures. The following offers a snapshot of the diversity and richness of the nation's annual events calendar.

### January

**Burns Night**
Haggis, neeps and tatties and an "address tae the haggis" is

accompanied to the skirl of bagpipes as families and dedicated Burns societies settle down across the land and indeed across the world to toast the birth of Rabbie Burns, the nation's most famous poet, on 25 January 1759; www.rabbie-burns.com/www.worldburnsclub.com
**Up-Helly-Aa**
On the last Tuesday of January, scores of Shetland Islanders dressed in Viking costume lead an atmospheric torchlit procession through the streets of Lerwick followed by the burning of a Viking longship.

### February

**Fort William Mountain Film Festival**
From footage of sea-kayaking adventures in the Outer Hebrides to climbing in Dumbarton, this action-packed festival attracts scores of outdoor enthusiasts and film buffs alike. Tel: (01397) 700707;
www.mountainfilmfestival.co.uk

### March

Spring into Easter at events organised by Scotland's five winter ski resorts; www.ski-scotland.com

### April

**The Glasgow Art Fair.** Scotland's National Art Fair. See also www.glasgowartfair.com
Malt lovers should head for the Highlands for the **Spirit of Speyside Whisky Festival;** www.spiritofspeyside.com
Alternatively, head to the Northern Isles for the **Shetland Folk Festival;**
www.shetlandfolkfestival.com

### May

Head for Loch Fyne as 200 yachts battle for supremacy in the **Bell Lawrie Scottish Series,** and for nightly festivities in the picturesque fishing port of Tarbert; www.clyde.org

### June

**St Magnus Festival,** Orkney. A spectacular, week-long celebration of the arts. Tel: (01856) 871445;
www.stmagnusfestival.com

### July

**The Open** (Golf) Championship returns to Turnberry in 2009 and St Andrews in 2010.
**The Wickerman Festival,** Dumfries and Galloway. This is one of Scotland's hottest music festivals. Tel: (01738) 450442;
www.thewickermanfestival.co.uk
**Hebridean Celtic Festival,** Outer Hebrides. Tel: (01851) 621234;
www.hebceltfest.com
**'T in the Park,** Kinross, Fife. Over 100 bands and thousands of pop

## VAT Refunds

Visitors to Scotland from non-EU countries can obtain a refund of value-added tax (currently 17.5 percent), which is added to most purchases. Many large stores will deduct the VAT from purchases at time of sale if the goods are being shipped abroad directly from the store. In other cases, obtain a receipt which can be stamped by Customs officers who will inspect the goods at ports or airports of exit; the receipt can then be sent to the store, which will mail a VAT refund cheque.

music fans converge outside Kinross for two days of non-stop partying; www.tinthepark.com

### August

**Piping Live!**, Glasgow. You'll hear many a skirl of the pipes at this extravaganza. Tel: (0845 241 4400; www.pipingfestival.co.uk
Equestrian-lovers will enjoy the spectacular Perthshire setting of the **Blair Castle International Horse Trials**. www.blairhorsetrials.co.uk .

### September

**Fort William Mountain Bike World Cup**. Almost 20,000 spectators converge on Lochaber to watch the thrills and spills of the world's best in action; www.fortwilliamworldcup.com
Alternatively, join members of the Royal Family for bagpipes, caber-tossing and Highland dancing at the renowned Braemar Highland Gathering; www.braemargathering.org

### October

First held in 1892, the **Am Mòd Nàiseanta Rioghail** (Royal National Mod) is Scotland's main festival of the Gaelic language, arts and culture. This competition-based festival is held annually in October and always at a different Scottish location. Tel: (01463) 709705; www.the-mod.co.uk
Alternatively, try to spot Nessie as you run all 26.2 miles of the annual **Loch Ness Marathon**; www.lochnessmarathon.com
However, if it's wet 'n' wild action you are after, then head for the Inner Hebridean Isle of Tiree to watch some of the world's best windsurfers defy gravity at the **Tiree Wave Classic**. Visit www.tireewaveclassic.com
Of course, there's also always the chance to understand why the population of Mull trebles for four days during the acclaimed **Tour of Mull Rally**; www.2300club.org

### November

**St Andrews Day**. On 30 November, Scots celebrate their patron saint.

### December

Join thousands of festive revellers to welcome in the **New Year** in Glasgow's George Square or Edinburgh's Princes Street. Note: it's strongly advised to purchase tickets in advance. www.glasgowshogmanay.org.uk and www.edinburghshogmanay.org

## Listings Magazines

### Edinburgh

*The List* is a listings magazine covering Edinburgh and Glasgow. It is published fortnightly and has a website at www.list.co.uk. For a guide to gigs in the city try the *Gig Guide* (www.gigguide.co.uk).

### Glasgow

*Itchy,* the Glasgow entertainment guide, is available at most bookshops in the city.

## NIGHTLIFE

### Clubs, Pubs and Bars

Pubs and clubs are very popular with the locals everywhere in Scotland and are especially crowded around the end of the working day and at weekends. The scene is lively and while the drinking man's bar still exists, most pubs now have a relaxed and friendly atmosphere. Thanks to changes in Scottish licensing laws, even children are welcome in many pubs.
In **Edinburgh**, the places to go are Cowgate and Grassmarket in the Old Town, and Broughton Street and George Street in the New Town. Most city-centre bars stay open until 1am, some even until 3am.
**Glasgow** is a vibrant and exciting city. It is said to have the largest population of gays and lesbians in the UK outside of London, and the gay nightlife scene is particularly active. The main clubs are around the main shopping area of Buchanan and Argyle Street, with some in Sauchiehall Street.

### Casinos

Both Edinburgh and Glasgow provide opportunities for you to gamble away your money. The law requires you become a member of a casino about 24 hours before you play. Membership is free. Men are expected to wear casual but smart dress.

### Edinburgh

**Stanley Berkeley Casino Club**
2 Rutland Place
Tel: (0131) 228 4446
**Gala Maybury Casino**
5 South Maybury
Tel: (0131) 338 4444
**Stanley Edinburgh Leisure**
56 York Place
Tel: (0131) 624 2121
**Cascades Casino**
Ocean Terminal, Leith
Tel: (0131) 553 7505

### Glasgow

**Gala Chevalier Casino**
95 Hope Street
Tel: (0141) 226 3856
**Gala Casino**
528 Sauchiehall Street
Tel: (0141) 332 8171
**Gala Riverboat Casin**
61 Broomielaw
Tel: (0141) 226 6000

## SHOPPING

### City Shopping

**Glasgow** is the UK's second shopping city (after London) in terms of retail space. With a plethora of attractive, modern shopping centres *(see page 178)* and a wide choice of designer boutiques, the city is ideal for the compulsive shopper.
In **Edinburgh**, the length of the Royal Mile is dotted with shops selling everything associated with Scotland, including Highland dress and tartan, Scottish heraldry, Celtic design jewellery, bagpipes, Scottish woollens, whisky and haggis. For shopping with a more international flavour, Princes Street is the main thoroughfare, concentrating on fashion chains, bookshops and several department stores, including the classy, independently-owned Jenners.

### Rural Luxury

However, the equally upmarket Harvey Nichols store, located on the fashionable Mulberry Walk off St Andrew Square is now giving Jenners a run for its money. While Glasgow and Edinburgh dominate in terms of retail space, Inverness, Dundee and Aberdeen all have major retail developments, too.
If large mall shopping isn't your idea of holiday fun, there are three distinct high-class shopping experiences to be found north of Perth. House of Bruar, located just off the A9 on the northern fringes of Blair Atholl, is where fine tweeds and

country outfitters mingle with delectable delights in the sprawling delicatessen and bustling café.

Forty miles (64 km) further north, in the new Macdonald Hotels Highland Resort, a line of designer boutiques that wouldn't look out of place in fashionable Knightsbridge is also to be found while Falls of Shin, beyond Lairg, offers yet more luxury browsing on product ranges from Harrods.
**House of Bruar**: 7 days, all year. Tel: (01796) 483236; www.houseofbruar.com
**Fall of Shin** (only Harrods outlet in Scotland): 7 days, all year. Tel: (01549) 402231; www.fallsofshin.co.uk
**Macdonald Aviemore Highland Resort**: "The Brands are Gathering", international luxury brands in the Highlands, 7 days. Tel: (0870) 124 4124.

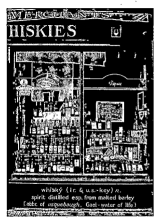

**ABOVE:** whiskies galore for sale.

However, if you'd rather browse for Scottish quality products online and save the hassle of lugging presents home, arguably the pick of the bunch is to be found at "Papa Stour" (www.papastour.com), where you can find everything from cowhide sporrans to real antlers from the Highlands.

### Opening Hours

Most shops stay open 9am–5.30pm, with some shops in the larger cities opening until late on Thursday evenings. In the smaller towns, there is often an early closing day, though few towns are without a "wee shoppie" which stays open at all hours and can provide food, drink and assorted necessities. Supermarkets are usually open to at least 8pm, later on Thursday and Friday. In bigger towns and cities you'll find shops now stay open on Sundays and late at night.

### What to Buy

There is a wide range of "typical" Scottish products, from tartan and heather-embellished souvenirs to cashmere and Highland crafts.

### Textiles and Knitwear

Though the industry is in decline, woollens production is still very much in evidence in the Borders region, where you can tour a number of mills and make reduced price purchases at the factory shops, including **Lochcarron of Scotland**, Huddersfield Street, Galashiels. Similarly, there is a Woollen Mill Trail in Clackmannanshire, near Stirling, where a quarter of Scottish woollens were once produced.

Look out for cashmere and Harris tweeds as well as lamb's wool. Shetland knitwear, including Fair Isle jumpers, is also justly renowned. Sadly, the art of the Harris tweed is a dying tradition.

### Glassware

There are a number of high-quality glass and crystal producers in Scotland, including Caithness Glass, Selkirk Glass, Edinburgh Crystal and Stuart Crystal. There's also Caithness Glass visitor centre, where you can buy beautiful paperweights.

### Ceramics and Crafts

There are many regional potteries producing distinctive, high-quality lines, such as Highland Stoneware. Look out for local outlets, especially in the Highlands and Islands.

### Celtic-Style Jewellery

Contemporary silver or gold jewellery with Celtic-influenced designs is very popular and widely available, with varying quality. Ortak from Orkney is particularly popular. www.ortak.co.uk.

### Scotch Whisky

Malt whisky is a major Scottish export. Many of the whiskies you see will be Moray whiskies, produced in the Speyside region, where over half the country's distilleries are located. There you can go on a "malt whisky trail" of over seven distilleries and their on-site shops, including the famous Glenfiddich distillery in Dufftown. Whiskies from the Northern Highlands and Islay whiskies from the west coast island are also renowned. Islay has eight distilleries.

### Speciality Foods

Delicatessens abound to tempt you with haggis (if you don't read the list of ingredients), smoked salmon and other smoked produce, cheeses, marmalade, porridge and oatcakes, butter shortbread and a number of other Scottish-made delectables – see the feature on *pages 121–3*. If you are self-catering, then fresh fish, often very fresh, can be an excellent buy. In the northwest, look out for fresh, hot smoked salmon.

### Outdoor Equipment

With a burgeoning outdoor adventure sports market, it's little wonder that the country boasts several excellent specialist adventure sports stockists. TISO (www.tiso.com) and Nevisport (www.nevisport.co.uk) both stock a wide range of outdoor equipment. However, far from those heading into Scotland's snowy backcountry, Mountain Spirit in Aviemore (tel: (01479) 811 788; www.mountainspirit.co.uk) is the place to buy and hire ski-touring, Nordic, telemark and mountaineering equipment.

## SPORTS

### Participant Sports

Thanks to the Land Reform (Scotland) Act 2003, visitors to Scotland can enjoy some of the most enlightened access laws in Europe. Add the fact that the nation boasts natural terrain of thousands of miles of rugged coastline, remote beaches, deep glens, rushing rivers and the highest mountains (Munros) in the UK, and it's easy to understand why Scotland is rapidly becoming one of the best destinations in Europe to enjoy a myriad of outdoor sports. Whatever the weather, fishing, mountain-biking, walking, horse-riding, sailing and surfing are just some of the popular activities to be enjoyed in its great outdoors.

Wildlife enthusiasts, too, flock to these shores *(see Birdwatching, page 352)* to enjoy wild sea and landscapes teeming with rare species. Indeed, within the boundaries of the Cairngorms National Park (www.cairngorms.co.uk) alone, over 25 percent of the UK's most threatened bird, animal and

### Hot Air Ballooning

Hot air balloon flights over Edinburgh, Lothians, Borders and Fife. For more information contact: **Alba Ballooning**, 12 Gladstone Terrace, tel: 667 4251, www.albaballooning.co.uk.

plant species can be found. Hikers and watersport enthusiasts also enjoy the forests, lochs and mountains of the Loch Lomond and Trossachs National Park.

VisitScotland's website (www.visitscotland.com) provides a host of information about available activities across the country, key destinations and reputable tour operators.

Alternatively, you can call its hotline on tel: (0845) 225 5121 (freephone +44 (0)1506 832222 from the rest of the world), or request a specific brochure about golf, sailing, fishing, walking or cycling from its head office. Write to: VisitScotland, Ocean Point, 94 Ocean Drive, Edinburgh EH6 6JH.

## Golf

Scotland is the home of golf, and, some would claim, the nation's national sport.

There are hundreds of courses, most of them open to the public. Even the most famous courses, such as St Andrews, Carnoustie and Turnberry, are public "links" courses, and anyone prepared to pay the appropriate fee and who can produce a handicap certificate (usually about 20 for men, 30 for ladies) is entitled to play on them.

It is advisable to book ahead at the "name" courses. At **St Andrews** half of all start times on the Old Course (closed on Sunday) are allocated by ballot. To be included, contact the starter before 2pm on the day before you wish to play. A handicap certificate (24 for men, 36 for women) or a letter of introduction is required. If the Old Course is fully booked, there are five other courses to choose from. Tel: (01334) 466 666 or log on to these websites for more information; www.standrews.co.uk; www.visitscotland.com/golf

### Walking

Scotland is a paradise for walkers, and walking is a rapidly growing tourism sector. There are 284 mountains over 3,000 ft (900 metres) – these are called Munros – and across the country you can find a wide range of climbs and walks suitable for the expert or the novice. The mountains, although not that high, should not be treated lightly. A peak which, when bathed in brilliant sunshine, looks an easy stroll can, a few minutes later, be covered by swirling mist, and can become a death trap. The importance of proper equipment (compass and maps) and clothing cannot be over-emphasised.

VisitScotland publishes an annual advice brochure, *Walk Scotland*. Scottish Natural Heritage (tel: (0131) 447 4784; fax: (0131) 446 2277; www.snh.org.uk) has free leaflets on *The West Highland Way*, from Glasgow to Fort William (95 miles/152 km), and another entitled *Scottish Hill Tracks*.

### Further Information
### The Mountaineering Council of Scotland
The Old Granary
West Mill Street
Perth PH1 5QP
Tel: (01738) 638227
Fax: (01738) 442095
www.mountaineering-scotland.org.uk
### Ramblers Association Scotland
Kingfisher House
Auld Mart Business Park, Milnathort
Kinross, KY13 9DA
Tel: (01577) 861222
Fax: (01577) 861333
www.ramblers.org.uk/scotland

### Fishing

Some of Britain's best fishing is found in Scotland. Rivers and lochs of all shapes and sizes can be fished for salmon and trout. Salmon

fishing need not be as expensive as most people believe, and trout fishing is available in far greater supply than is ever utilised. Local permits must be obtained; details are available from tourist offices.

The salmon-fishing season varies from river to river, starting from January in some places and as late as March in others and running until October. The trout season is from mid-March to early October. Fishing for migratory fish (salmon and sea trout) is forbidden on Sunday.

Sea fishing is found around the entire coast, particularly Orkney and the Shetland Islands. Shark, halibut, cod, hake and turbot are just a few of the species that can be caught.

### Surfing

The water may be colder than Brazil and Australia but with powerful Atlantic waves battering Scotland's coastline and the north and eastern coastlines, dotted with reef breaks, also enjoying consistent sizeable swells, it's unsurprising that Scotland is one of the hottest emerging surf destinations in Europe.

The Isle of Lewis, Tiree and Machrahanish on the west coast are remote, popular destinations while the east coast beaches of Fraserburgh and Pease/Coldingham Bay (East Lothian) attract legions of hardy surfers. Yet it's the renowned Thurso East in the north of Scotland that is really making waves. In April 2007, some of the world's best surfers could be seen shredding its waves during the O'Neill Highland Surf Open. See also; www.c2cadventure.com

### Sea-Kayaking

With miles of coastline, dozens of remote and uninhabited islands, countless sea lochs and a rich diversity of marine life including otter, whales and dolphins to observe, Scotland is paradise for paddlers who seek adventure and tranquillity.

Whether you are a beginner or an expert, increasing numbers of operators are offering day, weekend and even week-long trips off the coast. Indeed, at weekends between April and October it's not unusual to see cars with kayaks on the roof driving out of the cities.

Some argue that the Uists of the Outer Hebrides, complete with turquoise waters and white sands offer some of Europe's best sea kayaking. The Shetland Islands could also make such a claim.

**Canoe Scotland** is a useful first point of contact for suitable locations to learn/hire. Tel: (0131) 317 7314; www.canoescotland.com

## Birdwatching

More than 450 species of birds have been recorded, and some regions attract the rarest of species. Enormous seabird colonies can be seen on coastal cliffs and the islands. Outstanding are Shetland, Orkney, Handa Island, Isle of May, St Abb's Head, and Islay. Birds of prey, from the buzzard to the merlin, are often seen in the Highlands, where golden eagles and the osprey can also be spotted. Ornithological information can be obtained from: the **RSPB Scottish Office**, Dunedin House,

25 Ravelston Terrace, Edinburgh EH4 3TP. Tel: (0131) 311 6500. www.rspb.org.uk
The **Scottish Ornithologists' Club** Harbour Point, Newhailes Road, Musselburgh, EH21 6SJ Tel: (0131) 653 0653. www.the-soc.fsnet.co.uk
The **Scottish Wildlife Trust** (Cramond House, Cramond Glebe Road, Edinburgh EH4 6NS. Tel: (0131) 312 7765 www.swt.org.uk also manages many bird reserves.

There are also excellent sea-kayaking operators who offer tours and lessons. Try **Sea Kayak Shetland** (tel: (01595) 859647), **Wilderness Scotland** (tel: (0131) 625 6635), **Skyak Adventures** (Isle of Skye, www.skyakadventures.com) and **Uist Outdoor Centre**, North Uist (tel: (01876) 500 480; www.seakayakouterhebrides.co.uk).

### Skiing

Despite erratic snowfall in recent years, Scotland's five ski centres (Cairngorm, The Lecht, Glenshee, Glencoe and Nevis Range) continue to survive, albeit with at least three now also diversifying into activities such as hiking, mountain biking and even go-karting to balance the books. However, when the snow does fall (the main season is between January and April), groomed pistes and miles of challenging off-piste terrain become the playground for skiers, boarders and ski-mountaineers. See also www.ski-scotland.com

### Mountain Biking

If one sport has emphatically captured the imagination of the Scottish public and activity-minded visitors to Scotland alike, it's the humble mountain bike. While in the early 1990s, keen mountain bikers were forced to seek out their own trails through glens and forests, today there are over a dozen purpose-built mountain-bike centres offering mile upon mile of graded track (green for easy, black for experts) through forests, open countryside, and even down mountainsides. Such has been the explosion of interest in the sport that since 2002 alone the Forestry Commission Scotland (FCS), the largest landowner of public land in Scotland (www.forestry.gov.uk/scotland), has invested over £4 million in trail building projects.

Glentress (tel: (01721) 721736; www.thehubintheforest.co.uk) by Peebles reportedly attracted over 250,000 riders to its trails and continues to be one of Scotland's top tourist attractions. Its sprawling, marked trails (and wonderful café) are part of the 7Stanes trail network (www.7stanes.gov.uk) that stretches across the Borders and Dumfries and Galloway.

While Wolftrax at Laggan in the Central Highlands (tel: (01528) 544786; www.basecampmtb.com) and the Cairngorms (tel: (01479) 810111; www.bothybikes.co.uk; www.mountainebikers.org.uk) are both highly popular centres, it's the Witch's Trail cross-country route and

**ABOVE:** skiing down the slopes of Glencoe in the Scottish Highlands.

spectacular 1.6 miles (2.6 km) downhill course in the shadow of Ben Nevis which annually attracts thousands of amateur riders (tel: (01397) 705589; www.ridefortwilliam.co.uk). In September 2007, Fort William hosted the Mountain Bike World Championships.

### Diving

Scuba-divers won't be disappointed when they visit Scotland. Fish and plants abound in the clear waters which bathe the Scottish coast.

Outstanding sub-aqua areas with good facilities and experienced locals are the waters around Oban, the Summer Isles near Ullapool, Scapa Flow in Orkney and St Abb's Head on the southern part of the east coast. Information can be obtained from the **Scottish Sub-Aqua Club**
The Cockburn Centre
40 Bogmor Place
Glasgow G51 4TQ
Tel: (0141) 425 102
www.scotsac.com

## Spectator Sports

The most popular spectator sports are football (soccer), golf and rugby.

### Football

Rangers and Celtic are the two rival football teams which dominate the top of the Scottish Premier League;
**Rangers Football Club**
Ibrox Stadium, Glasgow
Tel: (0870) 600 1972
www.rangers.co.uk
**Celtic Football Club**
Celtic Park, Glasgow
Tel: (0845) 671 1888
www.celticfc.co.uk

Scotland's national football stadium is at **Hampden Park**, Glasgow. Tel: (0141) 620 4000, or (0141) 616 6100 for the museum.

International rugby matches are played at **Murrayfield Stadium** in Edinburgh. Tel: (0131) 346 5000; www.sru.org.uk.

### Shinty

Many Scots are fiercely proud of the heritage of this ancient Celtic sport of the camanachd or "curved stick". It demands stamina, speed and courage from the eleven players in two opposing teams who defend their goal on a football-like pitch. Fort William and Kingussie are among the most famous teams which compete in the annual shinty league and vie for the honour of contesting the greatest shinty prize of all, the Camanachd Cup. Contact the Camanachd Association, tel: (01463) 715931 (www.shinty.com) in Inverness for information about fixtures.

### Curling

It's an indigenous sport almost as old as the hills themselves and, like shinty, firmly embedded in the Scottish sporting culture. Played by teams on ice rinks across the land, between September and March thousands of men and women of all ages descend on rinks to "throw" and "sweep" their weighty granite-fashioned curling stones from the "hack". Two teams vie with each other to place their "stones" inside the "house" of concentric rings. Over the years, Scottish curlers have won European, World and Olympic medals in the sport. Tel: (0131) 333 3003; www.royalcaledoniancurlingclub.org

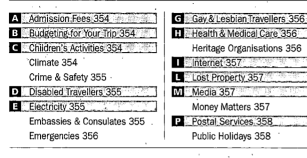

# A HANDY SUMMARY OF PRACTICAL INFORMATION, ARRANGED ALPHABETICALLY

## A dmission Fees

Libraries and many museums and galleries in Scotland are free to enter, including the Kelvingrove Museum and Art Gallery in Glasgow and the National Museums in Edinburgh. The National Trust for Scotland (NTS) and Historic Scotland (HS) *(see Heritage, page 356)* do charge admission to many of their properties. Some, like Edinburgh Castle, can cost as much as £11, so it's definitely worth asking about child-and-family discounts. The NTS offers substantial admission discounts to its members, so joining may be a worthwhile investment if you're planning to visit many properties. The Historic Scotland Explorer Pass is also a cost-saving option.

## B udgeting for Your Trip

Scotland is a relatively compact country. However, while even the outermost islands are easily reached, fuel costs continue to be high. Expect to pay over 80p per litre of fuel and much more in the Highlands – ironic, considering the oil is produced by the rigs just over

Aberdeen and Shetland's horizon. While bus travel is inexpensive (Glasgow–Edinburgh for under £5), the same return journey by train can cost over £15. There are accommodation and food options for every budget, from the almost five-figure cost of a 5-star dining experience and a suite at the Gleneagles Hotel to paying less than £10 to pitch your tent in one of dozens of campsites the length and breadth of the country.

However, as a rule of thumb, budget at least £25 per day for travel and food, and, depending on how you like to travel, £10–£80 per night for accommodation *(see Money Saving Tips, page 9).*

## C hildren's Activities

Scotland is a child-friendly nation, but attitudes definitely vary from place to place. For example, in cities and larger towns, some of the more established bistros and cafés generally welcome kids and are equipped with high chairs. However, many a parent has found their evening plans disrupted when their tiny offspring are deemed unwelcome at restaurants. In truth, access

sometimes depends as much on the attitude of the owner of the establishment as the law, though Scottish pubs must obtain a special license to permit U-16s into their bar. Invariably, parents will find the remoter parts of the Highlands and Islands much more accommodating, though it's worthwhile considering self-catering as a cast-iron eating and accommodation option,

That said, there are literally scores of child-friendly attractions across the country, from the child-orientated interpretive walks and interactive displays to be found at Forestry Commission centres (www.forestry.gov.uk/Scotland) to the renowned Landmark Forest Theme Park in Carrbridge (Speyside) that comes complete with treetop and red squirrel trail (tel: (0800) 731 3446; www.landmark-centre.co.uk). Parents will find many tourist attractions, restaurants, hotels and bus/train routes offer substantially reduced rates for children.

## Climate

No matter what you say about Scottish weather, you are bound to be wrong. There are those who rave

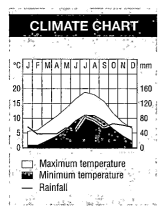

## CLIMATE CHART

| °C | J | F | M | A | M | J | J | A | S | O | N | D | mm |
|----|---|---|---|---|---|---|---|---|---|---|---|---|----|

☐ Maximum temperature
▨ Minimum temperature
— Rainfall

about the cloudless two weeks they spent on Skye; others have made several visits and have yet to see the Cuillins.

But it can be said that the west is generally wetter and warmer than the east. Summers are cool, with July temperatures averaging 55–59°F (13–15°C), though often peaking above 68°F (20°C) in the afternoon. Winters are cold, with January temperatures averaging 37–41°F (3–5°C), frost at night, and the higher mountains sometimes remaining snow-covered for months. Rainfall is heavy, except on the east coast, and exceeds 100 inches (2,540 mm) in the Western Highlands. January, April, May and June are usually drier than July, August and September, but take an umbrella whenever you go.

### Crime & Safety

Sadly, and like any other country in the world, crime does exist in Scotland, though serious crime is predominantly confined to the major cities. In truth, pickpockets and credit card fraud are two of the greatest risks a visitor must guard against. Tourists should avoid carrying large sums of cash on their person and keep a close eye on their handbag.

Scotland's city centre streets are generally safe to walk around in the evening, though women travelling on their own should remain especially vigilant. Exercise common sense and avoid dimly lit streets. If eating or partying late into the night, it's advisable to call a taxi to get back to your hotel.

Should you be concerned for your safety, the emergency services (police, ambulance and fire) can be reached on tel: 999. Note that this is an emergency number only.

Note, too, that airport terminals carry out stringent security checks on passengers. Ensure you allow yourself plenty of time to get through security for your flight. This includes domestic short-hop flights to the Highlands and Islands.

### D isabled Travellers

Recent legislation means that all new buildings in Scotland must have appropriate facilities for disabled travellers, including wheelchair access. **First Scotrail** (tel: (0845) 605 7021; www.firstscotrail.com) has ramps at station platforms for wheelchair-users to access trains, and such passengers also receive discounts on train travel. Visit its website and click on "Special Needs" for further details.

While buses don't offer such facilities, **Caledonian MacBrayne** (www.calmac.co.uk) shore staff will assist wheelchair-users in negotiating the gangway. There are also wheelchairs on board many vessels.

Sadly, while disabled toilet facilities are now commonplace in restaurants and cafés, it remains difficult for some disabled visitors to access some of the historic sites, though various (lower) parts of both Stirling and Edinburgh castles are accessible to wheelchair users (www.historic-scotland.gov.uk).

While there remains much work to be done, there are B&Bs, hotels and self-catering establishments across the country that provide facilities for disabled travellers. See **Association of Scotland's Self Caterers** (tel: (08705) 168571; www.assc.co.uk) for a list of such self-catering properties, or check out the VisitScotland website (www.visitscotland.com) for information.

Further advice on travel and services available for disabled visitors can be accessed from **Capability Scotland** (tel: (0131) 313 5510; fax: (0131) 346 2529; www.capability-scotland.org.uk).

### E lectricity

220 volts is standard. Hotels usually have dual 220/110-volt sockets for razors. If you are visiting from abroad, you will probably need an adaptor to link other small electrical appliances to the three-pin sockets universal in Britain; it is usually easier to find these at home before leaving than in Scotland.

### Embassies & Consulates

With the re-establishment of a Scottish Parliament in Edinburgh, many countries have opened consular offices in the capital *(if phoning from outside area use code: 0131).*
**Australia** Forsyth House, 93 George Street, EH2
Tel: 243 2589
**Czech Republic**
12a Riselaw Crescent, EH10
Tel: 447 9509
**Denmark**
48 Melville Street, EH3
Tel: 220 0300
**France**
11 Randolph Crescent, EH3
Tel: 225 7954
**Germany**
16 Eglinton Crescent, EH12
Tel: 337 2323
**Iceland**
45 Queen Street, EH2
Tel: 220 5775
**India**
17 Rutland Square, EH1
Tel: 229 2144

**BELOW:** the Royal Scottish Academy, Edinburgh has free admission.

**Ireland**
16 Randolph Crescent, EH3
Tel: 226 7711
**Italy**
32 Melville Street, EH3
Tel: 226 3631
**Japan**
2 Melville Crescent, EH3
Tel: 225 4777
**Jordan**
45 Queen Street, EH2
Tel: 226 4243
**The Netherlands**
1–2 Thistle Street, EH2
Tel: 220 3226
**Norway**
86 George Street, EH2
Tel: 333 0618
**Poland**
2 Kinnear Road, EH3
Tel: 552 0301
**Russia**
58 Melville Street, EH3
Tel: 225 7098
**Spain**
63 North Castle Street, EH2
Tel: 220 1843
**Sweden**
22 Hanover Street, EH2
Tel: 220 6050
**Switzerland**
255c Colinton Road, EH14
Tel: 441 4044
**Taipei**
1 Melville Street, EH3
Tel: 0131 220 6886
**Ukraine**
8 Windsor Street, EH7
Tel: 556 0023

## Emergencies

For emergency services such as police, ambulance, the fire service or lifeboat service dial **999**.

## G ay & Lesbian Travellers

All of Scotland's cities have a gay and lesbian scene, though arguably it's in Glasgow and Edinburgh where the most nightclubs and bars targeting this sector of the community are to be found. Edinburgh's Broughton Street and Glasgow's Merchant City are the two main "pink" areas of the respective cities. The best sources of information on your travels are to be found in the pages of the weekly entertainment magazine; *The List* (www.list.co.uk) and in the pages of the *Scotsgay* newspaper (www.scotsgay.co.uk). For various advice and support services, visitors should contact the Glasgow Lesbian, Gay, Bisexual and Transgender Centre on Bell Street (open Mon–Sun; tel: (0141) 552 4958; www.glgbt.org.uk).

## H ealth & Medical Care

It is advisable to have medical insurance. Citizens of European Union countries are entitled to medical treatment under reciprocal arrangements, and similar agreements exist with some other countries. No matter which country you come from, you will receive immediate emergency treatment free at a hospital casualty department.

Although Scotland isn't normally associated with mosquitoes, an aggressive breed of biting midge exists, especially in warm, humid conditions in parts of the west coast, and calls for a tough repellent from June to September.

## Heritage Organisations

**The National Trust for Scotland** is Scotland's premier conservation body, caring for over 100 buildings or areas of significant heritage interest. Its properties range from single boulders, such as the Bruce Stone in Galloway, through magnificent houses and castles including Culzean, Crathes and Fyvie, to large areas of outstanding countryside. These last include Glencoe, Mar Lodge in the Cairngorms, Kintail and Goat Fell on Arran. Some properties are available for holiday lets.

Membership allows free admission to all its properties and those owned by the English National Trust. Contact the NTS at:
28 Charlotte Square, Edinburgh EH2 4ET. Tel: (0131) 243 9300, www.nts.org.uk.
**Historic Scotland**
This government body looks after more than 300 sites of historical or archaeological interest. Its portfolio ranges from the magnificent Borders abbeys up to Stone Age sites in

**BELOW:** one of Scotland's most historic and scenic glens, Glencoe.

Orkney and Shetland.

Membership gain free admission to HS properties. Further information from: Longmore House, Salisbury Place, Edinburgh EH9 1SH. Tel: (0131) 668 8800/8831, www.historic-scotland.gov.uk.

# Internet

Scotland is well and truly on the internet highway, with even some of the remotest locations supported by dial-up, broadband or even Wi-Fi services. However, don't yet expect blanket coverage across the Highlands. While many of the higher-graded hotels and guest houses offer internet facilities as standard (often for a charge), many of the smaller B&Bs have yet to follow suit. However, from Ullapool to Stranraer, public libraries across Scotland offer free (for at least 15 minutes) internet access on condition that you register on arrival.

There are of course, innumerable internet cafés around the country where you pay around £1 per 30 minutes or 60 minutes to surf the internet and access your email. Some also serve as Wi-Fi hotspots; ideal for the visitor who arrives with his or her laptop in tow. Unfortunately, just as one internet café business opens, it seems another shuts, making a mockery of attempts to list systematically key locations in cities and towns. As a general rule, many are found in the student areas of a city. In Glasgow, Woodlands Road near Glasgow University is one such location, while Clerk Street and Rose Street in Edinburgh both support internet cafés.

# Lost Property

It's not always a case of "finder's keepers" – Network Rail (www.nationalrailco.uk) has stations with lost property and left luggage facilities. At Glasgow Central (train station) the left luggage office is open daily on the main concourse between 7am–11pm (tel: (0141) 221 8597). The same number should be called to try to locate lost property in and around the station.

In Edinburgh, the lost property department at Waverley Station is on platform 1 (tel: (0131) 550 2333). Note that lost property (including that which is left in taxis) found in and around the city centre may be handed in to the police HQ at Fettes Avenue (tel: (0131) 311 3141). Travellers in Aberdeen trying to track down their misplaced item(s) should contact the Lost and Found

Department, Grampian Police, Queen Street (tel: (0845) 600 5700). It's open 9am–4.45pm weekdays only.

While there's a left luggage (deposited items will be hand-searched) at Inverness Train Station (open Mon–Sat, 8.45am–6pm; Sun noon–6.30pm), there is no lost property facility.

# Media

## Newspapers

There are two quality dailies. *The Scotsman,* printed in Edinburgh, and *The Herald,* printed in Glasgow, both have good coverage of Scottish and other UK and foreign news, as well as material on the arts and business. Dundee prints the quirky *Courier.* Much of the Highlands is covered by the *Press and Journal,* printed in Aberdeen. It tries to live down its reputation for excessive parochialism, epitomised by the spurious headline on what proved to be a story about the sinking of the *Titanic:* "Aberdeen man lost at sea."

The most popular is the tabloid *Daily Record,* a stablemate of England's *Daily Mirror.* English dailies circulate widely in Scotland, and many have Scottish editions.

The four main cities each have evening papers. Scotland's most unusual Sunday newspaper is the *Sunday Post,* from the same stable as Dundee's *Courier.* It defies classification: perhaps the most helpful comment on it would be that it tries to be useful and inoffensive. *Scotland on Sunday* and the *Sunday Herald* are the two quality home-grown Sunday newspapers.

Throughout Scotland, there are many local weekly papers which you may find both entertaining and informative if you are interested in a particular region, or simply interested in newspapers.

## Magazines

Scotland is poorly served by magazines. However, the *Scottish Field, Scots Magazine* and *Scotland Magazine* are good-quality monthly magazines which deal with Scottish topics. The *Edinburgh Review* is a literary review of consistent quality. *The List,* an Edinburgh-based listings magazine which appears every two weeks provides lively and comprehensive coverage of events in both Edinburgh and Glasgow.

## Radio and Television

Radio and TV are excellent, for the most part. Radio Scotland is the main BBC radio service, and national BBC radio stations also operate in

Scotland, so it is possible to hear excellent Radio 4 (FM 92.4–94.6/LW 198), a mixture of news, current affairs and light entertainment, as well as classical music on Radio 3 (FM 90.2–92.4). Classic FM (FM 99.9–101.99) serves up the more familiar classics and some intriguing and challenging quiz games. Radio 2 (FM 88–90.2) concentrates on light entertainment and sport. Sports fans will tune in to BBC Radio Scotland or Radio 5 Live (MW 693/909).

Radio 1 (FM 97.6–99.8), Virgin (MW 1215), Atlantic (LW 252) and local radio stations run by both the BBC and commercial companies offer wall-to-wall pop and light music, interspersed with terse news summaries. Local stations tend to provide an unimaginative diet of pop music but can be useful sources of local traffic news and other important information.

Television services are provided by the BBC and commercial companies. BBC1 is a general TV service, mirrored (with a more downmarket emphasis) by the commercial networks on Channels 3 (ITV) and 5. BBC2 caters to a more specialist audience and minority groups. Satellite and cable channels are usually available in the larger hotels.

Television reception is poor in some of the remoter areas and islands of Scotland.

# Money Matters

## Currency

The British pound is divided into 100 pence. The coins used are 1p, 2p, 5p, 10p, 20p, 50p, £1 and £2. Although the £1 coin is widely used, £1 notes (issued by the Royal Bank of Scotland) still circulate along with notes of £5, £10, £20, £50 and £100. (Technically, Scottish notes are legal tender in England and Wales, but some shops will not accept them; English banks will readily change them for you.)

## Traveller's Cheques

Traveller's cheques can be cashed at banks, bureaux de change and many hotels, though the best rates are normally available at banks.

## Credit Cards

MasterCard and Visa are the most widely accepted credit cards, followed by American Express and Diners Club. Small guest houses and Bed & Breakfast places may not take credit cards, preferring payment in cash.

## Banks

Scotland has its own banks: the Royal Bank of Scotland, the Bank of

Scotland and the Clydesdale Bank. They still issue their own notes – although the Royal Bank is the only one to issue the £1 note – which circulate alongside Bank of England notes.

Don't expect consistent opening hours. As a rough guide, most banks open from between 9 and 9.45am to between 4 and 4.45pm (5.30pm on Thursday). In rural areas, banks may close between 12.30pm and 1.30pm and may not be open later on Thursday. However, you will also find "travelling banks" – large trucks which go round the smaller villages at set times each week and can provide most banking services. These times are advertised locally.

Building societies, unlike banks, often open on Saturday morning.

**ABOVE:** the postal service is a lifeline in some of the more remote parts.

### P ostal Services

Main post offices are open 9am–5.30pm Monday–Friday, and 9am–12.30pm on Saturday. Sub-post offices (which often form part of another shop) keep similar hours, though they usually close for one half-day during the week.

### Public Holidays

Local, public and bank holidays can be frustrating for visitors, but generally there will be a supermarket open somewhere during the major public holidays, except for **25** and **26 December**, **1** and **2 January** and **Good Friday**. If you are having difficulty, try petrol stations, many of which have good small shops on the premises and are open until late, or even for 24 hours.

Other national holidays in Scotland are **May Day** (first Monday in May), **Spring Holiday** (Monday in late May) and **Summer Holiday** (first Monday in August).

### R eligion

Scotland supports a diverse mix of communities from across the world. While Christianity (both Catholicism and Presbyterianism) is followed by the majority of inhabitants, Islamic, Sikh, Buddhist and Jewish services are among the others to be found in Scotland.

Sunday is the traditional "day of rest" in Scotland, though the diminishing numbers who attend church (or kirk as it's called in Scotland) would suggest this rest isn't being taken in church. However, most churches will welcome visitors who simply turn up at the door on a

Sunday morning. Further information can be found at;
www.churchofscotland.org.uk
The website www.upmystreet.com is also a useful reference point for locating churches, mosques and synagogues in the town or region of Scotland you will be visiting. The following religious contacts will be able to provide practical advice on their areas of worship.
**Catholic Church**
5 St Vincent Place
Glasgow G1 2DH
Tel: (0141) 221 1168
**Church of Scotland**
121 George Street
Edinburgh EH2
Tel: (0131) 225 5722
**Baptist Union of Scotland**
14 Aytoun Road
Glasgow G41 5RT
Tel: (0141) 423 6169
E-mail: admin@scottishbaptist.org.uk
**Edinburgh Buddhist Centre**
10 Viewforth
Edinburgh EH10
Tel: (0131) 228 3333
**Glasgow Buddhist Centre**
329 Sauchiehall Street
Glasgow G2 3HW
Tel: (0141) 333 0524
**Scottish Episcopal Church**
General Senate Office
21 Grosvenor Crescent
Edinburgh EH12 5EE
Tel: (0131) 225 6357
**Hindu Mandir & Cultural Centre**
Tel: (0131) 667 6064
**Jehovah's Witnesses**
10 Pennywell Road
Edinburgh EH4
Tel: (0131) 343 3005
**Jewish Synagogue & Community Centre**
4 Salisbury Road
Edinburgh EH16 5AB

Tel: (0131) 667 3144
**Sikh Temple**
1 Sheriff Brae
Edinburgh EH6 6ZZ
Tel: (0131) 553 7207
**UK Islamic Mission**
19 Carrington Street
Glasgow G4 9AJ
Tel: (0141) 331 1119

### S enior Travellers

If you are aged 60 or over, it's always worthwhile enquiring about discounts on buses, trains and at attractions. In Scotland, a Senior Rail Card (www.senior-railcard.co.uk) costs £20 and can often save the holder almost 30 percent of the standard cost of a train journey. Swimming pools, leisure centres and the National Trust for Scotland (www.nts.org.uk) are among other locations where proving you're an OAP can prove beneficial to the wallet.

In addition to discounted fares, the most readily accessed seats on buses and trains are reserved for use by senior travellers. Unfortunately, that doesn't always mean that the young person already sitting there will be willing to vacate their seat.

Saga (www.saga.co.uk) is among many tour operators now catering for the "grey market".

### T elecommunications

When dialling from abroad, the international access code for the UK is 44, followed by the area code without the initial 0 (Edinburgh 131, Glasgow 141, Aberdeen 1224, etc.).

To reach other countries from Scotland, first dial the **international access code 00**, then the country

TRANSPORT

code (e.g. Australia 61, France 33, Germany 49, Japan 81, the Netherlands 31, Spain 34, US and Canada 1). If using a US credit phone card, dial the company's access number: Sprint 00 801 15; AT&T 00 801 10; MCI 00 801 11.

The minimum charge for a call made at a public telephone is 20 pence. Most telephones accept only cardphone cards, which can be purchased at post offices and shops in various denominations. Public call boxes are becoming rarer as mobile phone use increases.

Direct dialling is possible to most parts of the world.

## Time Zones

Scotland, like the rest of the UK, follows Greenwich Mean Time (GMT). In spring the clock is moved forward one hour for British Summer Time (BST), and in autumn moved back to GMT. Especially in the far north, this means that it is light until at least 10pm in midsummer.

When it is noon GMT, it is:
4am in Los Angeles
7am in New York and Toronto
noon in London and Dublin
2pm in Cape Town
10pm in Melbourne and Sydney

## Tourist Information

### In Scotland

General postal enquiries should be made to VisitScotland, OceanPoint One, 94 Ocean Drive, Leith, Edinburgh EH6 6JH. Tel: (0845) 225 5121.

VisitScotland has its Edinburgh and Scotland Tourist Information Centre at 3 Princes Street in the centre of Edinburgh (tel: (0845) 225 5121). Other tourist information is provided by 14 area **Tourist Boards** throughout Scotland. Their main information centres, with the areas covered, are:

**Aberdeen and Grampian Tourist Board**: 27 Albyn Place, Aberdeen AB10 1YL. Tel: (01224) 288828. Fax: (01224) 581367; www.castlesandwhisky.com. (Aberdeen City, Moray and Aberdeenshire.)
**Angus and City of Dundee Tourist Board**: 21 Castle Street, Dundee DD1 3AA. Tel: (01382) 527527. Fax: (01382) 527550; www.angusanddundee.co.uk. (Angus and the City of Dundee.)
**Argyll, the Isles, Loch Lomond, Stirling and Trossachs Tourist Board**: 7 Alexandra Place, Dunoon, Argyll PA23 8AB. Tel: (01369) 701000. Fax: (01369) 706085; www.scottish.heartlands.org. (Argyll and

Bute, Clackmananshire, Dumbarton and Clydebank, Falkirk and Stirling.)
**Ayrshire and Arran Tourist Board**: 15 Skye Road, Prestwick KA9 2TA. Tel: (01292) 678100. Fax: (01292) 471832; www.ayrshire-arran.com.
**Dumfries and Galloway Tourist Board**: 64 Whitesands, Dumfries DG1 2RS. Tel: (01387) 253862. Fax: (01387) 245555; www.dumfriesandgalloway.co.uk.
**Edinburgh and Lothians Tourist Board**: 3 Princes Street (Waverley Market), Edinburgh EH2 2QP. Tel: (0845) 225 5121; email: info@visitscotland.com. (City of Edinburgh, East Lothian, Midlothian, West Lothian.)
**Greater Glasgow and Clyde Valley Tourist Board**: 11 George Square, Glasgow G2 1DY. Tel: (0141) 204 4400. Fax: (0141) 204 4772; www.seeglasgow.com. (City of Glasgow, East Dunbartonshire, Inverclyde, Lanarkshire, Renfrewshire.)
**The Highlands of Scotland Tourist Board**: Grampian Road, Aviemore PH22 1PP. Tel: (01479) 810797; email: aviemoretic@host.co.uk. (Caithness, Inverness-shire, Ross-shire, Sutherland and the Island of Skye.)
**Kingdom of Fife Tourist Board**: Haig House, Haig Business Park, Markinch, Fife KY7 6AQ. Tel: (01592) 750066. Fax: (01592) 611180; www.standrews.com/fife.
**Orkney Tourist Board**: 6 Broad Street, Kirkwall, Orkney KW5 1NX. Tel: (01856) 872856. Fax: (01856) 875056; www.visitorkney.com.
**Perthshire Tourist Board**: Lower City Mills, West Mill Street, Perth PH3 1LQ. Tel: (01738) 450600. Fax: (01738) 444863; www.perthshire.co.uk. (Perthshire and Kinross.)
**Scottish Borders Tourist Board**: Murray's Green, Jedburgh, Roxburghshire, TD8 6BE. Tel: (0870) 608 0404. Fax: (01750) 21886; www.scot-borders.co.uk.
**Shetland Islands Tourism**: Market Cross, Lerwick, Shetland ZE1 0LU. Tel: (01595) 693434. Fax: (01595) 695807; www.visitshetland.com.
**Western Isles Tourist Board**: 26

Cromwell Street, Stornoway, Isle of Lewis HS1 2DD. Tel: (01851) 703088. Fax: (01851) 705244; www.with.co.uk. (Lewis, Harris, North Uist, Benbecula, South Uist and Barra.)
In addition, most towns have **Tourist Information Centres (TICs)**; not all are open in the winter months.

### In London

**VisitBritain**
Thames Tower, Blacks Road, London W6 9EL
Tel: (020) 8846 9000
Fax: (020) 8563 0302
E-mail: visitbritain@visitbritain.org www.visitbritain.com
Information about Scotland is available through the British Tourist Authority offices.

### Outside the United Kingdom

**Australia**: VisitBritain, Level 2, 15 Blue Street, Sydney NSW 2000.
Tel: (2) 9021 4400
Fax: (2) 9377 4499
E-mail: visitbritainaus@visitbritain.org www.visitbritain.com.au
**Canada**: VisitBritain, 5915 Airport Road, Suite 120, Mississauga, Ontario L4V 1T1.
Tel: (1) 888 847 4885
Fax: (905) 405 8490
www.visitbritain.com/ca
**Ireland**: VisitBritain, 3rd floor, 22–24 Newmount House, Lower Mount Street, Dublin 2.
Tel: (1) 670 8000
Fax: (1) 670 8244
E-mail: contactus@visitbritain.org
**New Zealand**: VisitBritain, Level 17, NZI House, 151 Queen Street, Auckland 1.
Tel: (0800) 700 741
www.visitbritain.com/nz
**South Africa:**
E-mail: johannesburg@visitbritain.org www.visitbritain.com/za
**US (New York City)**: VisitBritain, 7th Floor, 551 Fifth Avenue, New York, NY.
Tel: (1) 800 462 2748
E-mail: travelinfo@visitbritain.org www.travelbritain.org

## Useful Numbers

● Directory enquiries are provided by several companies. Numbers include **118500, 118888, 118811, 118118**
● International directory enquiries **118505** or **118866** or **118899**
● Operator assistance **100** for UK calls, **155** for international calls
● Emergencies – police, fire and ambulance **999**

## Tours

From literary tours of Edinburgh's New and Old Town and wildlife tours on Mull to specialist adventure breaks by bike, foot and kayaking in the rugged Highlands, visitors are spoilt for choice with specialist tours.

The following are just a few of dozens to be found through local tourist information centres.
**Mercat Tours**
28 Blair Street, Edinburgh
Tel: (0131) 225 5445

ACCOMMODATION
EATING OUT
ACTIVITIES
A–Z

Literary and ghost tours promise delight and fright.

**Islay Birding**
Port Charlotte, Isle of Islay
Tel: (01496) 850010
Award-winning operator who also runs bushcraft courses involving night navigation and sleeping in caves!

**Wilderness Scotland**
3a St Vincent Street, Edinburgh
Tel: (0131) 625 6635
www.wildernessscotland.com
Another award-winnning operator who promises adventure and wildlife in abundance, as small groups explore the remotest corners of Scotland's Highlands and Islands by sea-kayak, mountain bike, skis or on your own two feet.

**Haggis Adventures**
Tel: (0131) 557 9393
www.haggisadventures.com
Especially designed for travellers on a budget. Visitors are taken into the furthest reaches of the Highlands aboard their distinctive yellow "haggis" buses.

## Visas & Passports

Your best starting point for a visa-related enquiry concerning entry to the UK is to contact the UK Foreign and Commonwealth Offices visa website (www.ukvisas.gov.uk).

Citizens of most EU countries don't require a visa (just a passport) to visit Scotland. For all other nationalities, it's best to check with the British consulate in your own country before travelling to access the latest advice on the documentation required to holiday/study/work in the UK.

## Water

It's the vital ingredient for Scotland's national drink, fills the nation's many lochs and reservoirs and runs freely from every household and hotel tap. While the taste varies across the country, the good news is that water drunk from the cold tap (unless stated otherwise) should be refreshing and perfectly safe to drink. However, if you would rather have the bottled variety, there's now also a bewildering array of mineral water brands on the market, including Highland Spring.

If you want to tap into further information about Scotland's water resource visit www.scottishwater.co.uk.

## Websites

The following website addresses could prove useful on your travels throughout Scotland:

### Travel
**www.visitscotland.com**; Scotland's national tourism agency.
**www.visitbritain.com**; the UK's tourism agency with links to Scotland.
**www.undiscoveredscotland.co.uk**; a very informative online guide to Scotland.
**www.seeglasgow.com**; the official destination marketing agency for Glasgow.
**www.lochnessexpress.com**; this shuttle ferry down the entire length of Loch Ness takes 1½ hours and will carry bikes (up to 16) for free.

### Eating and drinking
**www.smws.co.uk**; Scotch Malt Whisky Society.
**www.5pm.co.uk**; for last-minute deals on restaurant and bar food.
**www.whisky-heritage.co.uk**; everything you wanted to know about the distillation of Scotland's favourite tipple.

### Accommodation
**www.syha.org.uk**; Scottish Youth Hostel Association.
**www.assc.co.uk**; the Association of Scotland's self-caterers.

### Entertainment
**www.thelist.co.uk**; *The List* magazine highlights the latest and best entertainment venues and gigs across the Central Belt.
**www.eventscotland.org**; a handy reference for key forthcoming festivals and sports events to be staged in Scotland.

### Outdoors
**www.visitscotland.com/walking**; for everything from walking guides and operators to over 800 suggested walking routes.
**www.forestry.gov.uk/scotland**; Forestry Commission Scotland.
**www.snh.org.uk**; Scottish Natural Heritage works with various conservation agencies to protect sensitive areas of fauna and flora throughout the country.
**www.wildernessscotland.com**; for the traveller who seeks a tour operator who really does venture off the beaten track.
**www.met-office.gov.uk**; find out the latest weather reports around the country, including sea and mountain conditions.

## Weights & Measures

Britain is only halfway to accepting the metric system: beer comes in pints and half-pints, and shop assistants will sell you "a quarter" of sweets or "half a pound" of cheese; yet pre-packaged goods cite weights in grams. Road signs give distances in miles, but fuel is sold in litres.

## What to Wear

Given the climate, it follows that you should never be without a raincoat or a warm sweater. Neither should you be without light clothes in summer. For those attracted to the excellent opportunities for hill-walking and rock-climbing, it is essential to come properly prepared. In the mountains the weather can change very quickly.

Each year people suffer serious and needless injury through setting out without adequate clothing equipment; the Highlands are no place to go on a serious hill-walk in a T-shirt and light trainers.

**BELOW:** be prepared when out walking as weather conditions can quickly change.

# FURTHER READING

## History

**The Scottish Enlightenment – The Scots Invention of the Modern World.** A. Herman. Fourth Estate.
**Mary Queen of Scots.** Antonia Fraser. Weidenfeld & Nicolson.
**Bonnie Prince Charlie.** Fitzroy MacLean. Canongate.
**A Concise History of Scotland.** Fitzroy MacLean. Thames and Hudson.
**Culloden** and **The Highland Clearances.** John Prebble. Secker & Warburg.
**A History of the Scottish People 1560–1830.** T.C. Smout. Fontana.
**A Century of the Scottish People 1830–1950.** T.C. Smout. Fontana.
**Scotland's Story.** Tom Steel. Fontana.

## Poetry

Many editions are available of Robert Burns' poems.
**Last Poetic Gems.** William McGonagall. Winter/Duckworth. Scotland's (and perhaps the world's) worst poet, who has become something of a cult.
**Selected Poems.** William Dunbar. Fyfield Books.

## Miscellaneous

**Aberdeen, An Illustrated Architectural Guide.** W.A. Brogden. Scottish Academic Press.
**A Companion to Scottish Culture.** David Daiches (ed). Arnold.
**Edinburgh: A Travellers' Companion.** David Daiches. Arnold.
**Exploring Scotland's Heritage.** Her Majesty's Stationery Office.
**Four Scottish Journeys.** Andrew Eames. Hodder & Stoughton.
**Glasgow.** David Daiches. Andre Deutsch.
**Glasgow Observed.** John Donald. John Donald Publishers.
**The Heart of Glasgow.** Jack House. Richard Drew Publishing.
**Hebridean Connection.** Derek Cooper. Futura.
**In Search of Scotland.** H.V. Morton. Methuen.
**A Journey to the Western Isles of Scotland** and **The Journal of a Tour to the Hebrides.** Dr Samuel Johnson and James Boswell. Two accounts of the same trip made in the 18th century by the great lexicographer and his biographer. Oxford University Paperbacks.
**The Munros: Scottish Mountaineering Club Hillwalkers' Guide.** Donald Bennet and Rab Anderson. Scottish Mountaineering Club.
**The Northeast Lowlands of Scotland.** John R. Allan. Robert Hale.
Berry, Simon and Hamish Whyte.
**Scotland: An Anthology.** Douglas Dunn. Fontana.
**The Patter: A Guide to Current Glasgow Usage.** Michael Munro. Glasgow District Libraries.
**Portrait of Aberdeen and Deeside.**

## Feedback

We do our best to ensure the information in our books is as accurate and up-to-date as possible. The books are updated on a regular basis, using local contacts, who painstakingly add, amend and correct as required. However, some mistakes and omissions are inevitable and we are ultimately reliant on our readers to put us in the picture. We would welcome your feedback on any details related to your experiences using the book "on the road". Maybe we recommended a hotel that you liked (or another that you didn't), as well as interesting new attractions, or facts and figures you have found out about the country itself. The more details you can give us (particularly with regard to addresses, e-mails and telephone numbers), the better. We will acknowledge all contributions, and we'll offer an Insight Guide to the best letters received.

Please write to us at:
Insight Guides
PO Box 7910
London SE1 1WE
United Kingdom
Or send e-mail to:
insight@apaguide.co.uk

Graham Cuthbert. Robert Hale.
**Road to the Isles.** Derek Cooper. Futura.

## Fiction

**Kidnapped.** Robert Louis Stevenson. Penguin. An historical novel set in the aftermath of the Jacobite rebellion.
**Knots and Crosses.** Ian Rankin. Orion. The first book in the Inspector Rebus series.
**The Prime of Miss Jean Brodie.** Muriel Spark. Penguin. An unconventional school teacher instructs her girl pupils on the ways of love and life.
**A Scots Quair** (Sunset Song, Cloud Howe, Grey Granite). Lewis Grassic Gibbon. Canongate. A trilogy following the life of Chris Guthrie, a woman from northeast Scotland at the turn of the 20th century.
**The Thirty-Nine Steps.** John Buchan. Penguin. The best-known of Buchan's thrillers, set against the Scottish landscape.
**Trainspotting.** Irvine Welsh. Vintage. A horrifying look at Edinburgh's drug scene.
**Waverley.** Sir Walter Scott. Penguin Classics.
**Whisky Galore.** Compton Mackenzie. Vintage Classics. A comic novel about a wreck of a cargo of whisky.

## Other Insight Guides

Companion volumes to Insight Guide: Scotland include Insight Guide: Edinburgh and Insight Guide: Glasgow. Both provide a complete cultural background, supplemented by stunning photography. Insight Guide: Great Gardens of Britain and Ireland includes full coverage of Scotland's many fine gardens.

Compact Guides to Scotland, the Scottish Highlands, Edinburgh, and Glasgow are designed for portability; packing in all the information you'll need, plus cross-referenced maps and photography.

Insight Pocket Guide: Scotland contains a local author's recommendations for places to go and things to do. It includes carefully timed itineraries and is designed for readers with limited time to spare.

TRANSPORT · ACCOMMODATION · EATING OUT · ACTIVITIES · A–Z

# ART & PHOTO CREDITS

## PICTURE SPREADS

# INDEX

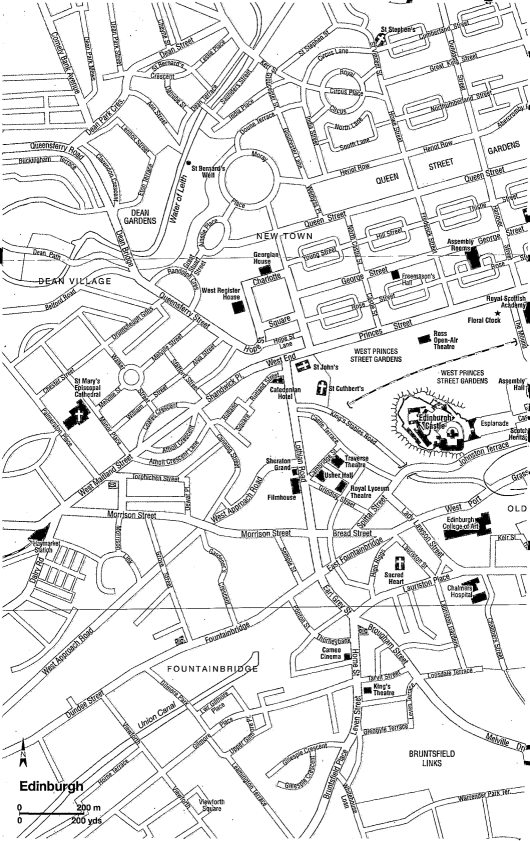